MUSASHI #9

volume 7

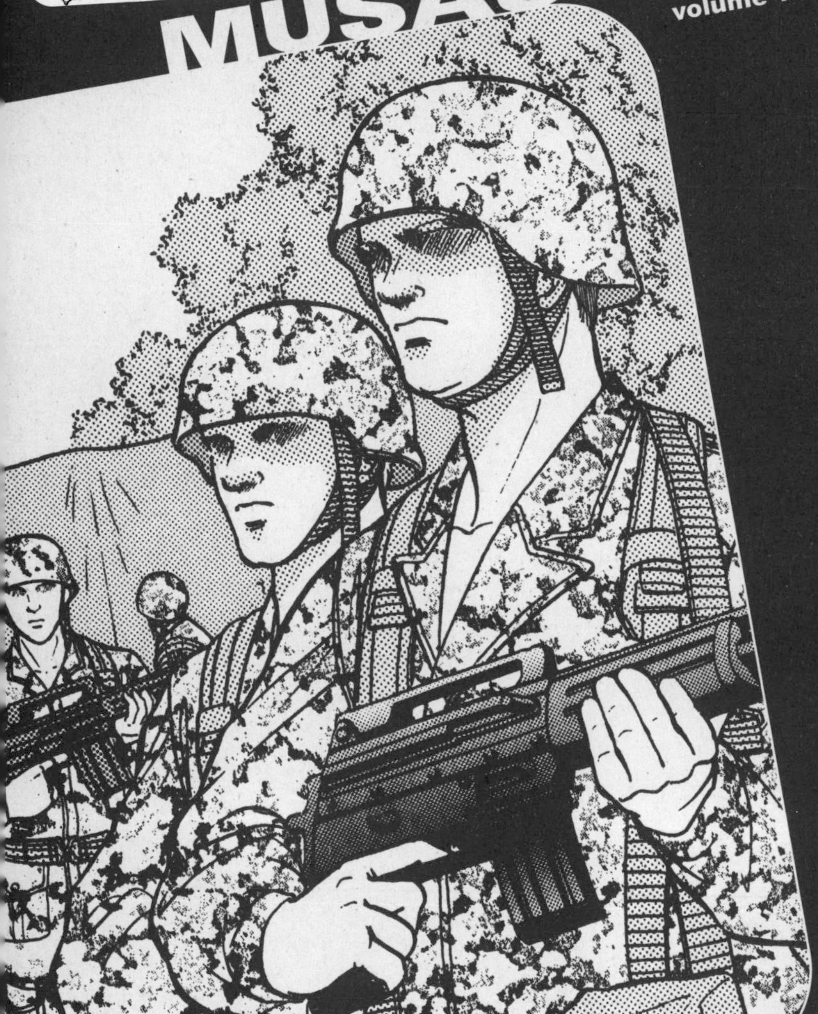

by Miyuki Takahashi

The history of mankind has
been one of wars. Race.
Religion. Philosophy.
The causes are untold.

The combatants have their own
justifications, but on occasion,
some create a volatile
situation that threatens to
destroy the world.

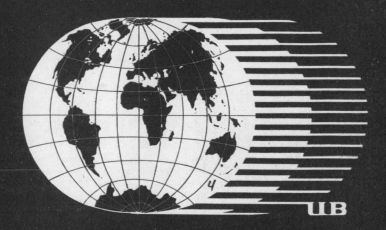

Ultimate Blue.
An organization shrouded in
complete secrecy. Also known
as "the other United Nations."
Nobody knows when it was
created. Nobody knows
where it is based.

The Blue of the Seas.
The Blue of the Skies.
The Blue of the Earth.

The last line of defense against chaos.

The story so far...

The history of mankind has been one of wars. Relentless warring would have doomed the planet to annihilation were it not for Ultimate Blue, a secret organization also known as "the other United Nations," and its team of super agents. **Musashi Nine**, or **Shinozuka Kou** as she is known, is one of them.

Musashi goes undercover at a high school to stop a gun-smuggling organization called "White Dragon." She befriends Tachibana Shingo, who has unwittingly come across critical evidence, and together they bring down the organization. They also succeed in apprehending Lau, an assassin who had sworn revenge.

The end of the organization also meant the end of Musashi's mission to protect Shingo--but not an end to their growing affection for one another. Knowing they belong in different worlds, Musashi fakes her own death, but...

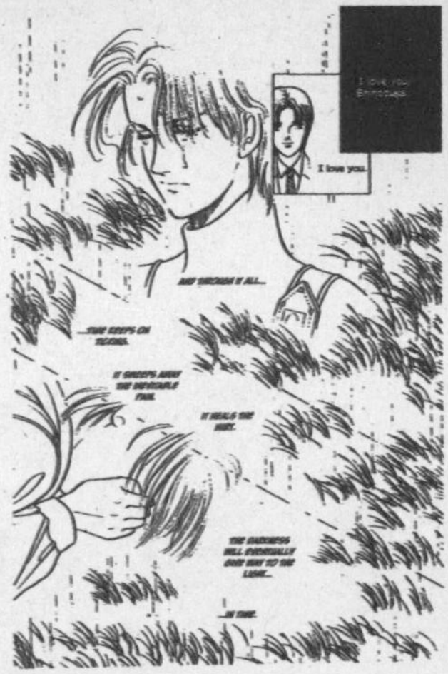
I love you.

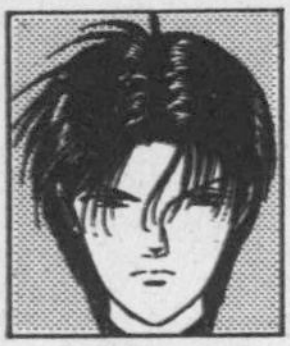

MUSASHI (SHINOZUKA KOU)

Ultimate Blue agent #9. Went undercover as Shinozuka Kou at a boys school, but is actually a girl. Faked her own death when capturing Lau, but her feelings for Shingo run deeper than she realizes.

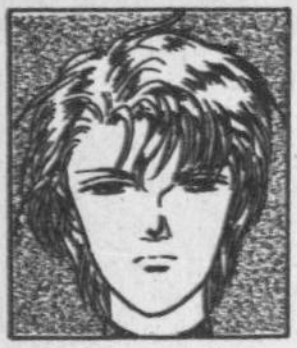

#7

Codename: Athena. A woman, but works undercover as a male officer in the American Navy. Very gifted advisor with considerable influence.

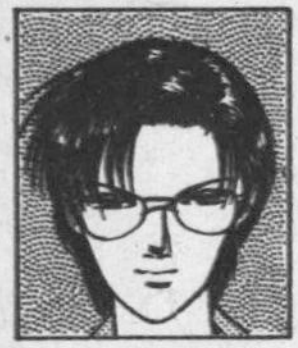

#19

Ultimate Blue agent. He assists Nine as her lieutenant and at times as her double. He catches on to the growing affection between #9 and Shingo, but ultimately chooses to tell Shingo of Musashi's "death."

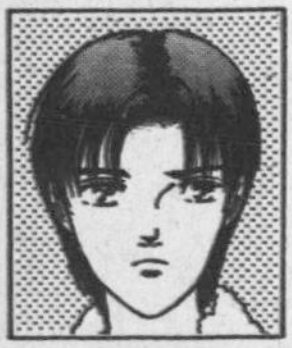

Tachibana Shingo

A hot-headed teenager befriended by Musashi when they avenged his best friend. He confessed his love to her and rightly suspects she faked her death.

contents

MUSASHI #9

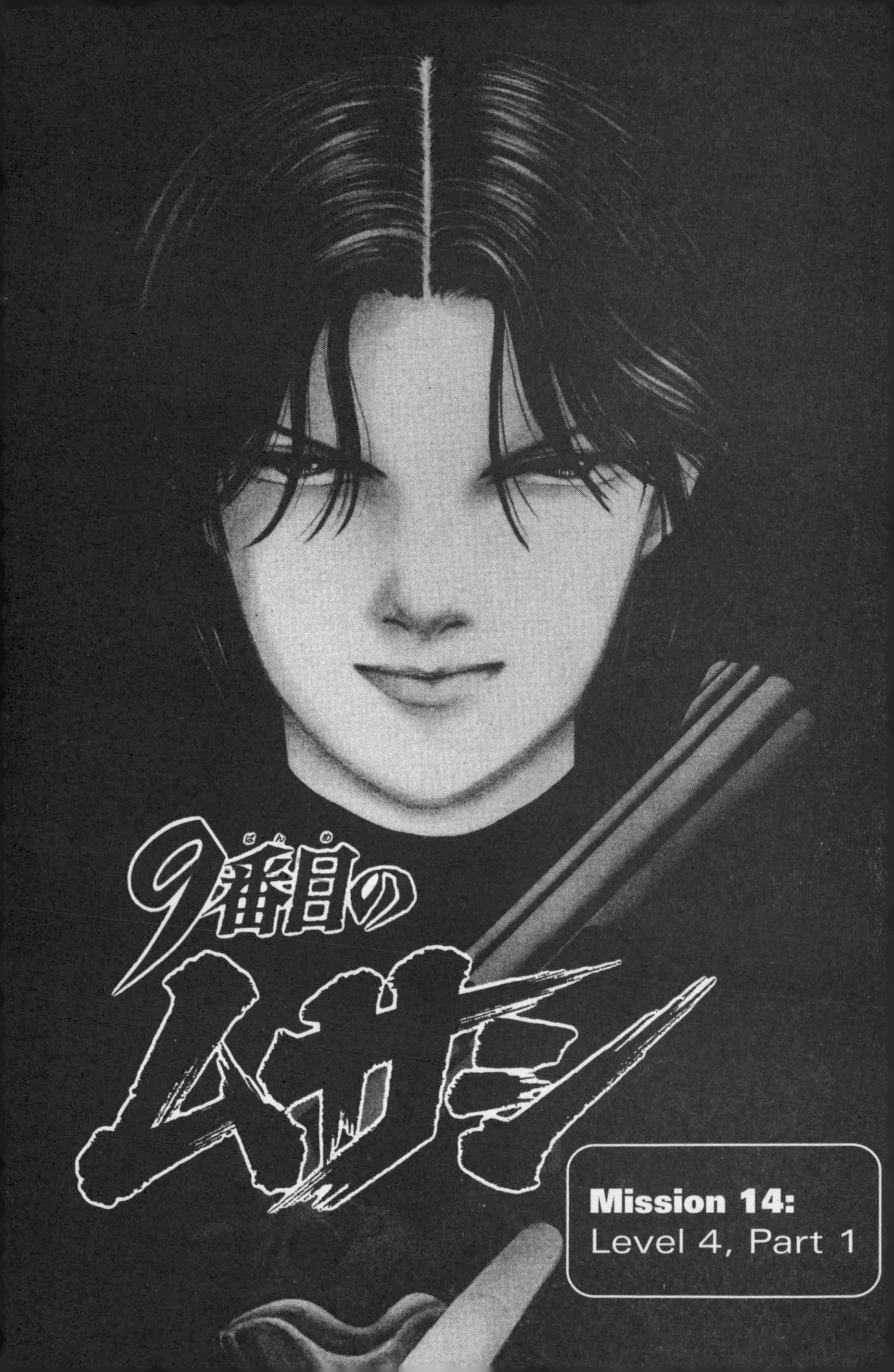
9番目の
ムサシ
Mission 14:
Level 4, Part 1

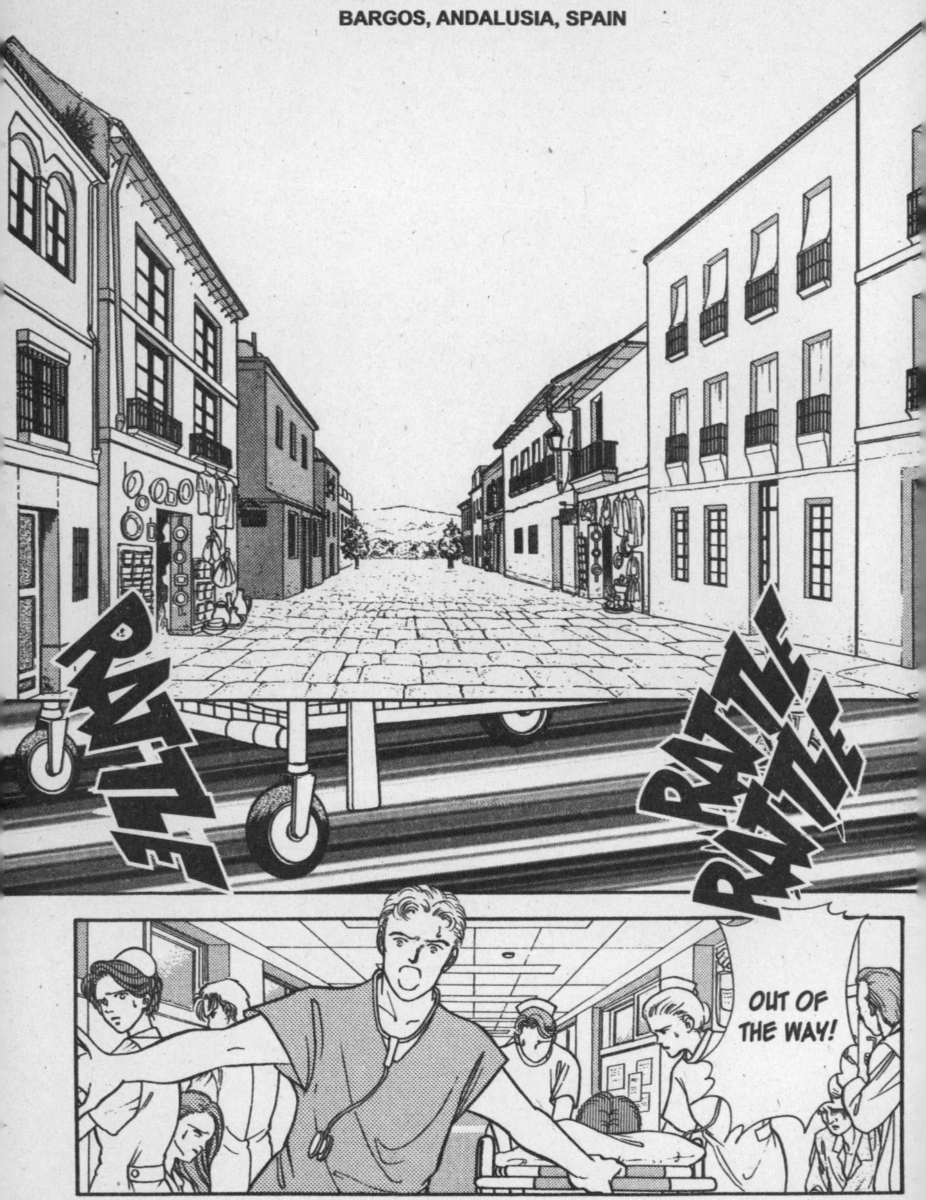
BARGOS, ANDALUSIA, SPAIN
RATTLE!
RATTLE RATTLE
OUT OF THE WAY!

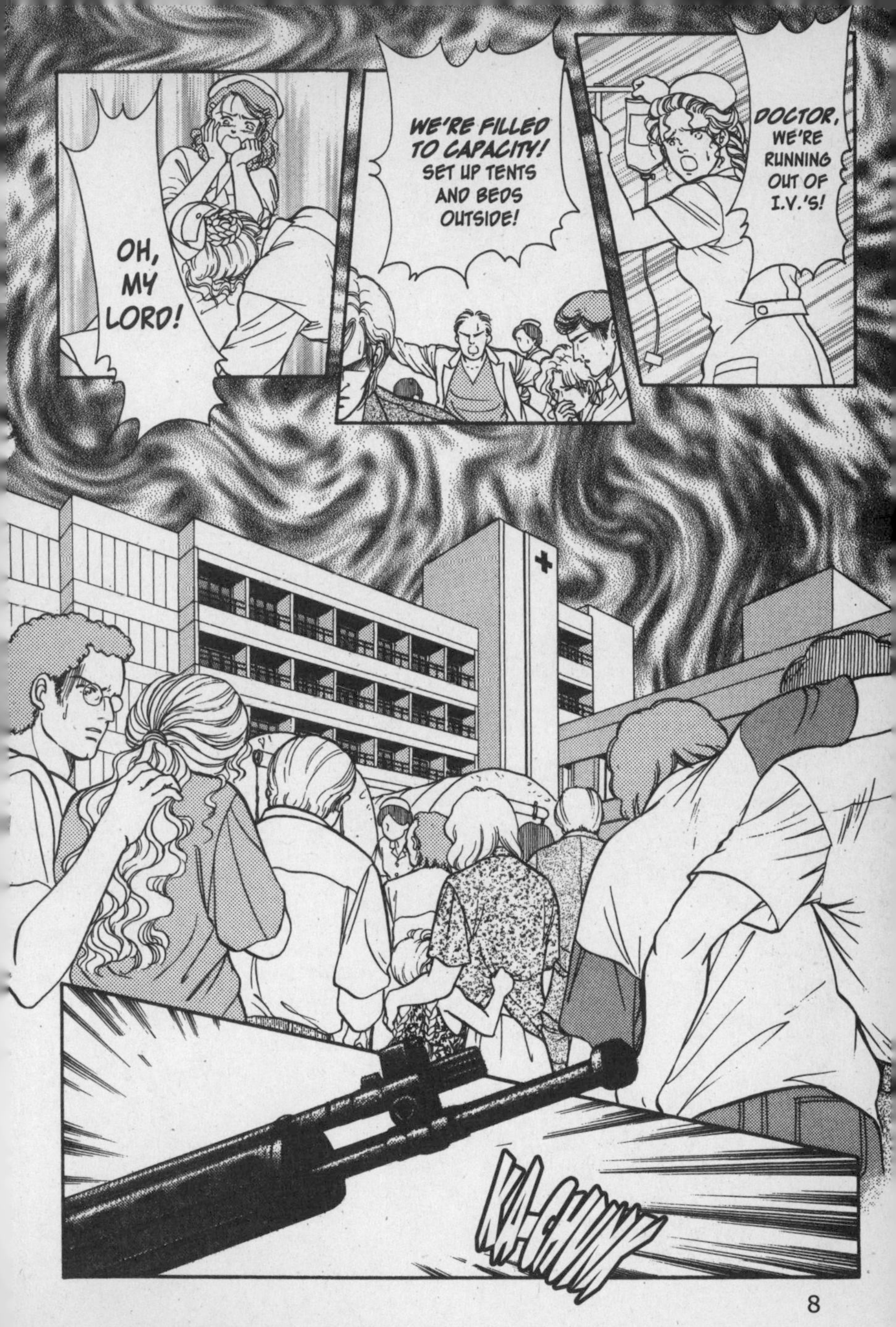
DOCTOR, WE'RE RUNNING OUT OF I.V.'S!
WE'RE FILLED TO CAPACITY! SET UP TENTS AND BEDS OUTSIDE!
OH, MY LORD!
KA-CHUNK

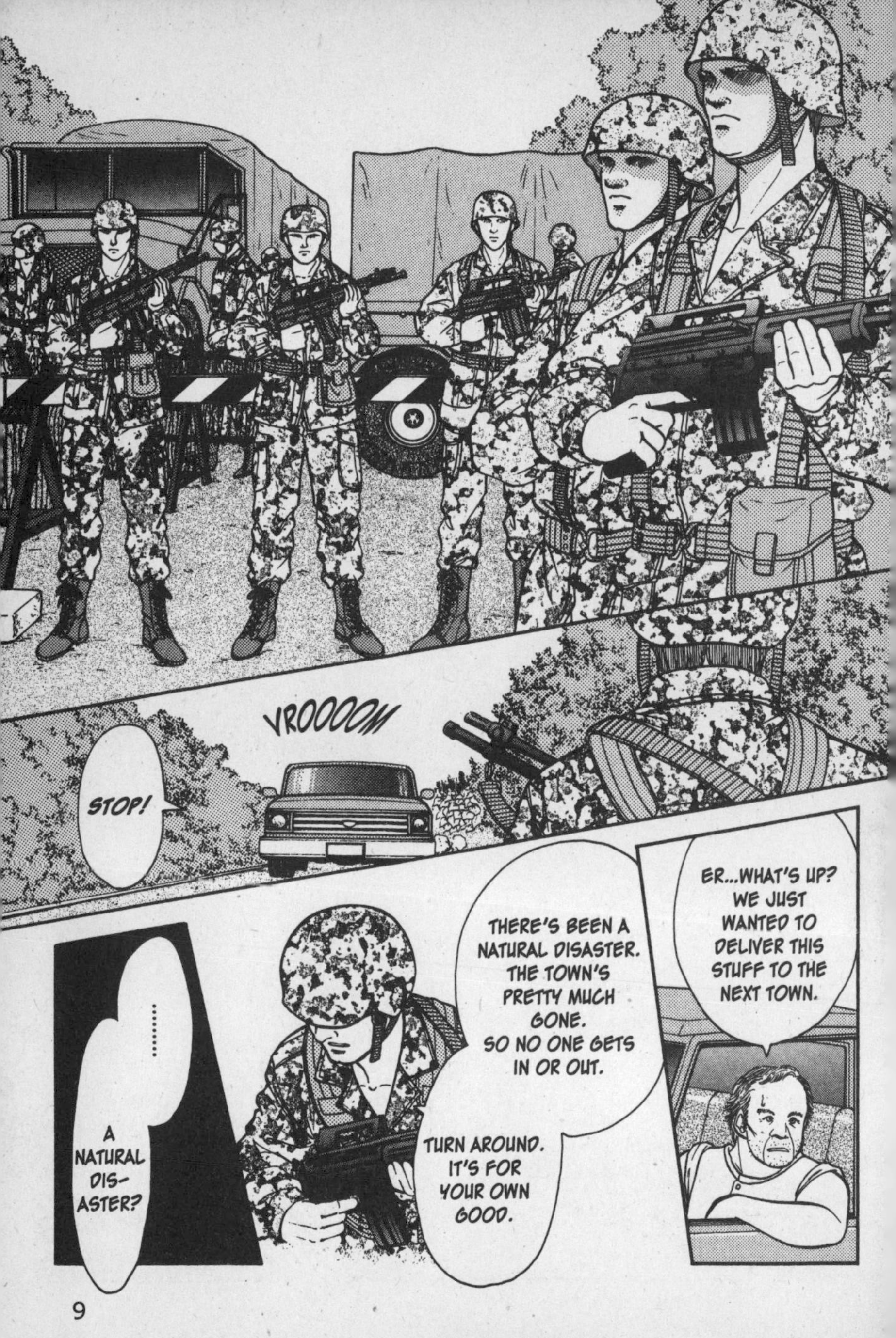
VROOOOM
STOP!
ER...WHAT'S UP? WE JUST WANTED TO DELIVER THIS STUFF TO THE NEXT TOWN.
THERE'S BEEN A NATURAL DISASTER. THE TOWN'S PRETTY MUCH GONE. SO NO ONE GETS IN OR OUT.
TURN AROUND. IT'S FOR YOUR OWN GOOD.
......
A NATURAL DIS-ASTER?

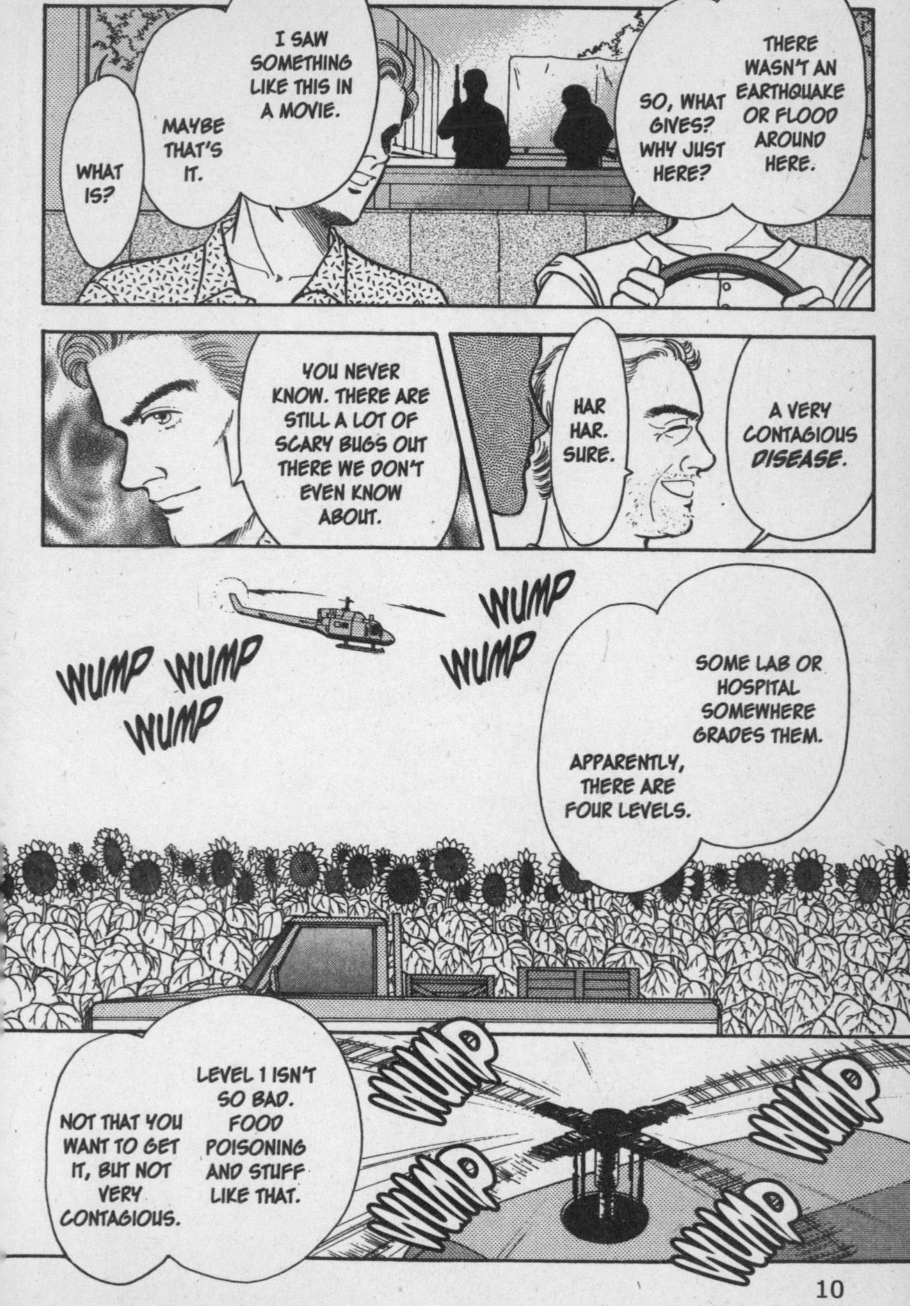
THERE WASN'T AN EARTHQUAKE OR FLOOD AROUND HERE.
SO, WHAT GIVES? WHY JUST HERE?
I SAW SOMETHING LIKE THIS IN A MOVIE.
MAYBE THAT'S IT.
WHAT IS?
A VERY CONTAGIOUS *DISEASE*.
HAR HAR. SURE.
YOU NEVER KNOW. THERE ARE STILL A LOT OF SCARY BUGS OUT THERE WE DON'T EVEN KNOW ABOUT.
WUMP WUMP
SOME LAB OR HOSPITAL SOMEWHERE GRADES THEM.
APPARENTLY, THERE ARE FOUR LEVELS.
WUMP WUMP WUMP
WUMP
WUMP
WUMP
LEVEL 1 ISN'T SO BAD. FOOD POISONING AND STUFF LIKE THAT.
NOT THAT YOU WANT TO GET IT, BUT NOT VERY CONTAGIOUS.
WUMP

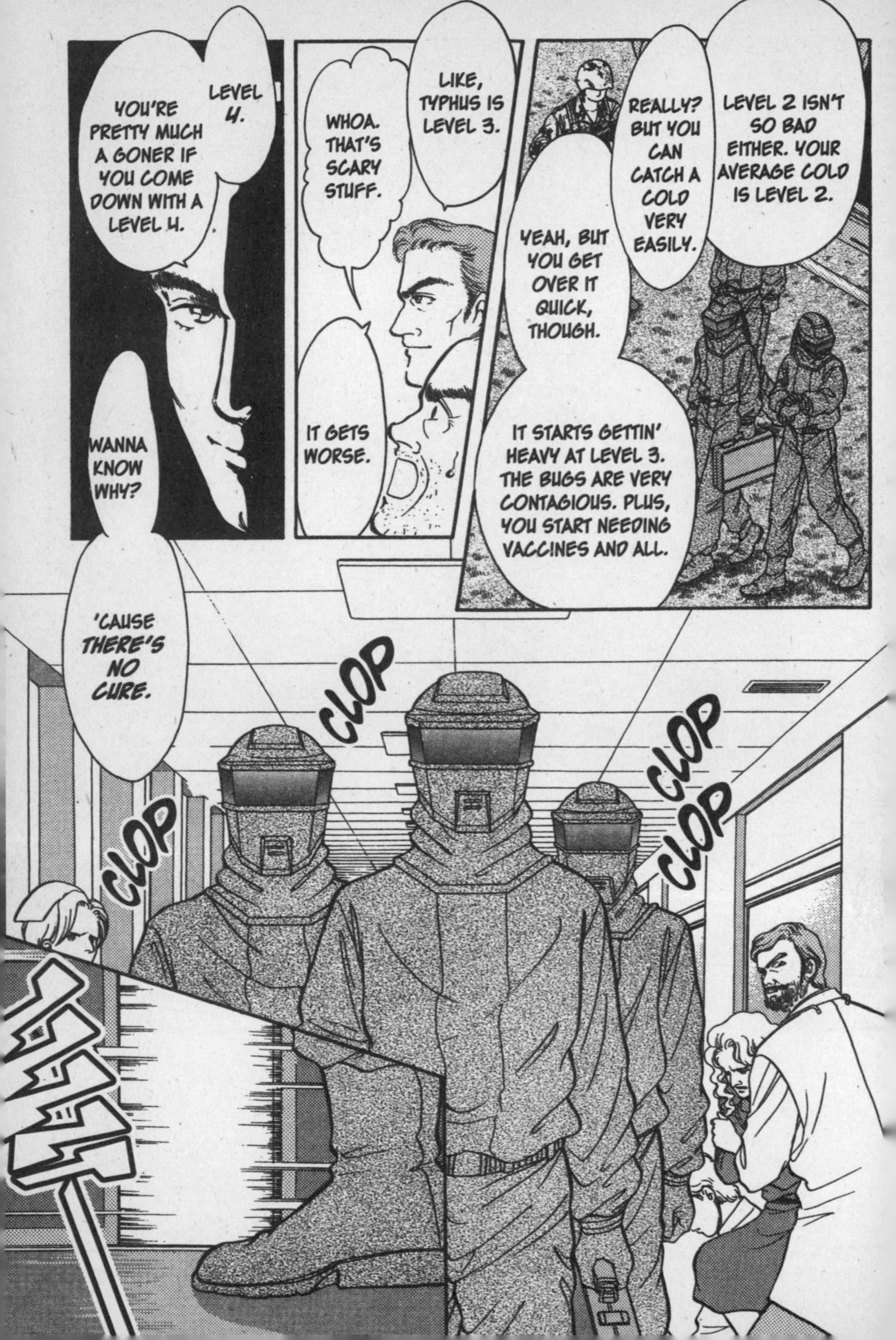

LEVEL 2 ISN'T SO BAD EITHER. YOUR AVERAGE COLD IS LEVEL 2.
REALLY? BUT YOU CAN CATCH A COLD VERY EASILY.
YEAH, BUT YOU GET OVER IT QUICK, THOUGH.
IT STARTS GETTIN' HEAVY AT LEVEL 3. THE BUGS ARE VERY CONTAGIOUS. PLUS, YOU START NEEDING VACCINES AND ALL.
LIKE, TYPHUS IS LEVEL 3.
WHOA. THAT'S SCARY STUFF.
IT GETS WORSE.
LEVEL 4.
YOU'RE PRETTY MUCH A GONER IF YOU COME DOWN WITH A LEVEL 4.
WANNA KNOW WHY?
'CAUSE THERE'S NO CURE.
CLOP CLOP
CLOP CLOP
CLOP
CLOP

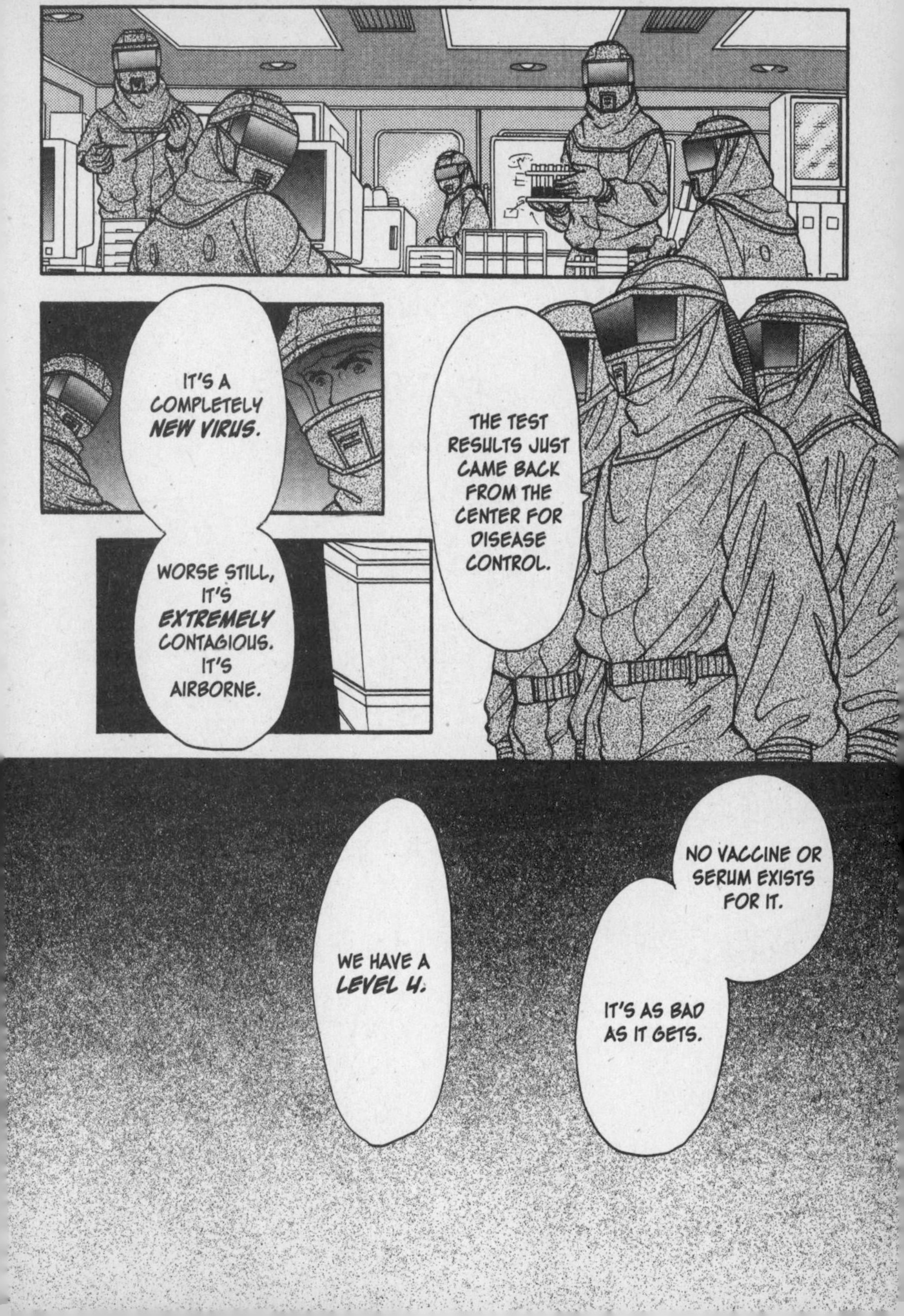
THE TEST RESULTS JUST CAME BACK FROM THE CENTER FOR DISEASE CONTROL.
IT'S A COMPLETELY *NEW VIRUS.*
WORSE STILL, IT'S *EXTREMELY* CONTAGIOUS. IT'S AIRBORNE.
NO VACCINE OR SERUM EXISTS FOR IT.
IT'S AS BAD AS IT GETS.
WE HAVE A *LEVEL 4.*

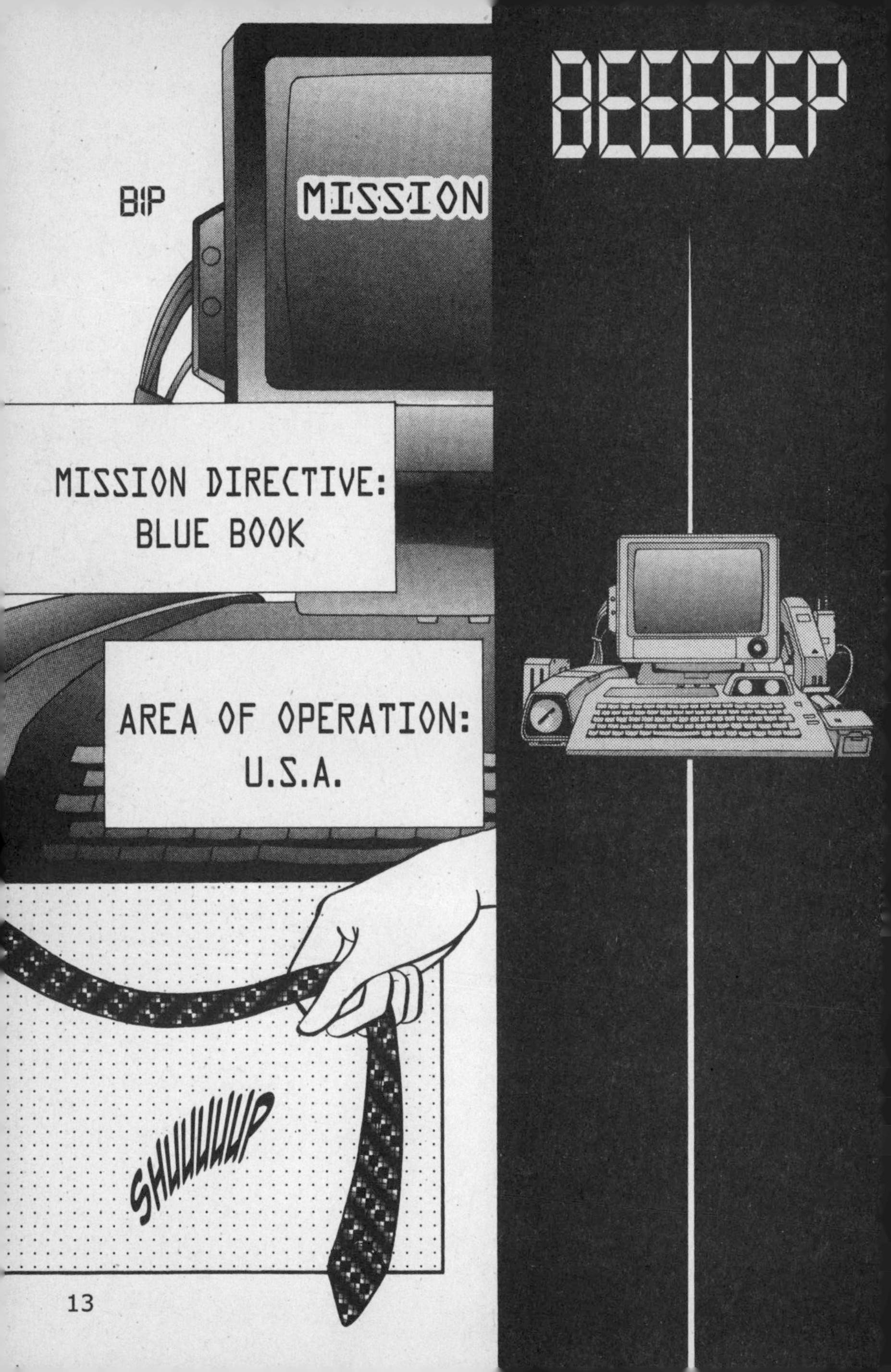
BEEEEEP
MISSION
BIP
MISSION DIRECTIVE: BLUE BOOK
AREA OF OPERATION: U.S.A.
SHUUUUUP

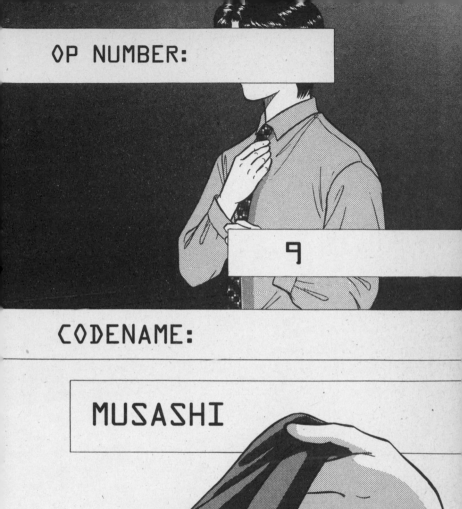

OP NUMBER:

9

CODENAME:

MUSASHI

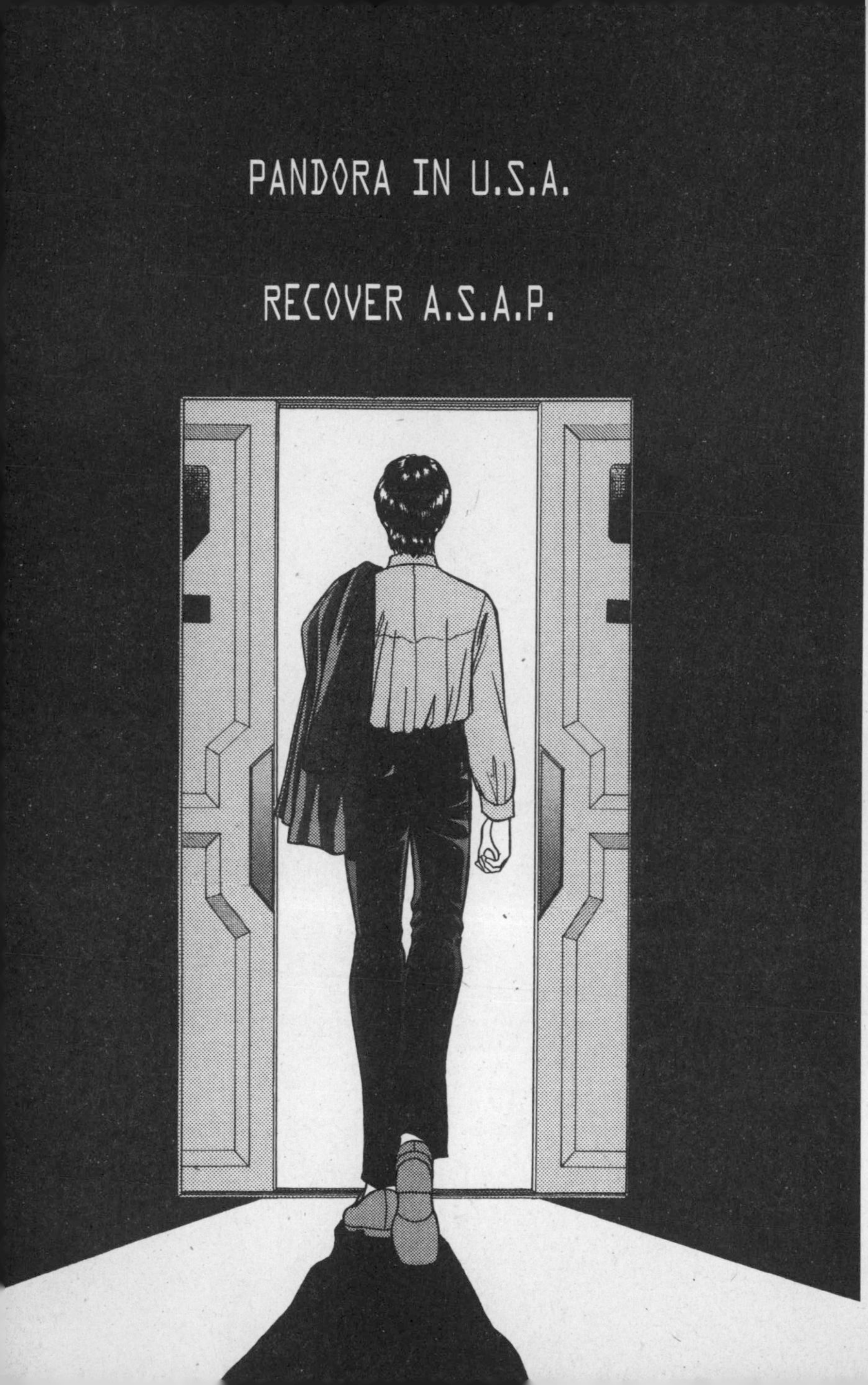
PANDORA IN U.S.A.
RECOVER A.S.A.P.

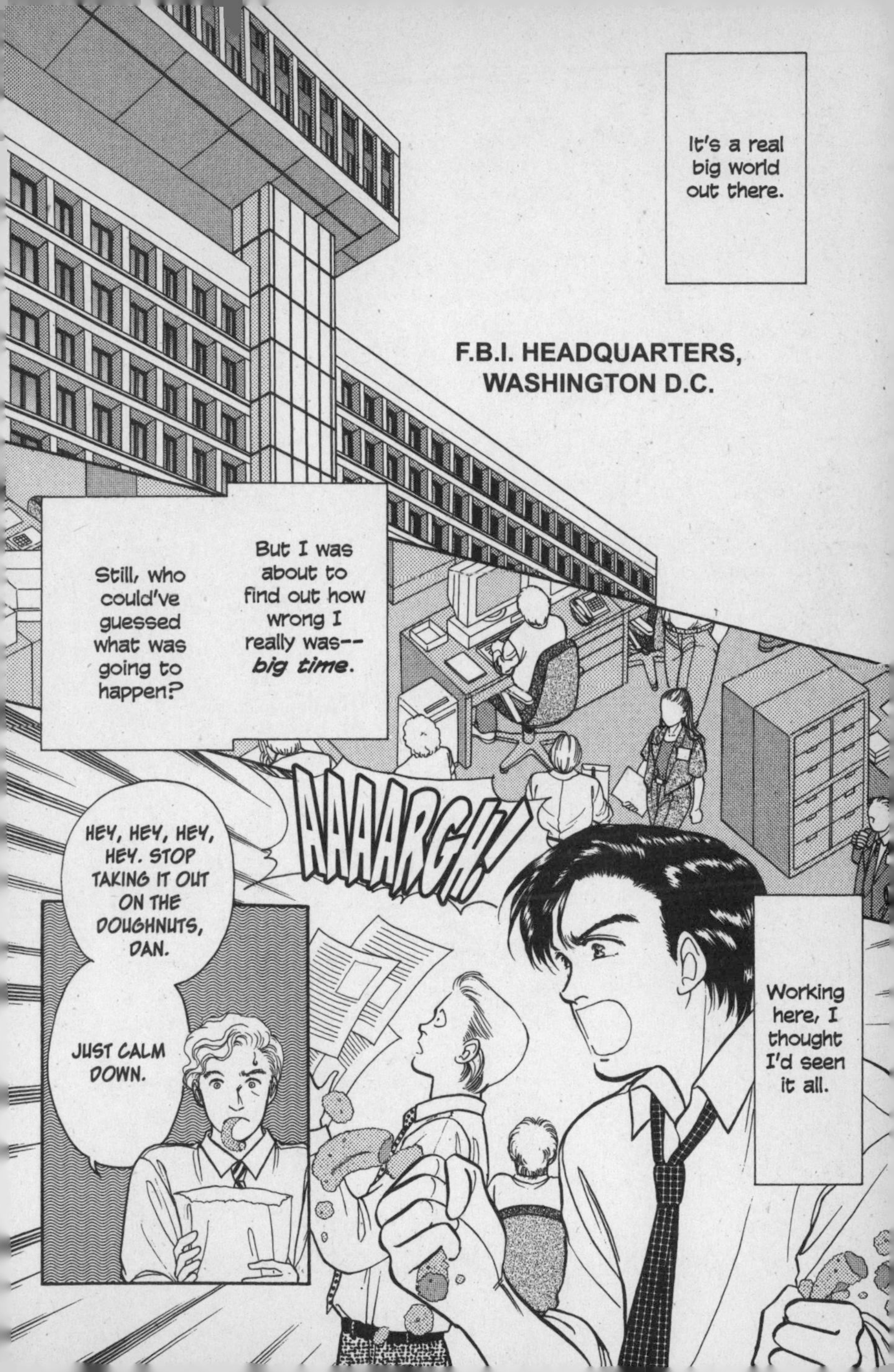
It's a real big world out there.
F.B.I. HEADQUARTERS, WASHINGTON D.C.
But I was about to find out how wrong I really was-- *big time*.
Still, who could've guessed what was going to happen?
Working here, I thought I'd seen it all.
AAAARGH!
HEY, HEY, HEY, HEY. STOP TAKING IT OUT ON THE DOUGHNUTS, DAN.
JUST CALM DOWN.

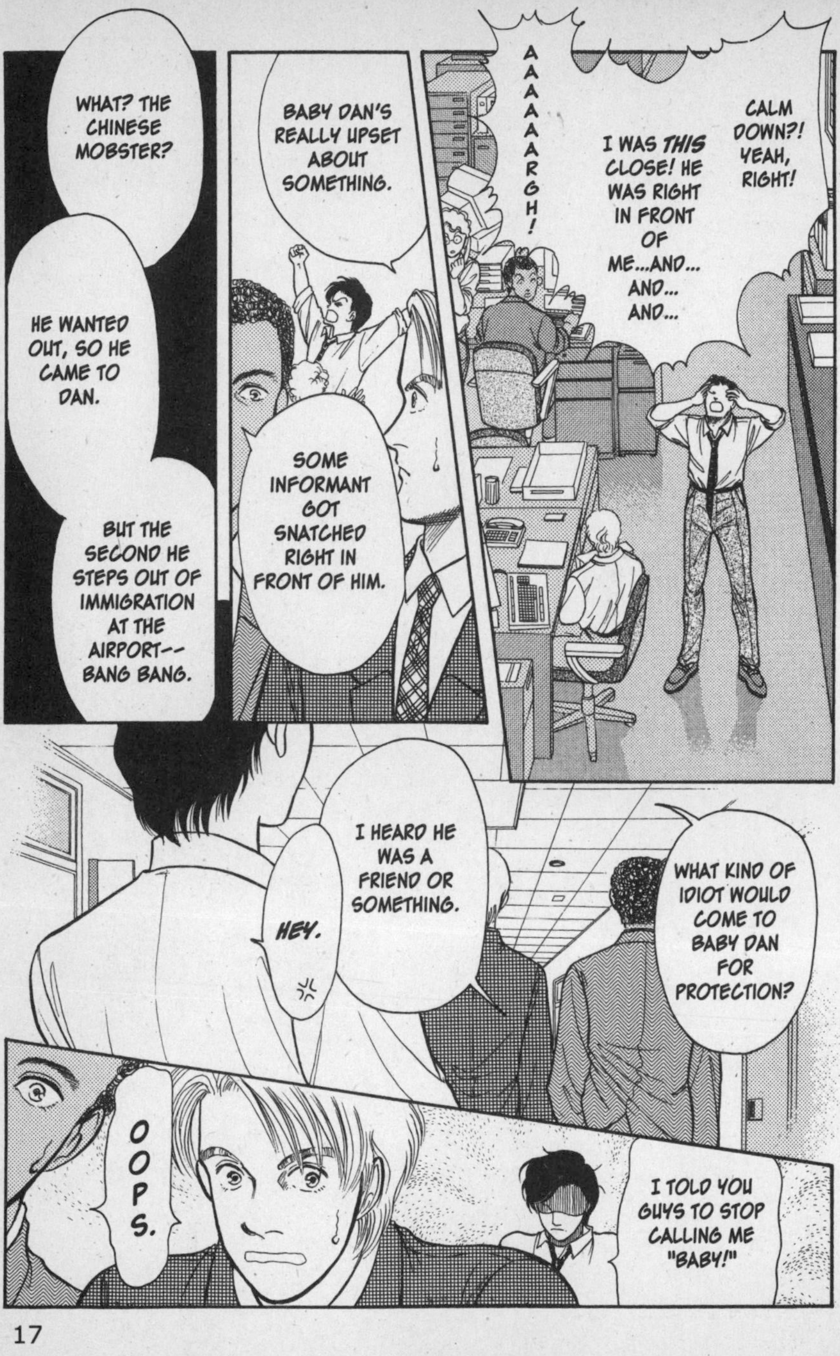

CALM DOWN?! YEAH, RIGHT!
I WAS *THIS* CLOSE! HE WAS RIGHT IN FRONT OF ME...AND... AND... AND...
AAAAAARGH!
BABY DAN'S REALLY UPSET ABOUT SOMETHING.
SOME INFORMANT GOT SNATCHED RIGHT IN FRONT OF HIM.
WHAT? THE CHINESE MOBSTER?
HE WANTED OUT, SO HE CAME TO DAN.
BUT THE SECOND HE STEPS OUT OF IMMIGRATION AT THE AIRPORT--BANG BANG.
WHAT KIND OF IDIOT WOULD COME TO BABY DAN FOR PROTECTION?
I HEARD HE WAS A FRIEND OR SOMETHING.
HEY.
I TOLD YOU GUYS TO STOP CALLING ME "BABY!"
OOPS.

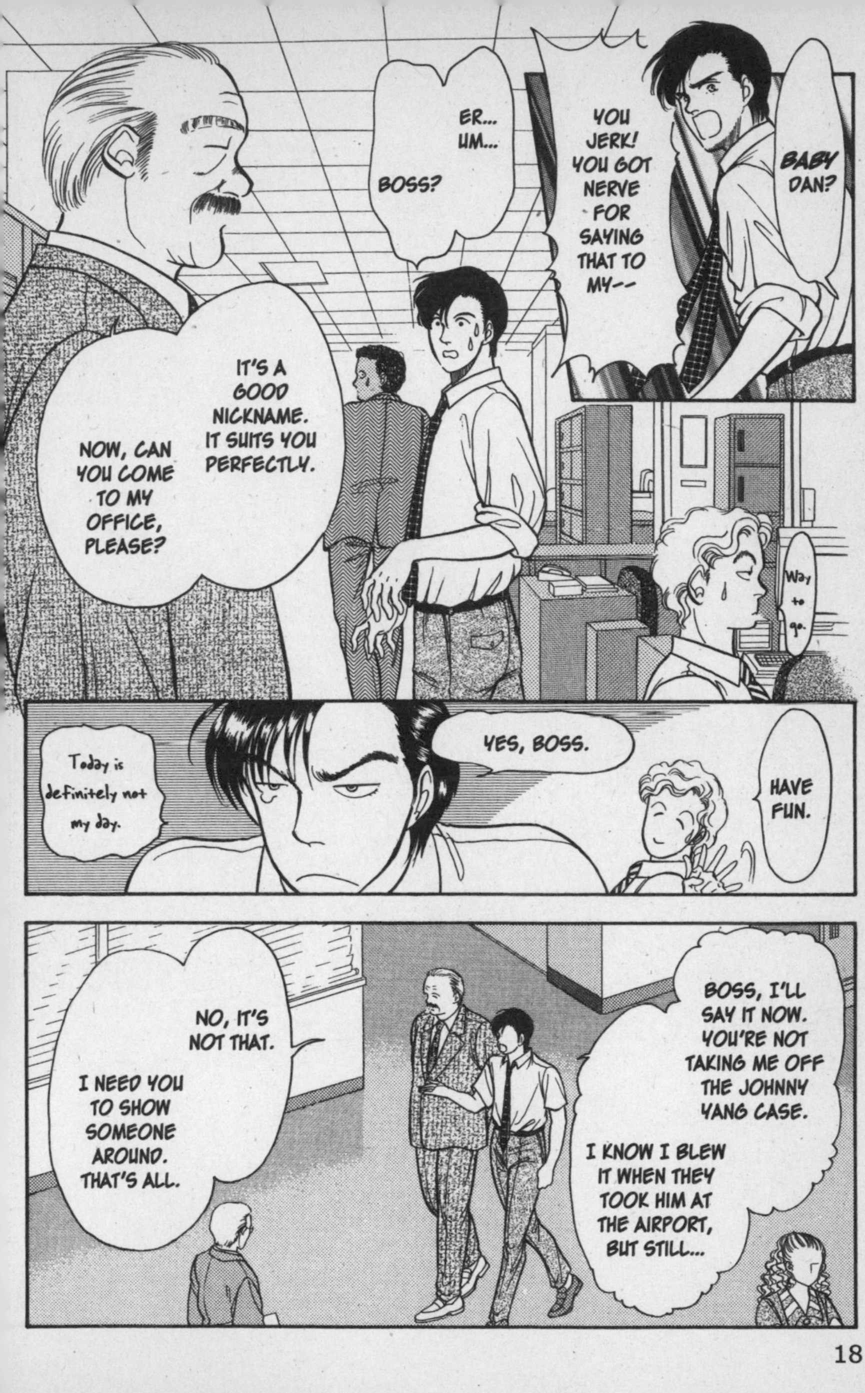
BABY DAN?
YOU JERK! YOU GOT NERVE FOR SAYING THAT TO MY--
ER... UM... BOSS?
IT'S A GOOD NICKNAME. IT SUITS YOU PERFECTLY.
NOW, CAN YOU COME TO MY OFFICE, PLEASE?
Way to go.
HAVE FUN.
YES, BOSS.
Today is definitely not my day.
BOSS, I'LL SAY IT NOW. YOU'RE NOT TAKING ME OFF THE JOHNNY YANG CASE.
I KNOW I BLEW IT WHEN THEY TOOK HIM AT THE AIRPORT, BUT STILL...
NO, IT'S NOT THAT.
I NEED YOU TO SHOW SOMEONE AROUND. THAT'S ALL.

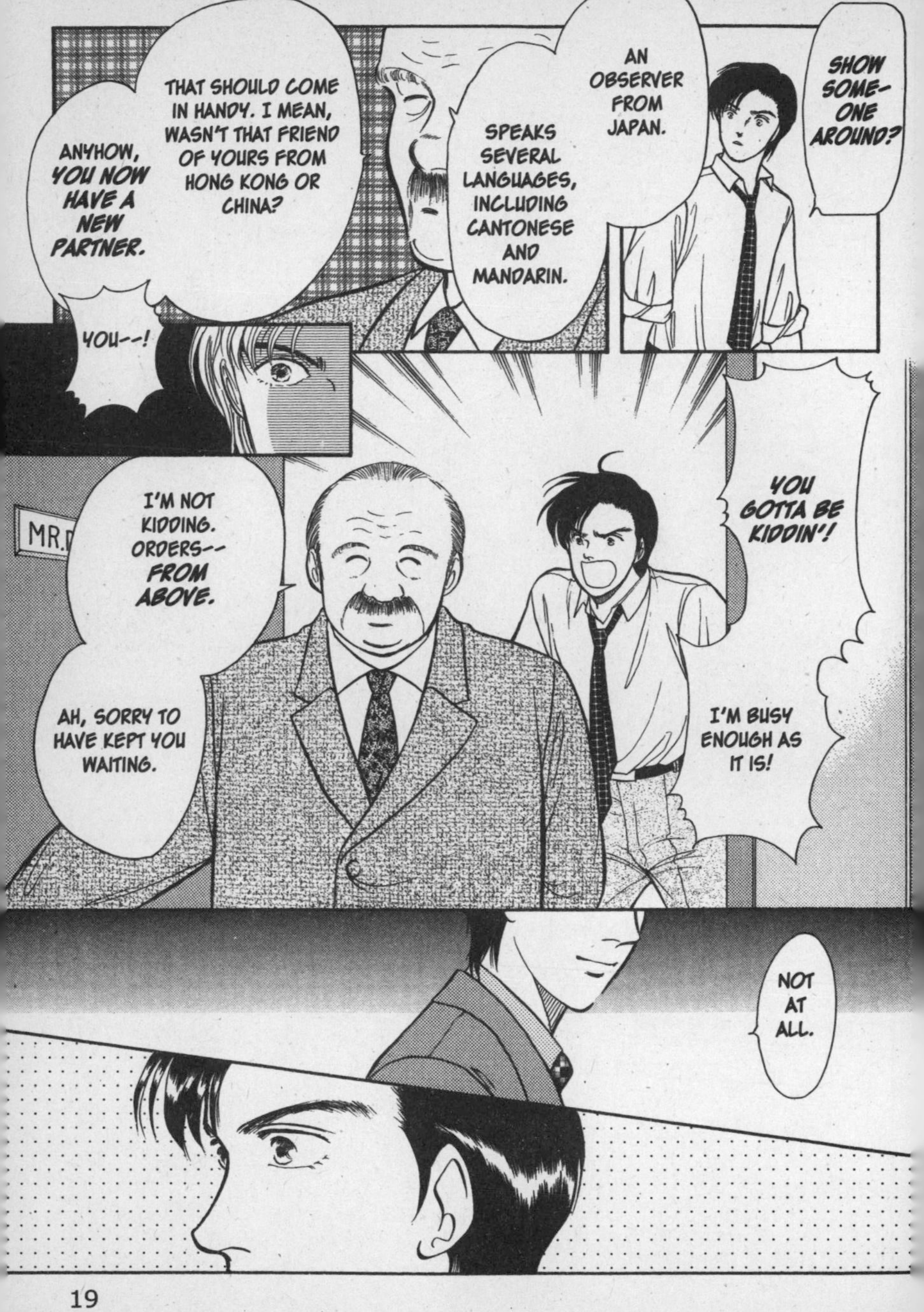
SHOW SOME-ONE AROUND?
AN OBSERVER FROM JAPAN.
SPEAKS SEVERAL LANGUAGES, INCLUDING CANTONESE AND MANDARIN.
THAT SHOULD COME IN HANDY. I MEAN, WASN'T THAT FRIEND OF YOURS FROM HONG KONG OR CHINA?
ANYHOW, YOU NOW HAVE A NEW PARTNER.
YOU--!
YOU GOTTA BE KIDDIN'!
I'M BUSY ENOUGH AS IT IS!
I'M NOT KIDDING. ORDERS--FROM ABOVE.
MR.
AH, SORRY TO HAVE KEPT YOU WAITING.
NOT AT ALL.

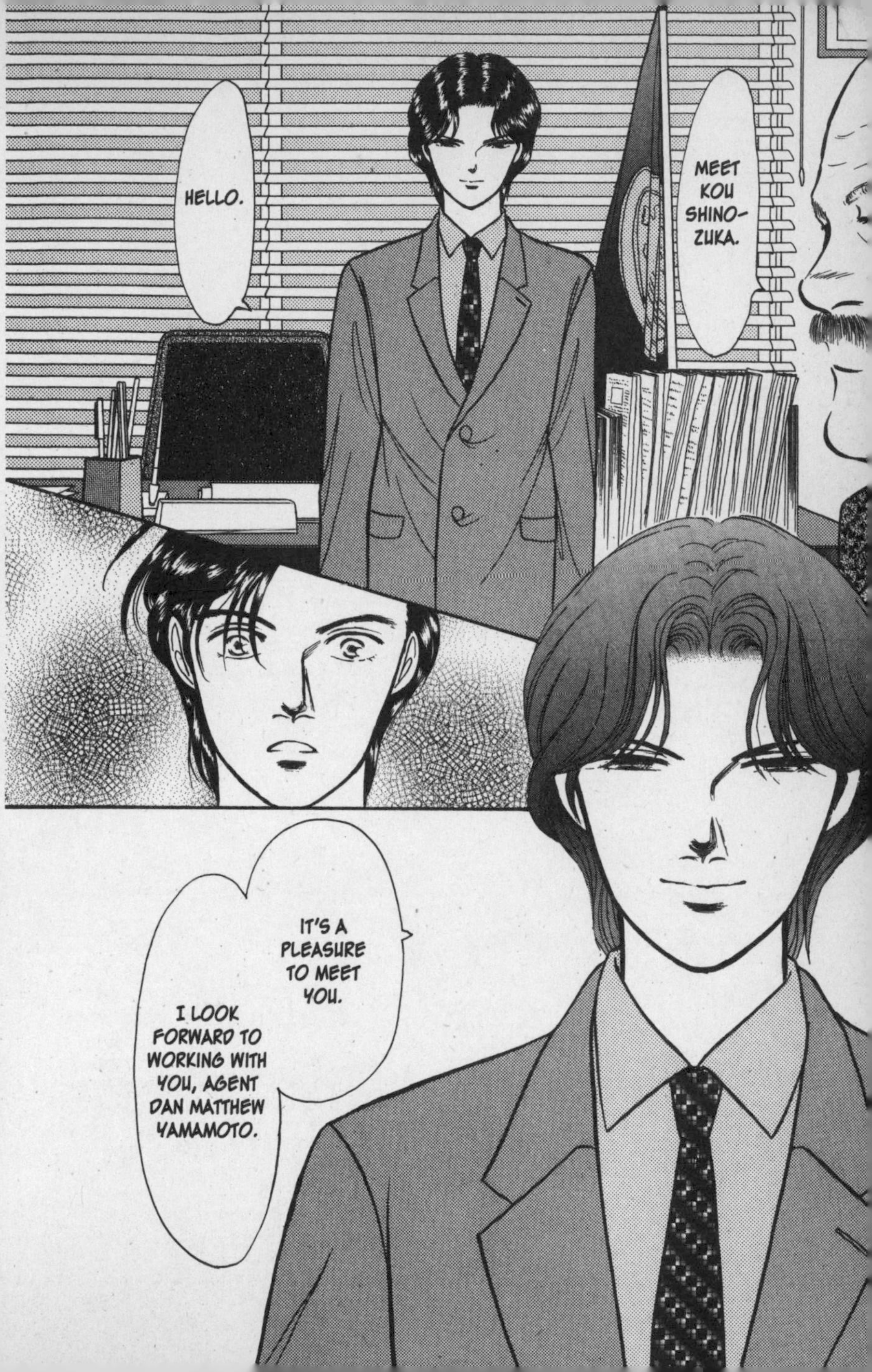
MEET KOU SHINOZUKA.
HELLO.
IT'S A PLEASURE TO MEET YOU.
I LOOK FORWARD TO WORKING WITH YOU, AGENT DAN MATTHEW YAMAMOTO.

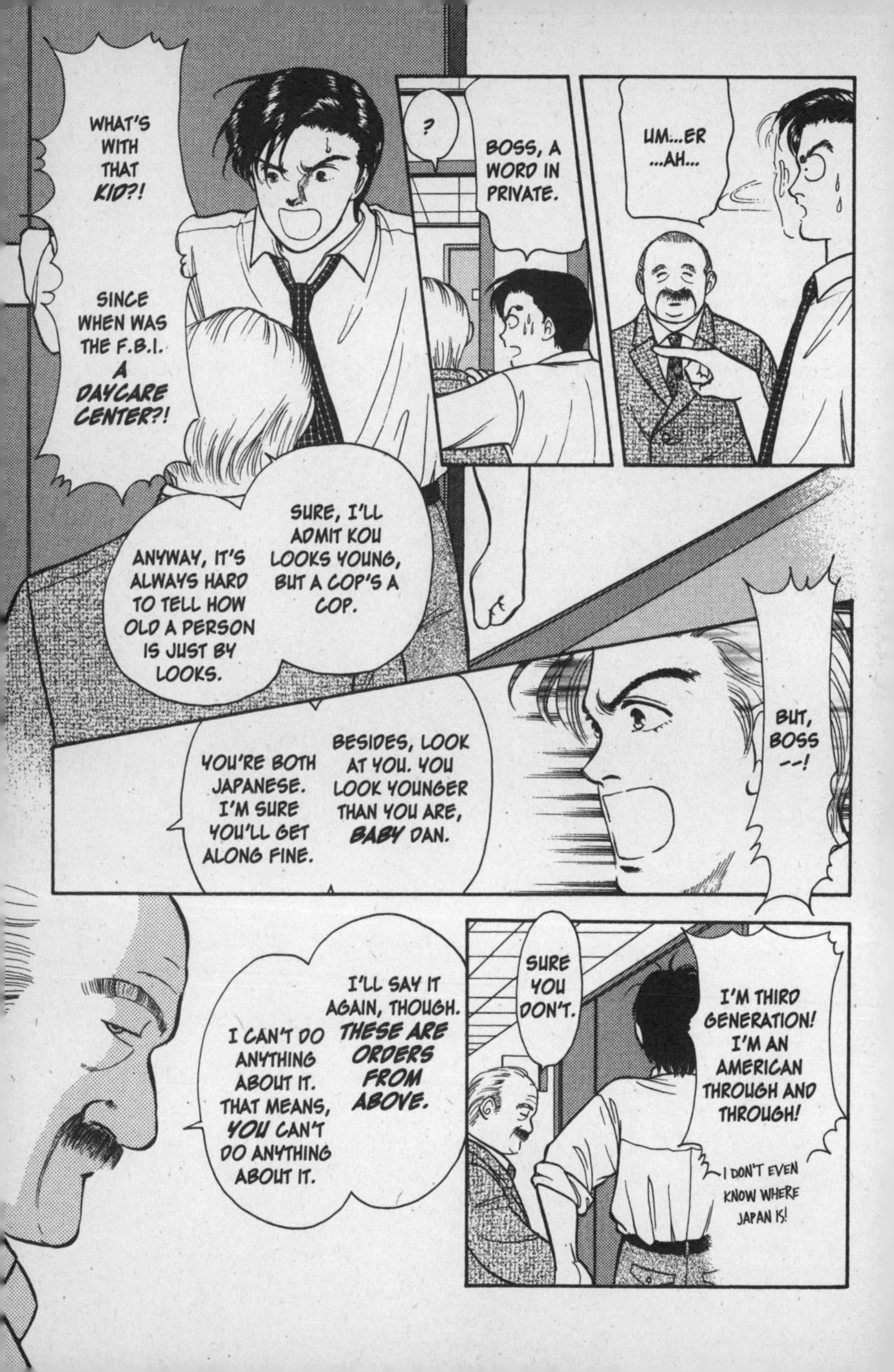
UM...ER ...AH...
?
BOSS, A WORD IN PRIVATE.
WHAT'S WITH THAT *KID?!*
SINCE WHEN WAS THE F.B.I. *A DAYCARE CENTER?!*
SURE, I'LL ADMIT KOU LOOKS YOUNG, BUT A COP'S A COP.
ANYWAY, IT'S ALWAYS HARD TO TELL HOW OLD A PERSON IS JUST BY LOOKS.
BUT, BOSS --!
BESIDES, LOOK AT YOU. YOU LOOK YOUNGER THAN YOU ARE, *BABY* DAN.
YOU'RE BOTH JAPANESE. I'M SURE YOU'LL GET ALONG FINE.
I'M THIRD GENERATION! I'M AN AMERICAN THROUGH AND THROUGH!
I DON'T EVEN KNOW WHERE JAPAN IS!
SURE YOU DON'T.
I'LL SAY IT AGAIN, THOUGH. *THESE ARE ORDERS FROM ABOVE.*
I CAN'T DO ANYTHING ABOUT IT. THAT MEANS, *YOU* CAN'T DO ANYTHING ABOUT IT.

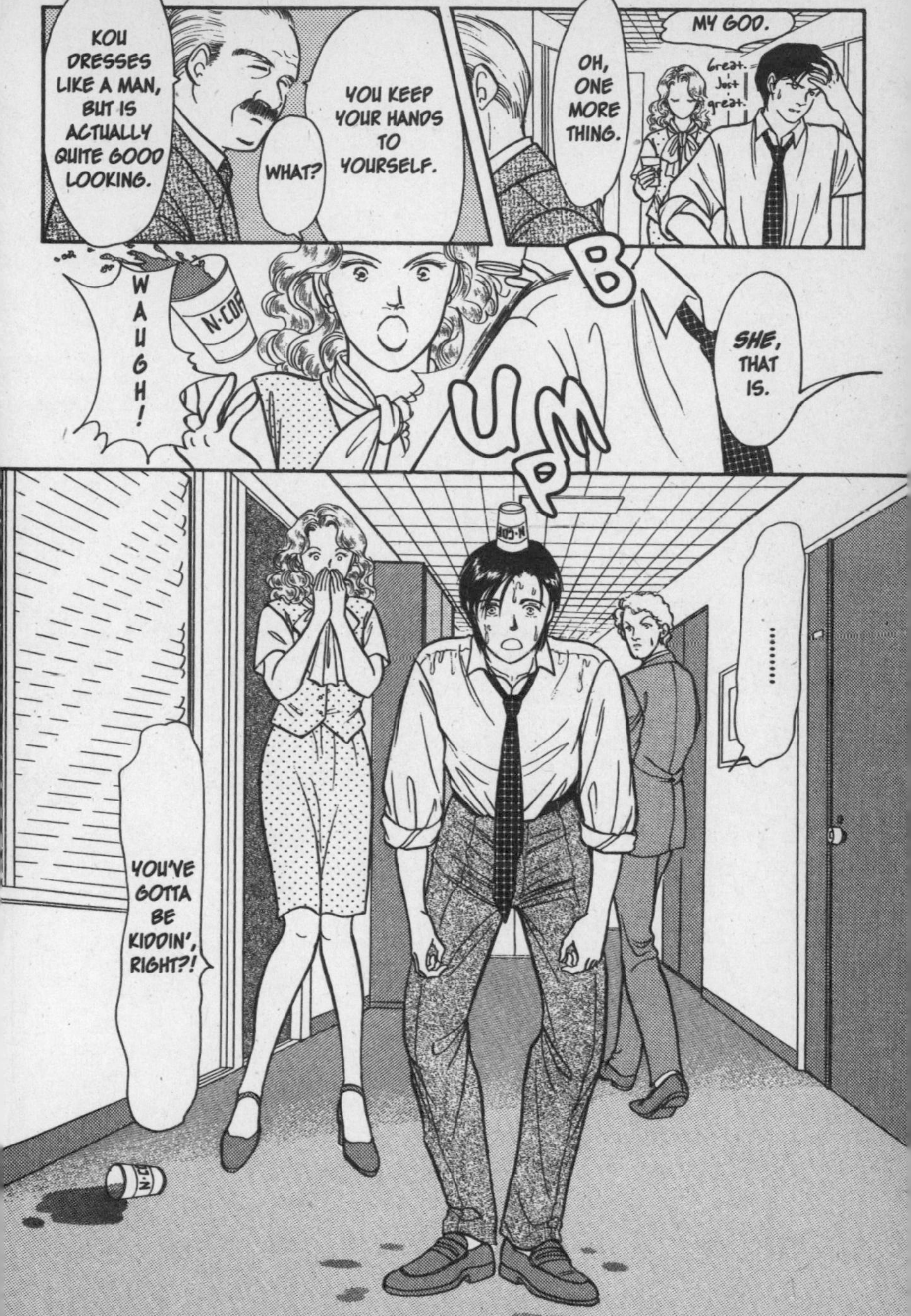
MY GOD.
Great. Just great.
OH, ONE MORE THING.
YOU KEEP YOUR HANDS TO YOURSELF.
WHAT?
KOU DRESSES LIKE A MAN, BUT IS ACTUALLY QUITE GOOD LOOKING.
SHE, THAT IS.
BUMP
N·COF
WAUGH!
N·COF
......
YOU'VE GOTTA BE KIDDIN', RIGHT?!
N·COF

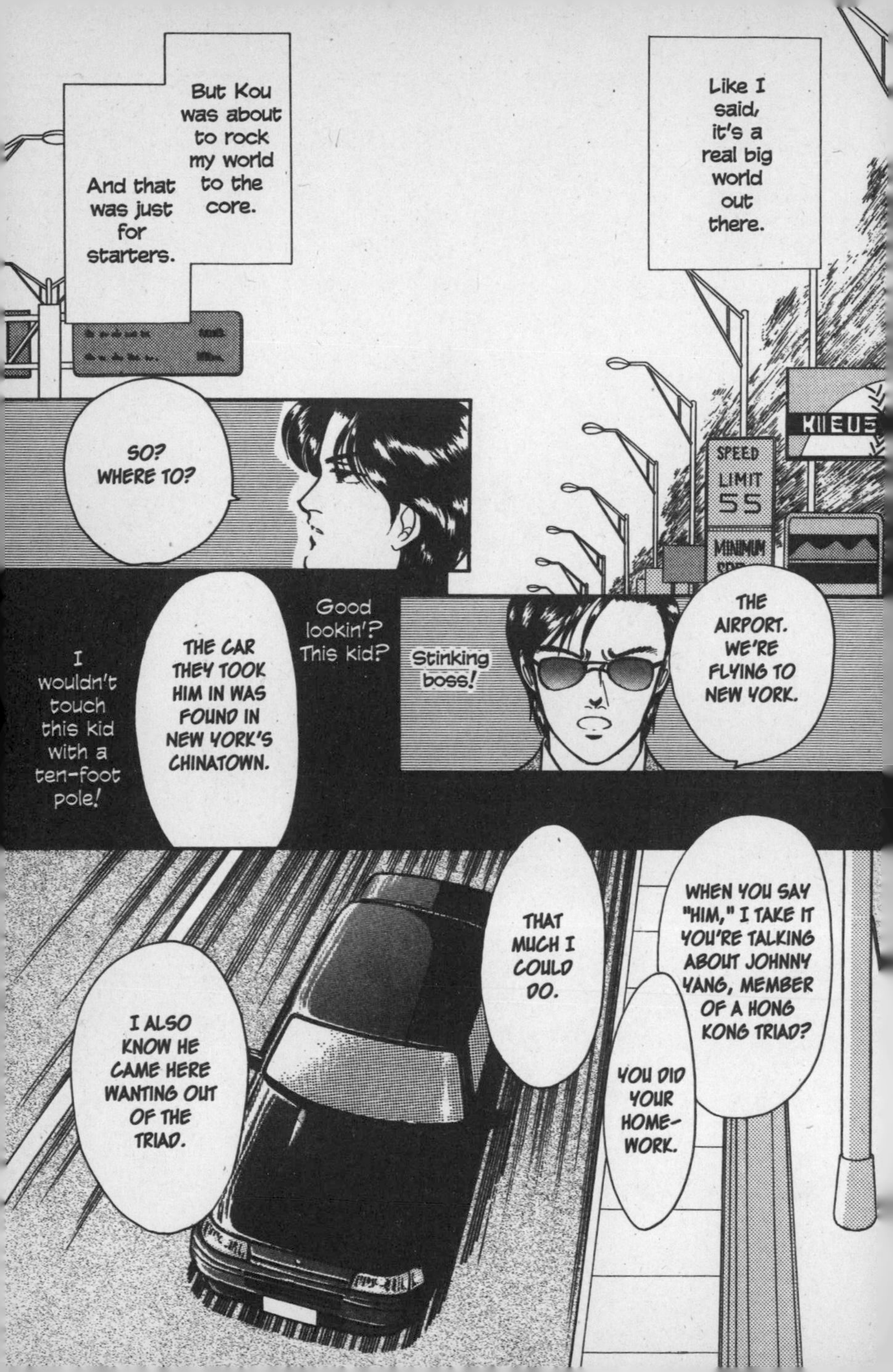
Like I said, it's a real big world out there.
But Kou was about to rock my world to the core.
And that was just for starters.
SPEED LIMIT 55
SO? WHERE TO?
THE AIRPORT. WE'RE FLYING TO NEW YORK.
Stinking boss!
Good lookin'? This kid?
THE CAR THEY TOOK HIM IN WAS FOUND IN NEW YORK'S CHINATOWN.
I wouldn't touch this kid with a ten-foot pole!
WHEN YOU SAY "HIM," I TAKE IT YOU'RE TALKING ABOUT JOHNNY YANG, MEMBER OF A HONG KONG TRIAD?
YOU DID YOUR HOME-WORK.
THAT MUCH I COULD DO.
I ALSO KNOW HE CAME HERE WANTING OUT OF THE TRIAD.

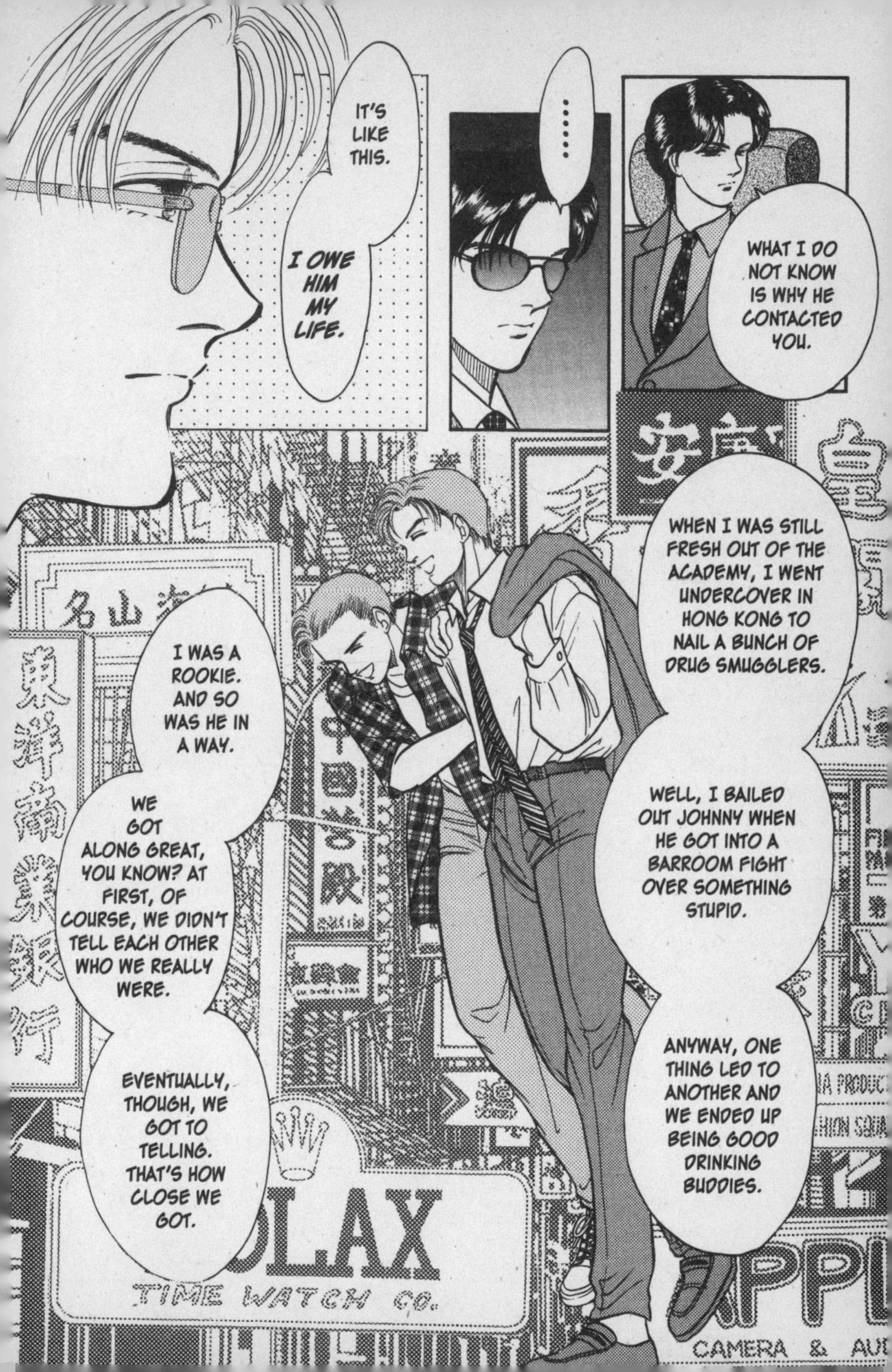

WHAT I DO NOT KNOW IS WHY HE CONTACTED YOU.
......
IT'S LIKE THIS.
I OWE HIM MY LIFE.
WHEN I WAS STILL FRESH OUT OF THE ACADEMY, I WENT UNDERCOVER IN HONG KONG TO NAIL A BUNCH OF DRUG SMUGGLERS.
WELL, I BAILED OUT JOHNNY WHEN HE GOT INTO A BARROOM FIGHT OVER SOMETHING STUPID.
ANYWAY, ONE THING LED TO ANOTHER AND WE ENDED UP BEING GOOD DRINKING BUDDIES.
I WAS A ROOKIE. AND SO WAS HE IN A WAY.
WE GOT ALONG GREAT, YOU KNOW? AT FIRST, OF COURSE, WE DIDN'T TELL EACH OTHER WHO WE REALLY WERE.
EVENTUALLY, THOUGH, WE GOT TO TELLING. THAT'S HOW CLOSE WE GOT.
TIME WATCH CO.

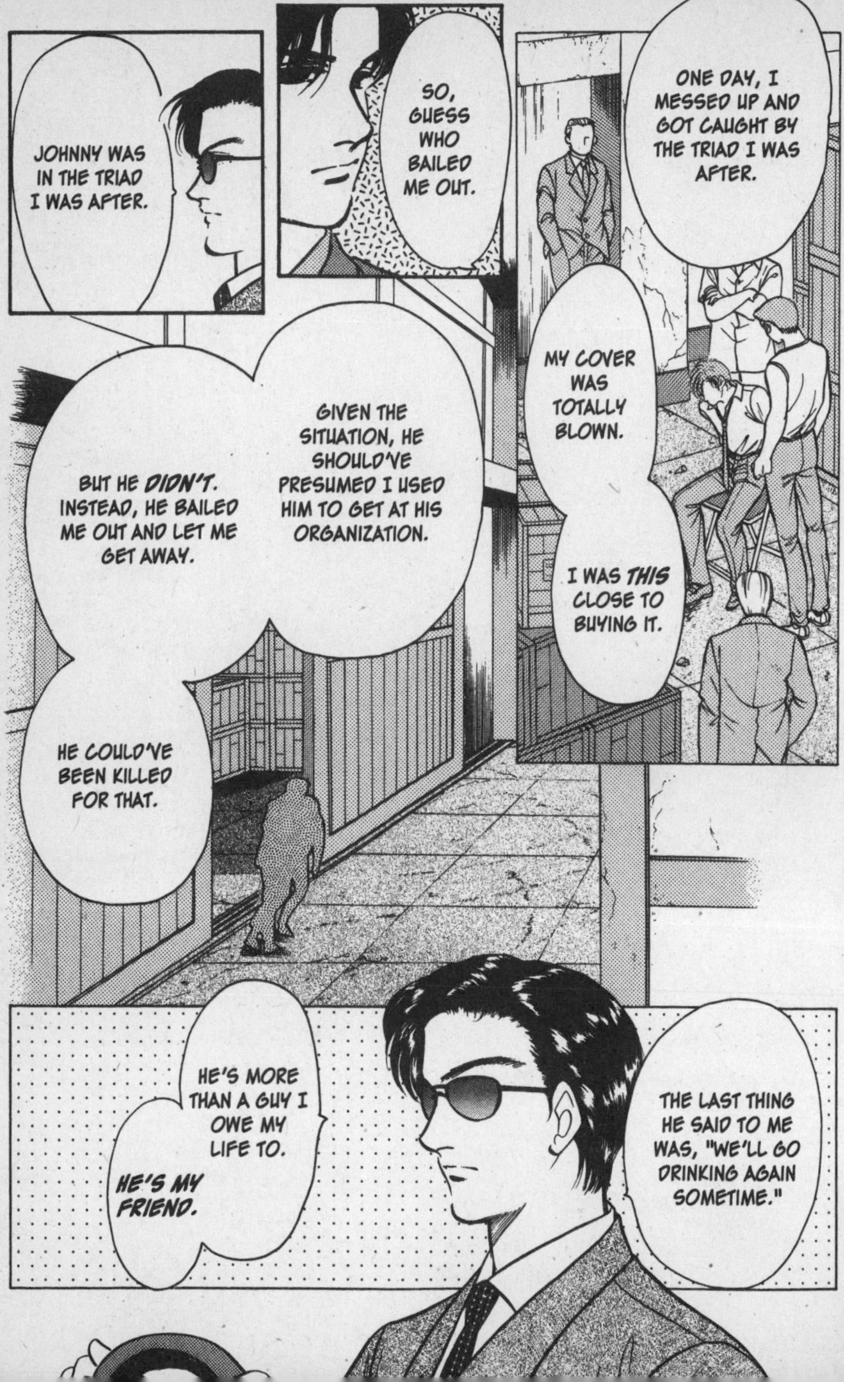
ONE DAY, I MESSED UP AND GOT CAUGHT BY THE TRIAD I WAS AFTER.
MY COVER WAS TOTALLY BLOWN.
I WAS *THIS* CLOSE TO BUYING IT.
SO, GUESS WHO BAILED ME OUT.
JOHNNY WAS IN THE TRIAD I WAS AFTER.
GIVEN THE SITUATION, HE SHOULD'VE PRESUMED I USED HIM TO GET AT HIS ORGANIZATION.
BUT HE *DIDN'T*. INSTEAD, HE BAILED ME OUT AND LET ME GET AWAY.
HE COULD'VE BEEN KILLED FOR THAT.
THE LAST THING HE SAID TO ME WAS, "WE'LL GO DRINKING AGAIN SOMETIME."
HE'S MORE THAN A GUY I OWE MY LIFE TO.
HE'S MY FRIEND.

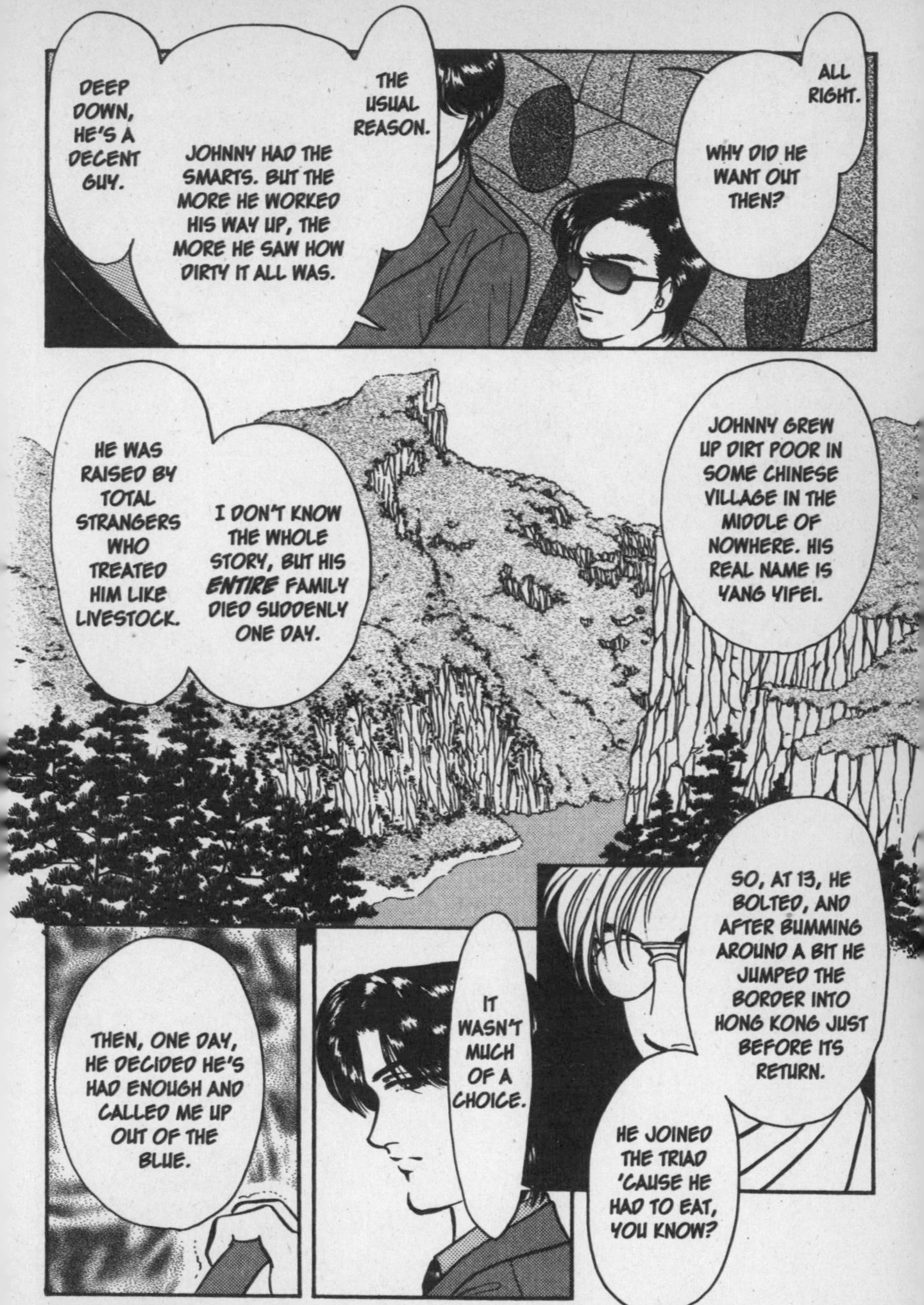
ALL RIGHT.
WHY DID HE WANT OUT THEN?
THE USUAL REASON.
JOHNNY HAD THE SMARTS. BUT THE MORE HE WORKED HIS WAY UP, THE MORE HE SAW HOW DIRTY IT ALL WAS.
DEEP DOWN, HE'S A DECENT GUY.
JOHNNY GREW UP DIRT POOR IN SOME CHINESE VILLAGE IN THE MIDDLE OF NOWHERE. HIS REAL NAME IS YANG YIFEI.
I DON'T KNOW THE WHOLE STORY, BUT HIS *ENTIRE* FAMILY DIED SUDDENLY ONE DAY.
HE WAS RAISED BY TOTAL STRANGERS WHO TREATED HIM LIKE LIVESTOCK.
SO, AT 13, HE BOLTED, AND AFTER BUMMING AROUND A BIT HE JUMPED THE BORDER INTO HONG KONG JUST BEFORE ITS RETURN.
HE JOINED THE TRIAD 'CAUSE HE HAD TO EAT, YOU KNOW?
IT WASN'T MUCH OF A CHOICE.
THEN, ONE DAY, HE DECIDED HE'S HAD ENOUGH AND CALLED ME UP OUT OF THE BLUE.

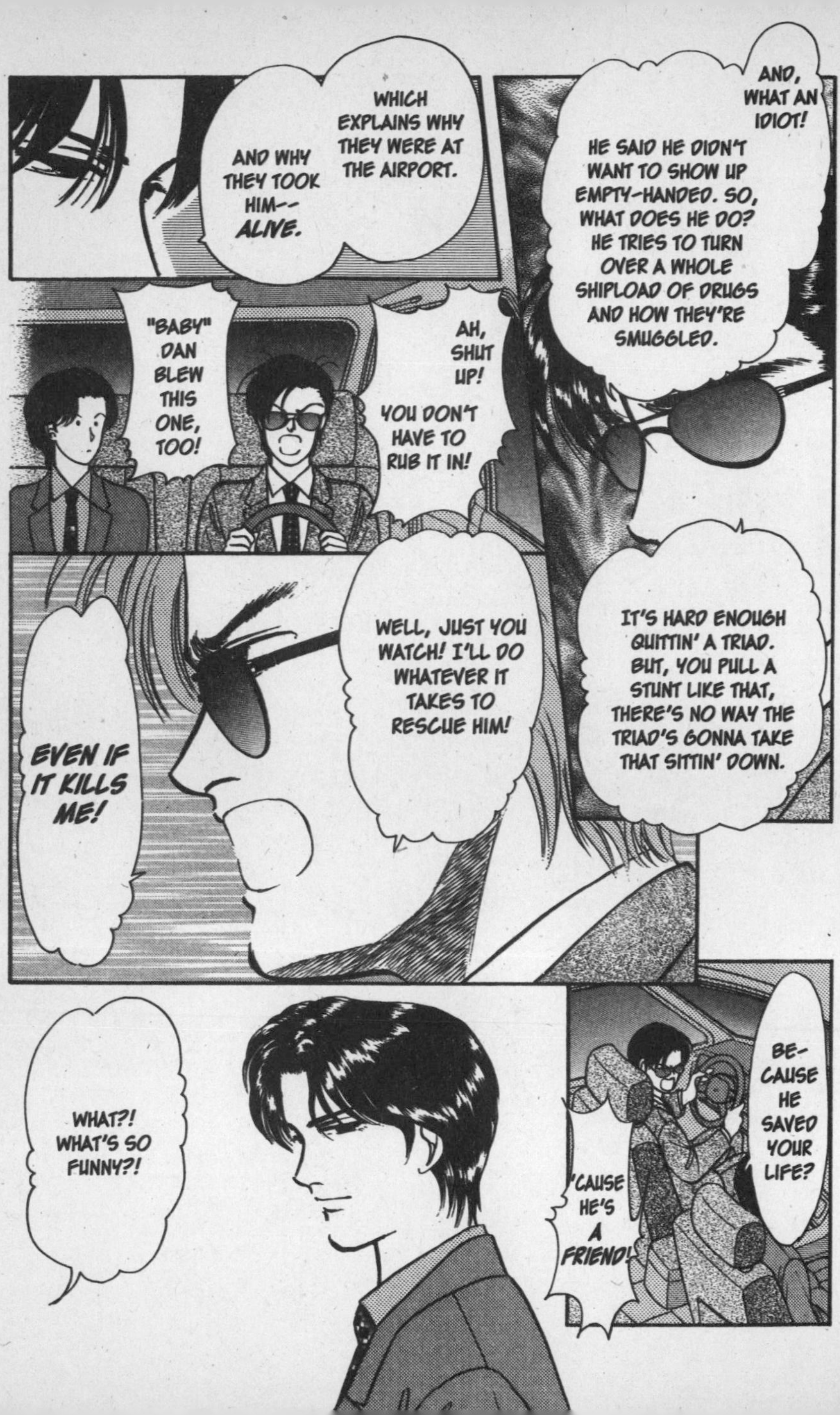
AND, WHAT AN IDIOT!
HE SAID HE DIDN'T WANT TO SHOW UP EMPTY-HANDED. SO, WHAT DOES HE DO? HE TRIES TO TURN OVER A WHOLE SHIPLOAD OF DRUGS AND HOW THEY'RE SMUGGLED.
IT'S HARD ENOUGH QUITTIN' A TRIAD. BUT, YOU PULL A STUNT LIKE THAT, THERE'S NO WAY THE TRIAD'S GONNA TAKE THAT SITTIN' DOWN.
WHICH EXPLAINS WHY THEY WERE AT THE AIRPORT.
AND WHY THEY TOOK HIM-- ALIVE.
"BABY" DAN BLEW THIS ONE, TOO!
AH, SHUT UP!
YOU DON'T HAVE TO RUB IT IN!
WELL, JUST YOU WATCH! I'LL DO WHATEVER IT TAKES TO RESCUE HIM!
EVEN IF IT KILLS ME!
BE-CAUSE HE SAVED YOUR LIFE?
'CAUSE HE'S A FRIEND!
WHAT?! WHAT'S SO FUNNY?!

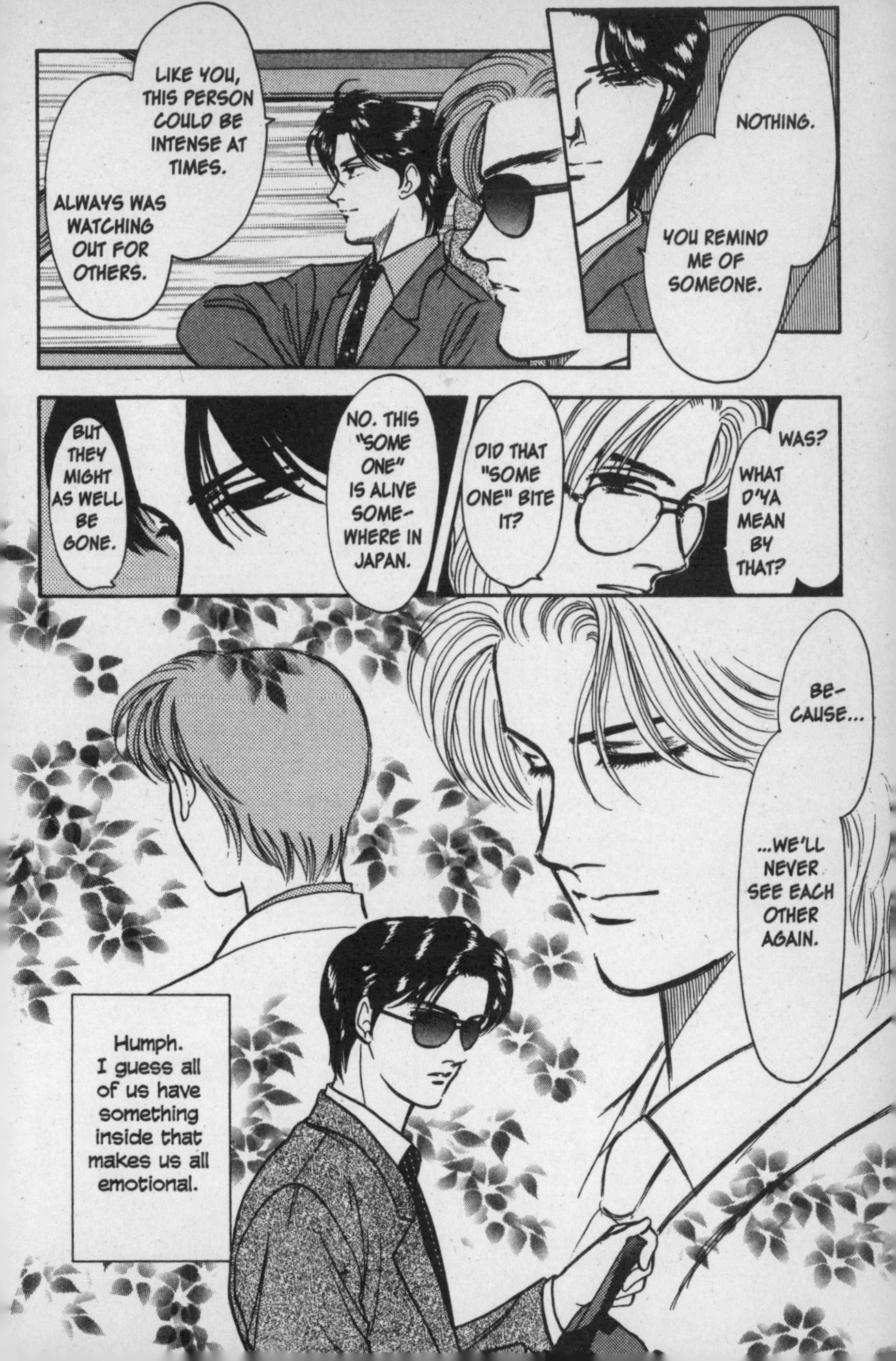
NOTHING.
YOU REMIND ME OF SOMEONE.
LIKE YOU, THIS PERSON COULD BE INTENSE AT TIMES.
ALWAYS WAS WATCHING OUT FOR OTHERS.
WAS? WHAT D'YA MEAN BY THAT?
DID THAT "SOME ONE" BITE IT?
NO. THIS "SOME ONE" IS ALIVE SOME-WHERE IN JAPAN.
BUT THEY MIGHT AS WELL BE GONE.
BE-CAUSE...
...WE'LL NEVER SEE EACH OTHER AGAIN.
Humph. I guess all of us have something inside that makes us all emotional.

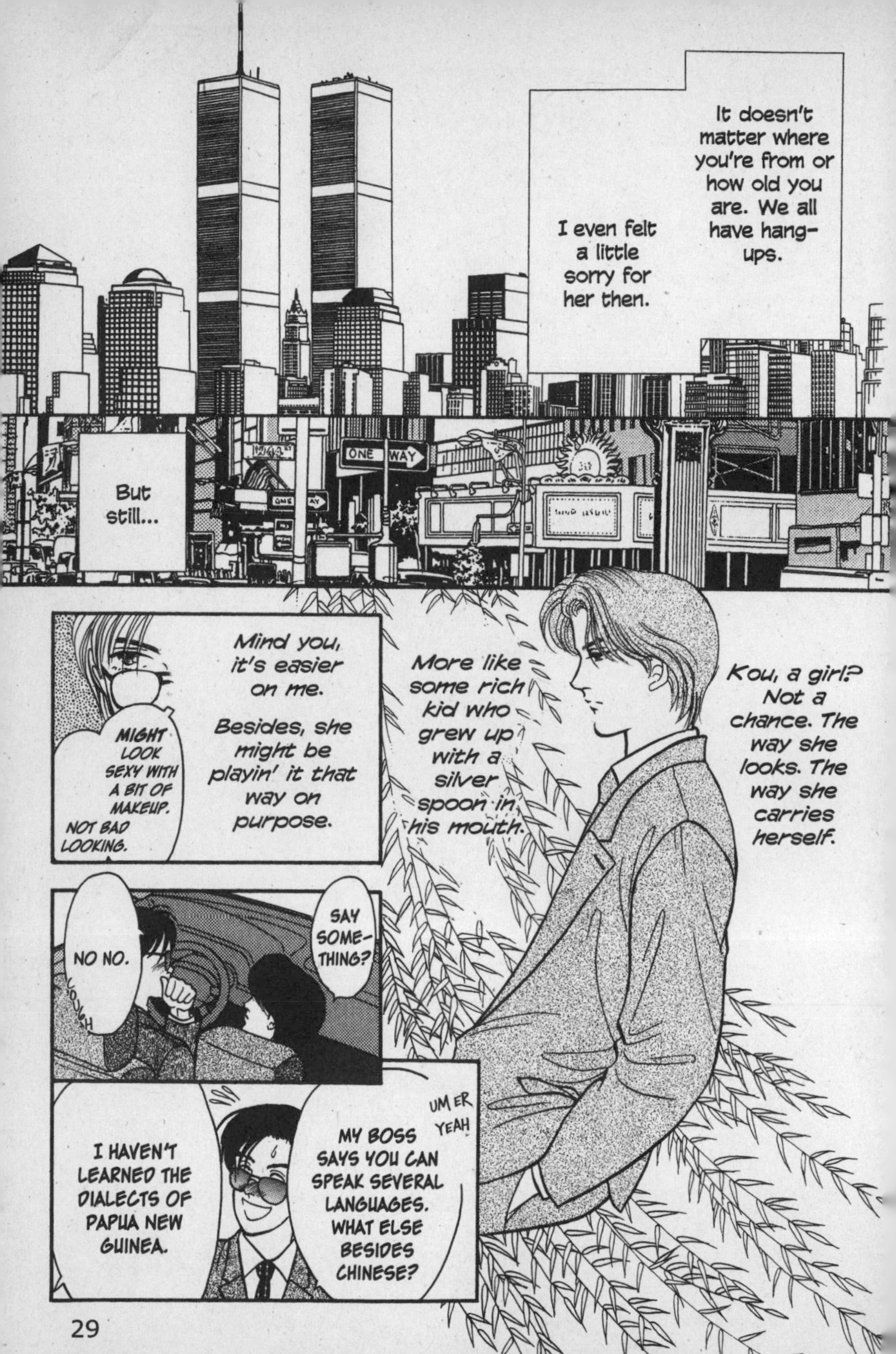
It doesn't matter where you're from or how old you are. We all have hang-ups.
I even felt a little sorry for her then.
ONE WAY
But still...
Kou, a girl? Not a chance. The way she looks. The way she carries herself.
More like some rich kid who grew up with a silver spoon in his mouth.
Mind you, it's easier on me.
Besides, she might be playin' it that way on purpose.
MIGHT LOOK SEXY WITH A BIT OF MAKEUP.
NOT BAD LOOKING.
SAY SOME-THING?
NO NO.
COUGH
UM ER YEAH
MY BOSS SAYS YOU CAN SPEAK SEVERAL LANGUAGES. WHAT ELSE BESIDES CHINESE?
I HAVEN'T LEARNED THE DIALECTS OF PAPUA NEW GUINEA.

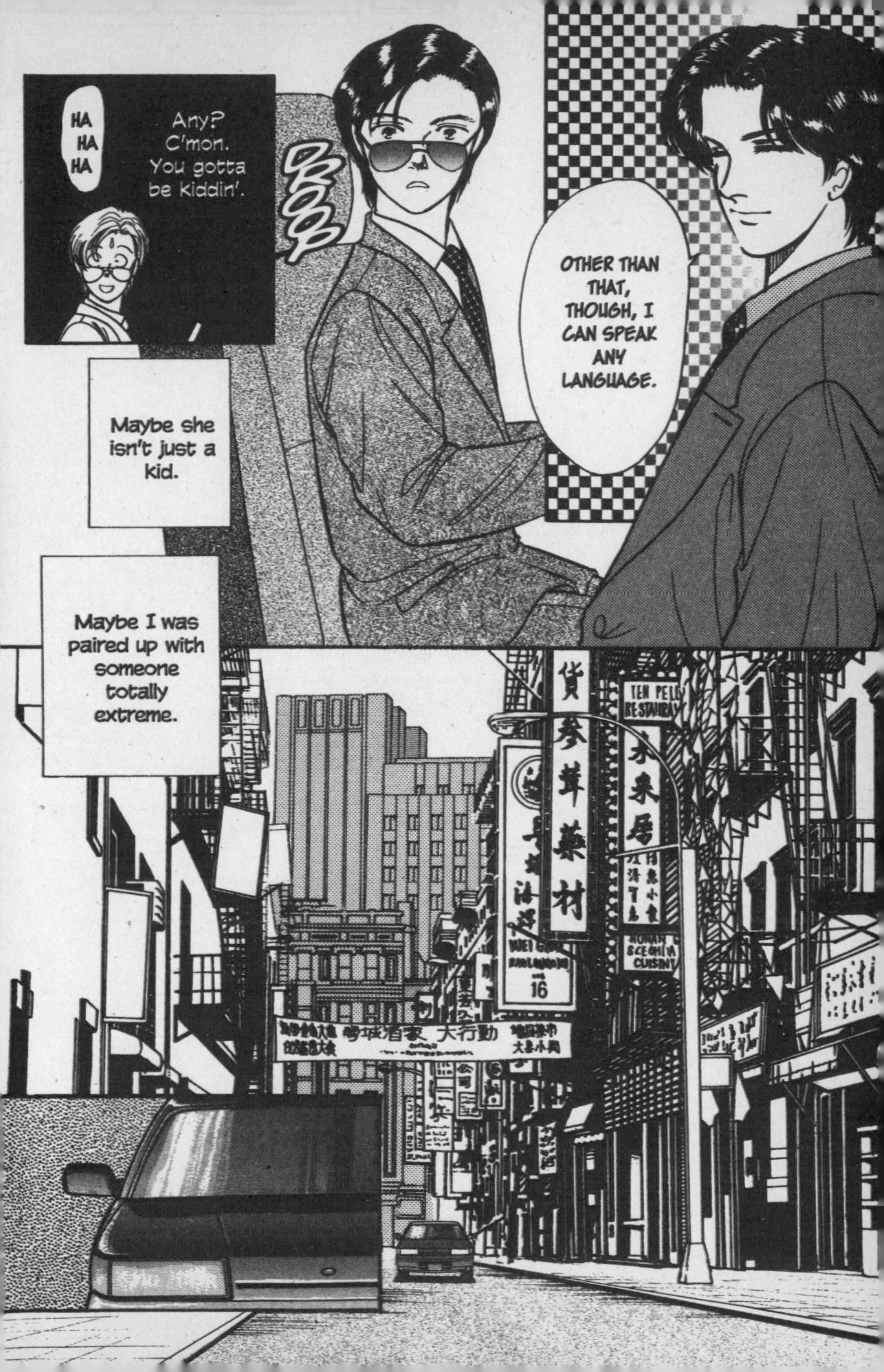

OTHER THAN THAT, THOUGH, I CAN SPEAK ANY LANGUAGE.
HA HA HA
Any? C'mon. You gotta be kiddin'.
Maybe she isn't just a kid.
Maybe I was paired up with someone totally extreme.

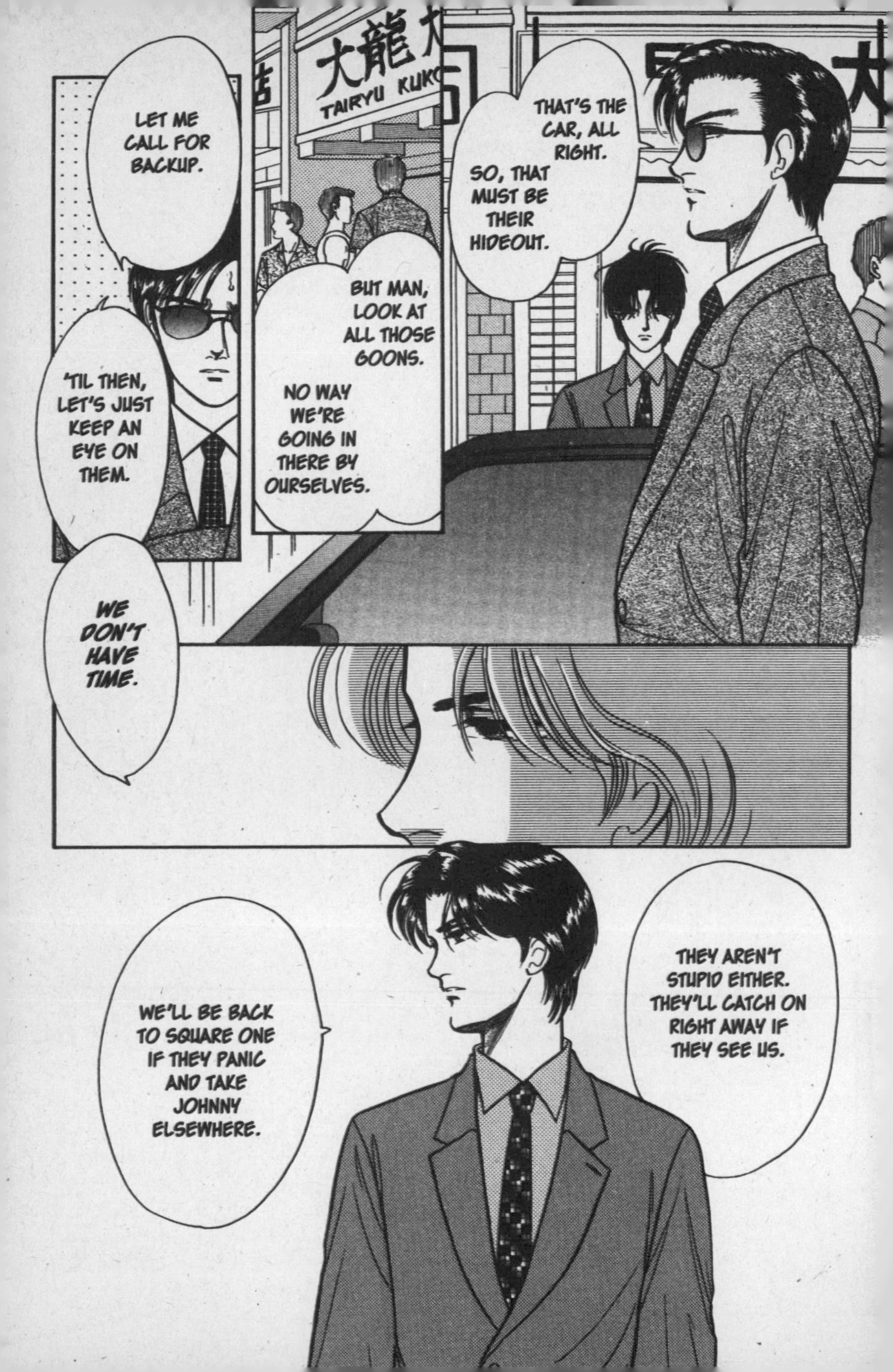
THAT'S THE CAR, ALL RIGHT.
SO, THAT MUST BE THEIR HIDEOUT.
大龍
BUT MAN, LOOK AT ALL THOSE GOONS.
NO WAY WE'RE GOING IN THERE BY OURSELVES.
LET ME CALL FOR BACKUP.
'TIL THEN, LET'S JUST KEEP AN EYE ON THEM.
WE DON'T HAVE TIME.
THEY AREN'T STUPID EITHER. THEY'LL CATCH ON RIGHT AWAY IF THEY SEE US.
WE'LL BE BACK TO SQUARE ONE IF THEY PANIC AND TAKE JOHNNY ELSEWHERE.

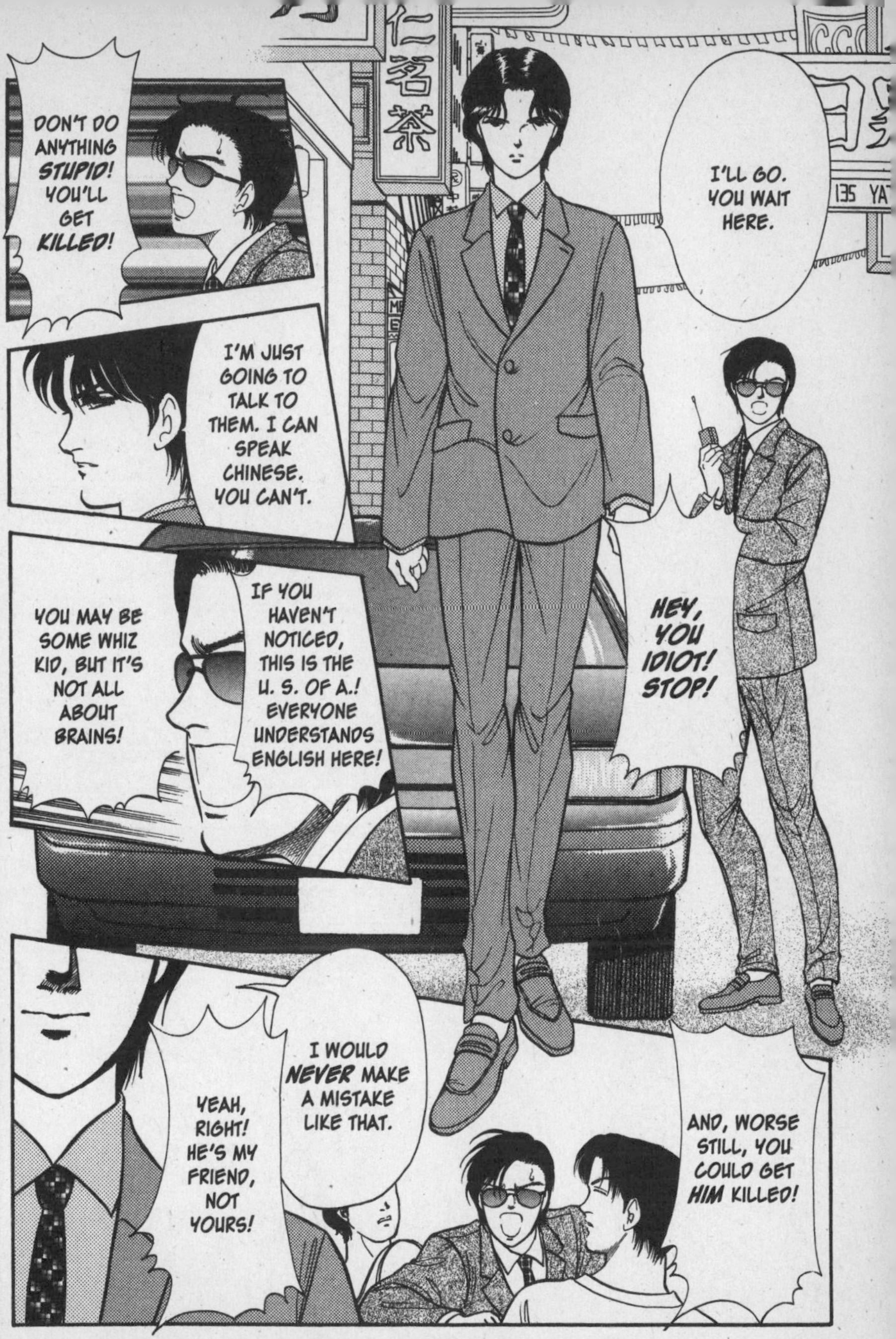
I'LL GO. YOU WAIT HERE.
HEY, YOU IDIOT! STOP!
DON'T DO ANYTHING STUPID! YOU'LL GET KILLED!
I'M JUST GOING TO TALK TO THEM. I CAN SPEAK CHINESE. YOU CAN'T.
IF YOU HAVEN'T NOTICED, THIS IS THE U. S. OF A.! EVERYONE UNDERSTANDS ENGLISH HERE!
YOU MAY BE SOME WHIZ KID, BUT IT'S NOT ALL ABOUT BRAINS!
AND, WORSE STILL, YOU COULD GET HIM KILLED!
I WOULD NEVER MAKE A MISTAKE LIKE THAT.
YEAH, RIGHT! HE'S MY FRIEND, NOT YOURS!

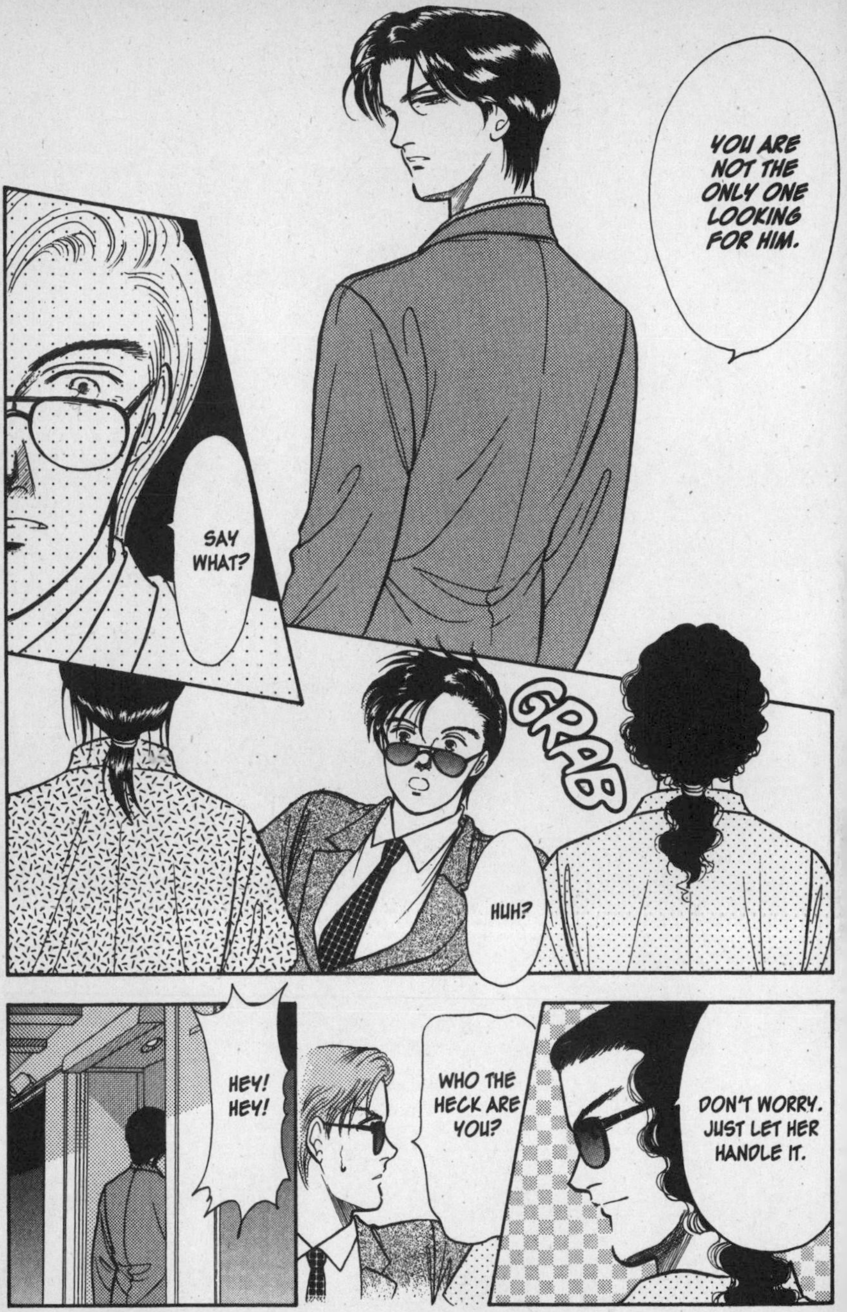
YOU ARE NOT THE ONLY ONE LOOKING FOR HIM.
SAY WHAT?
GRAB
HUH?
DON'T WORRY. JUST LET HER HANDLE IT.
WHO THE HECK ARE YOU?
HEY! HEY!

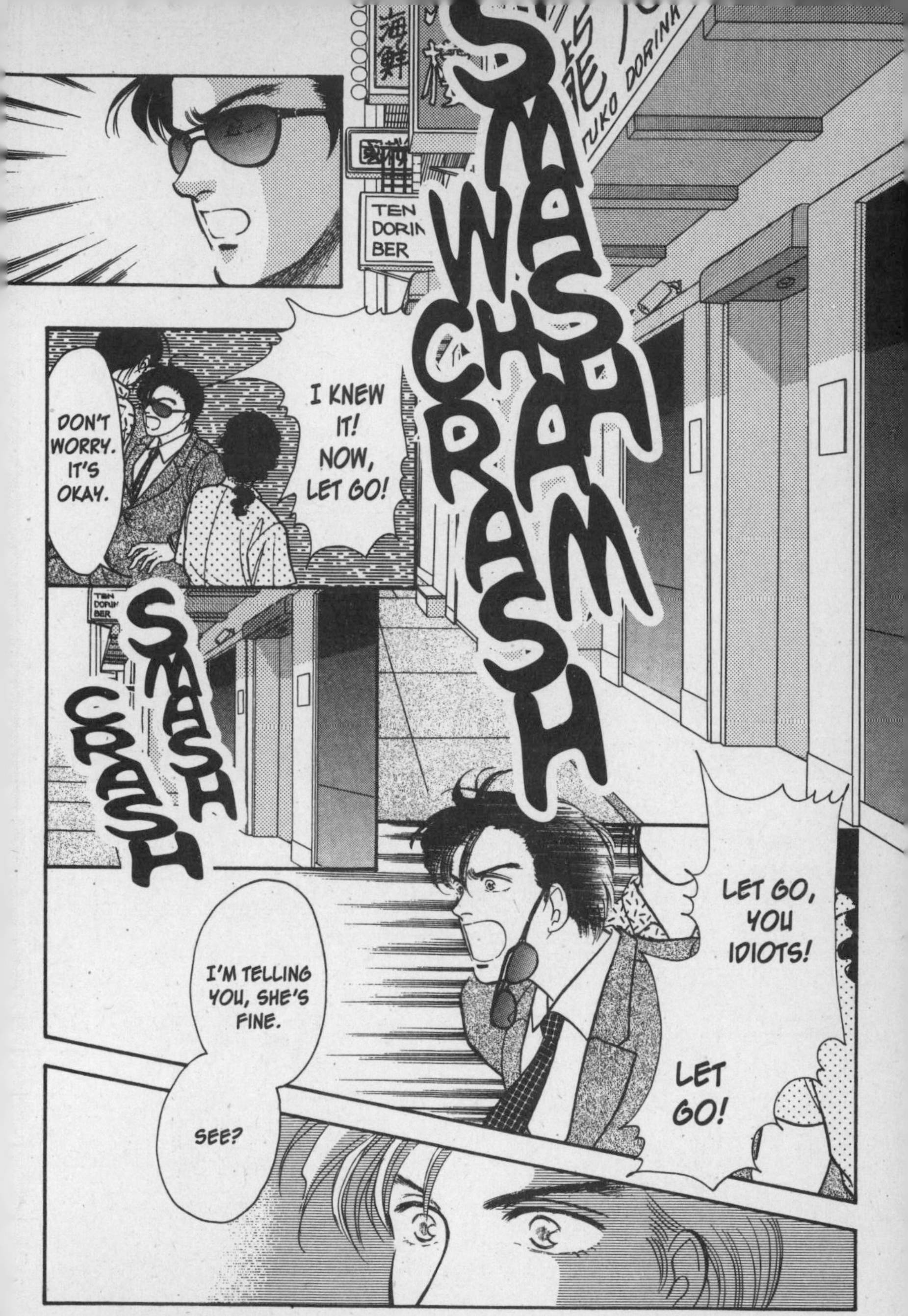
I KNEW IT! NOW, LET GO!
DON'T WORRY. IT'S OKAY.
SMASH
CRASH
LET GO, YOU IDIOTS!
LET GO!
I'M TELLING YOU, SHE'S FINE.
SEE?

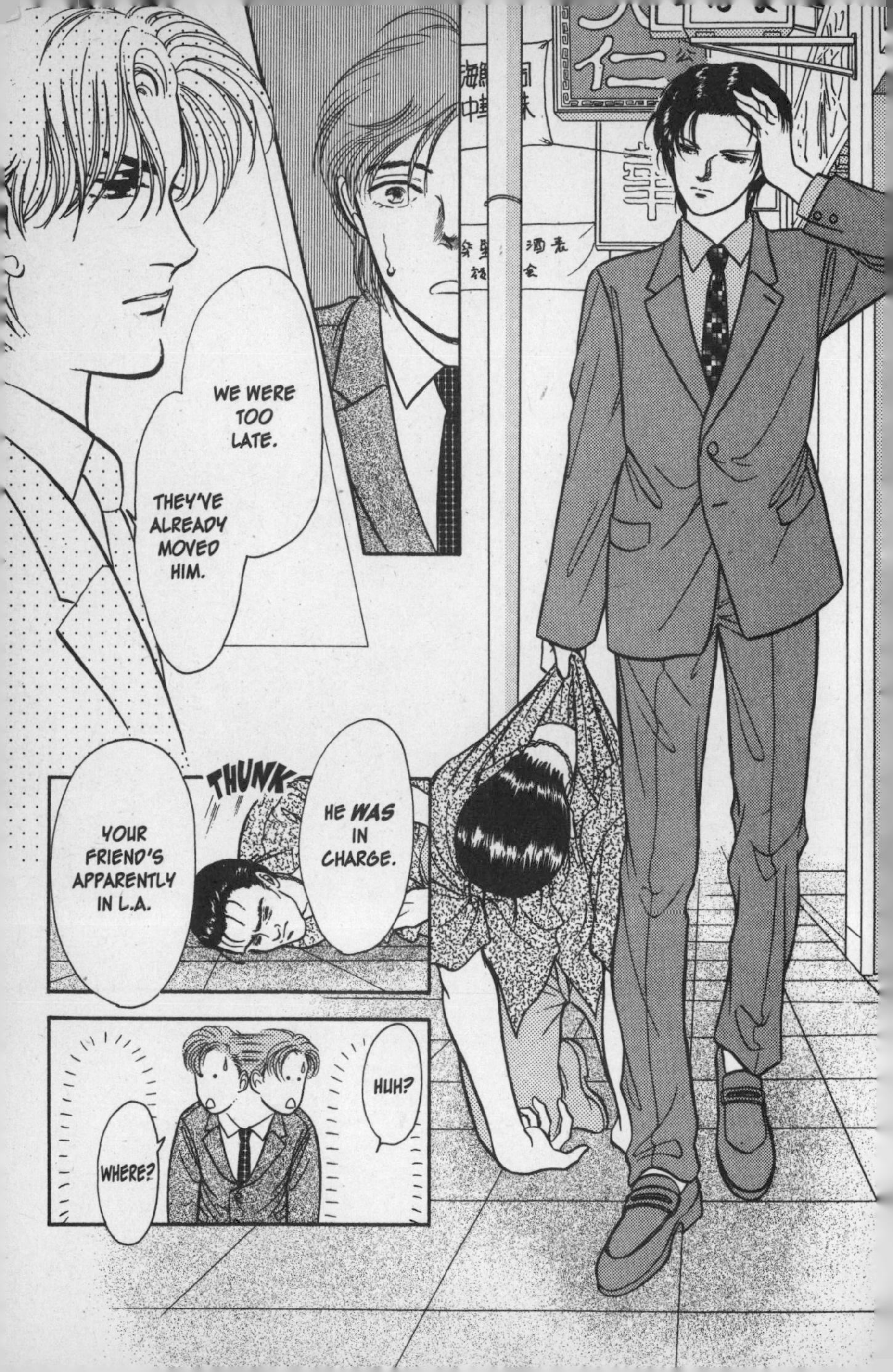
WE WERE TOO LATE.
THEY'VE ALREADY MOVED HIM.
THUNK
HE *WAS* IN CHARGE.
YOUR FRIEND'S APPARENTLY IN L.A.
HUH?
WHERE?

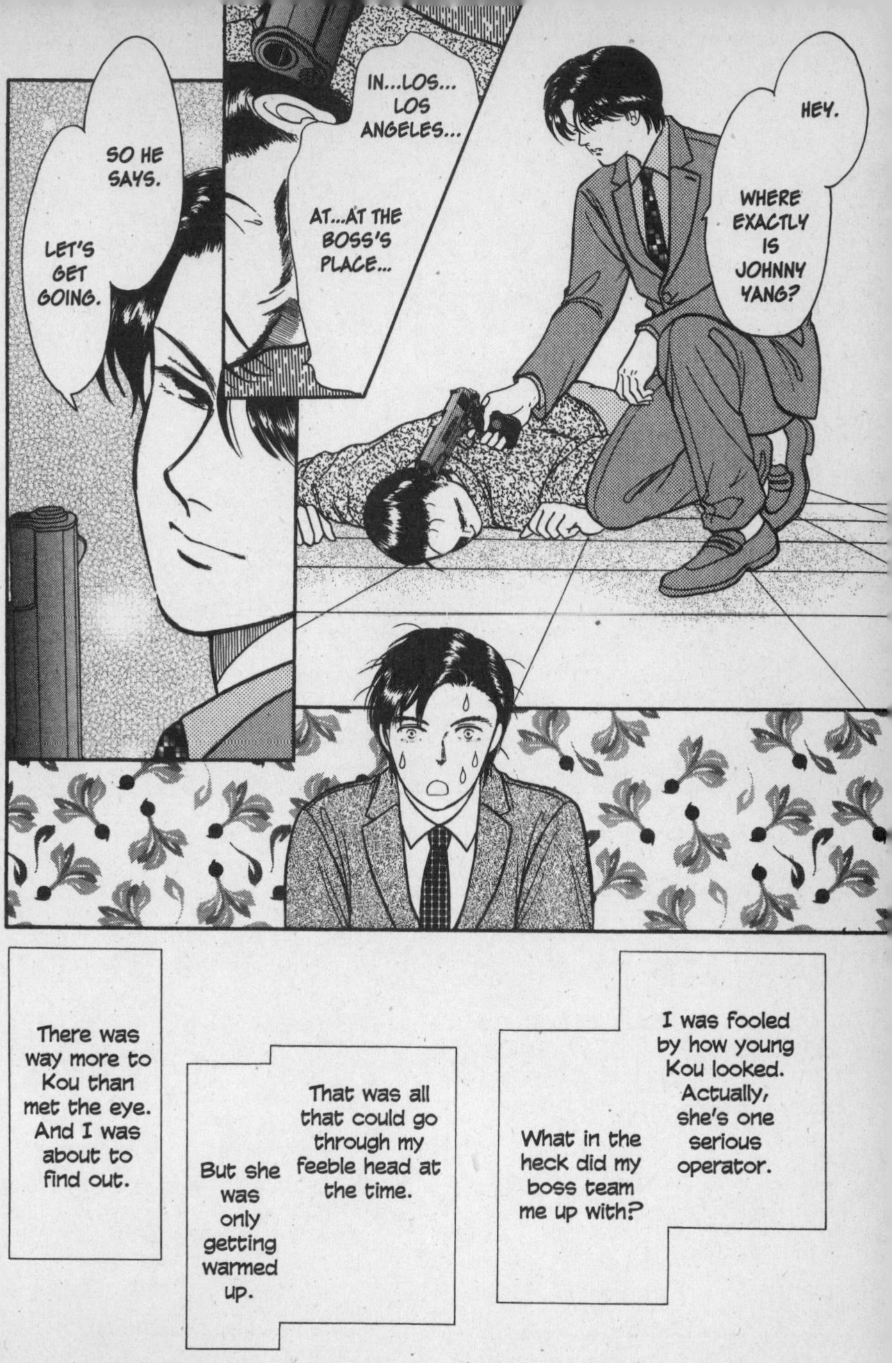
HEY.
WHERE EXACTLY IS JOHNNY YANG?
IN...LOS... LOS ANGELES...
AT...AT THE BOSS'S PLACE...
SO HE SAYS.
LET'S GET GOING.

I was fooled by how young Kou looked. Actually, she's one serious operator.

What in the heck did my boss team me up with?

That was all that could go through my feeble head at the time.

But she was only getting warmed up.

There was way more to Kou than met the eye. And I was about to find out.

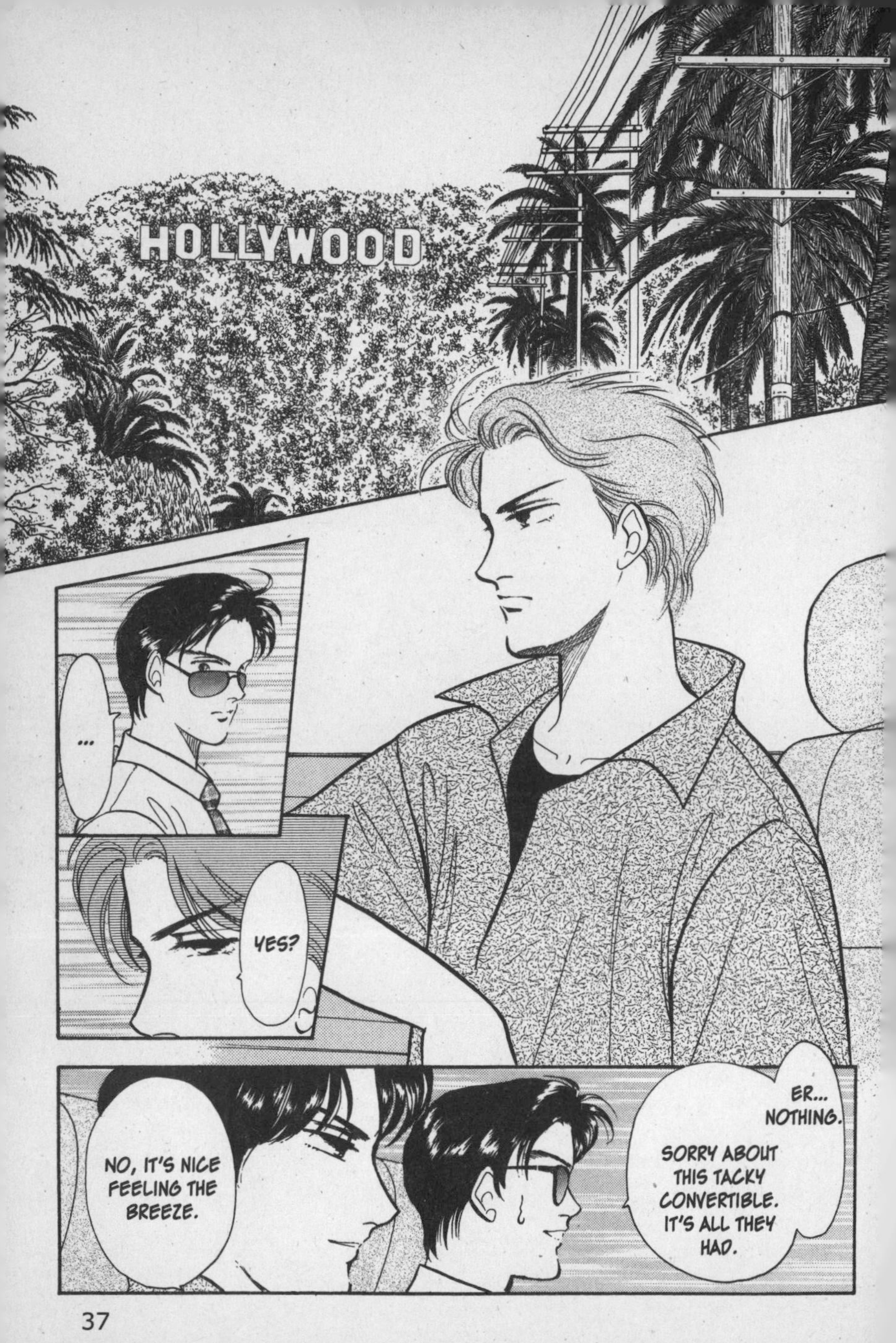
HOLLYWOOD
...
YES?
ER... NOTHING.
SORRY ABOUT THIS TACKY CONVERTIBLE. IT'S ALL THEY HAD.
NO, IT'S NICE FEELING THE BREEZE.

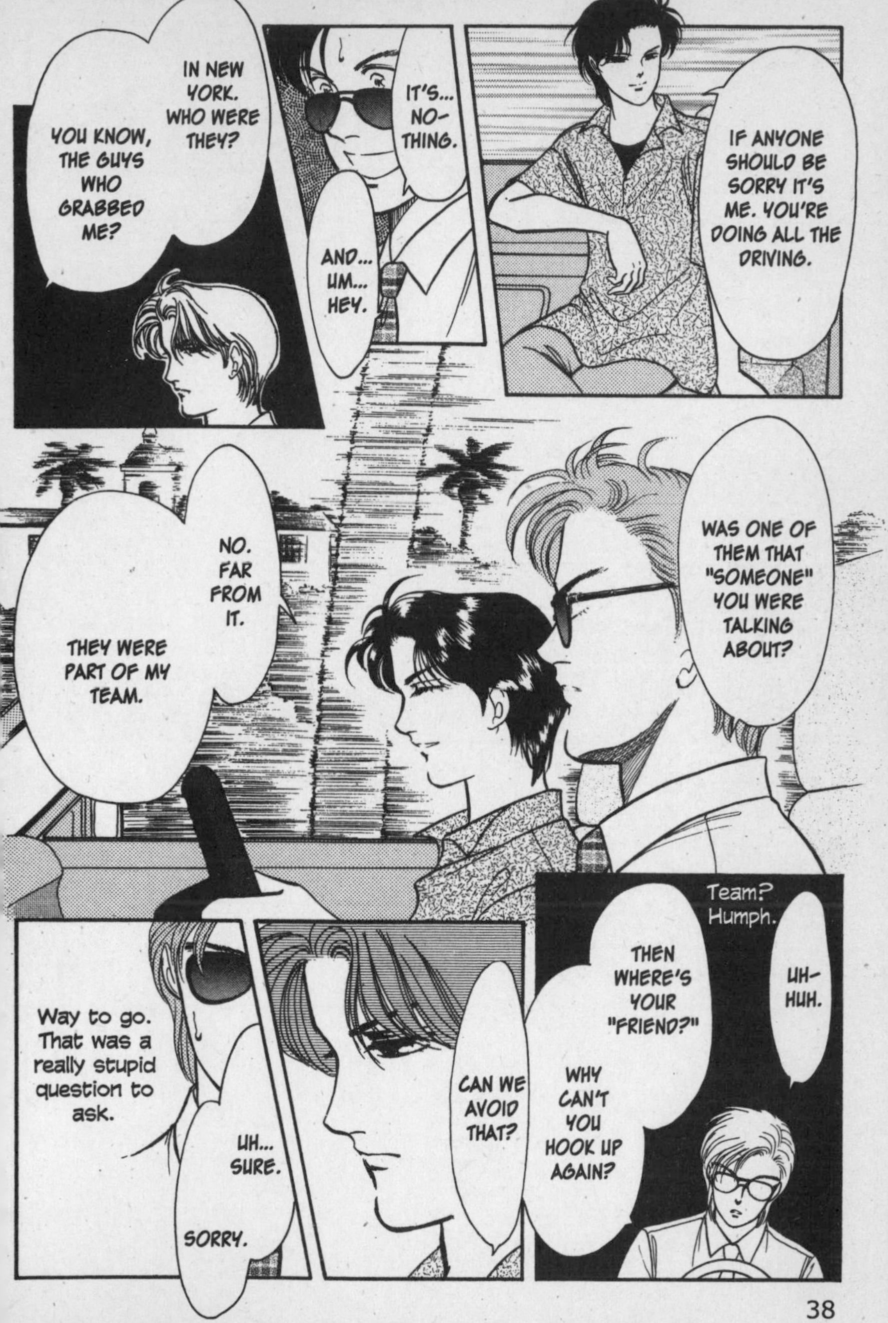
IF ANYONE SHOULD BE SORRY IT'S ME. YOU'RE DOING ALL THE DRIVING.
IT'S... NO-THING.
AND... UM... HEY.
YOU KNOW, THE GUYS WHO GRABBED ME? IN NEW YORK. WHO WERE THEY?
WAS ONE OF THEM THAT "SOMEONE" YOU WERE TALKING ABOUT?
NO. FAR FROM IT. THEY WERE PART OF MY TEAM.
Team? Humph.
UH-HUH.
THEN WHERE'S YOUR "FRIEND?" WHY CAN'T YOU HOOK UP AGAIN?
CAN WE AVOID THAT?
Way to go. That was a really stupid question to ask.
UH... SURE.
SORRY.

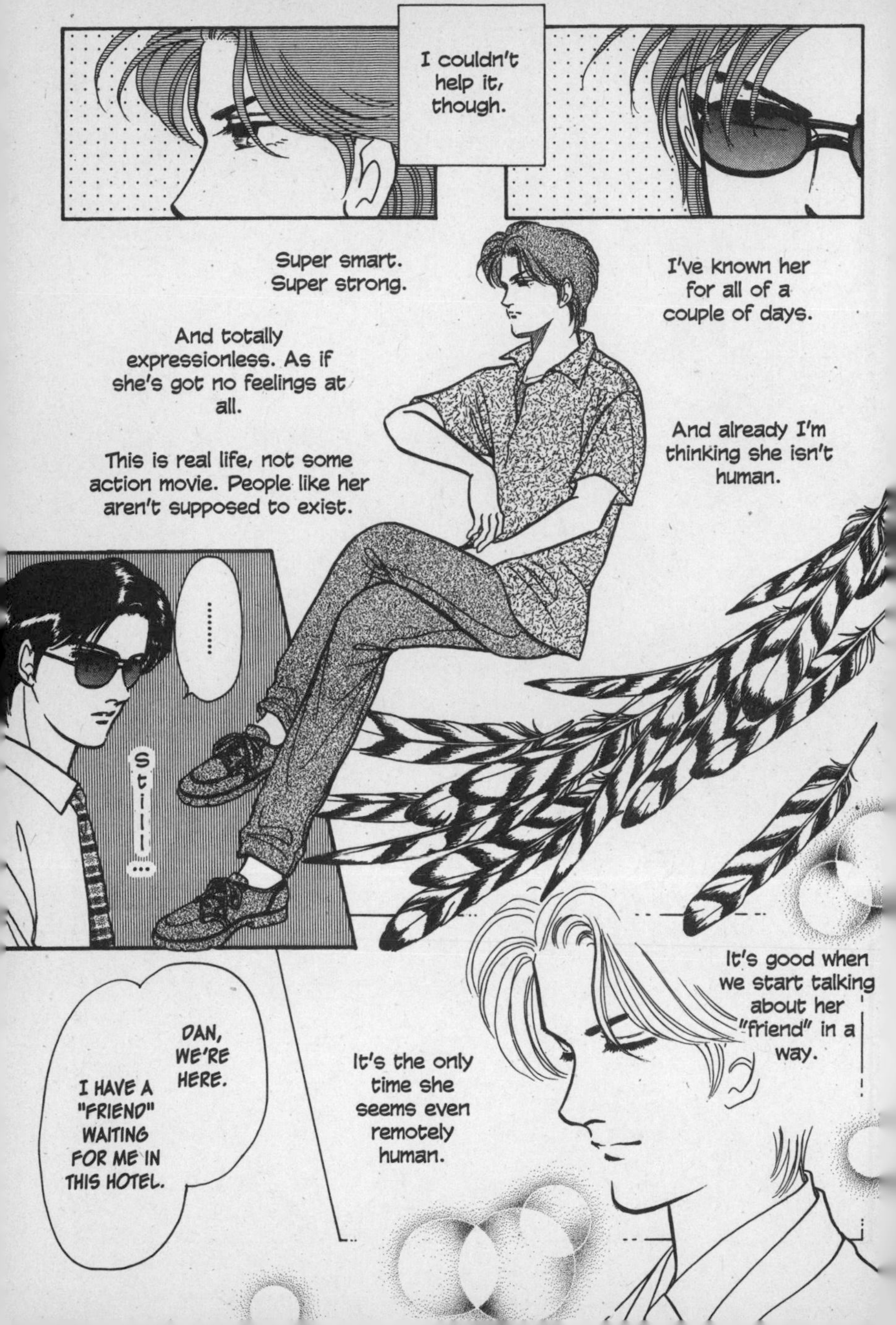
I couldn't help it, though.
I've known her for all of a couple of days.
And already I'm thinking she isn't human.
Super smart. Super strong.
And totally expressionless. As if she's got no feelings at all.
This is real life, not some action movie. People like her aren't supposed to exist.
......
Still...
It's good when we start talking about her "friend" in a way.
It's the only time she seems even remotely human.
DAN, WE'RE HERE.
I HAVE A "FRIEND" WAITING FOR ME IN THIS HOTEL.

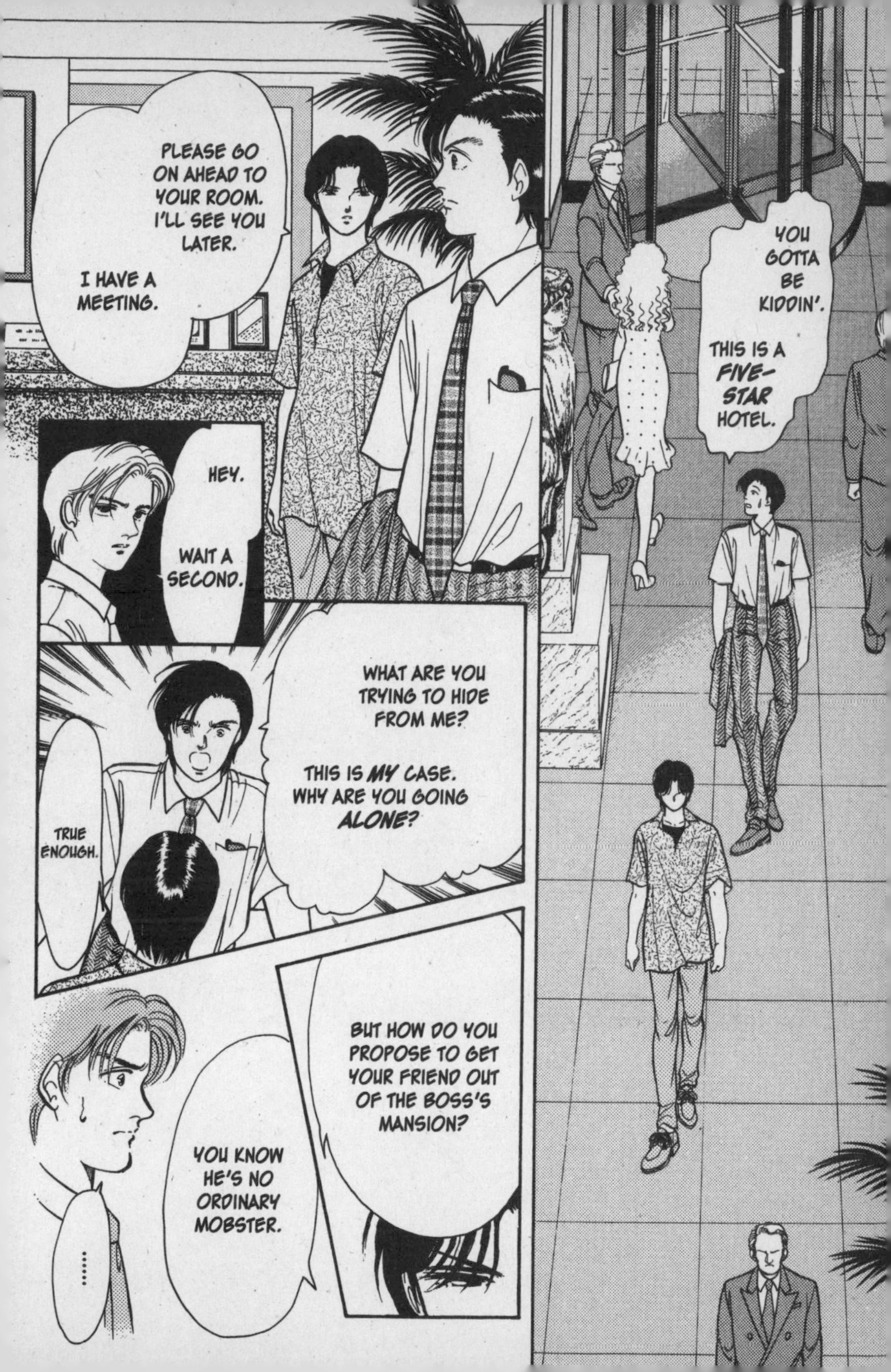
YOU GOTTA BE KIDDIN'.
THIS IS A *FIVE-STAR* HOTEL.
PLEASE GO ON AHEAD TO YOUR ROOM. I'LL SEE YOU LATER.
I HAVE A MEETING.
HEY.
WAIT A SECOND.
WHAT ARE YOU TRYING TO HIDE FROM ME?
THIS IS *MY* CASE. WHY ARE YOU GOING *ALONE?*
TRUE ENOUGH.
BUT HOW DO YOU PROPOSE TO GET YOUR FRIEND OUT OF THE BOSS'S MANSION?
YOU KNOW HE'S NO ORDINARY MOBSTER.
......

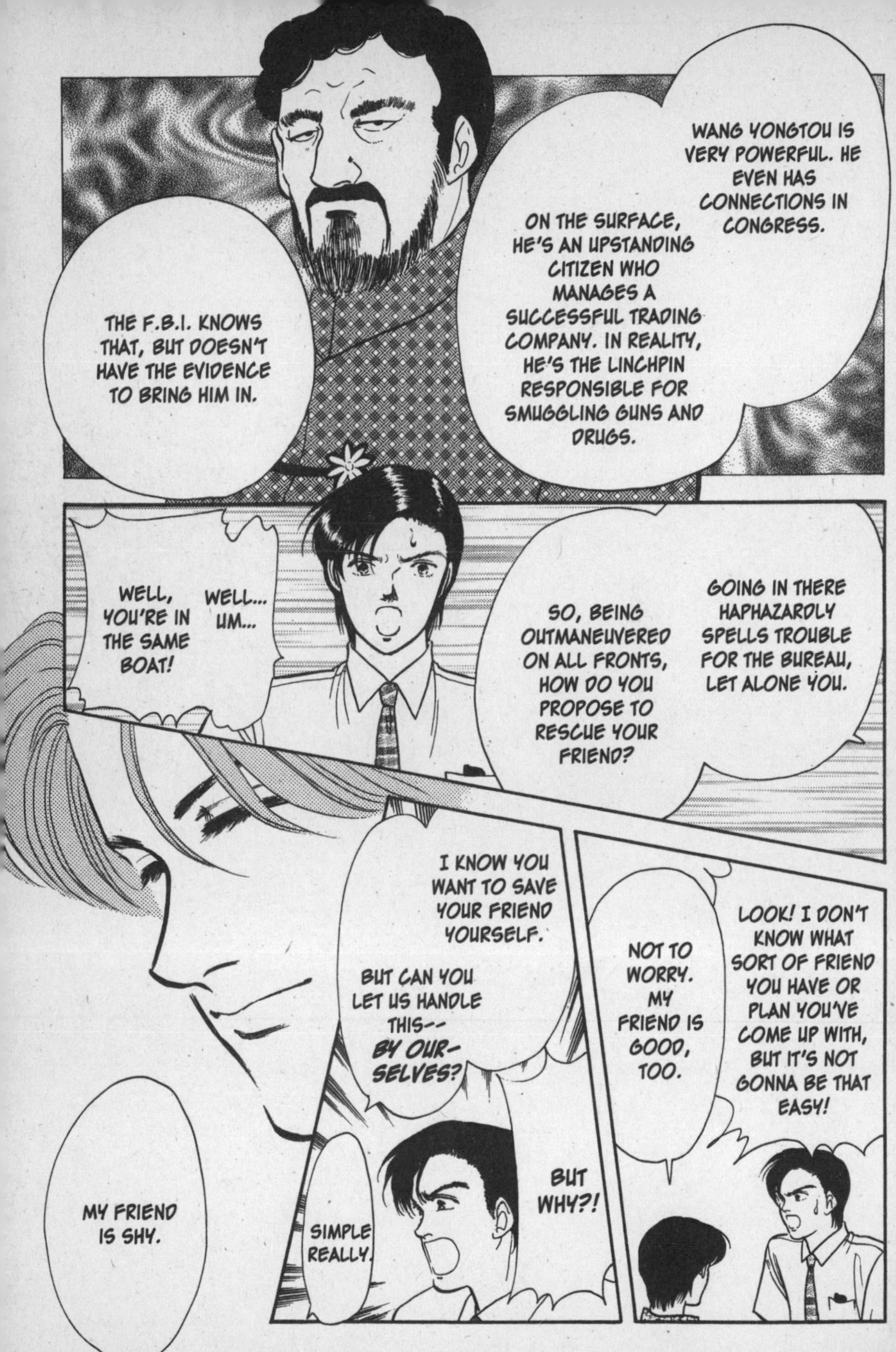
WANG YONGTOU IS VERY POWERFUL. HE EVEN HAS CONNECTIONS IN CONGRESS.
ON THE SURFACE, HE'S AN UPSTANDING CITIZEN WHO MANAGES A SUCCESSFUL TRADING COMPANY. IN REALITY, HE'S THE LINCHPIN RESPONSIBLE FOR SMUGGLING GUNS AND DRUGS.
THE F.B.I. KNOWS THAT, BUT DOESN'T HAVE THE EVIDENCE TO BRING HIM IN.
GOING IN THERE HAPHAZARDLY SPELLS TROUBLE FOR THE BUREAU, LET ALONE YOU.
SO, BEING OUTMANEUVERED ON ALL FRONTS, HOW DO YOU PROPOSE TO RESCUE YOUR FRIEND?
WELL... UM...
WELL, YOU'RE IN THE SAME BOAT!
LOOK! I DON'T KNOW WHAT SORT OF FRIEND YOU HAVE OR PLAN YOU'VE COME UP WITH, BUT IT'S NOT GONNA BE THAT EASY!
NOT TO WORRY. MY FRIEND IS GOOD, TOO.
I KNOW YOU WANT TO SAVE YOUR FRIEND YOURSELF.
BUT CAN YOU LET US HANDLE THIS-- *BY OUR-SELVES?*
BUT WHY?!
SIMPLE REALLY.
MY FRIEND IS SHY.

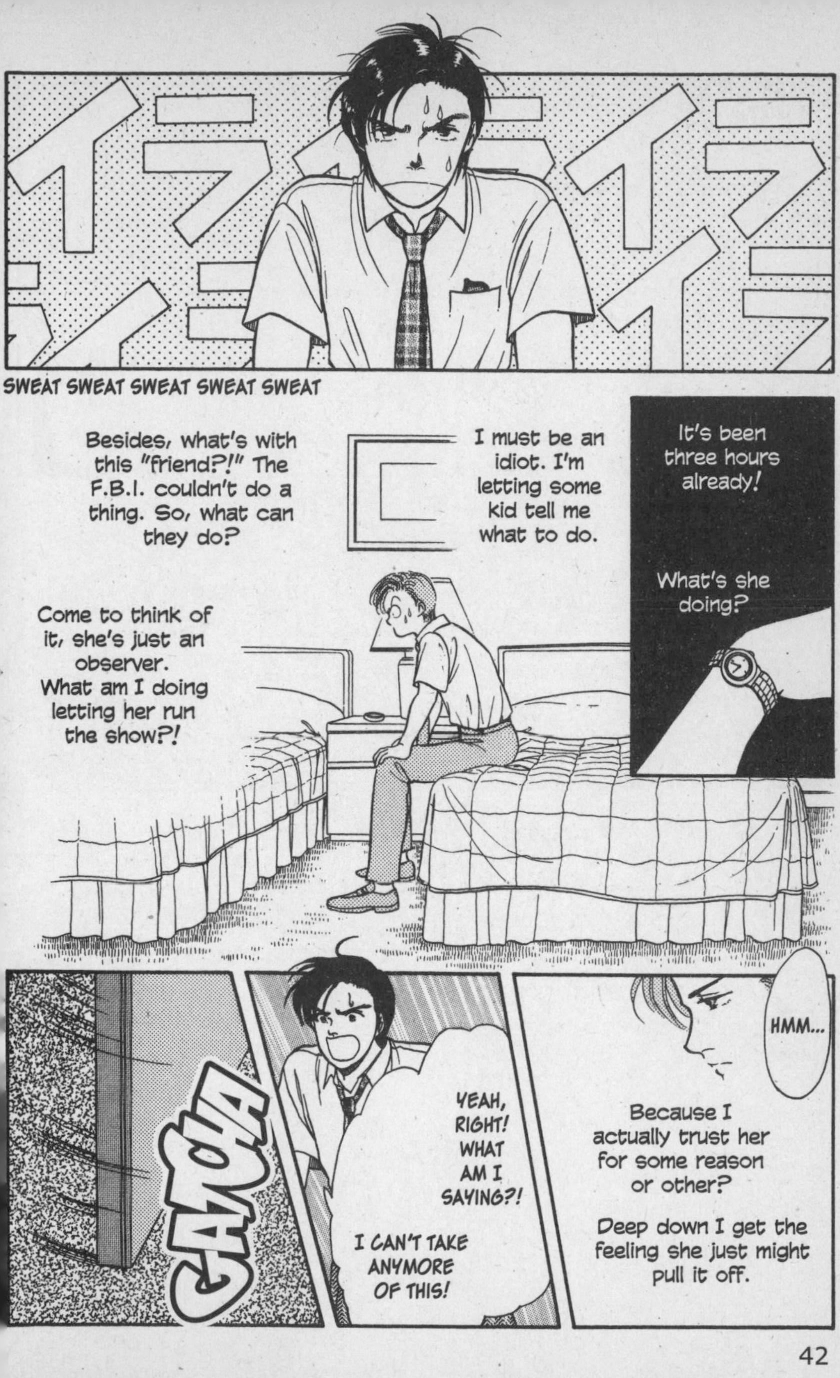
SWEAT SWEAT SWEAT SWEAT SWEAT
It's been three hours already!
What's she doing?
I must be an idiot. I'm letting some kid tell me what to do.
Besides, what's with this "friend?!" The F.B.I. couldn't do a thing. So, what can they do?
Come to think of it, she's just an observer. What am I doing letting her run the show?!
HMM...
Because I actually trust her for some reason or other?
Deep down I get the feeling she just might pull it off.
YEAH, RIGHT! WHAT AM I SAYING?!
I CAN'T TAKE ANYMORE OF THIS!
GATCHA

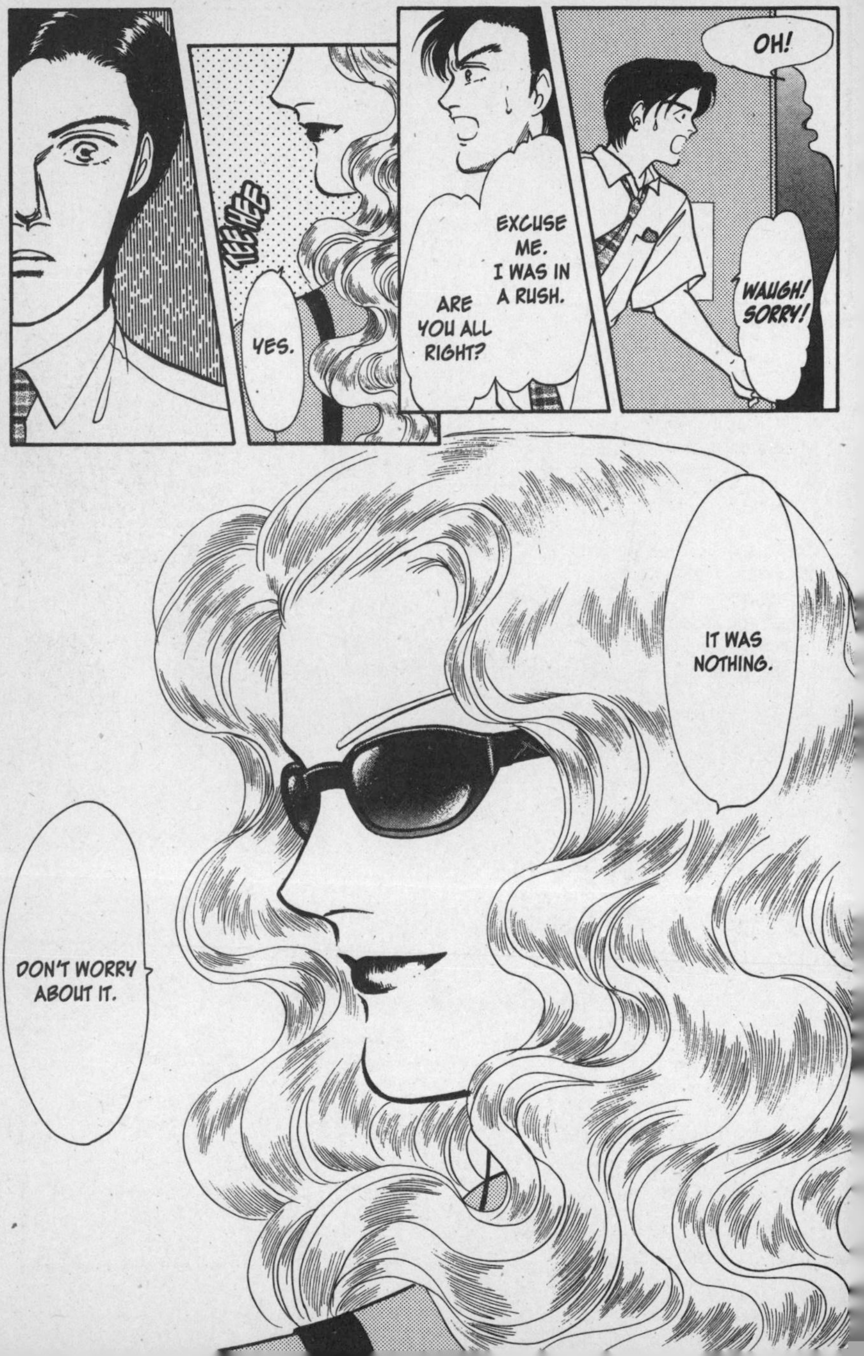
OH!
WAUGH! SORRY!
EXCUSE ME. I WAS IN A RUSH.
ARE YOU ALL RIGHT?
TEE HEE
YES.
IT WAS NOTHING.
DON'T WORRY ABOUT IT.

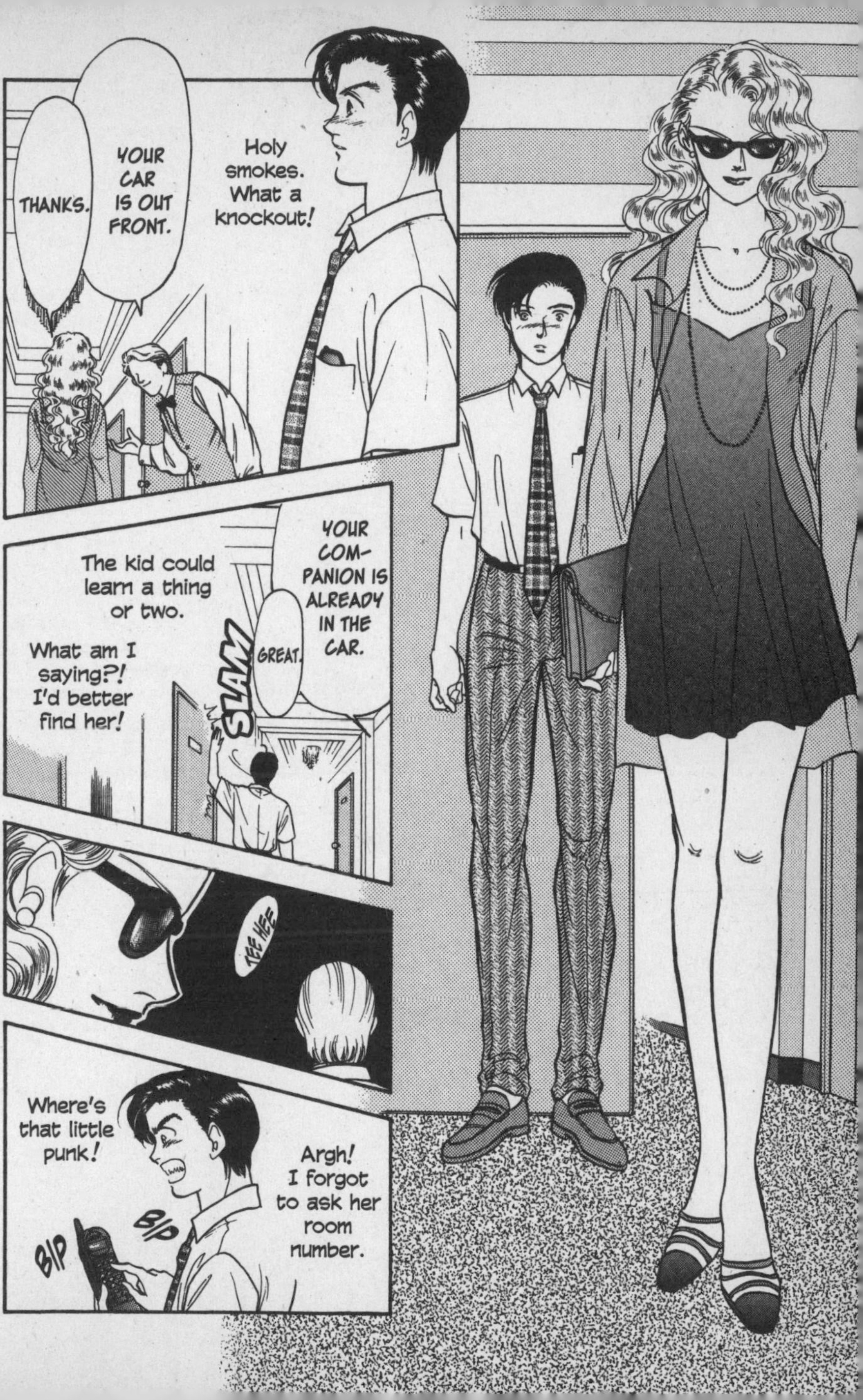

Holy smokes. What a knockout!
YOUR CAR IS OUT FRONT.
THANKS.
YOUR COMPANION IS ALREADY IN THE CAR.
GREAT.
SLAM
The kid could learn a thing or two.
What am I saying?! I'd better find her!
TEE HEE
Where's that little punk!
Argh! I forgot to ask her room number.
BIP
BIP

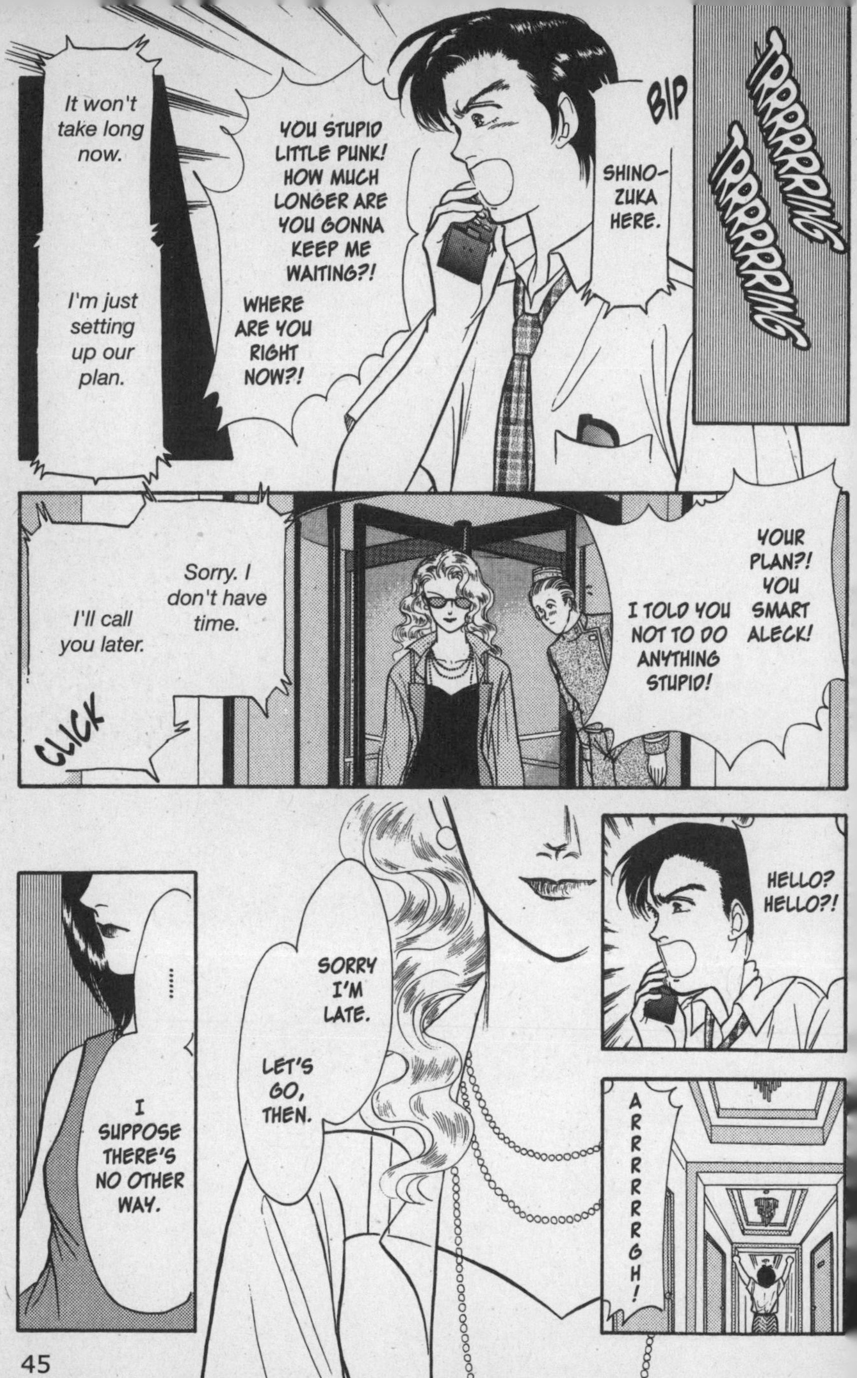
TRRRRRING TRRRRRING
BIP
SHINO-ZUKA HERE.
YOU STUPID LITTLE PUNK! HOW MUCH LONGER ARE YOU GONNA KEEP ME WAITING?!
WHERE ARE YOU RIGHT NOW?!
It won't take long now.
I'm just setting up our plan.
YOUR PLAN?! YOU SMART ALECK!
I TOLD YOU NOT TO DO ANYTHING STUPID!
Sorry. I don't have time.
I'll call you later.
CLICK
HELLO? HELLO?!
ARRRRRRGH!
SORRY I'M LATE.
LET'S GO, THEN.
......
I SUPPOSE THERE'S NO OTHER WAY.

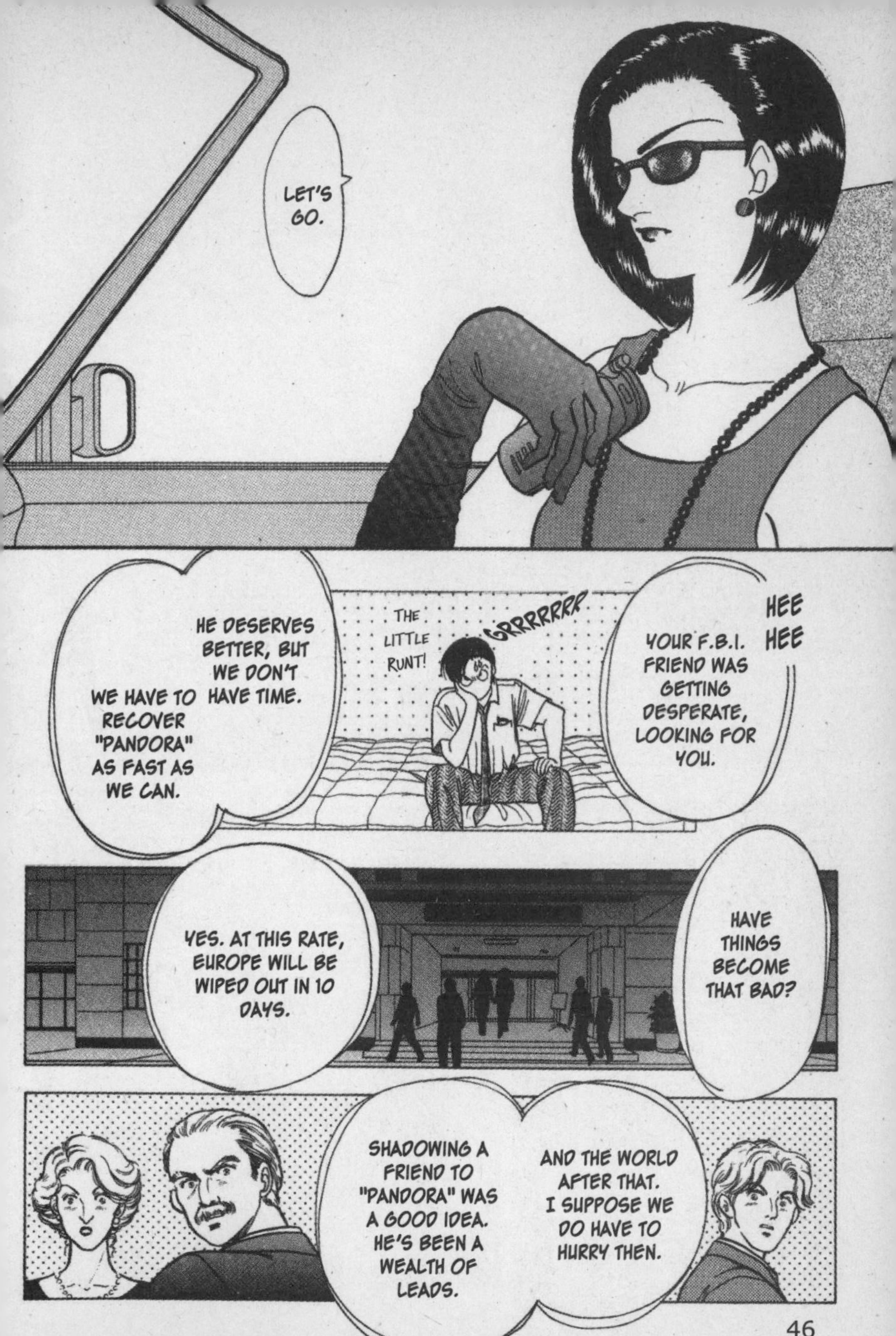
LET'S GO.
HEE HEE
YOUR F.B.I. FRIEND WAS GETTING DESPERATE, LOOKING FOR YOU.
THE LITTLE RUNT!
GRRRRRRR
HE DESERVES BETTER, BUT WE DON'T HAVE TIME.
WE HAVE TO RECOVER "PANDORA" AS FAST AS WE CAN.
HAVE THINGS BECOME THAT BAD?
YES. AT THIS RATE, EUROPE WILL BE WIPED OUT IN 10 DAYS.
AND THE WORLD AFTER THAT. I SUPPOSE WE DO HAVE TO HURRY THEN.
SHADOWING A FRIEND TO "PANDORA" WAS A GOOD IDEA. HE'S BEEN A WEALTH OF LEADS.

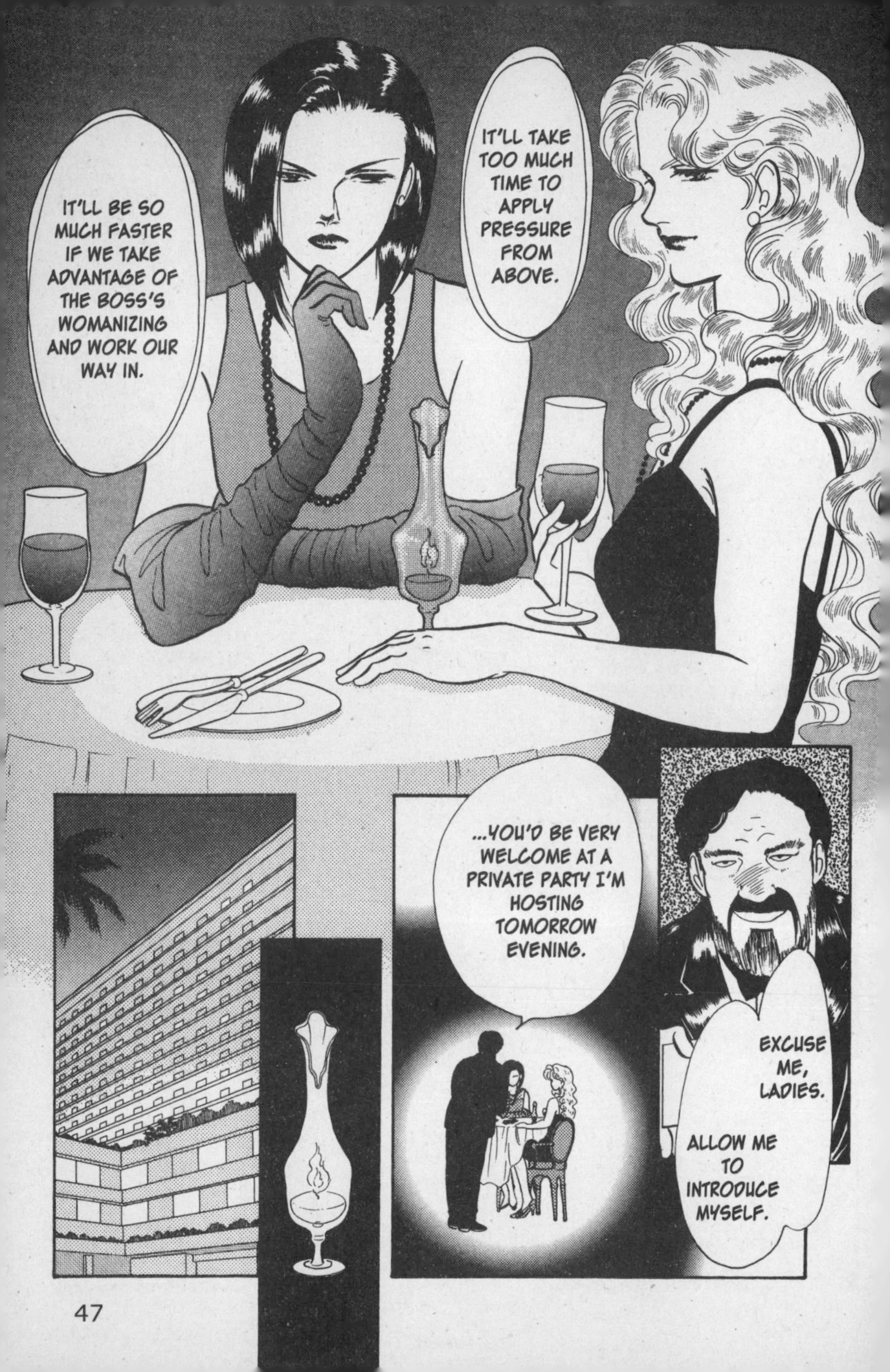
IT'LL TAKE TOO MUCH TIME TO APPLY PRESSURE FROM ABOVE.
IT'LL BE SO MUCH FASTER IF WE TAKE ADVANTAGE OF THE BOSS'S WOMANIZING AND WORK OUR WAY IN.
EXCUSE ME, LADIES.
ALLOW ME TO INTRODUCE MYSELF.
...YOU'D BE VERY WELCOME AT A PRIVATE PARTY I'M HOSTING TOMORROW EVENING.

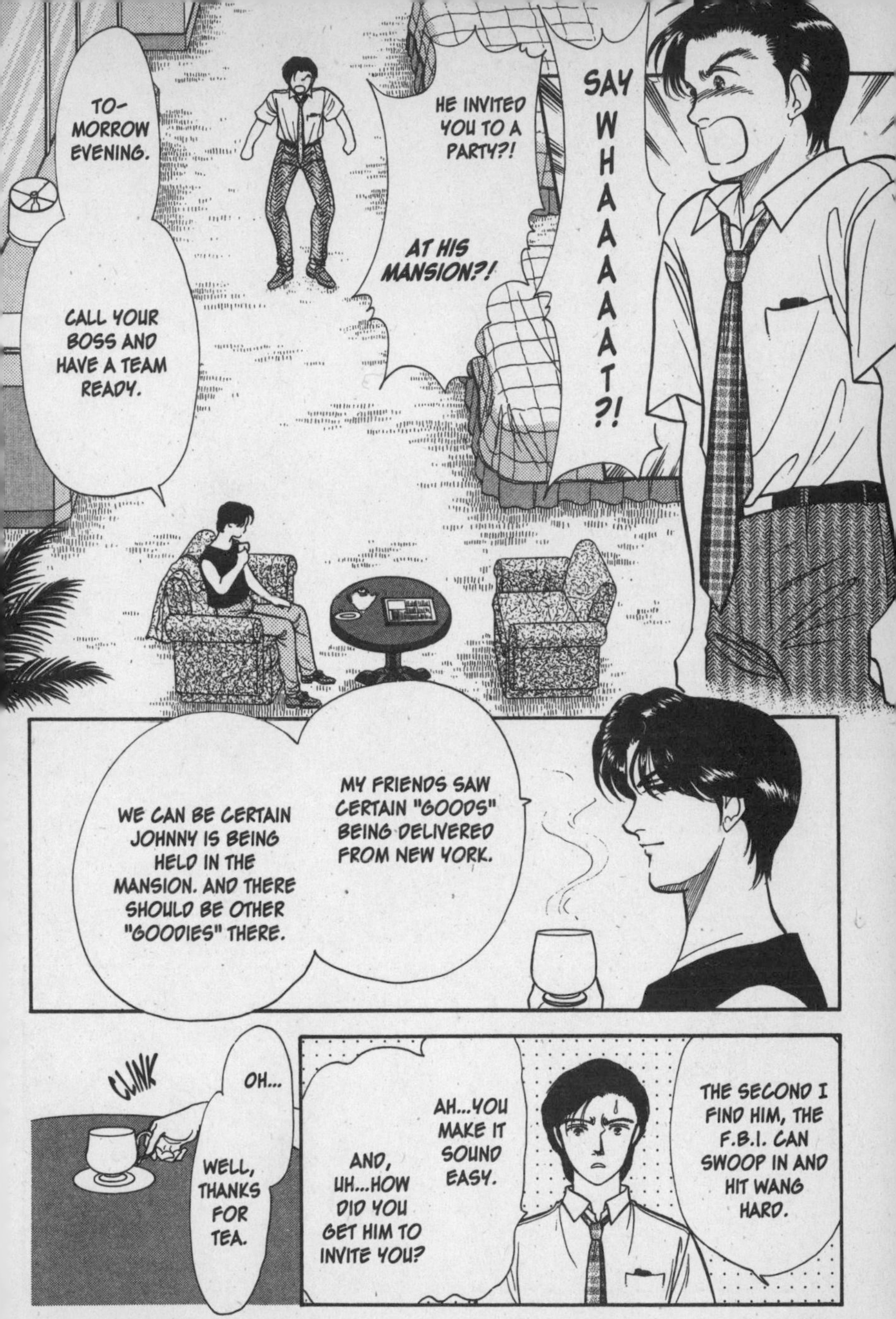
SAY WHAAAAAAT?!
HE INVITED YOU TO A PARTY?!
AT HIS MANSION?!
TO-MORROW EVENING.
CALL YOUR BOSS AND HAVE A TEAM READY.
MY FRIENDS SAW CERTAIN "GOODS" BEING DELIVERED FROM NEW YORK.
WE CAN BE CERTAIN JOHNNY IS BEING HELD IN THE MANSION. AND THERE SHOULD BE OTHER "GOODIES" THERE.
THE SECOND I FIND HIM, THE F.B.I. CAN SWOOP IN AND HIT WANG HARD.
AH...YOU MAKE IT SOUND EASY.
AND, UH...HOW DID YOU GET HIM TO INVITE YOU?
OH...
WELL, THANKS FOR TEA.
CLINK

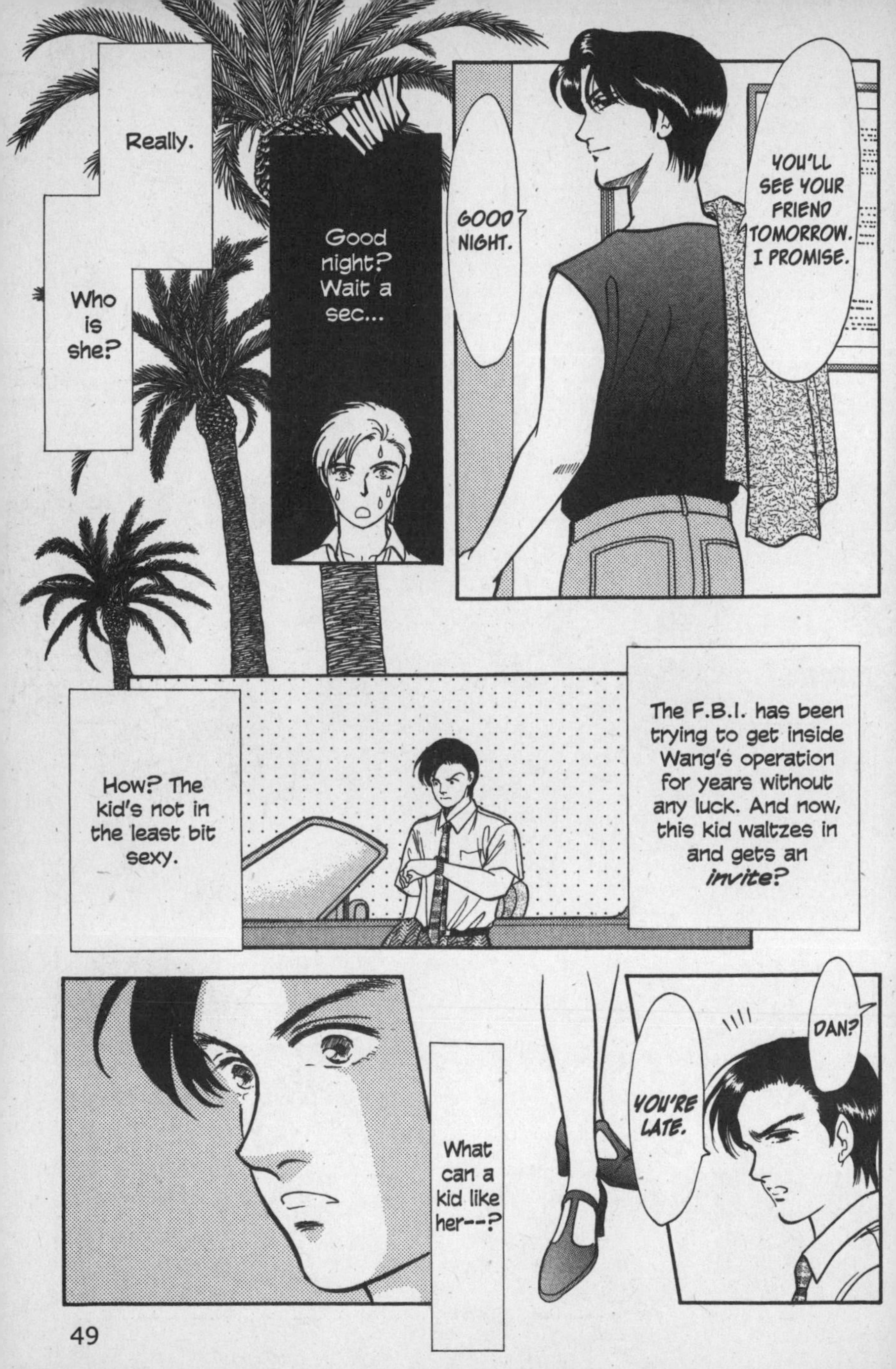
YOU'LL SEE YOUR FRIEND TOMORROW. I PROMISE.
GOOD NIGHT.
THUNK
Good night? Wait a sec...
Really.
Who is she?
The F.B.I. has been trying to get inside Wang's operation for years without any luck. And now, this kid waltzes in and gets an *invite?*
How? The kid's not in the least bit sexy.
DAN?
YOU'RE LATE.
What can a kid like her--?

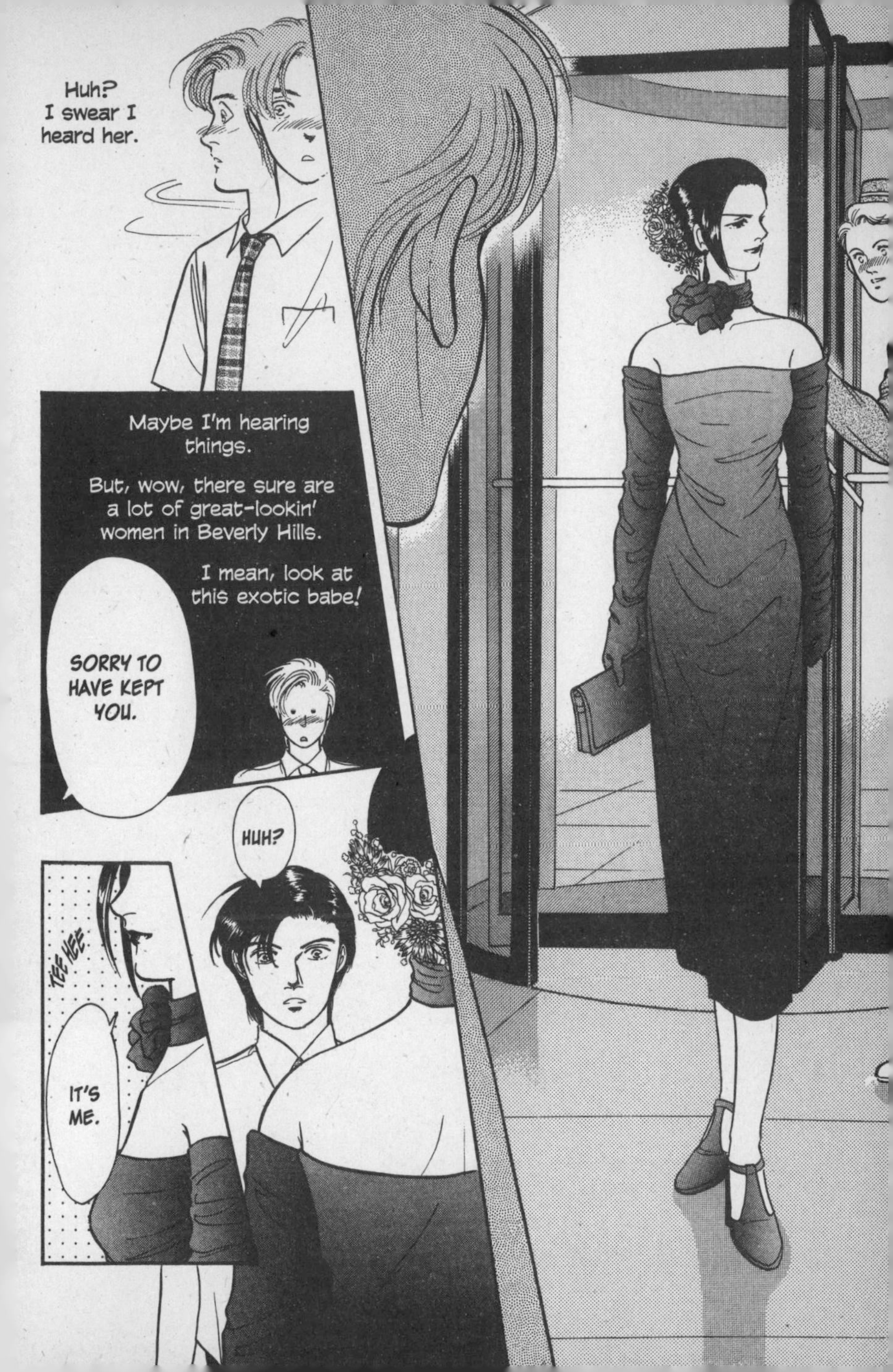
Huh? I swear I heard her.
Maybe I'm hearing things.
But, wow, there sure are a lot of great-lookin' women in Beverly Hills.
I mean, look at this exotic babe!
SORRY TO HAVE KEPT YOU.
HUH?
TEE HEE
IT'S ME.

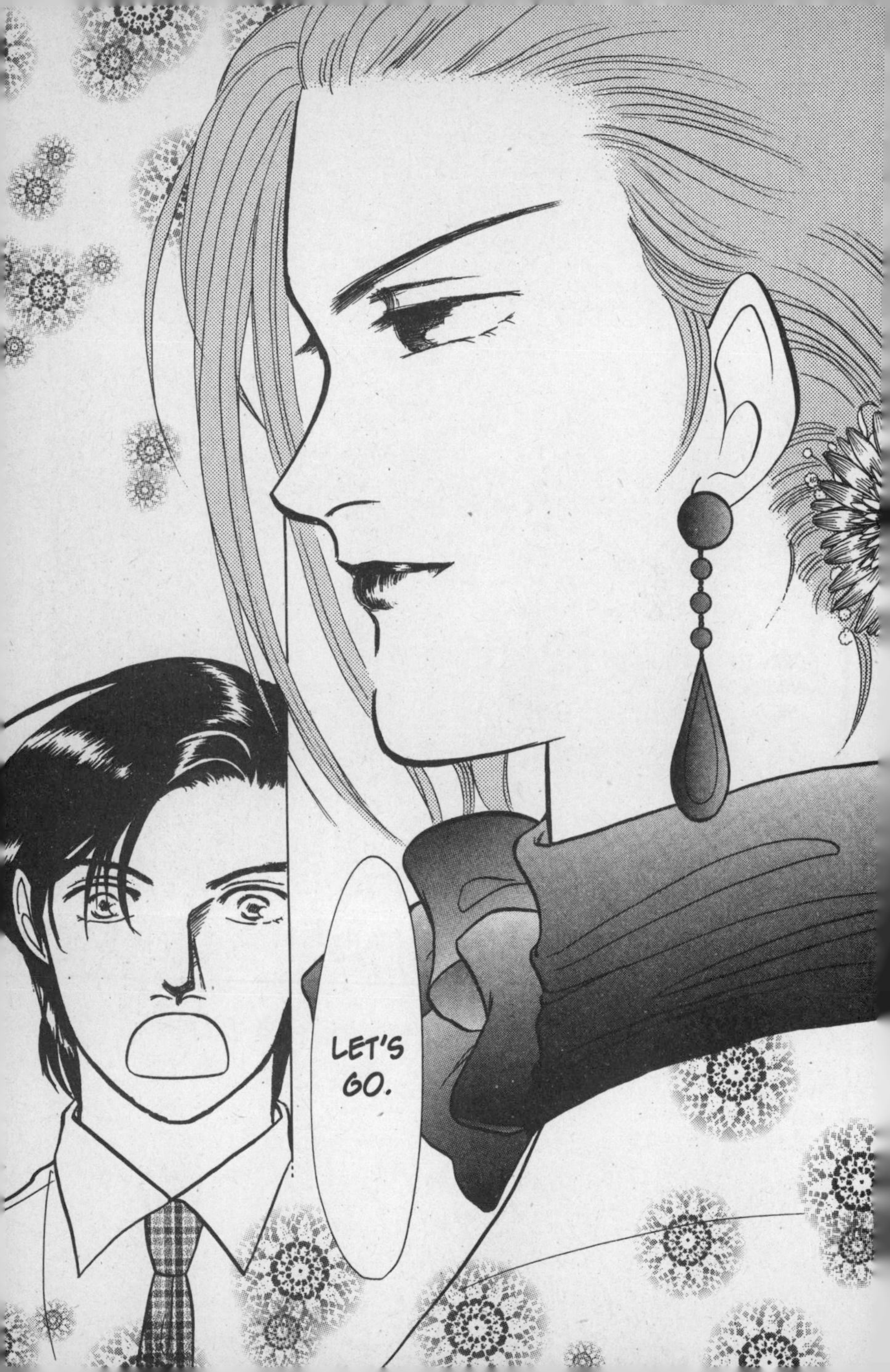
LET'S GO.

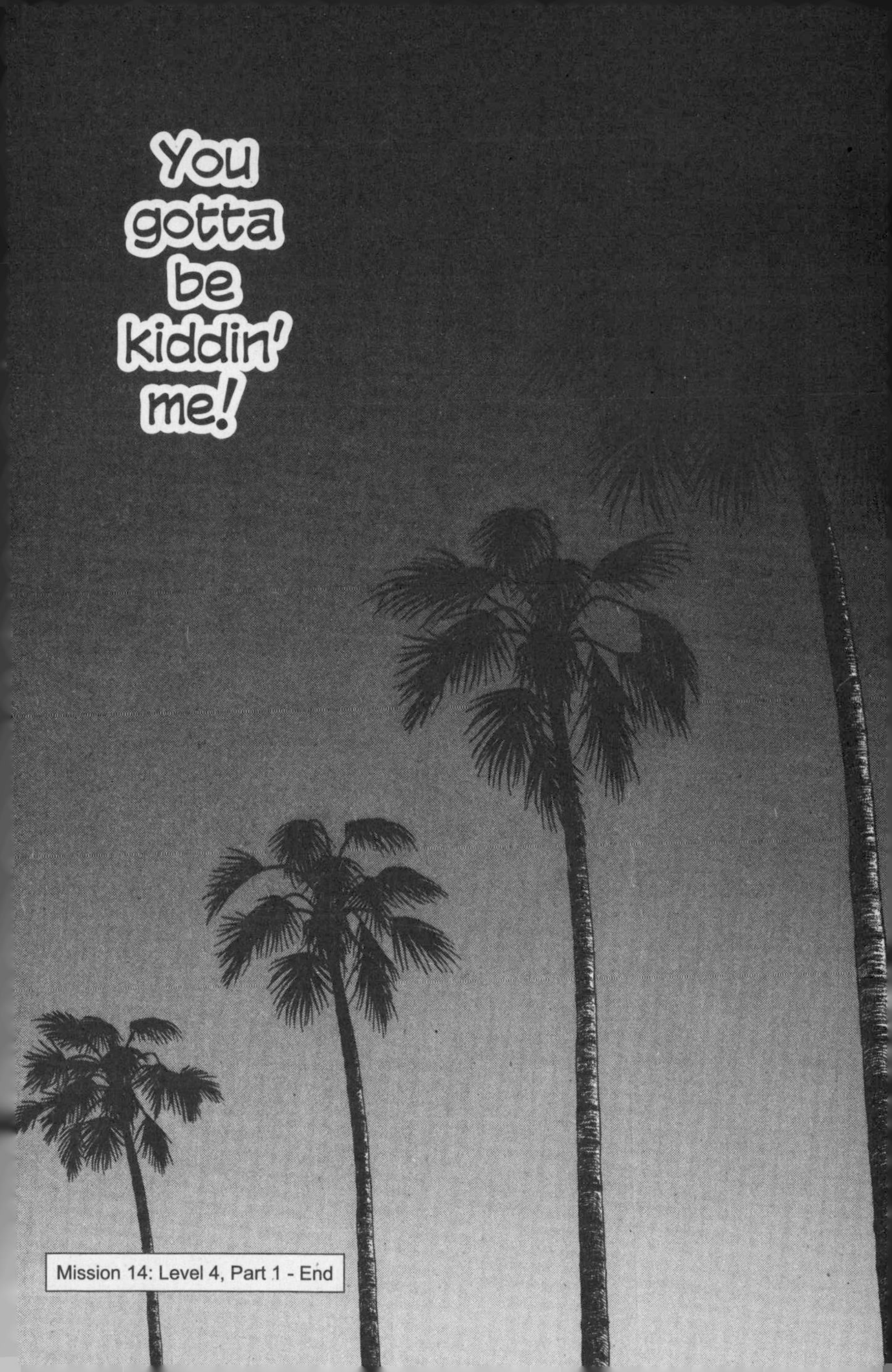
You gotta be kiddin' me!
Mission 14: Level 4, Part 1 - End

Mission 14: Level 4, Part 2

Kou dropped in out of the blue one day.

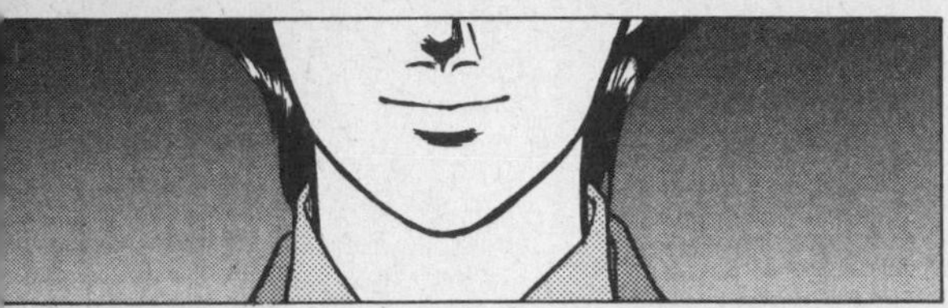

Dressed like a man, but looking like a kid who'd never taken a razor to his face.

I felt like jumping off the Hoover Building when I was told Kou was my new partner.
I thought it was all just a bad, bad joke.

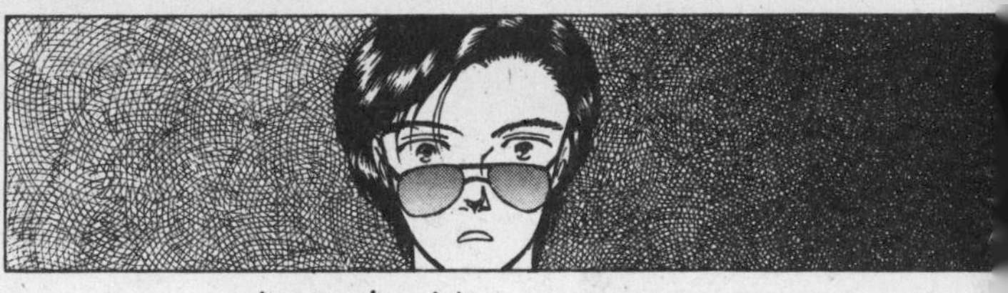

It wasn't a joke.

Nor was Kou some guy fresh out of some academy.

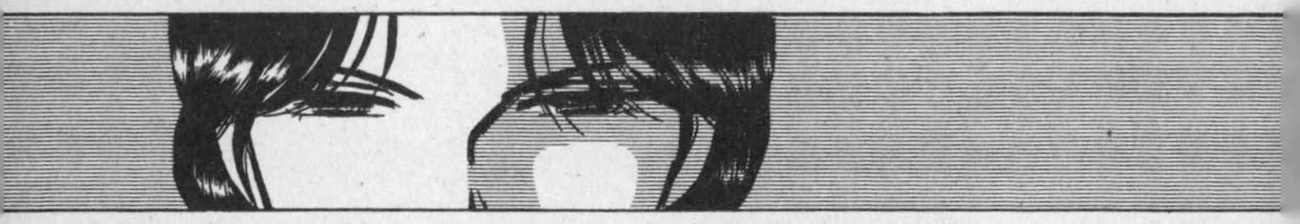

Kou was something else all together.

There was far more to ***her*** than I could've ever imagined.

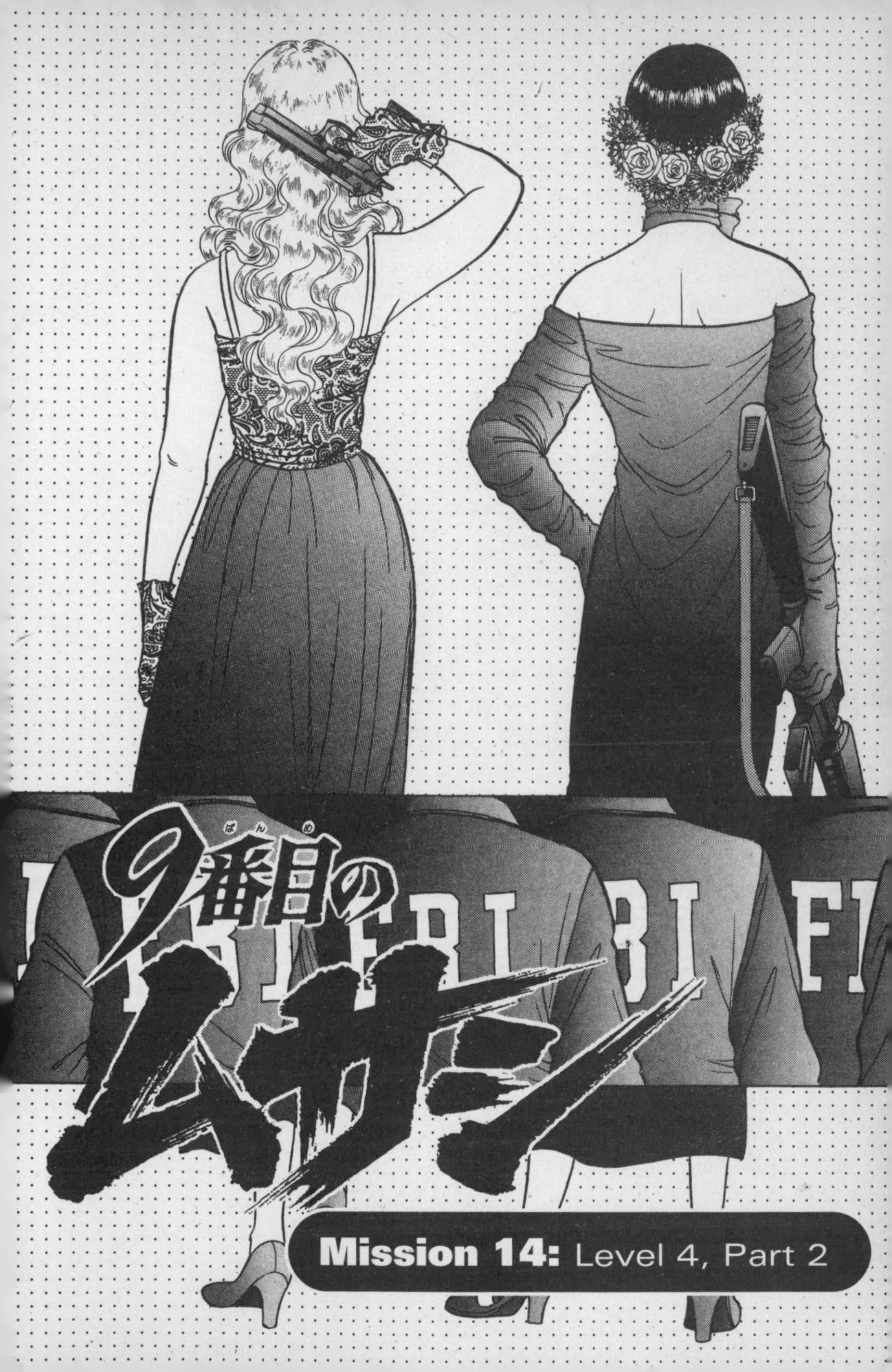
9番目のムサシ
Mission 14: Level 4, Part 2

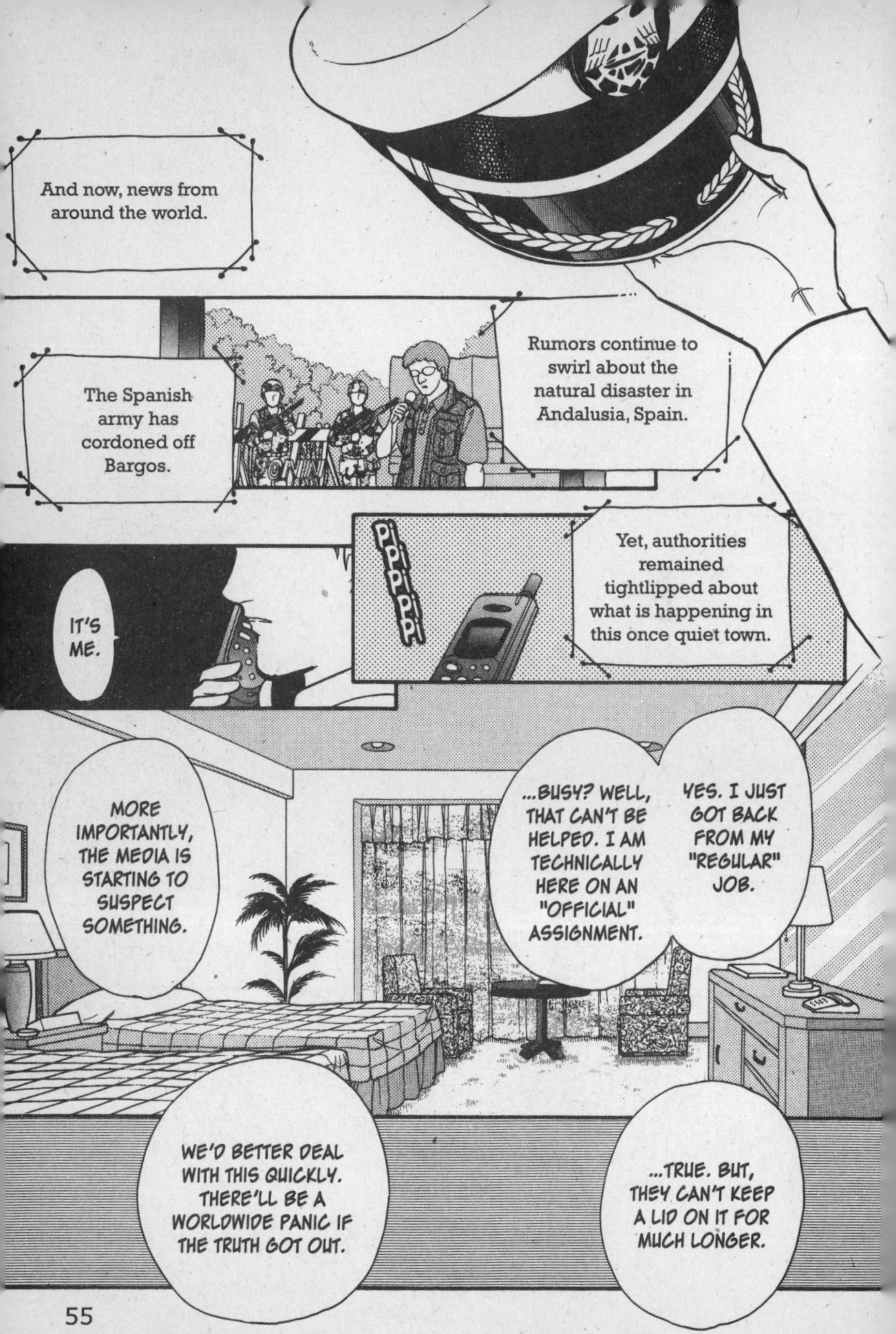
And now, news from around the world.
Rumors continue to swirl about the natural disaster in Andalusia, Spain.
The Spanish army has cordoned off Bargos.
PiPiPiPiPi
Yet, authorities remained tightlipped about what is happening in this once quiet town.
IT'S ME.
YES. I JUST GOT BACK FROM MY "REGULAR" JOB.
...BUSY? WELL, THAT CAN'T BE HELPED. I AM TECHNICALLY HERE ON AN "OFFICIAL" ASSIGNMENT.
MORE IMPORTANTLY, THE MEDIA IS STARTING TO SUSPECT SOMETHING.
...TRUE. BUT, THEY CAN'T KEEP A LID ON IT FOR MUCH LONGER.
WE'D BETTER DEAL WITH THIS QUICKLY. THERE'LL BE A WORLDWIDE PANIC IF THE TRUTH GOT OUT.

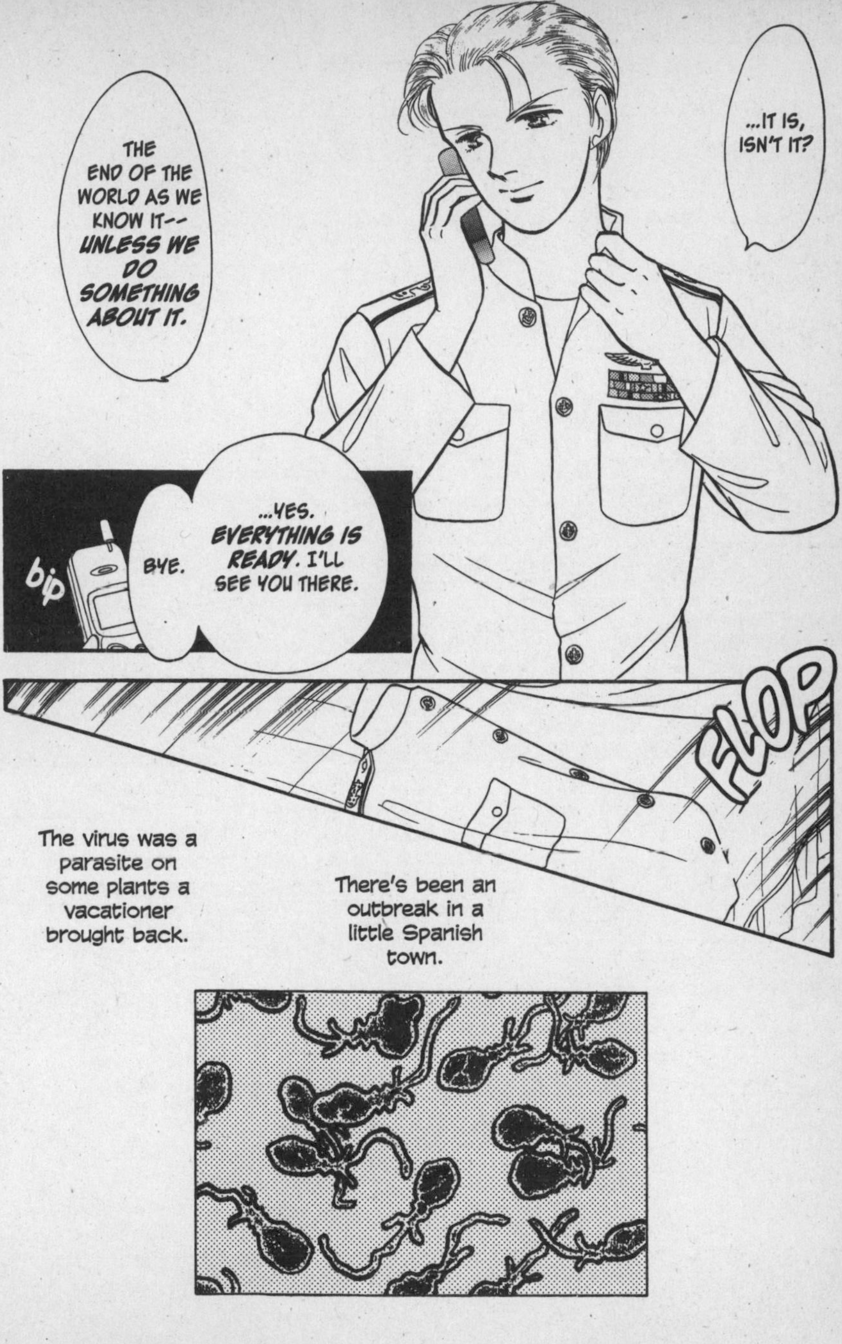
...IT IS, ISN'T IT?
THE END OF THE WORLD AS WE KNOW IT-- UNLESS WE DO SOMETHING ABOUT IT.
...YES. EVERYTHING IS READY. I'LL SEE YOU THERE.
BYE.
bip
FLOP
There's been an outbreak in a little Spanish town.
The virus was a parasite on some plants a vacationer brought back.

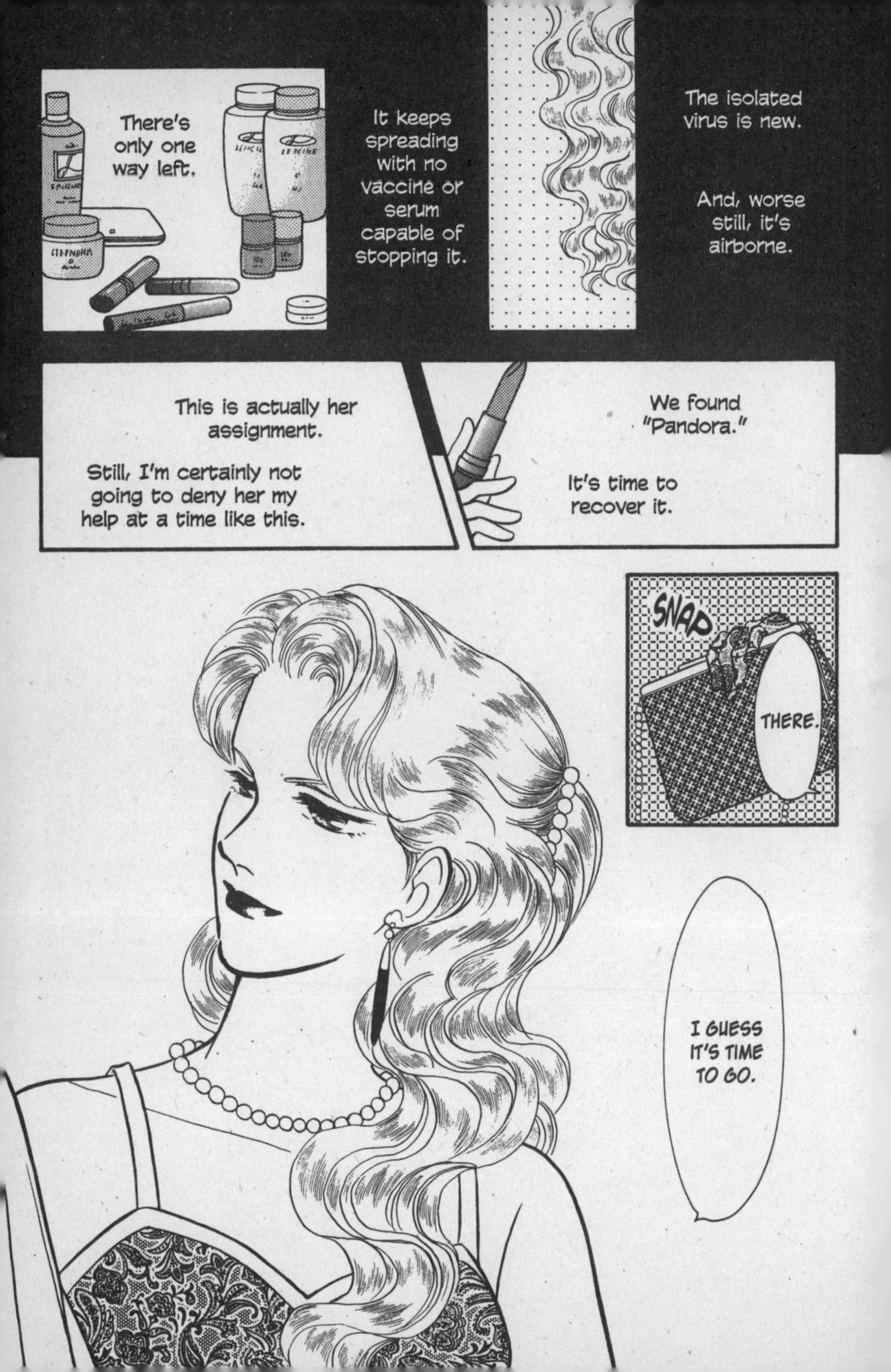
The isolated virus is new.
And, worse still, it's airborne.
It keeps spreading with no vaccine or serum capable of stopping it.
There's only one way left.
We found "Pandora."
It's time to recover it.
This is actually her assignment.
Still, I'm certainly not going to deny her my help at a time like this.
SNAP
THERE.
I GUESS IT'S TIME TO GO.

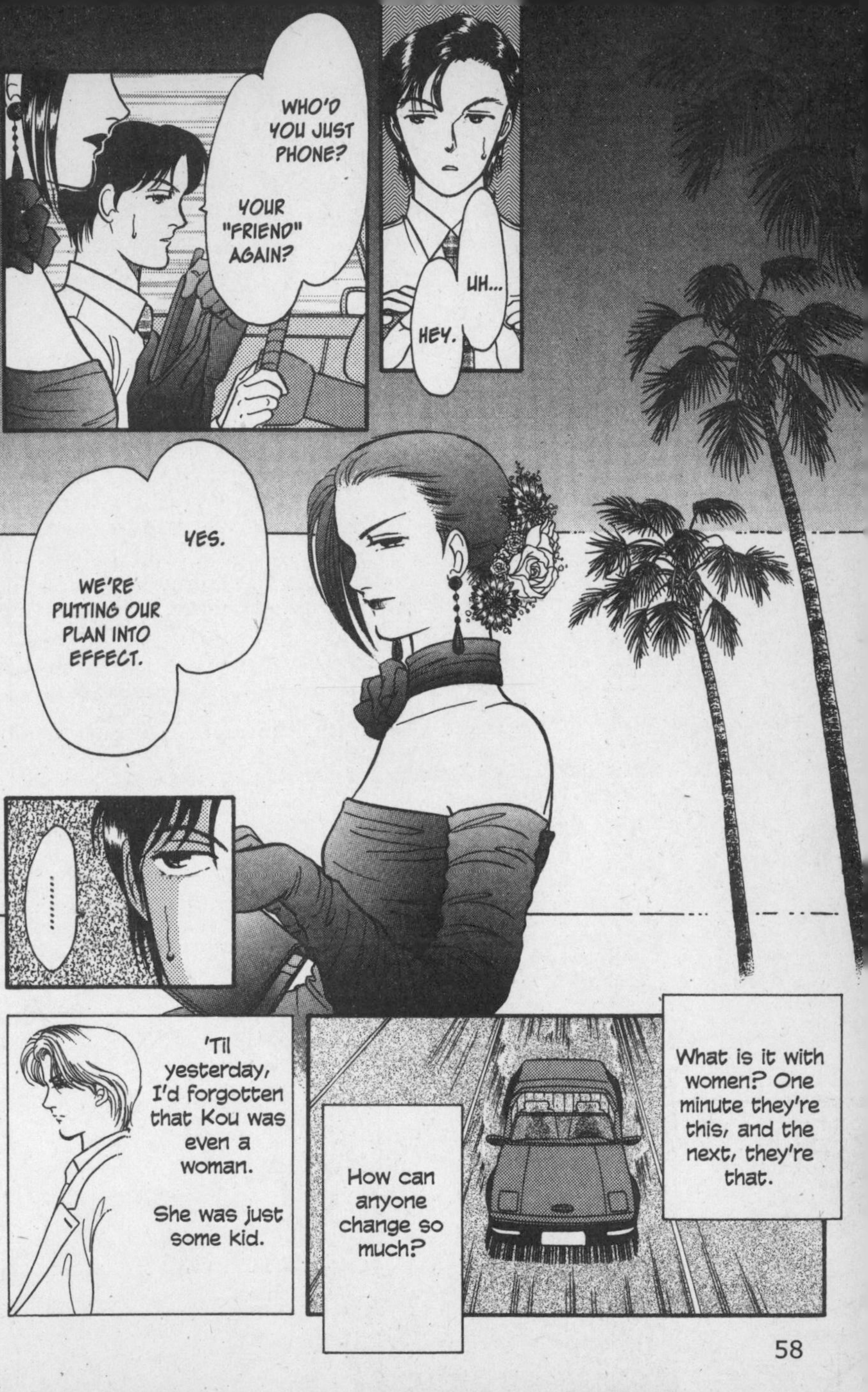
UH...
HEY.
WHO'D YOU JUST PHONE?
YOUR "FRIEND" AGAIN?
YES.
WE'RE PUTTING OUR PLAN INTO EFFECT.
......
What is it with women? One minute they're this, and the next, they're that.
How can anyone change so much?
'Til yesterday, I'd forgotten that Kou was even a woman.
She was just some kid.

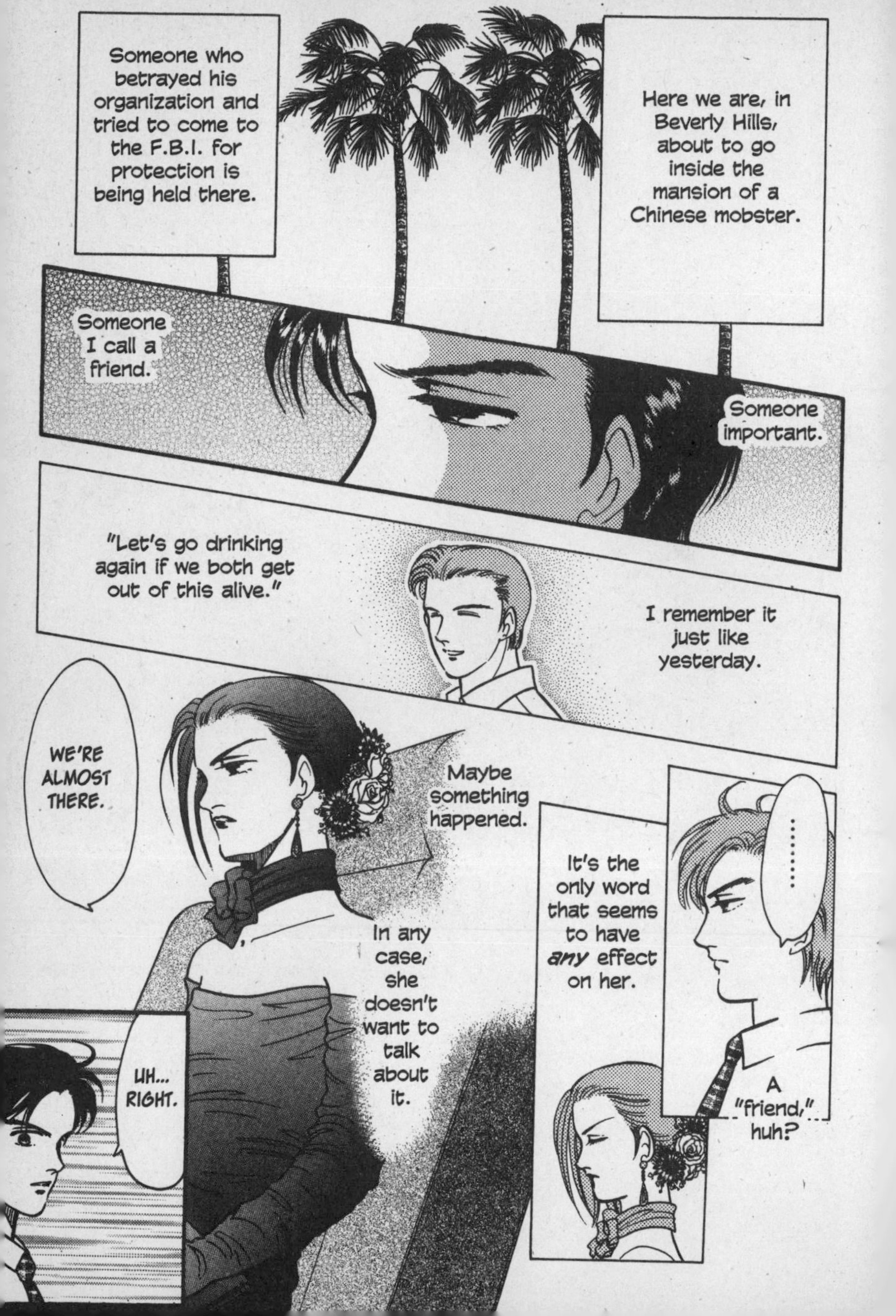

Here we are, in Beverly Hills, about to go inside the mansion of a Chinese mobster.
Someone who betrayed his organization and tried to come to the F.B.I. for protection is being held there.
Someone I call a friend.
Someone important.
"Let's go drinking again if we both get out of this alive."
I remember it just like yesterday.
......
A "friend," huh?
It's the only word that seems to have *any* effect on her.
Maybe something happened.
WE'RE ALMOST THERE.
UH... RIGHT.
In any case, she doesn't want to talk about it.

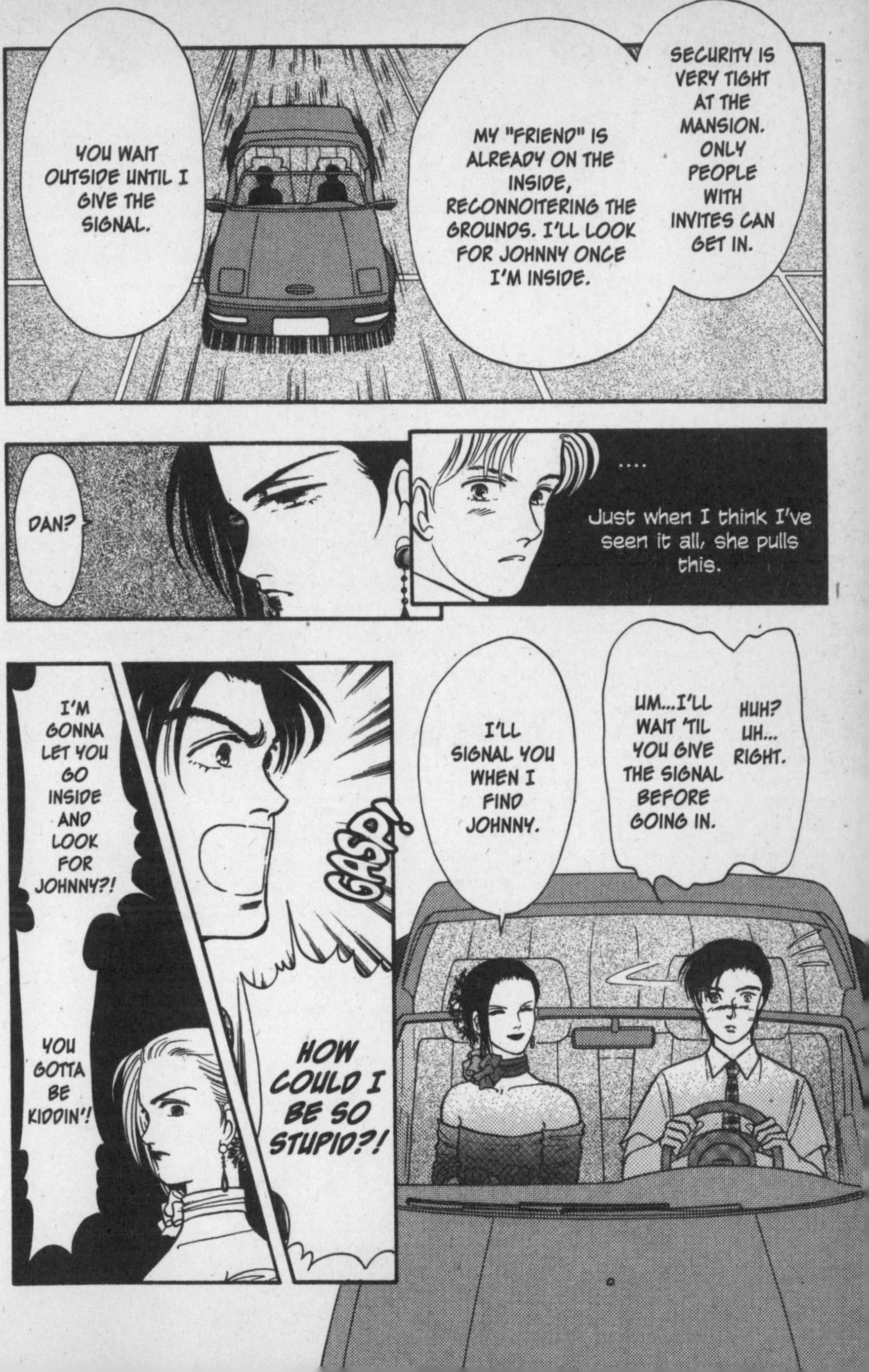
SECURITY IS VERY TIGHT AT THE MANSION. ONLY PEOPLE WITH INVITES CAN GET IN.
MY "FRIEND" IS ALREADY ON THE INSIDE, RECONNOITERING THE GROUNDS. I'LL LOOK FOR JOHNNY ONCE I'M INSIDE.
YOU WAIT OUTSIDE UNTIL I GIVE THE SIGNAL.
....
Just when I think I've seen it all, she pulls this.
DAN?
HUH? UH... RIGHT.
UM...I'LL WAIT 'TIL YOU GIVE THE SIGNAL BEFORE GOING IN.
I'LL SIGNAL YOU WHEN I FIND JOHNNY.
I'M GONNA LET YOU GO INSIDE AND LOOK FOR JOHNNY?!
GASP!
HOW COULD I BE SO STUPID?!
YOU GOTTA BE KIDDIN'!

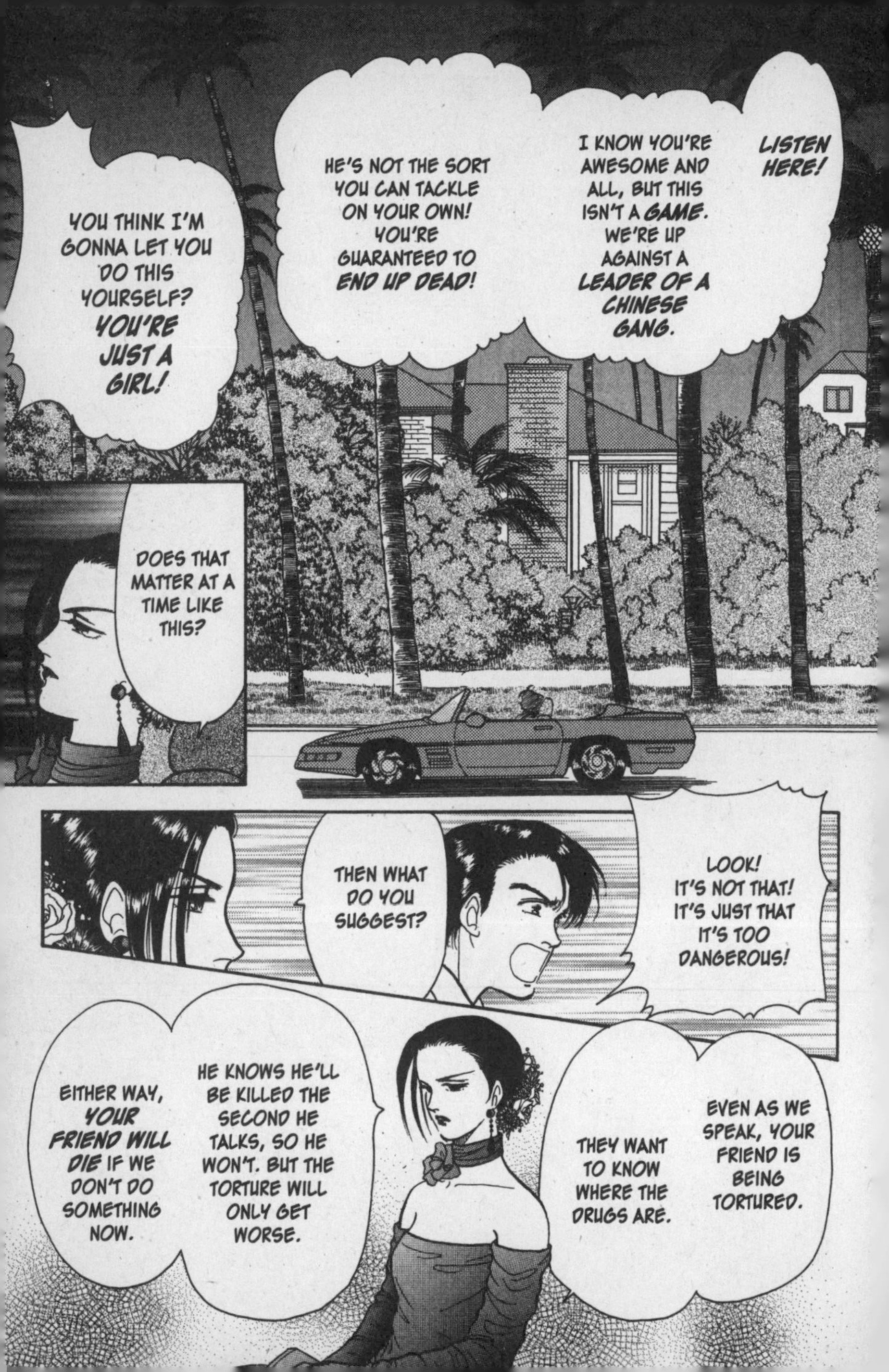
LISTEN HERE!
I KNOW YOU'RE AWESOME AND ALL, BUT THIS ISN'T A GAME. WE'RE UP AGAINST A LEADER OF A CHINESE GANG.
HE'S NOT THE SORT YOU CAN TACKLE ON YOUR OWN! YOU'RE GUARANTEED TO END UP DEAD!
YOU THINK I'M GONNA LET YOU DO THIS YOURSELF? YOU'RE JUST A GIRL!
DOES THAT MATTER AT A TIME LIKE THIS?
LOOK! IT'S NOT THAT! IT'S JUST THAT IT'S TOO DANGEROUS!
THEN WHAT DO YOU SUGGEST?
EVEN AS WE SPEAK, YOUR FRIEND IS BEING TORTURED.
THEY WANT TO KNOW WHERE THE DRUGS ARE.
HE KNOWS HE'LL BE KILLED THE SECOND HE TALKS, SO HE WON'T. BUT THE TORTURE WILL ONLY GET WORSE.
EITHER WAY, YOUR FRIEND WILL DIE IF WE DON'T DO SOMETHING NOW.

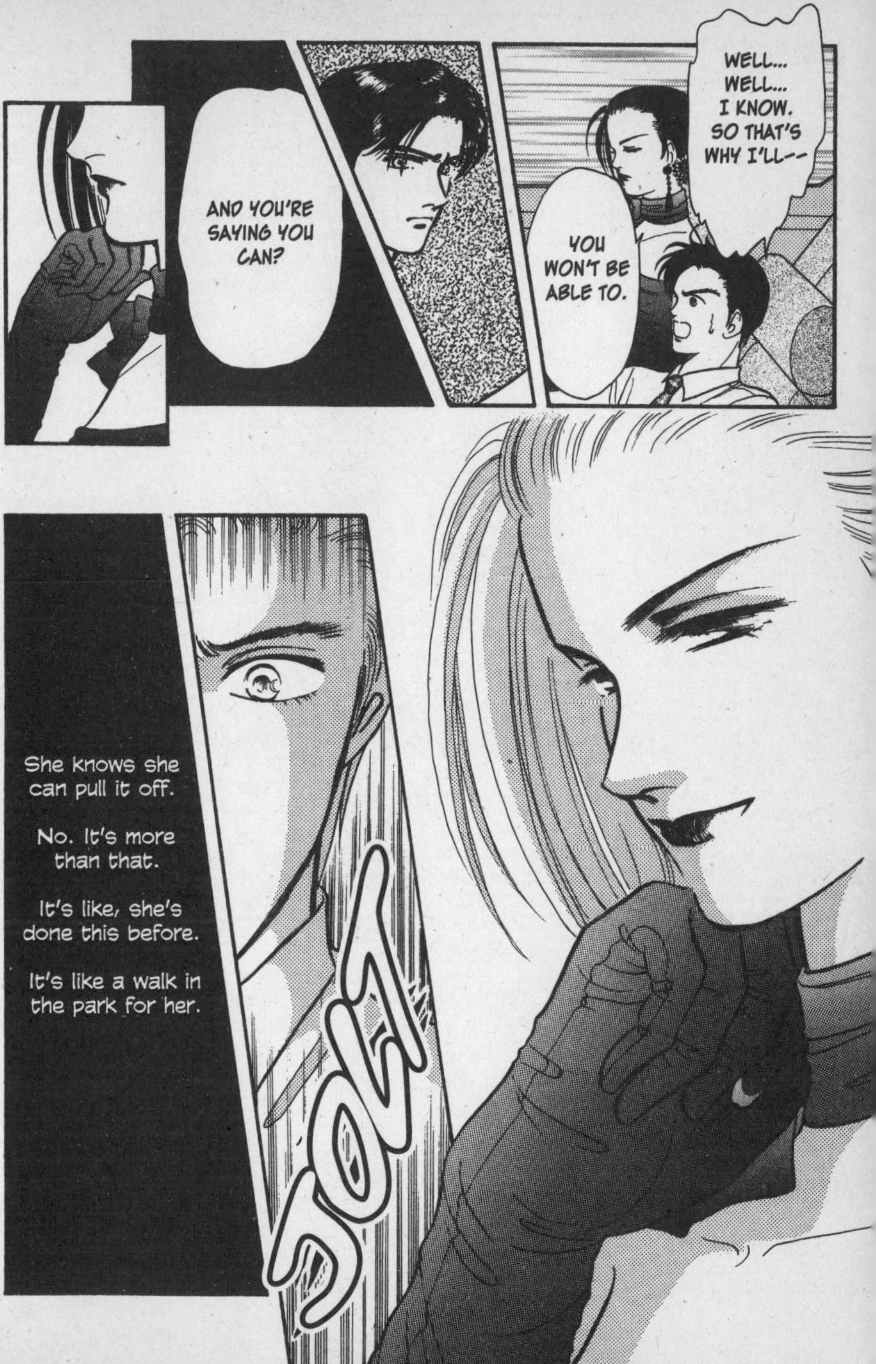
WELL... WELL... I KNOW. SO THAT'S WHY I'LL--
YOU WON'T BE ABLE TO.
AND YOU'RE SAYING YOU CAN?
She knows she can pull it off.
No. It's more than that.
It's like, she's done this before.
It's like a walk in the park for her.

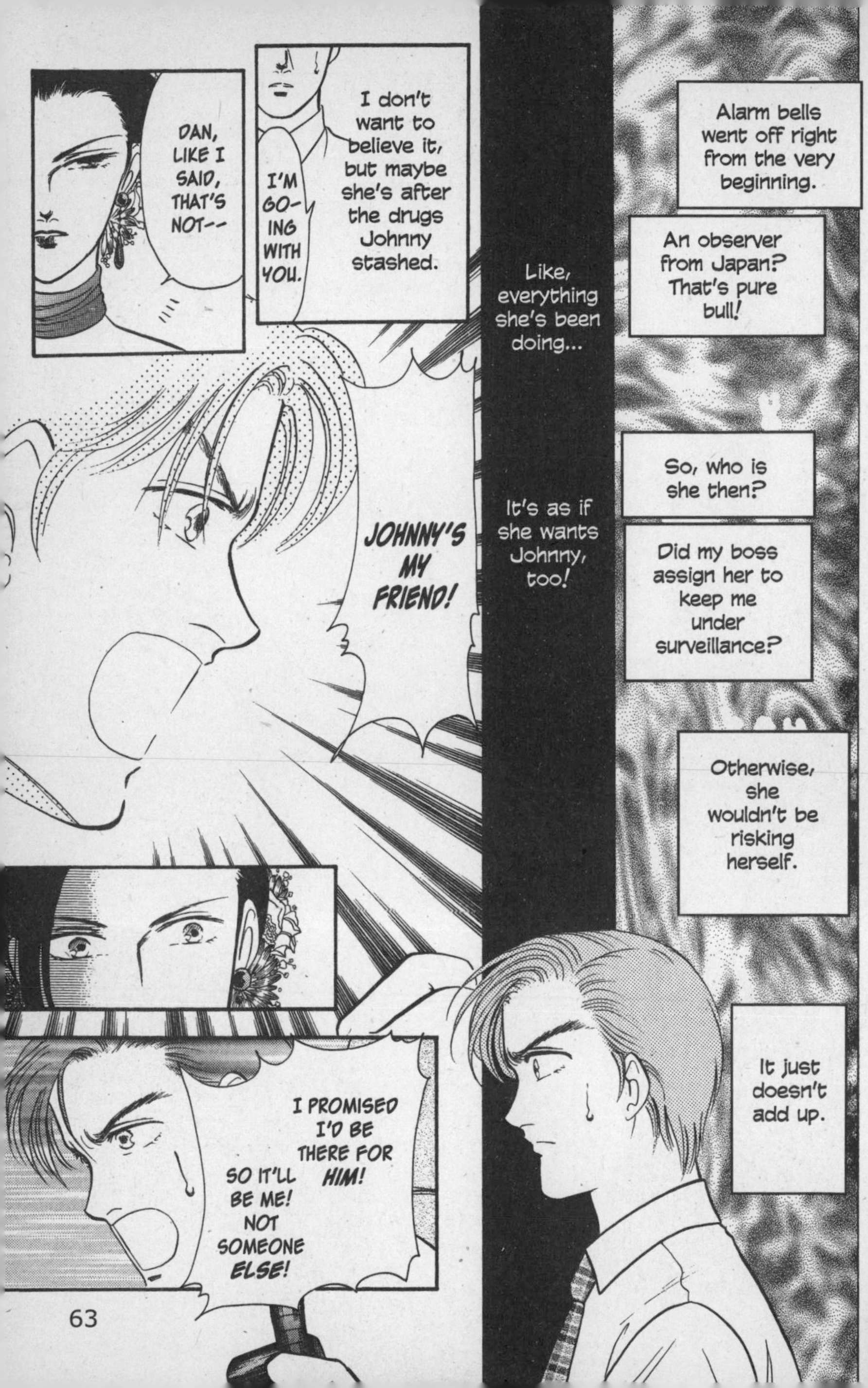

Alarm bells went off right from the very beginning.
An observer from Japan? That's pure bull!
So, who is she then?
Did my boss assign her to keep me under surveillance?
Otherwise, she wouldn't be risking herself.
It just doesn't add up.
Like, everything she's been doing...
It's as if she wants Johnny, too!
I don't want to believe it, but maybe she's after the drugs Johnny stashed.
I'M GO-ING WITH YOU.
DAN, LIKE I SAID, THAT'S NOT--
JOHNNY'S MY FRIEND!
I PROMISED I'D BE THERE FOR HIM!
SO IT'LL BE ME! NOT SOMEONE ELSE!

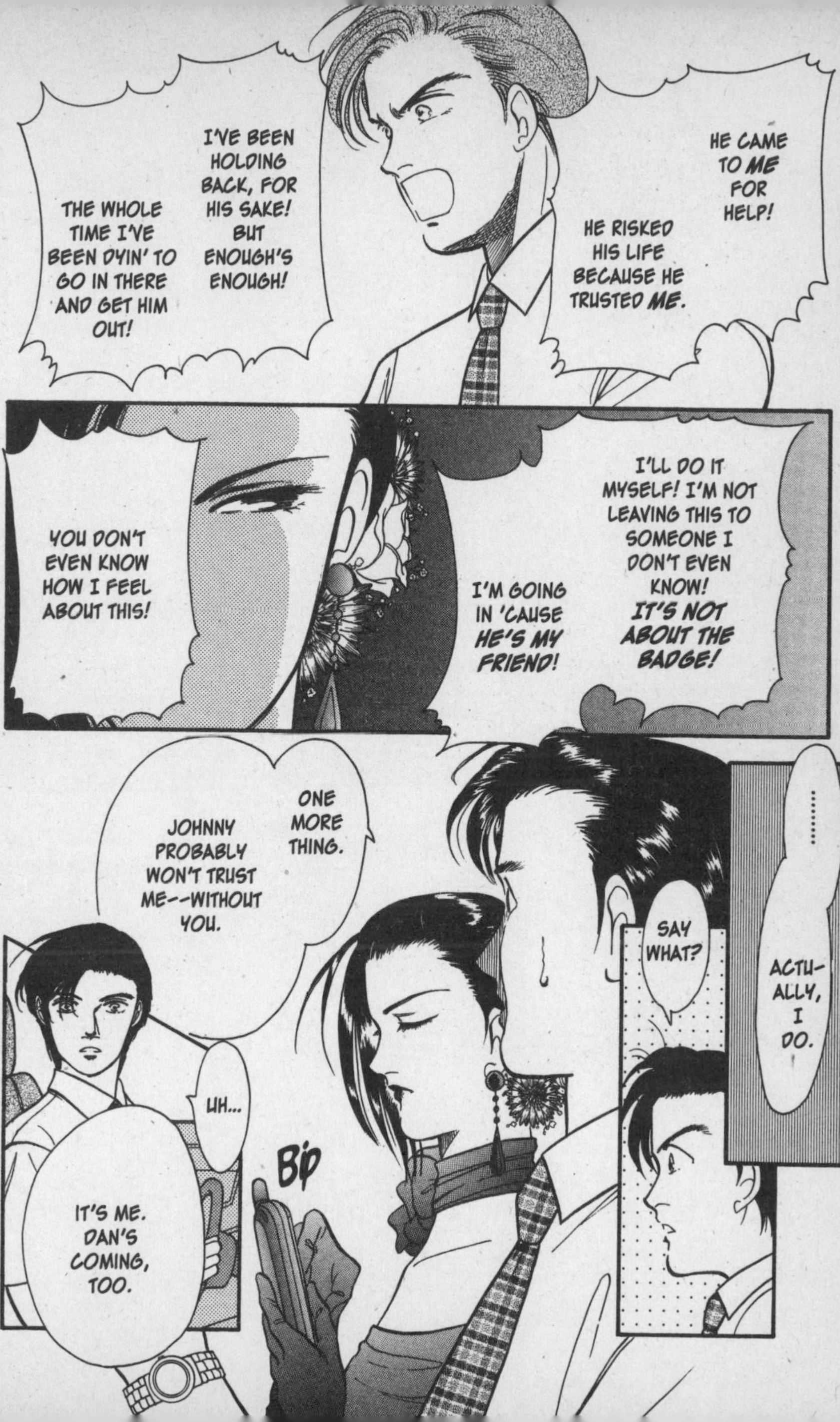
HE CAME TO ME FOR HELP!
HE RISKED HIS LIFE BECAUSE HE TRUSTED ME.
I'VE BEEN HOLDING BACK, FOR HIS SAKE! BUT ENOUGH'S ENOUGH!
THE WHOLE TIME I'VE BEEN DYIN' TO GO IN THERE AND GET HIM OUT!
I'LL DO IT MYSELF! I'M NOT LEAVING THIS TO SOMEONE I DON'T EVEN KNOW! IT'S NOT ABOUT THE BADGE!
I'M GOING IN 'CAUSE HE'S MY FRIEND!
YOU DON'T EVEN KNOW HOW I FEEL ABOUT THIS!
....
ACTU-ALLY, I DO.
SAY WHAT?
ONE MORE THING.
JOHNNY PROBABLY WON'T TRUST ME--WITHOUT YOU.
Bip
UH...
IT'S ME. DAN'S COMING, TOO.

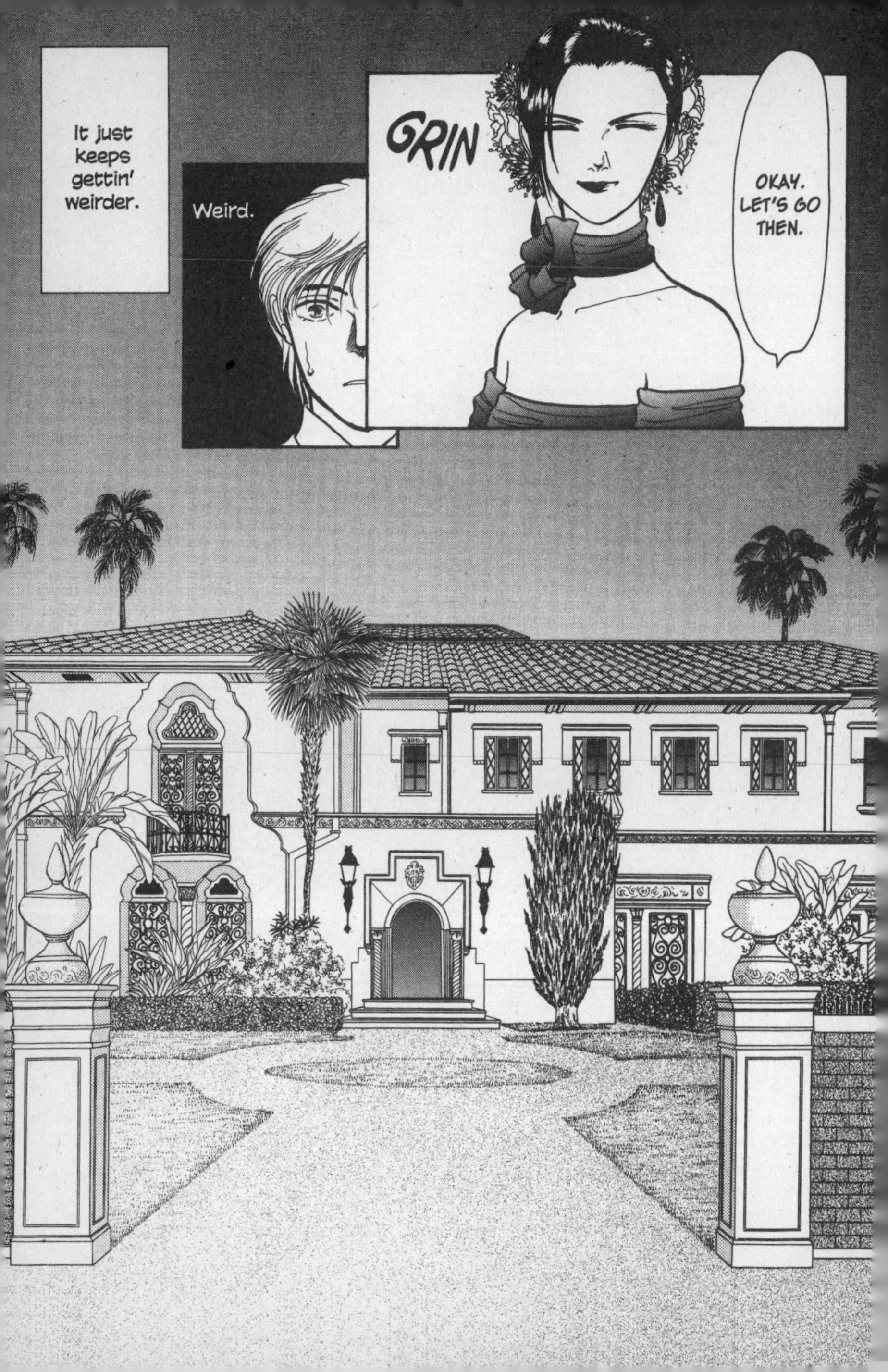
OKAY. LET'S GO THEN.
GRIN
Weird.
It just keeps gettin' weirder.

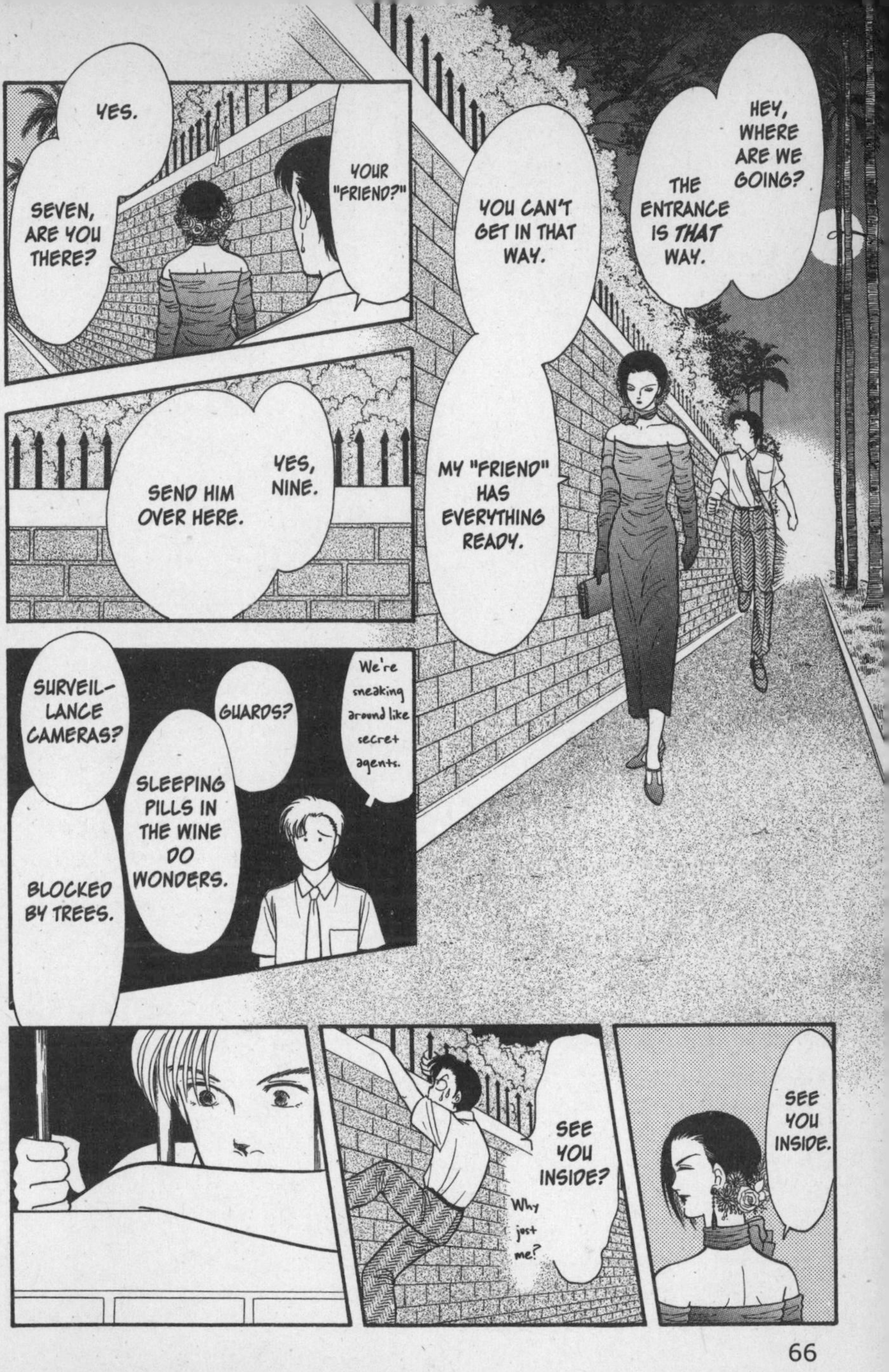

HEY, WHERE ARE WE GOING?
THE ENTRANCE IS *THAT* WAY.
YOU CAN'T GET IN THAT WAY.
MY "FRIEND" HAS EVERYTHING READY.
YOUR "FRIEND?"
SEVEN, ARE YOU THERE?
YES.
YES, NINE.
SEND HIM OVER HERE.
We're sneaking around like secret agents.
GUARDS?
SURVEIL-LANCE CAMERAS?
SLEEPING PILLS IN THE WINE DO WONDERS.
BLOCKED BY TREES.
SEE YOU INSIDE.
SEE YOU INSIDE?
Why just me?

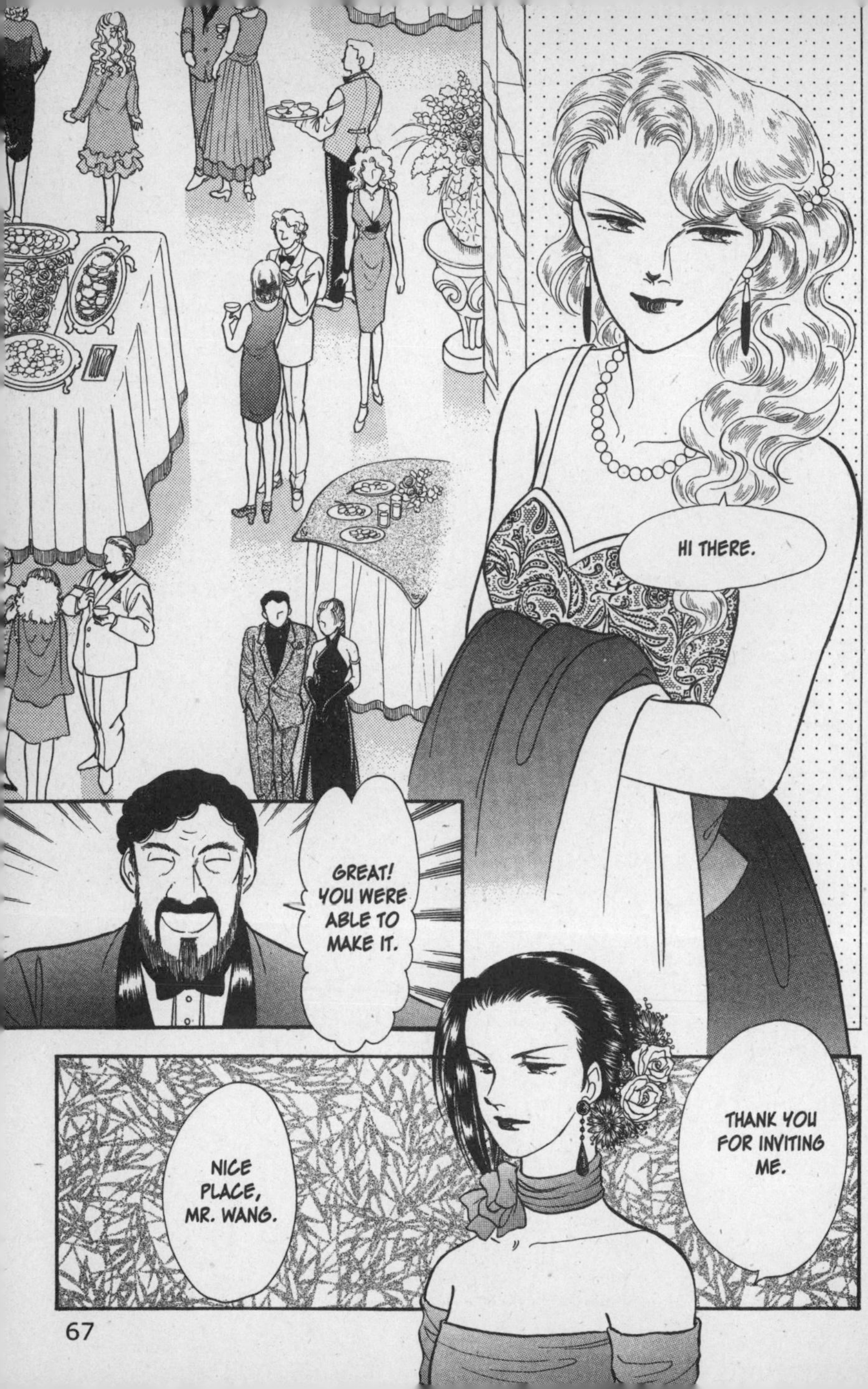
HI THERE.
GREAT! YOU WERE ABLE TO MAKE IT.
THANK YOU FOR INVITING ME.
NICE PLACE, MR. WANG.

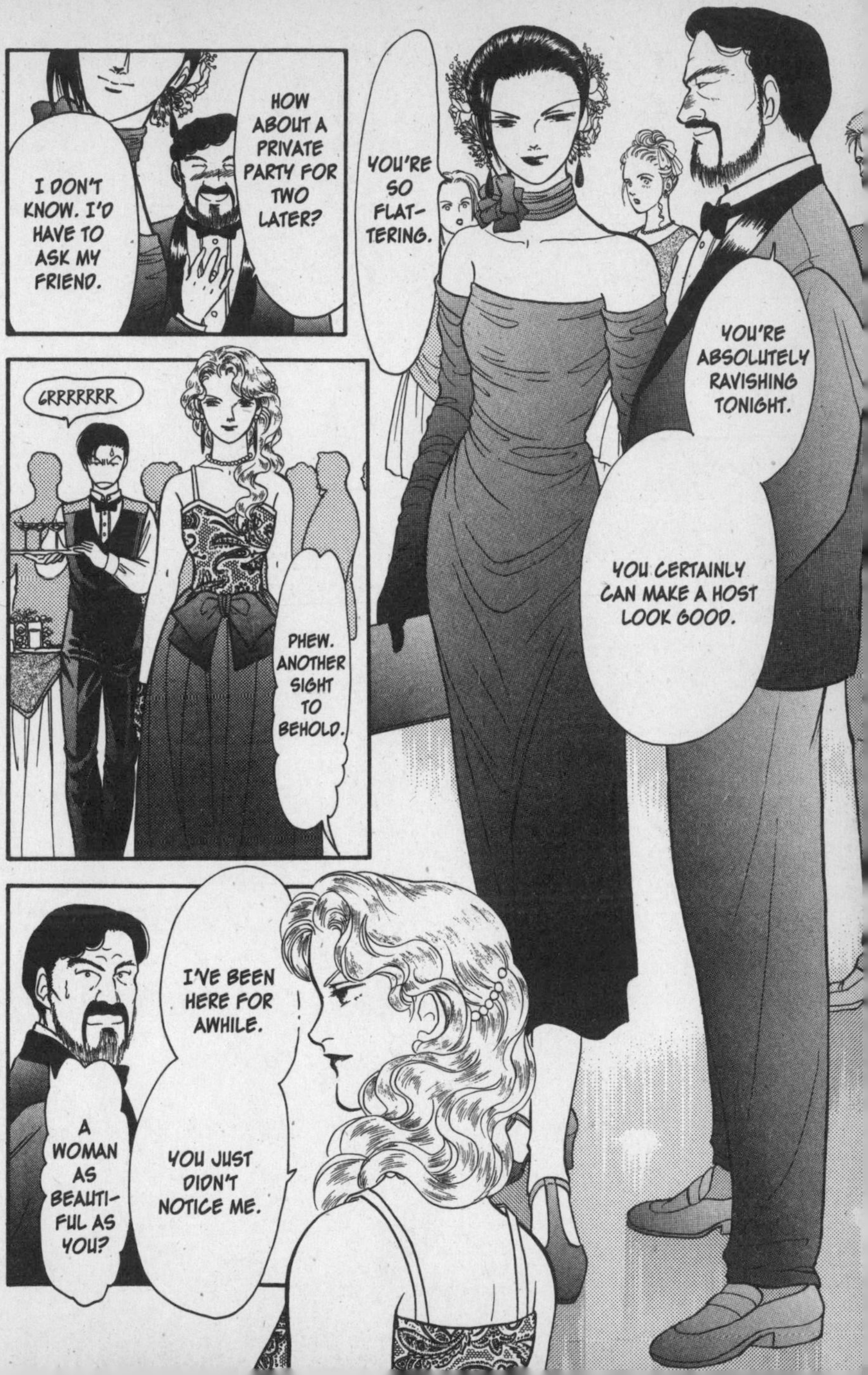
YOU'RE ABSOLUTELY RAVISHING TONIGHT.
YOU CERTAINLY CAN MAKE A HOST LOOK GOOD.
YOU'RE SO FLAT-TERING.
HOW ABOUT A PRIVATE PARTY FOR TWO LATER?
I DON'T KNOW. I'D HAVE TO ASK MY FRIEND.
PHEW. ANOTHER SIGHT TO BEHOLD.
GRRRRRRR
I'VE BEEN HERE FOR AWHILE.
YOU JUST DIDN'T NOTICE ME.
A WOMAN AS BEAUTI-FUL AS YOU?

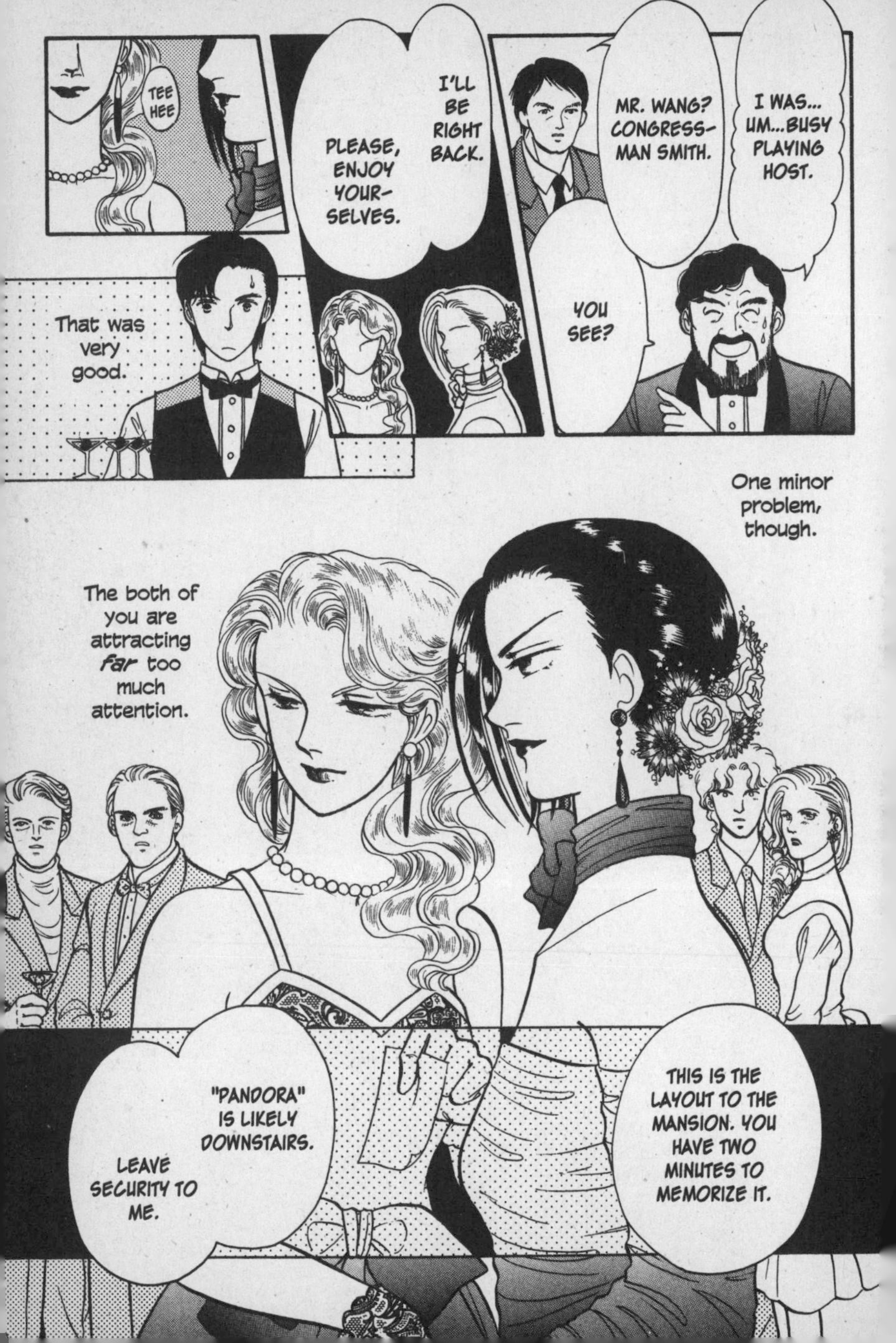
I WAS... UM...BUSY PLAYING HOST.
MR. WANG? CONGRESS-MAN SMITH.
YOU SEE?
I'LL BE RIGHT BACK.
PLEASE, ENJOY YOUR-SELVES.
TEE HEE
That was very good.
One minor problem, though.
The both of you are attracting *far* too much attention.
THIS IS THE LAYOUT TO THE MANSION. YOU HAVE TWO MINUTES TO MEMORIZE IT.
"PANDORA" IS LIKELY DOWNSTAIRS.
LEAVE SECURITY TO ME.

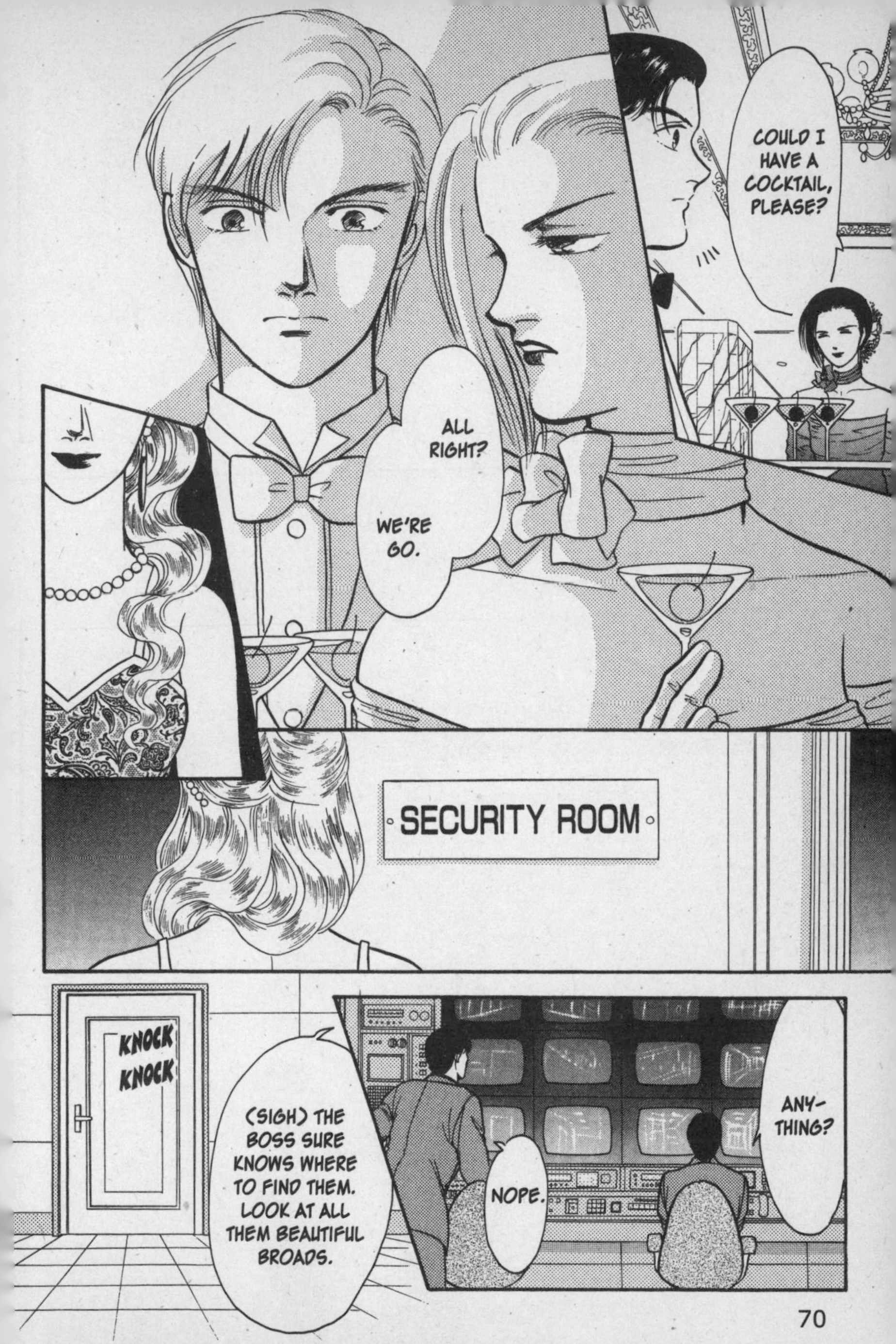
COULD I HAVE A COCKTAIL, PLEASE?
ALL RIGHT?
WE'RE GO.
SECURITY ROOM
ANY-THING?
NOPE.
(SIGH) THE BOSS SURE KNOWS WHERE TO FIND THEM. LOOK AT ALL THEM BEAUTIFUL BROADS.
KNOCK KNOCK

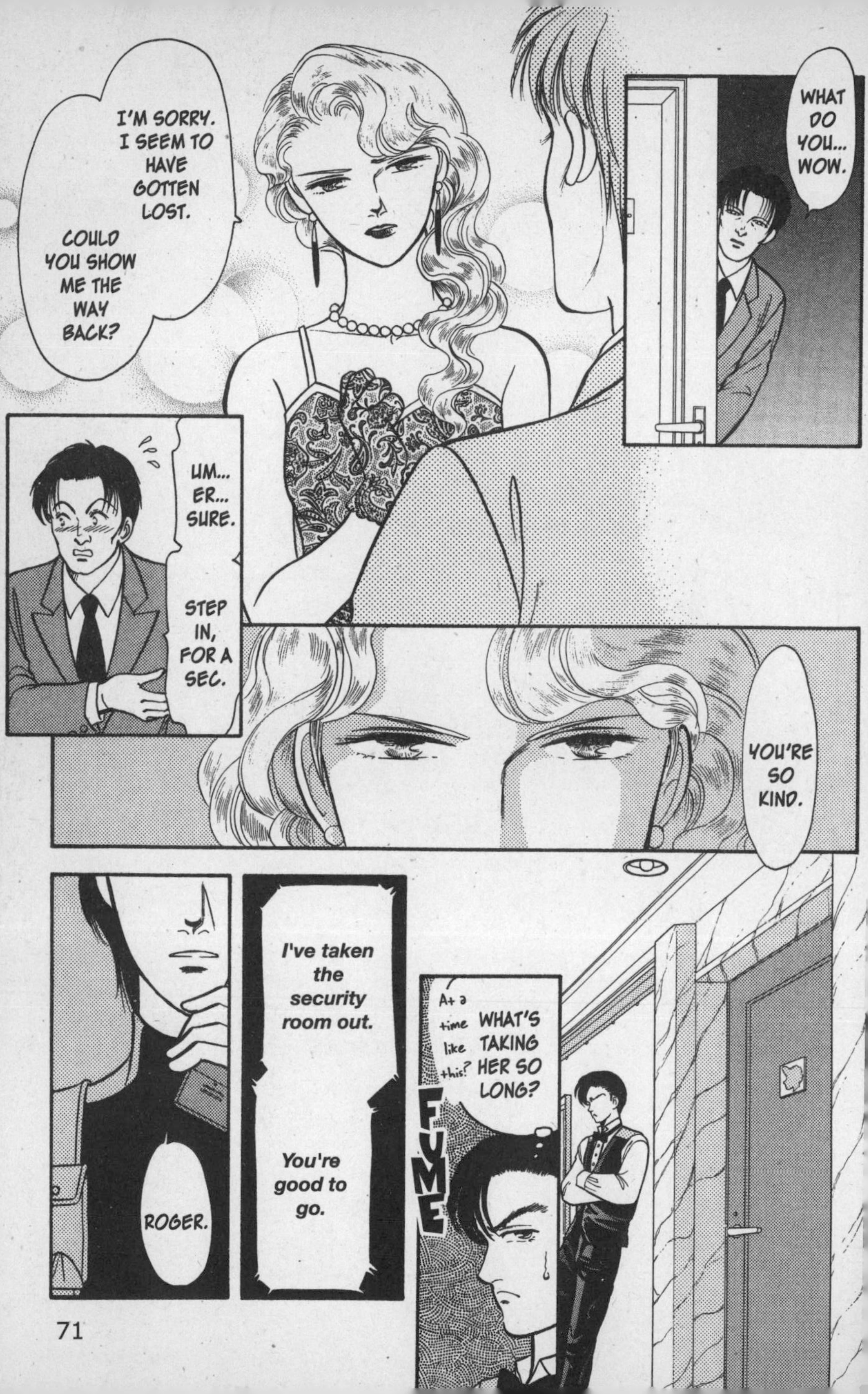

WHAT DO YOU... WOW.
I'M SORRY. I SEEM TO HAVE GOTTEN LOST.
COULD YOU SHOW ME THE WAY BACK?
UM... ER... SURE.
STEP IN, FOR A SEC.
YOU'RE SO KIND.
At a time like this?
WHAT'S TAKING HER SO LONG?
FUME
I've taken the security room out.
You're good to go.
ROGER.

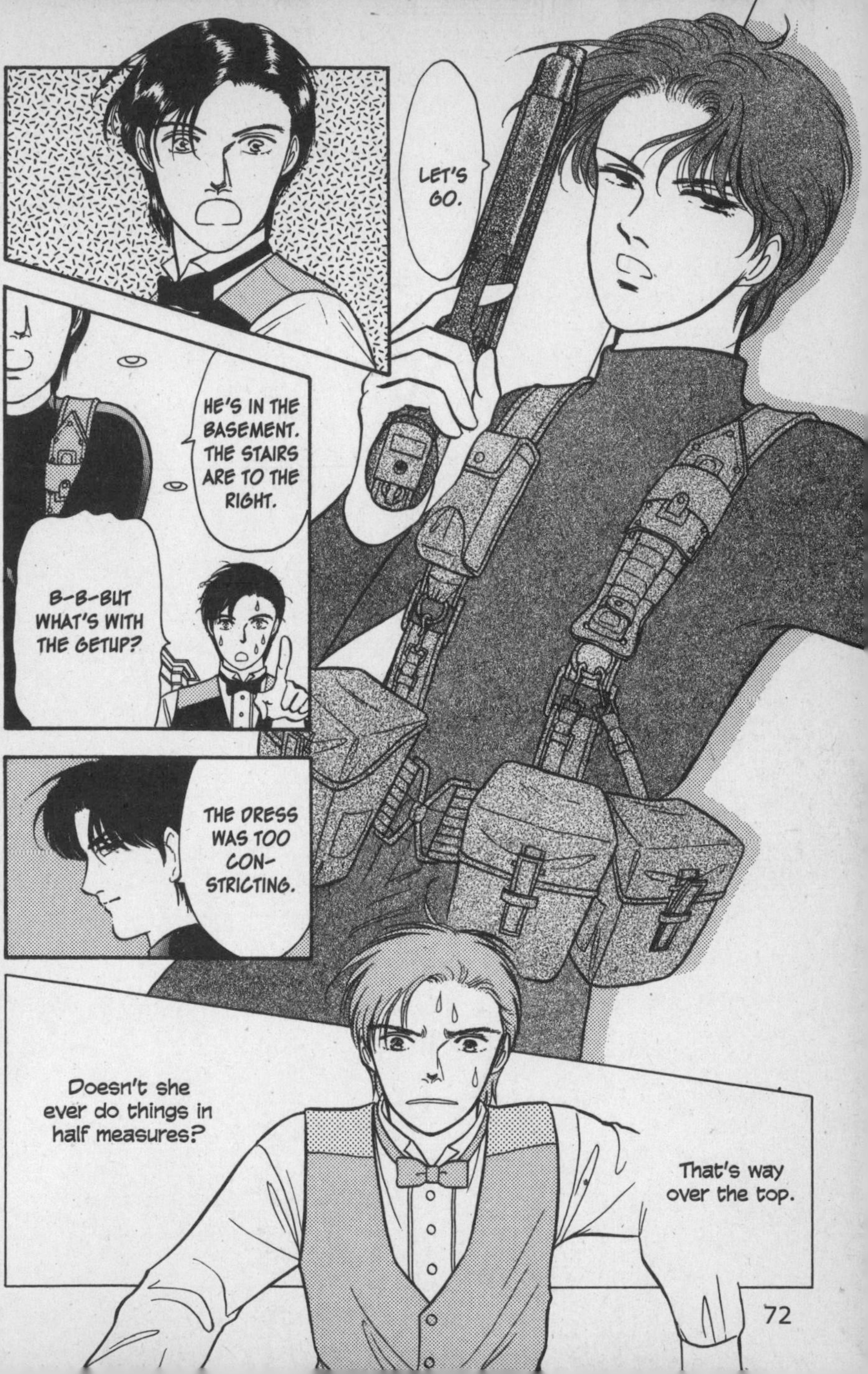
LET'S GO.
HE'S IN THE BASEMENT. THE STAIRS ARE TO THE RIGHT.
B-B-BUT WHAT'S WITH THE GETUP?
THE DRESS WAS TOO CON-STRICTING.
Doesn't she ever do things in half measures?
That's way over the top.

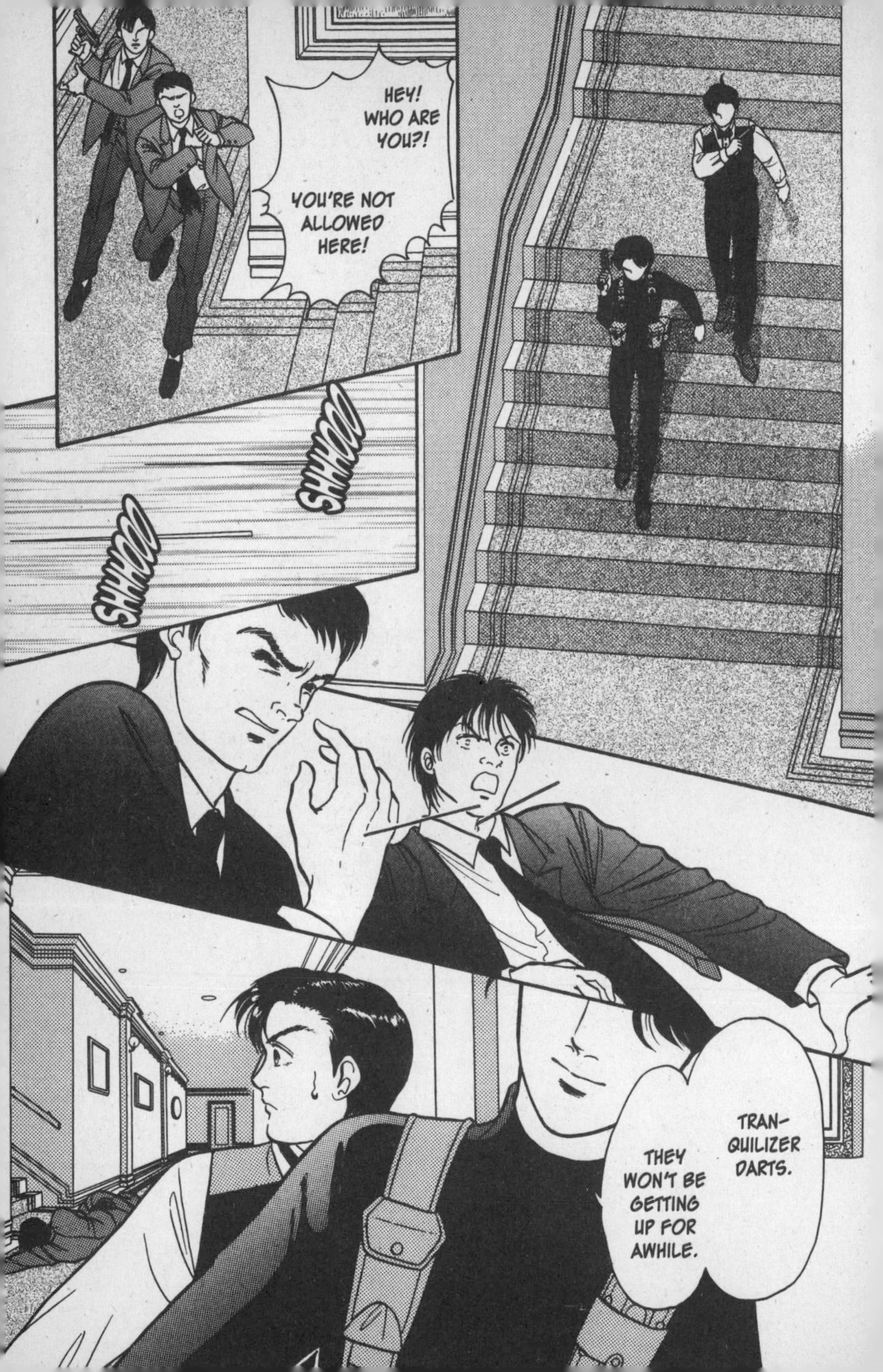
HEY! WHO ARE YOU?!
YOU'RE NOT ALLOWED HERE!
SHHOOO
SHHOOO
TRAN-QUILIZER DARTS.
THEY WON'T BE GETTING UP FOR AWHILE.

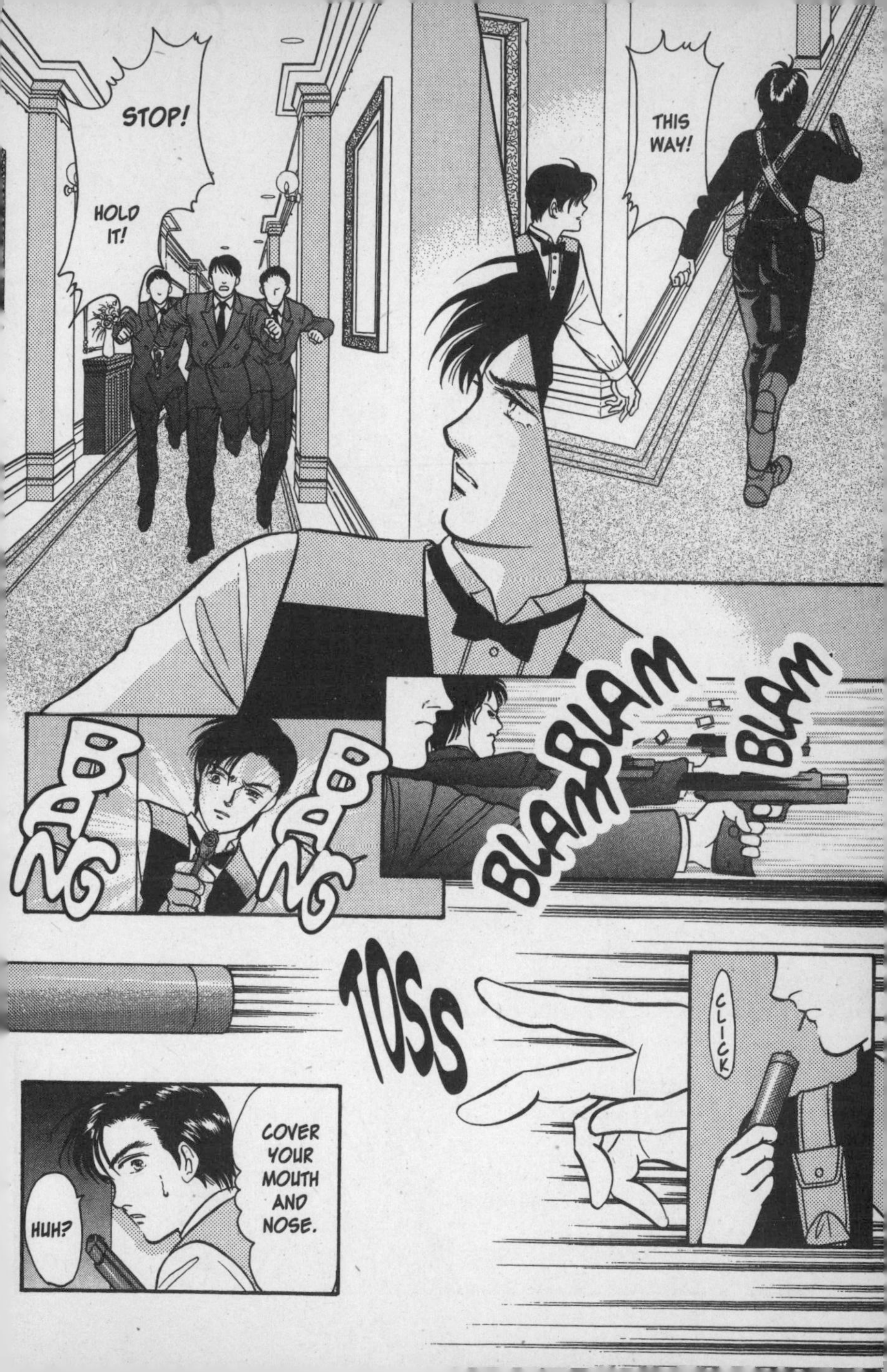

THIS WAY!
STOP!
HOLD IT!
BLAM
BLAM
BLAM
BLAM
BLAM
BANG
BANG
CLICK
TOSS
COVER YOUR MOUTH AND NOSE.
HUH?

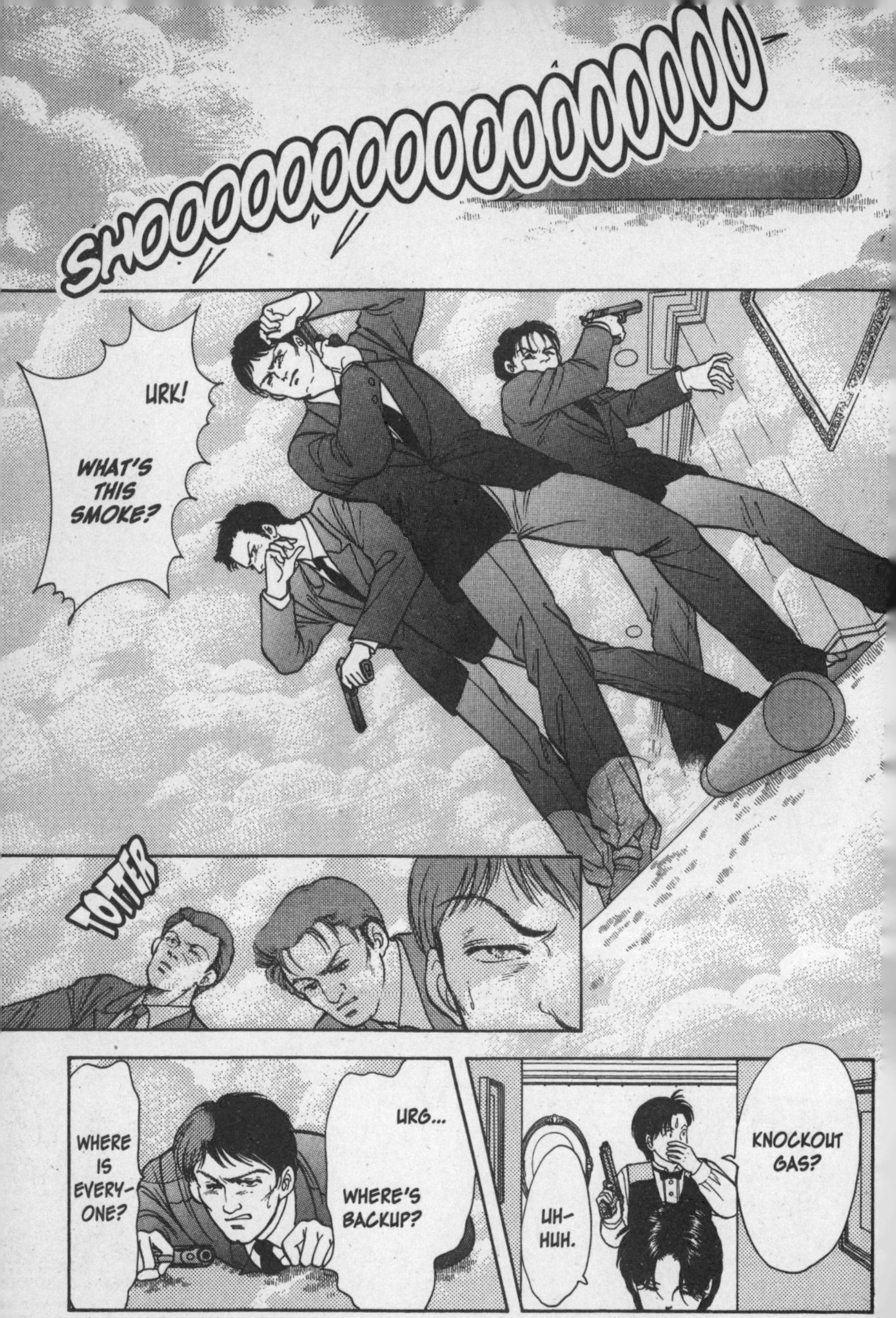
SHOOOOOOOOOOOOOOOOO
URK!
WHAT'S THIS SMOKE?
TOTTER
KNOCKOUT GAS?
UH-HUH.
URG...
WHERE'S BACKUP?
WHERE IS EVERY-ONE?

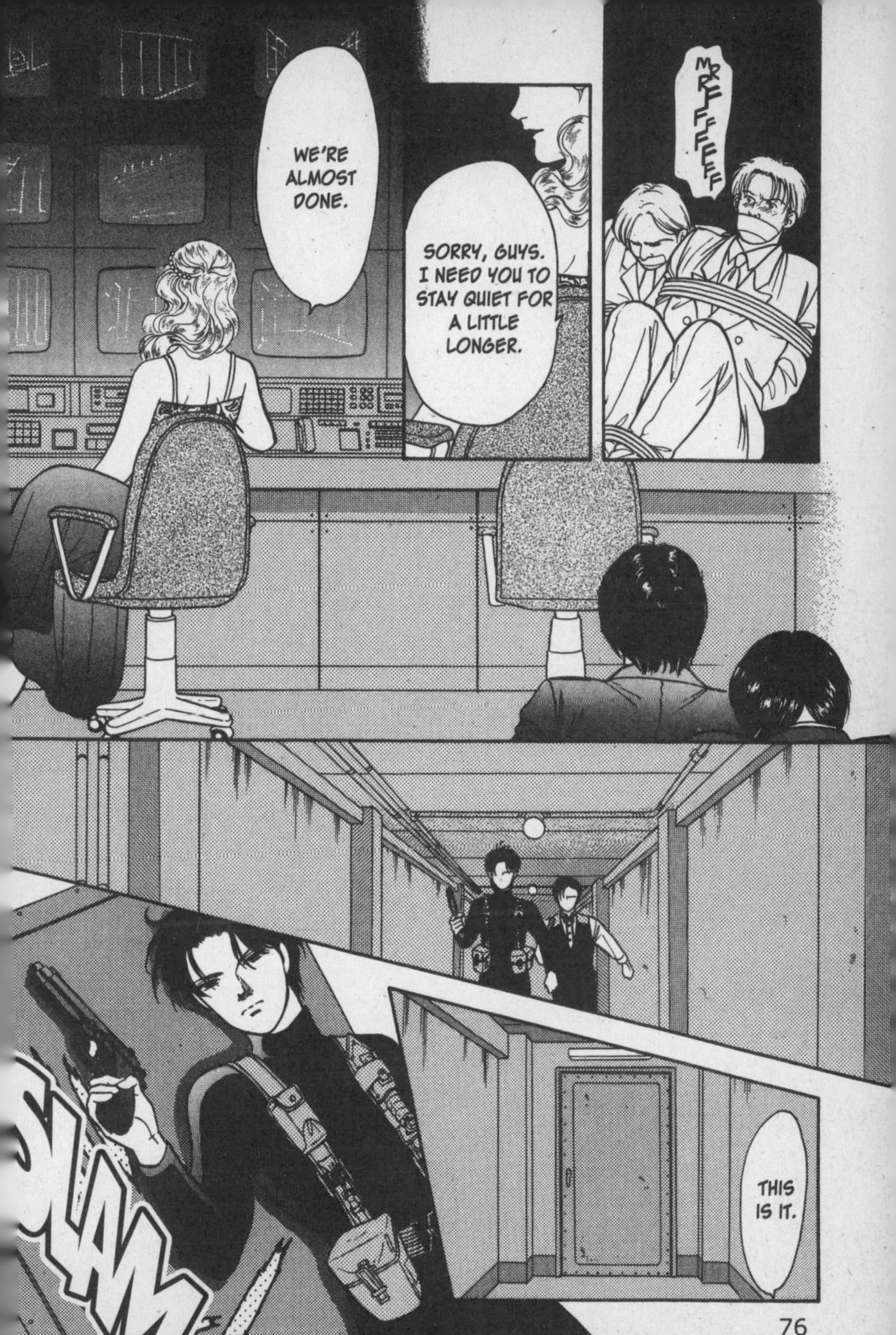
MRRFFFFFFF
SORRY, GUYS. I NEED YOU TO STAY QUIET FOR A LITTLE LONGER.
WE'RE ALMOST DONE.
THIS IS IT.
SLAM

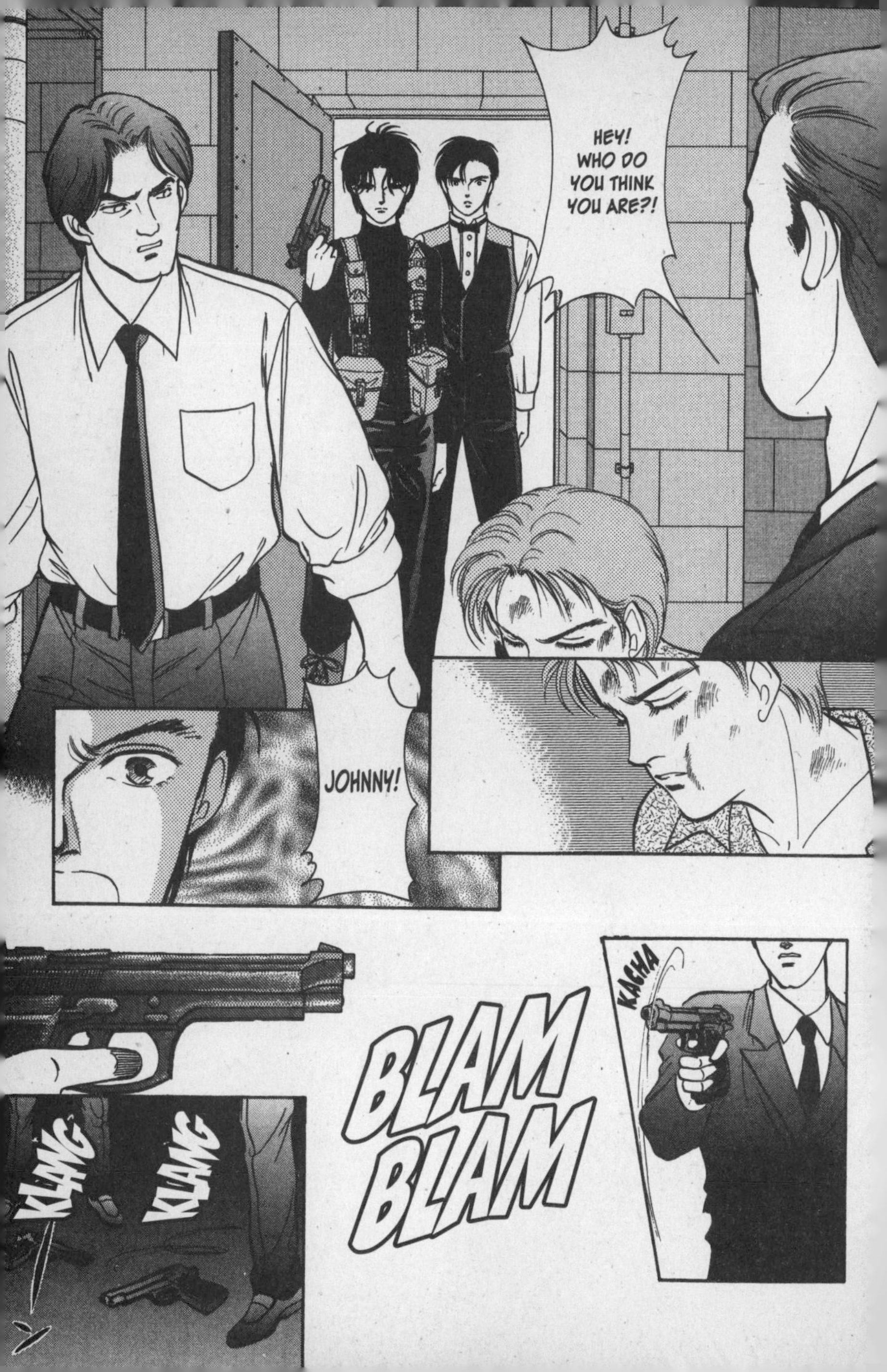
HEY! WHO DO YOU THINK YOU ARE?!
JOHNNY!
KACHA
BLAM BLAM
KLANG KLANG

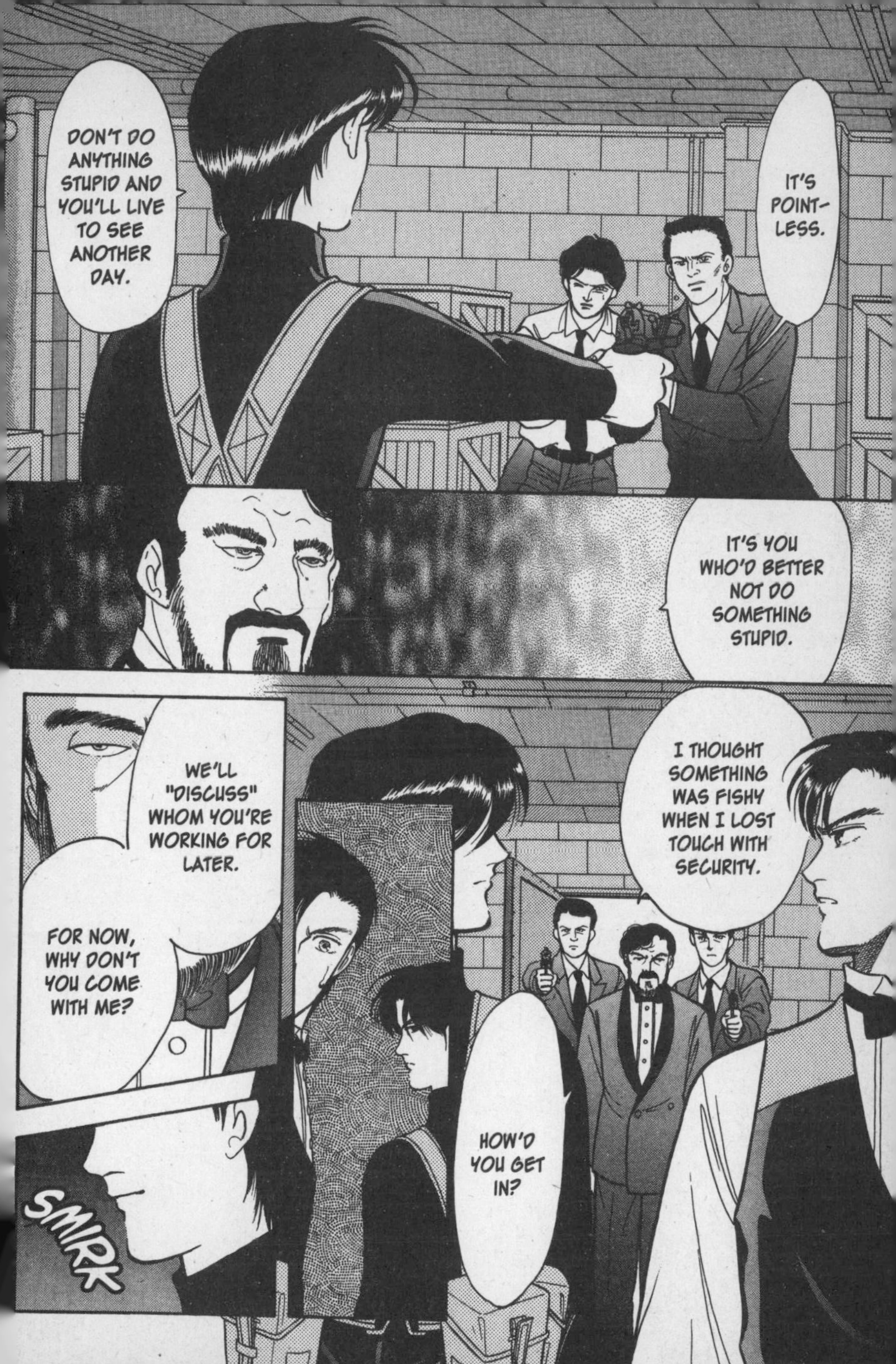
IT'S POINT-LESS.
DON'T DO ANYTHING STUPID AND YOU'LL LIVE TO SEE ANOTHER DAY.
IT'S YOU WHO'D BETTER NOT DO SOMETHING STUPID.
I THOUGHT SOMETHING WAS FISHY WHEN I LOST TOUCH WITH SECURITY.
HOW'D YOU GET IN?
WE'LL "DISCUSS" WHOM YOU'RE WORKING FOR LATER.
FOR NOW, WHY DON'T YOU COME WITH ME?
SMIRK

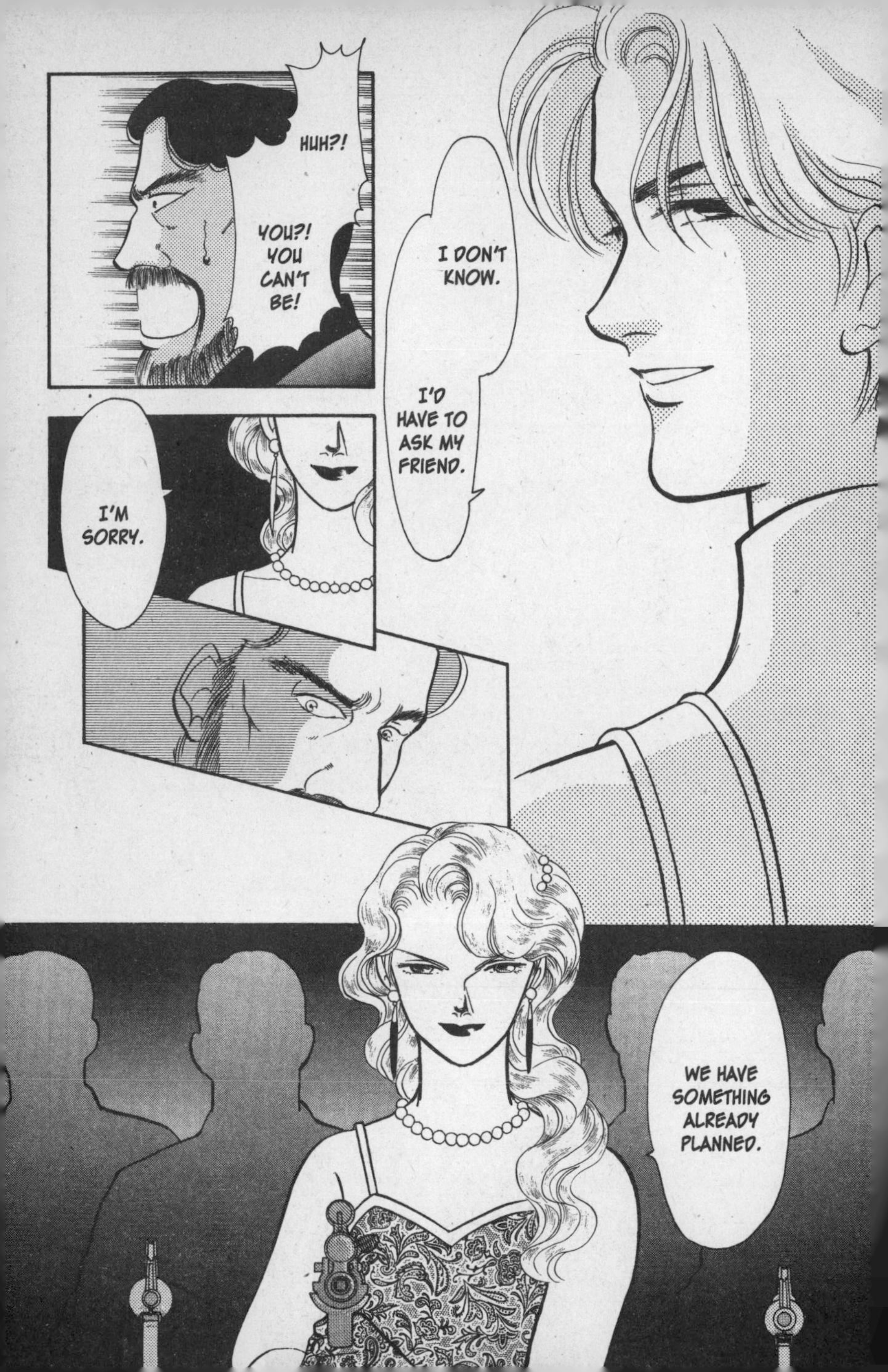
I DON'T KNOW.
I'D HAVE TO ASK MY FRIEND.
HUH?!
YOU?! YOU CAN'T BE!
I'M SORRY.
WE HAVE SOMETHING ALREADY PLANNED.

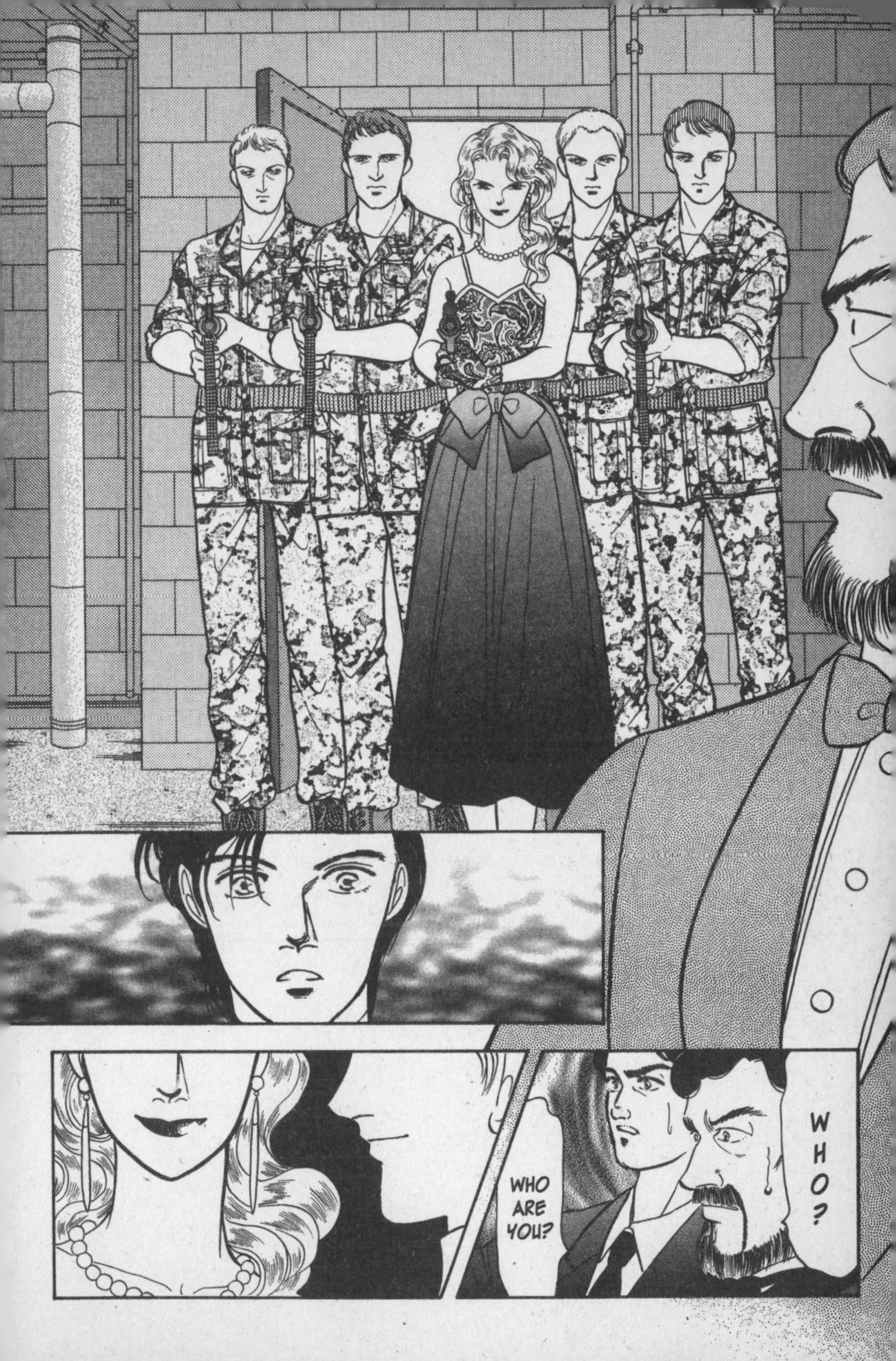
WHO?
WHO ARE YOU?

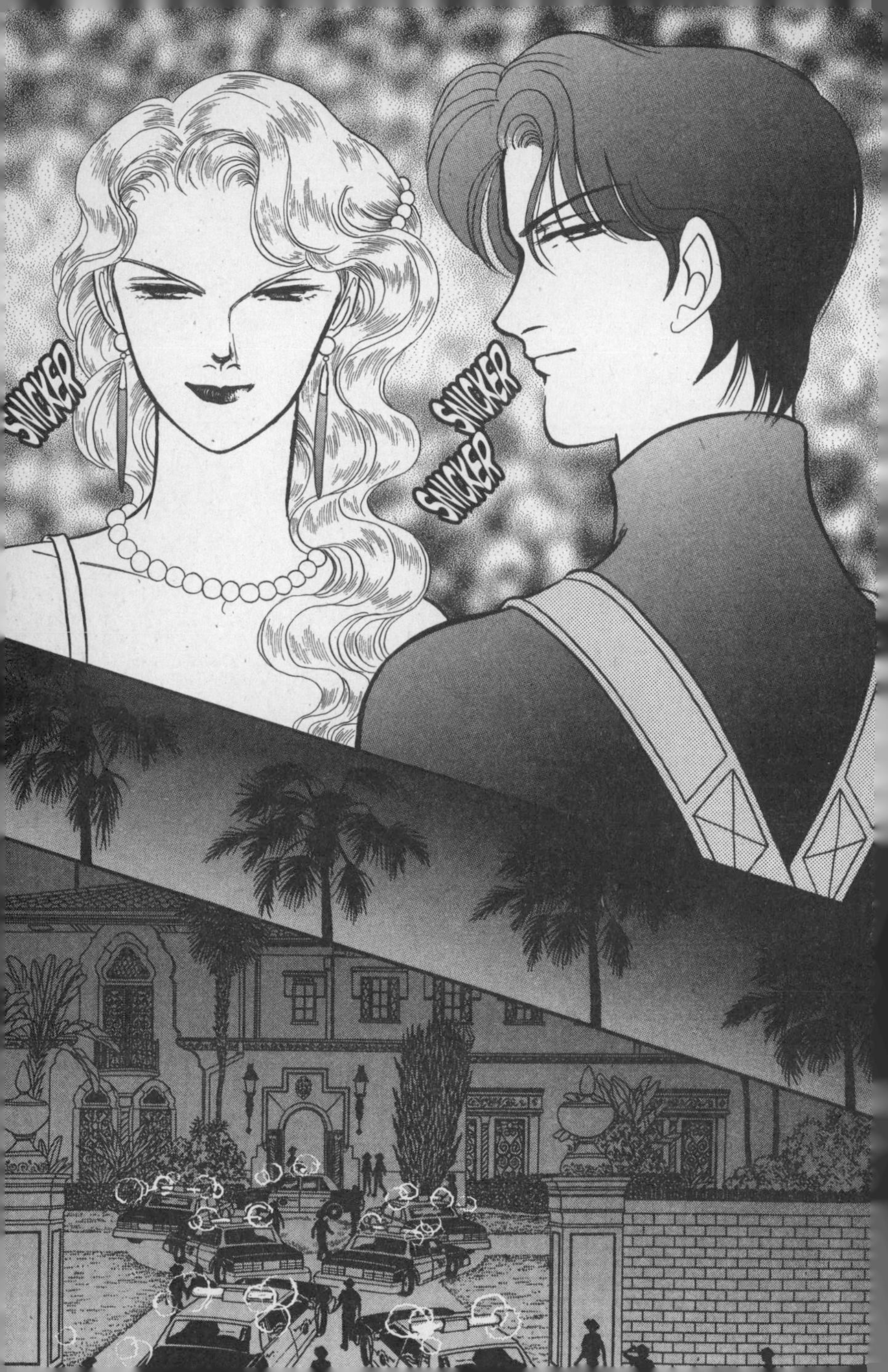
SNICKER
SNICKER
SNICKER

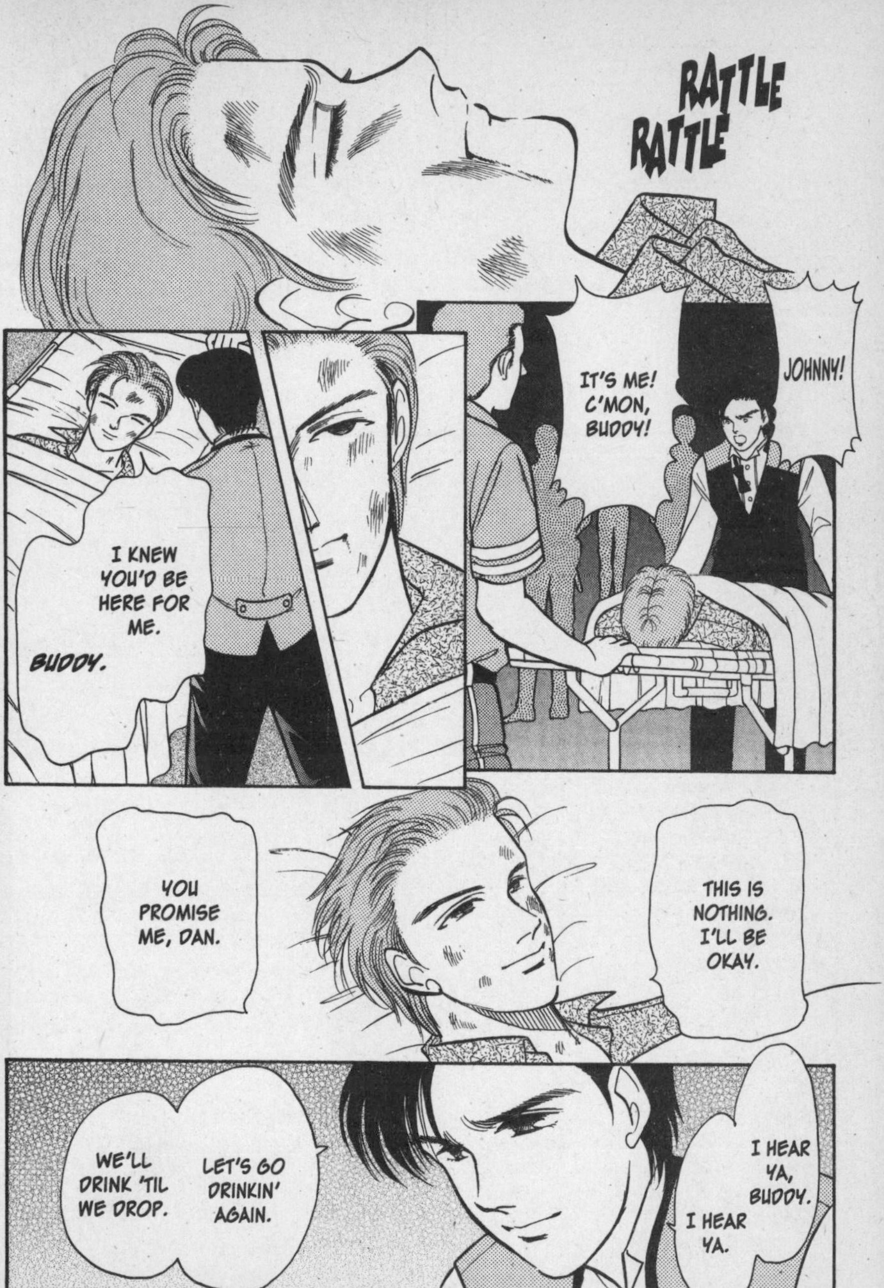
RATTLE
RATTLE
JOHNNY!
IT'S ME! C'MON, BUDDY!
I KNEW YOU'D BE HERE FOR ME.
BUDDY.
THIS IS NOTHING. I'LL BE OKAY.
YOU PROMISE ME, DAN.
I HEAR YA, BUDDY.
I HEAR YA.
LET'S GO DRINKIN' AGAIN.
WE'LL DRINK 'TIL WE DROP.

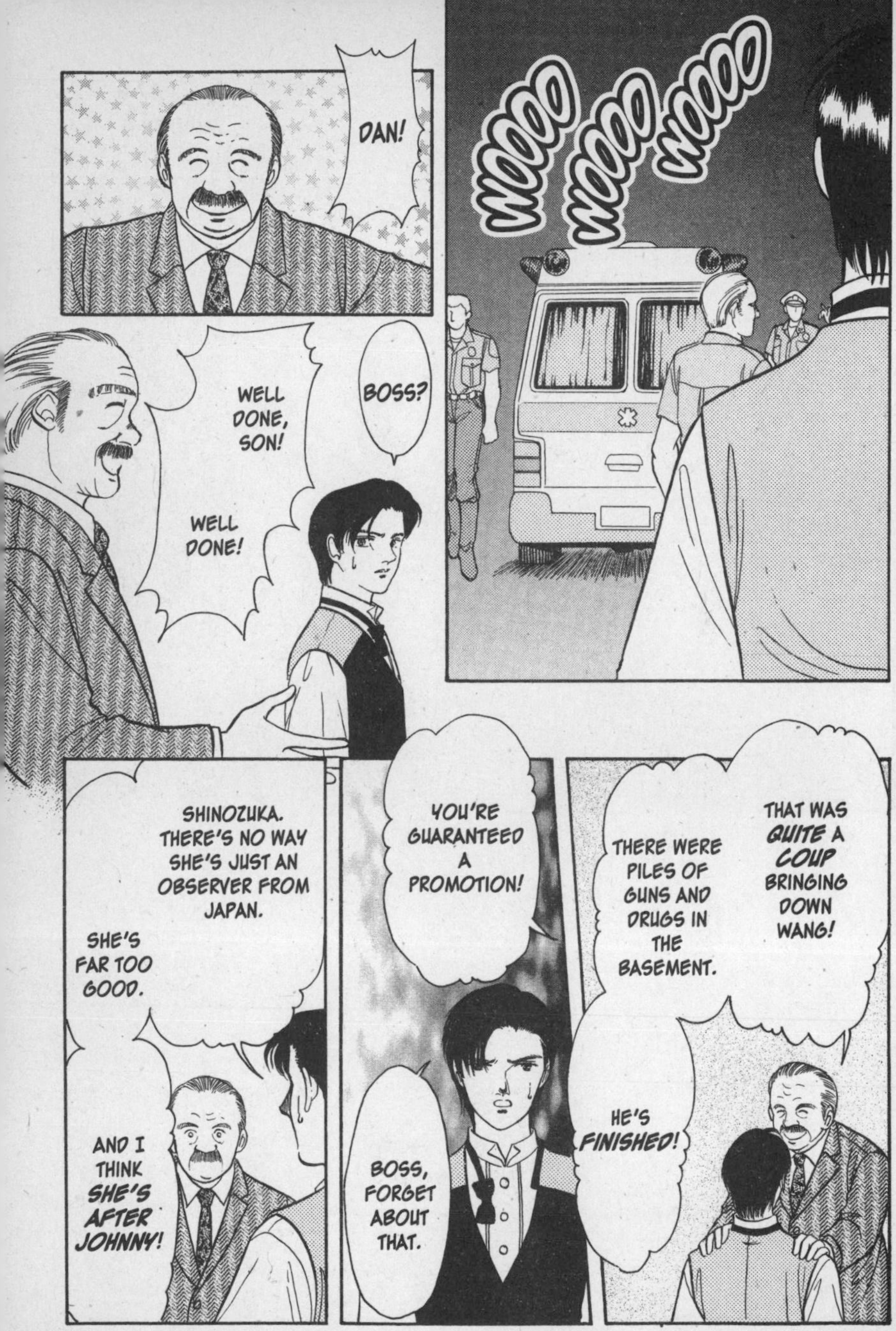
WOOOO
WOOOO
WOOOO
DAN!
BOSS?
WELL DONE, SON!
WELL DONE!
THAT WAS QUITE A COUP BRINGING DOWN WANG!
THERE WERE PILES OF GUNS AND DRUGS IN THE BASEMENT.
HE'S FINISHED!
YOU'RE GUARANTEED A PROMOTION!
BOSS, FORGET ABOUT THAT.
SHINOZUKA. THERE'S NO WAY SHE'S JUST AN OBSERVER FROM JAPAN.
SHE'S FAR TOO GOOD.
AND I THINK SHE'S AFTER JOHNNY!

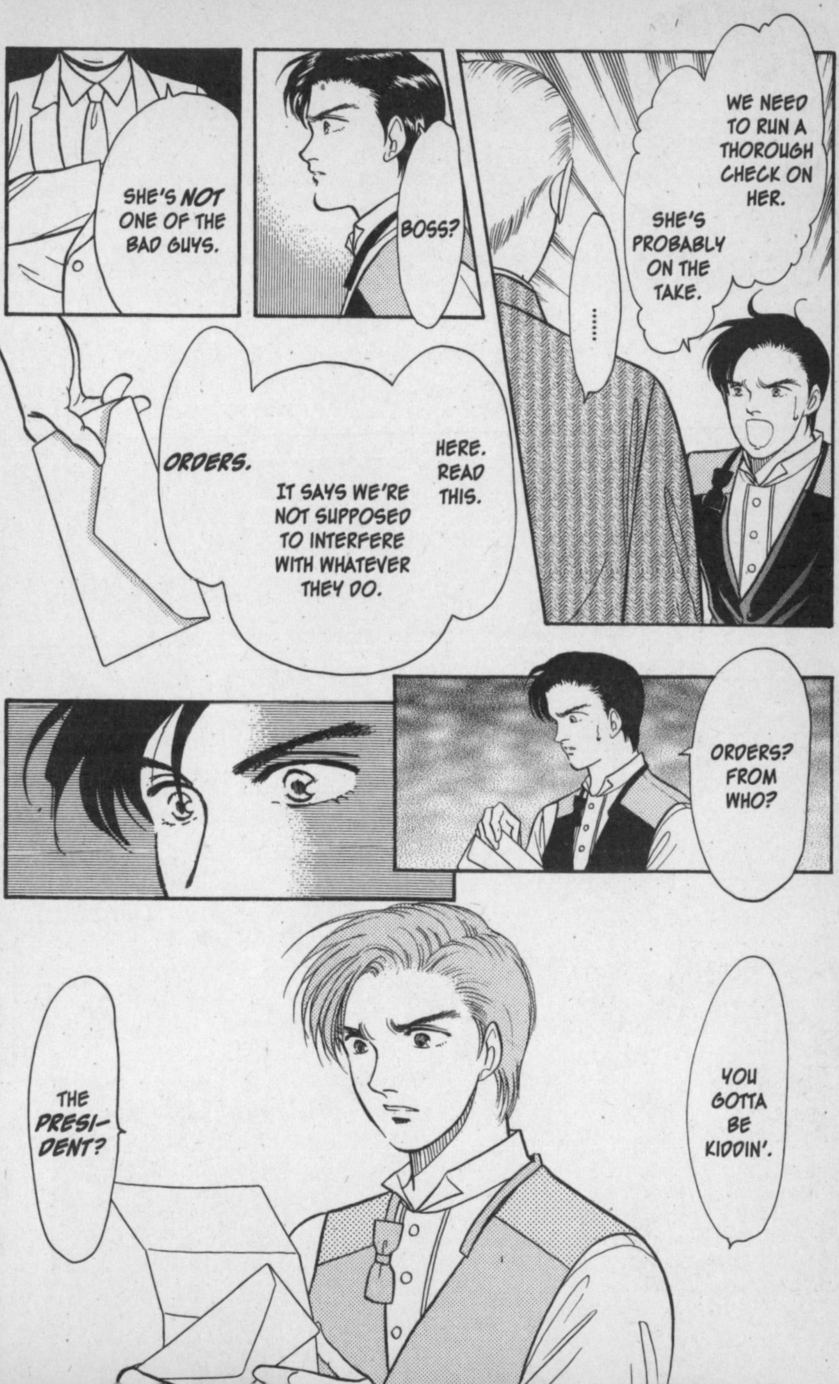
WE NEED TO RUN A THOROUGH CHECK ON HER.
SHE'S PROBABLY ON THE TAKE.
......
BOSS?
SHE'S NOT ONE OF THE BAD GUYS.
HERE. READ THIS.
IT SAYS WE'RE NOT SUPPOSED TO INTERFERE WITH WHATEVER THEY DO.
ORDERS.
ORDERS? FROM WHO?
YOU GOTTA BE KIDDIN'.
THE PRESIDENT?

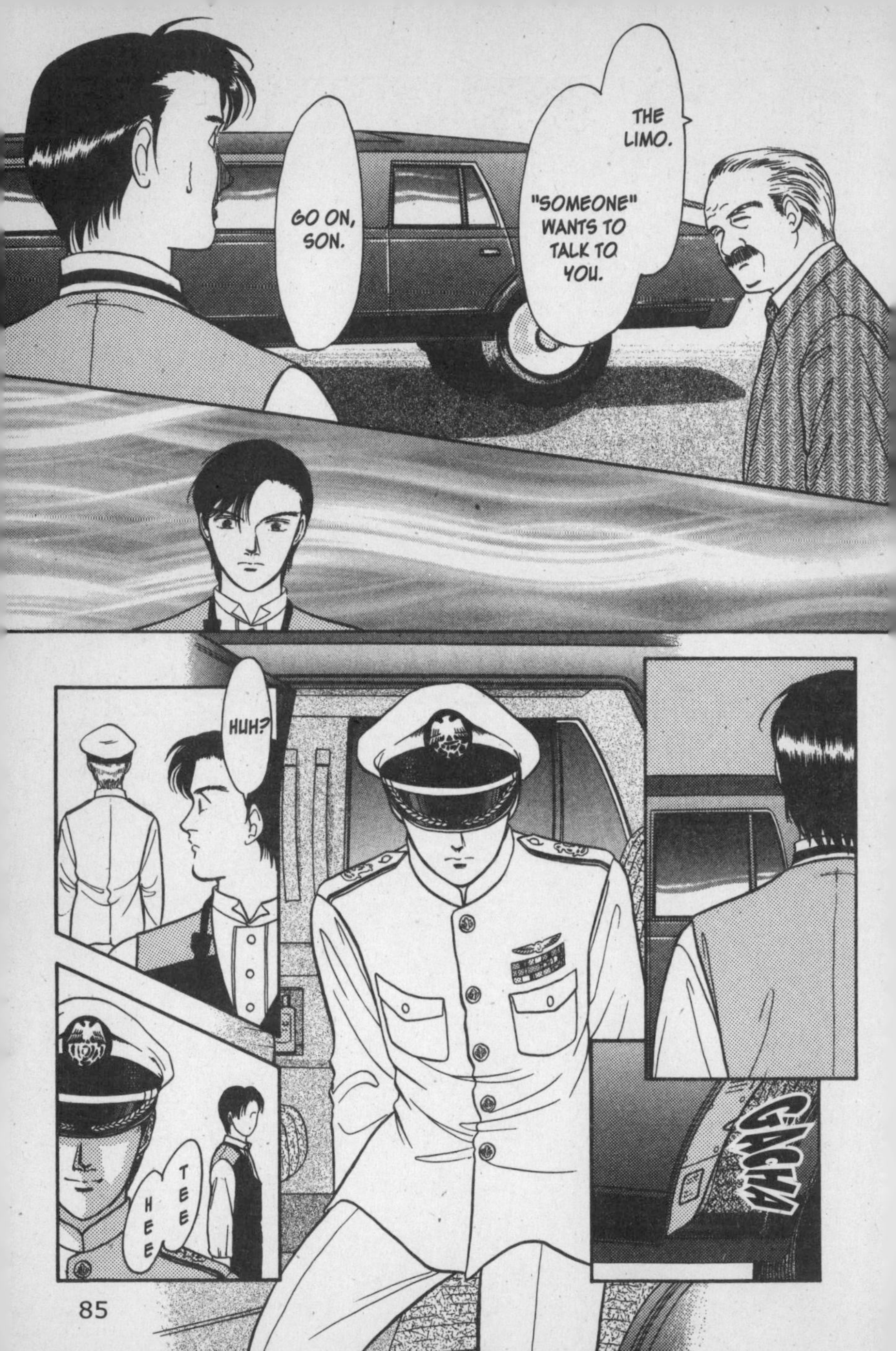
THE LIMO.
"SOMEONE" WANTS TO TALK TO YOU.
GO ON, SON.
GACHA
HUH?
HEE TEE

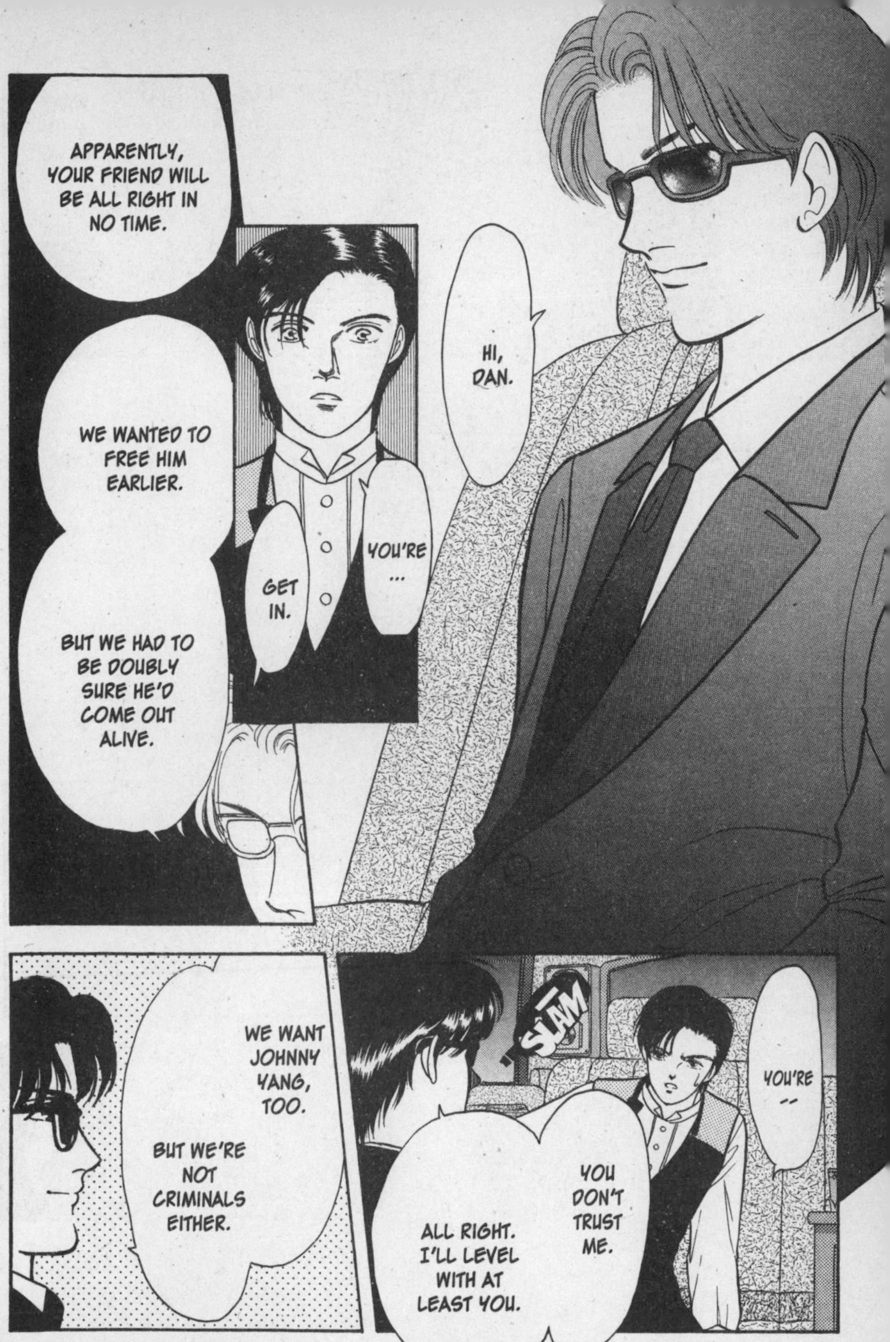
HI, DAN.
YOU'RE ...
GET IN.
APPARENTLY, YOUR FRIEND WILL BE ALL RIGHT IN NO TIME.
WE WANTED TO FREE HIM EARLIER.
BUT WE HAD TO BE DOUBLY SURE HE'D COME OUT ALIVE.
SLAM
YOU'RE --
YOU DON'T TRUST ME.
ALL RIGHT. I'LL LEVEL WITH AT LEAST YOU.
WE WANT JOHNNY YANG, TOO.
BUT WE'RE NOT CRIMINALS EITHER.

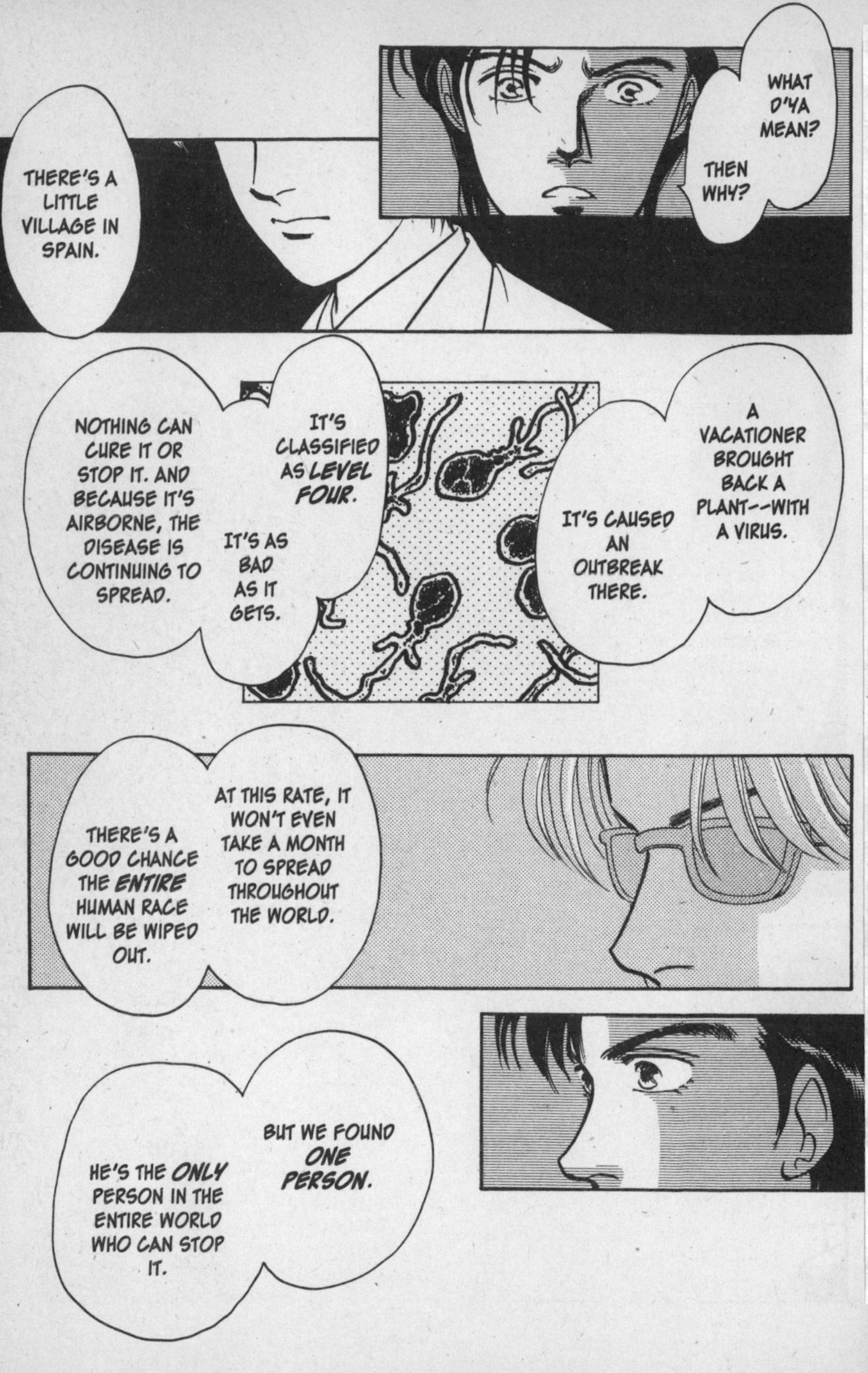
WHAT D'YA MEAN?
THEN WHY?
THERE'S A LITTLE VILLAGE IN SPAIN.
A VACATIONER BROUGHT BACK A PLANT--WITH A VIRUS.
IT'S CAUSED AN OUTBREAK THERE.
IT'S CLASSIFIED AS *LEVEL FOUR*.
IT'S AS BAD AS IT GETS.
NOTHING CAN CURE IT OR STOP IT. AND BECAUSE IT'S AIRBORNE, THE DISEASE IS CONTINUING TO SPREAD.
AT THIS RATE, IT WON'T EVEN TAKE A MONTH TO SPREAD THROUGHOUT THE WORLD.
THERE'S A GOOD CHANCE THE *ENTIRE* HUMAN RACE WILL BE WIPED OUT.
BUT WE FOUND *ONE PERSON*.
HE'S THE *ONLY* PERSON IN THE ENTIRE WORLD WHO CAN STOP IT.

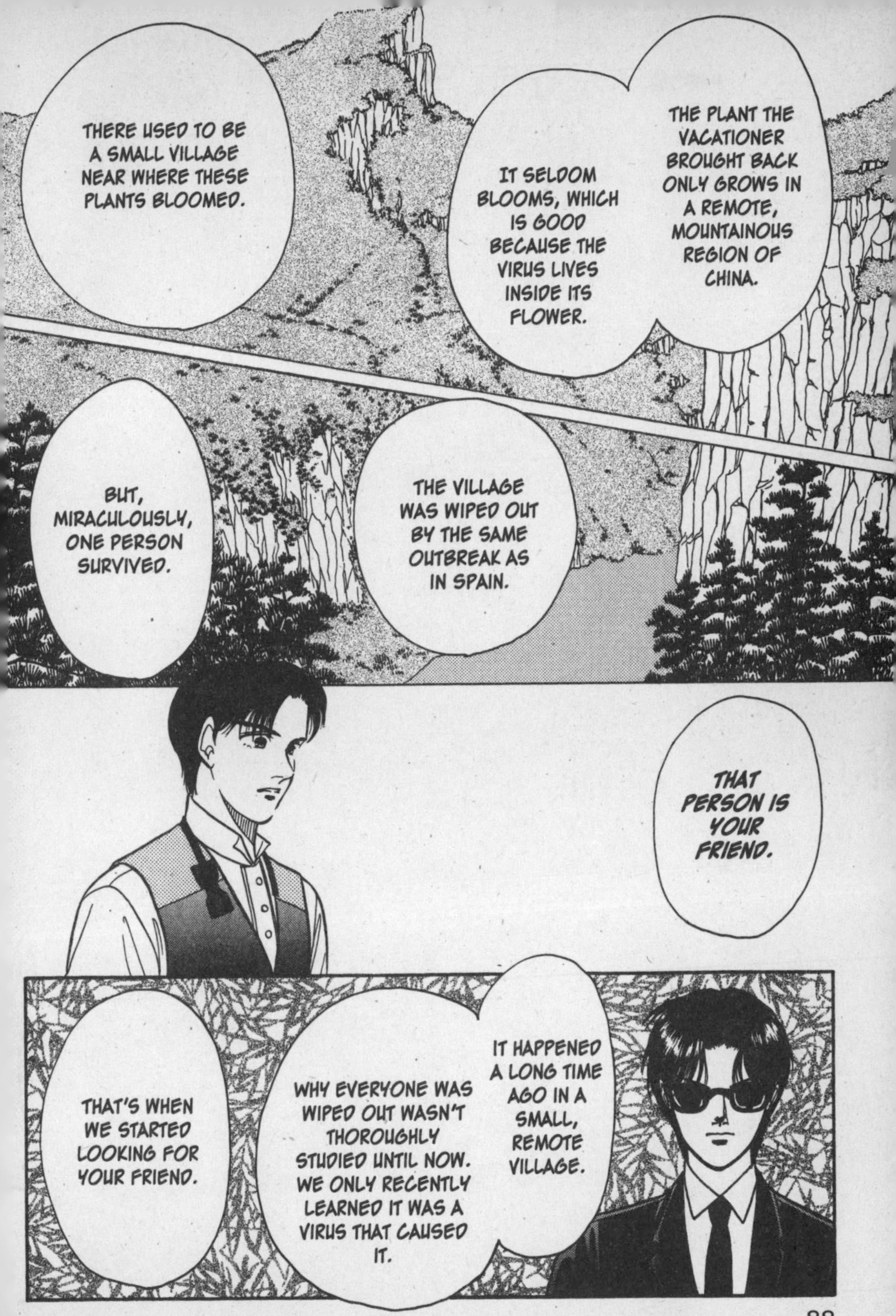
THE PLANT THE VACATIONER BROUGHT BACK ONLY GROWS IN A REMOTE, MOUNTAINOUS REGION OF CHINA.
IT SELDOM BLOOMS, WHICH IS GOOD BECAUSE THE VIRUS LIVES INSIDE ITS FLOWER.
THERE USED TO BE A SMALL VILLAGE NEAR WHERE THESE PLANTS BLOOMED.
THE VILLAGE WAS WIPED OUT BY THE SAME OUTBREAK AS IN SPAIN.
BUT, MIRACULOUSLY, ONE PERSON SURVIVED.
THAT PERSON IS YOUR FRIEND.
IT HAPPENED A LONG TIME AGO IN A SMALL, REMOTE VILLAGE.
WHY EVERYONE WAS WIPED OUT WASN'T THOROUGHLY STUDIED UNTIL NOW. WE ONLY RECENTLY LEARNED IT WAS A VIRUS THAT CAUSED IT.
THAT'S WHEN WE STARTED LOOKING FOR YOUR FRIEND.

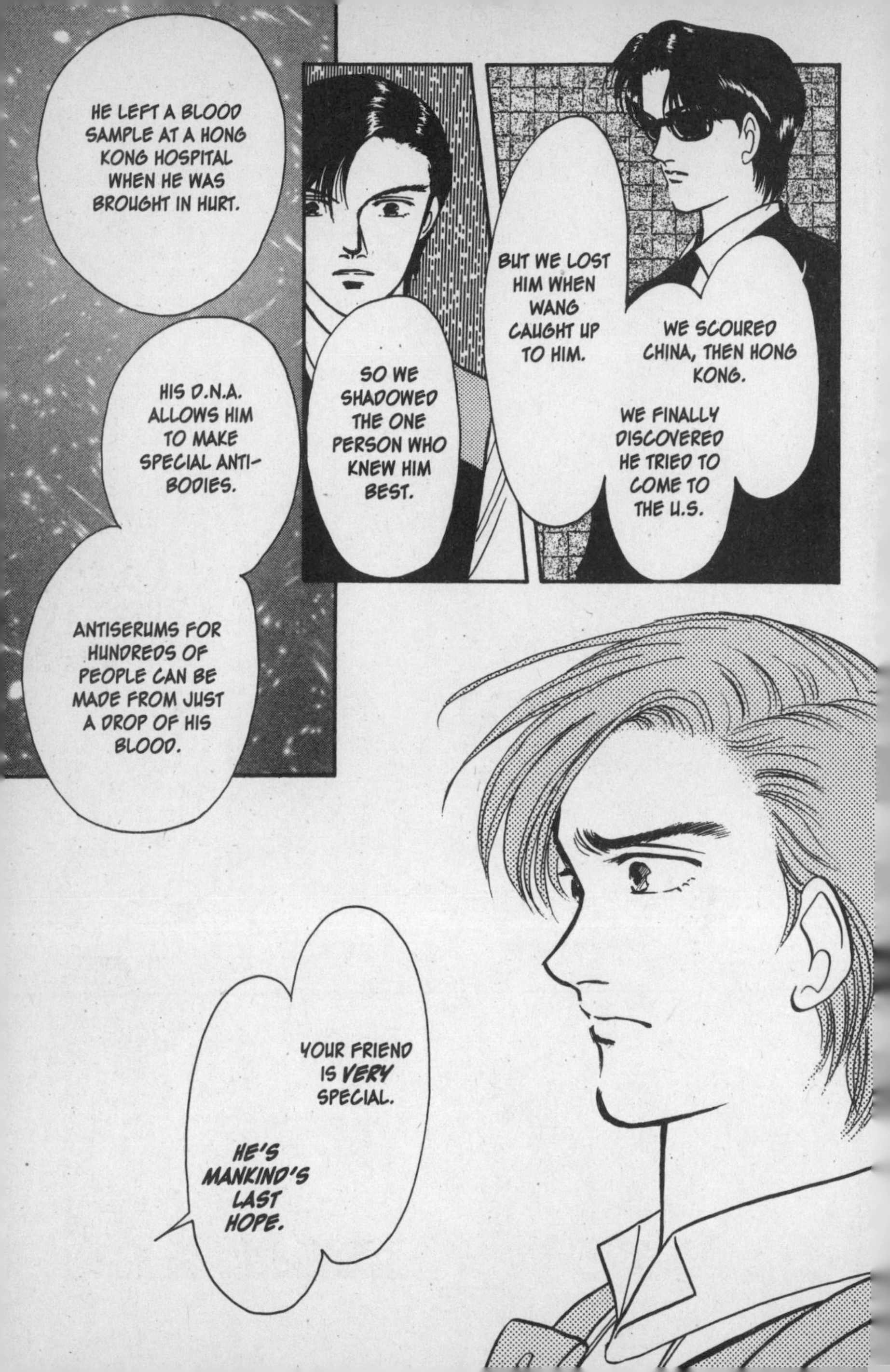
WE SCOURED CHINA, THEN HONG KONG.
WE FINALLY DISCOVERED HE TRIED TO COME TO THE U.S.
BUT WE LOST HIM WHEN WANG CAUGHT UP TO HIM.
SO WE SHADOWED THE ONE PERSON WHO KNEW HIM BEST.
HE LEFT A BLOOD SAMPLE AT A HONG KONG HOSPITAL WHEN HE WAS BROUGHT IN HURT.
HIS D.N.A. ALLOWS HIM TO MAKE SPECIAL ANTI-BODIES.
ANTISERUMS FOR HUNDREDS OF PEOPLE CAN BE MADE FROM JUST A DROP OF HIS BLOOD.
YOUR FRIEND IS VERY SPECIAL.
HE'S MANKIND'S LAST HOPE.

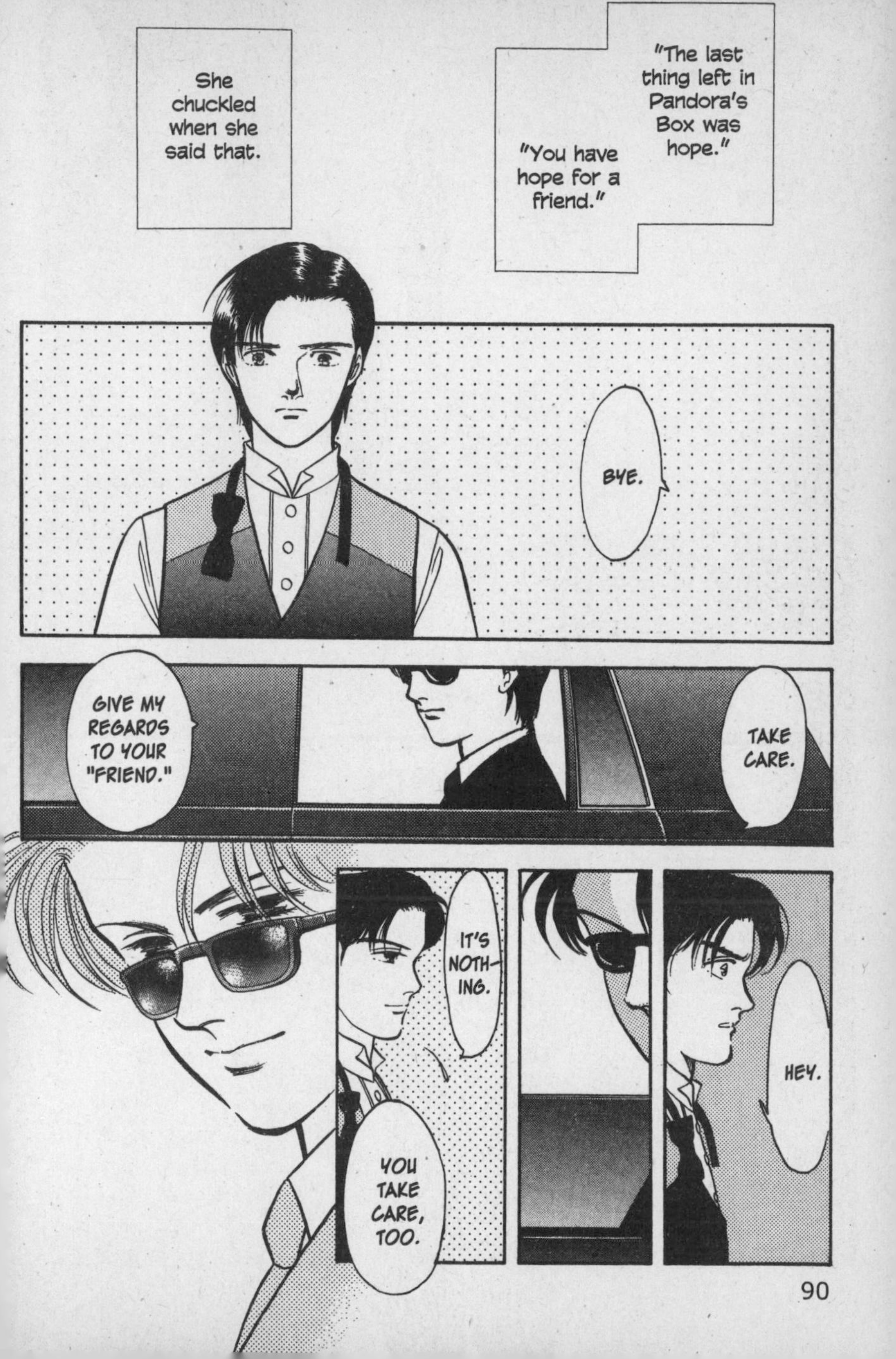
"The last thing left in Pandora's Box was hope."
"You have hope for a friend."
She chuckled when she said that.
BYE.
TAKE CARE.
GIVE MY REGARDS TO YOUR "FRIEND."
HEY.
IT'S NOTHING.
YOU TAKE CARE, TOO.

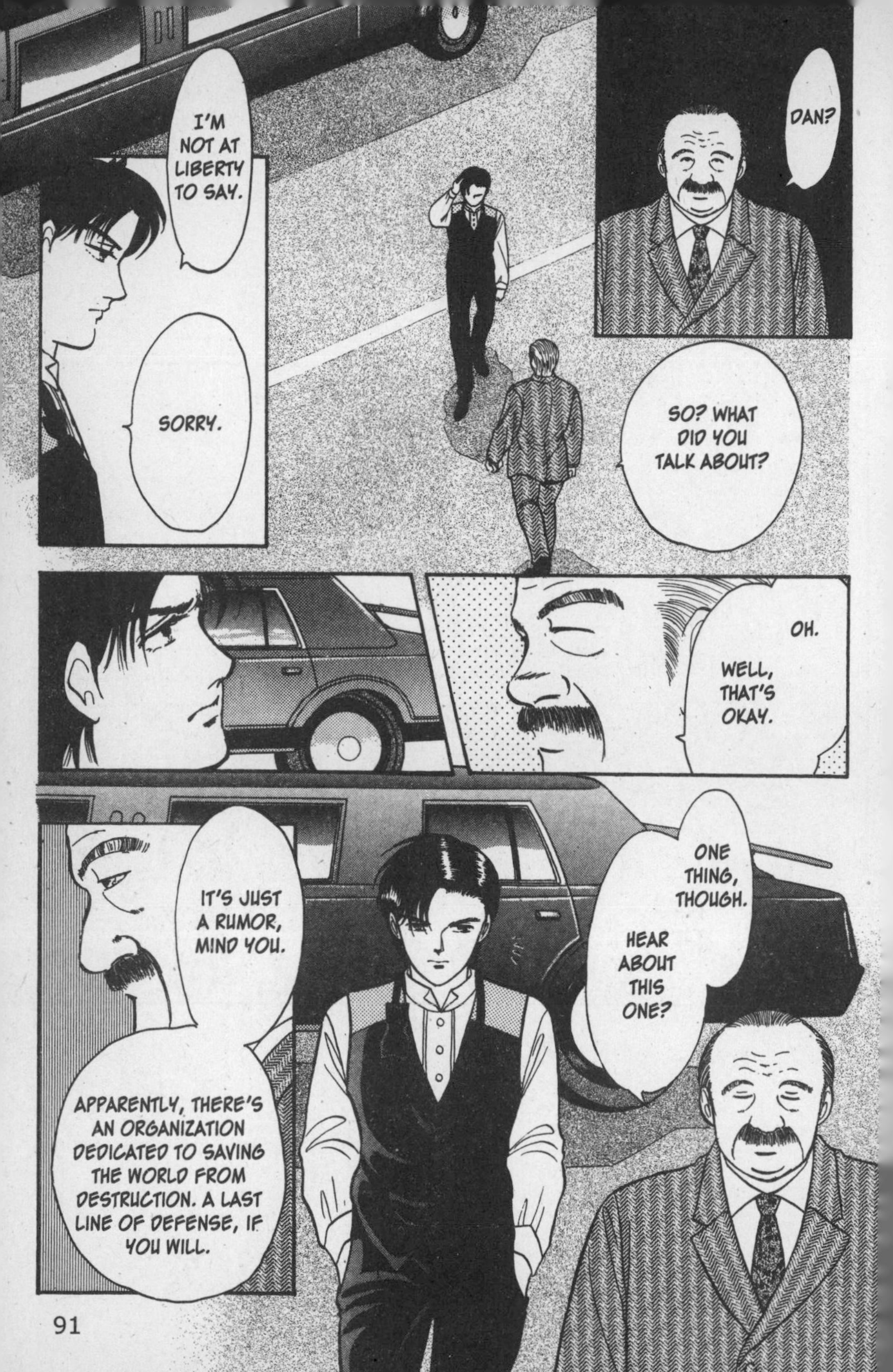
DAN?
SO? WHAT DID YOU TALK ABOUT?
I'M NOT AT LIBERTY TO SAY.
SORRY.
OH.
WELL, THAT'S OKAY.
ONE THING, THOUGH.
HEAR ABOUT THIS ONE?
IT'S JUST A RUMOR, MIND YOU.
APPARENTLY, THERE'S AN ORGANIZATION DEDICATED TO SAVING THE WORLD FROM DESTRUCTION. A LAST LINE OF DEFENSE, IF YOU WILL.

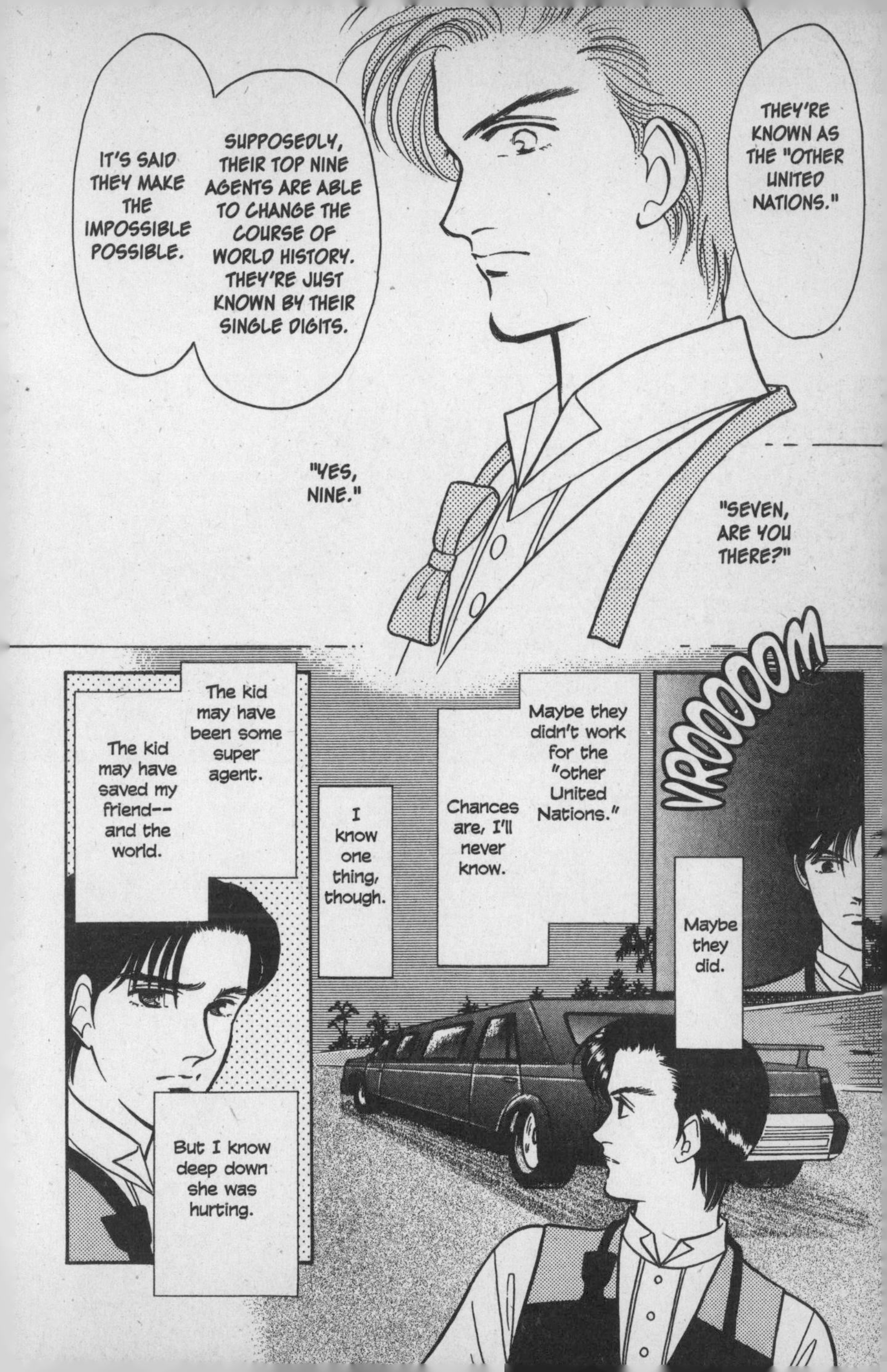
THEY'RE KNOWN AS THE "OTHER UNITED NATIONS."
SUPPOSEDLY, THEIR TOP NINE AGENTS ARE ABLE TO CHANGE THE COURSE OF WORLD HISTORY. THEY'RE JUST KNOWN BY THEIR SINGLE DIGITS.
IT'S SAID THEY MAKE THE IMPOSSIBLE POSSIBLE.
"SEVEN, ARE YOU THERE?"
"YES, NINE."
VROOOOOOM
Maybe they did.
Maybe they didn't work for the "other United Nations."
Chances are, I'll never know.
I know one thing, though.
The kid may have been some super agent.
The kid may have saved my friend-- and the world.
But I know deep down she was hurting.

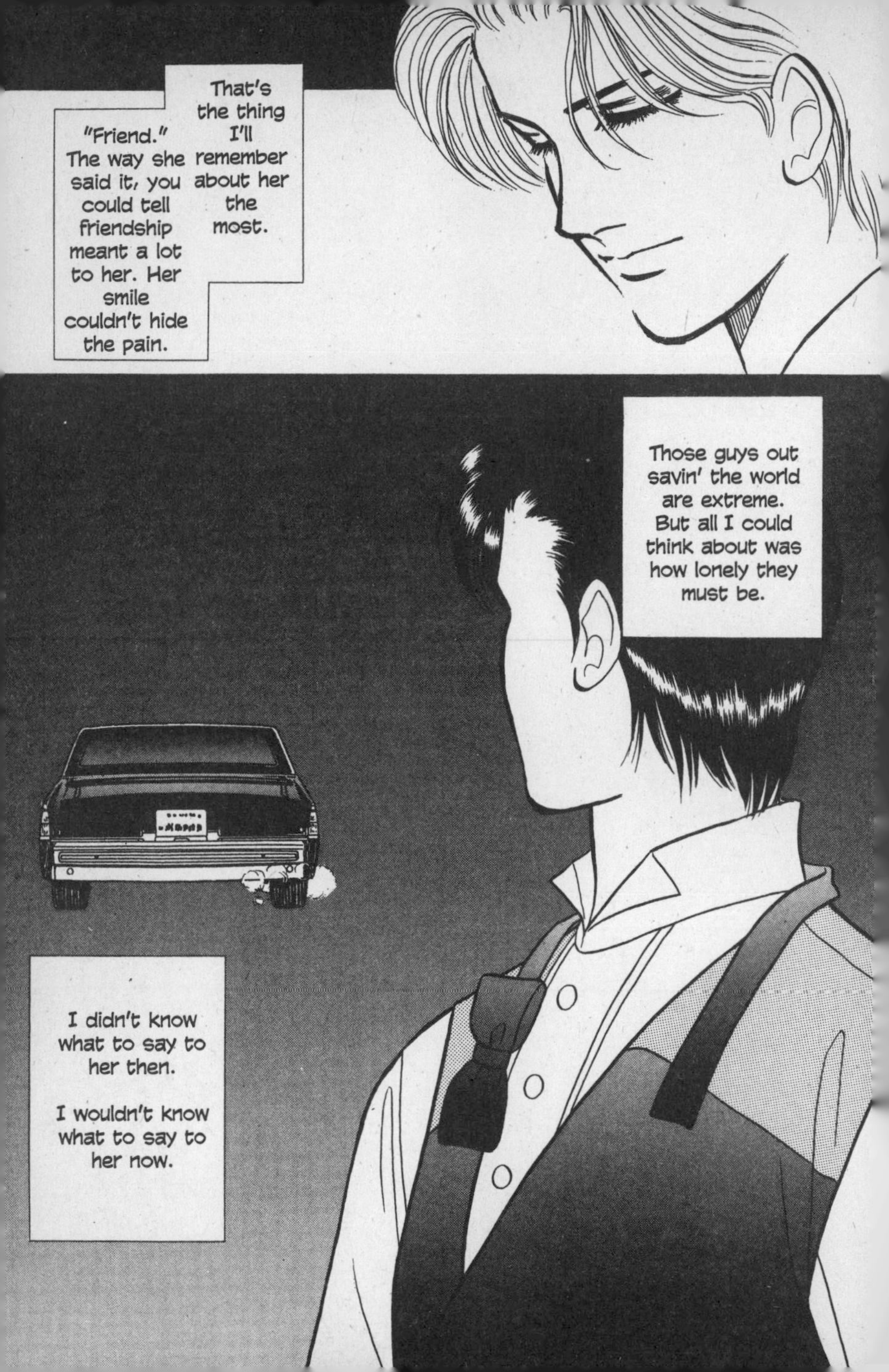
That's the thing I'll remember about her the most.
"Friend." The way she said it, you could tell friendship meant a lot to her. Her smile couldn't hide the pain.
Those guys out savin' the world are extreme. But all I could think about was how lonely they must be.
I didn't know what to say to her then.
I wouldn't know what to say to her now.

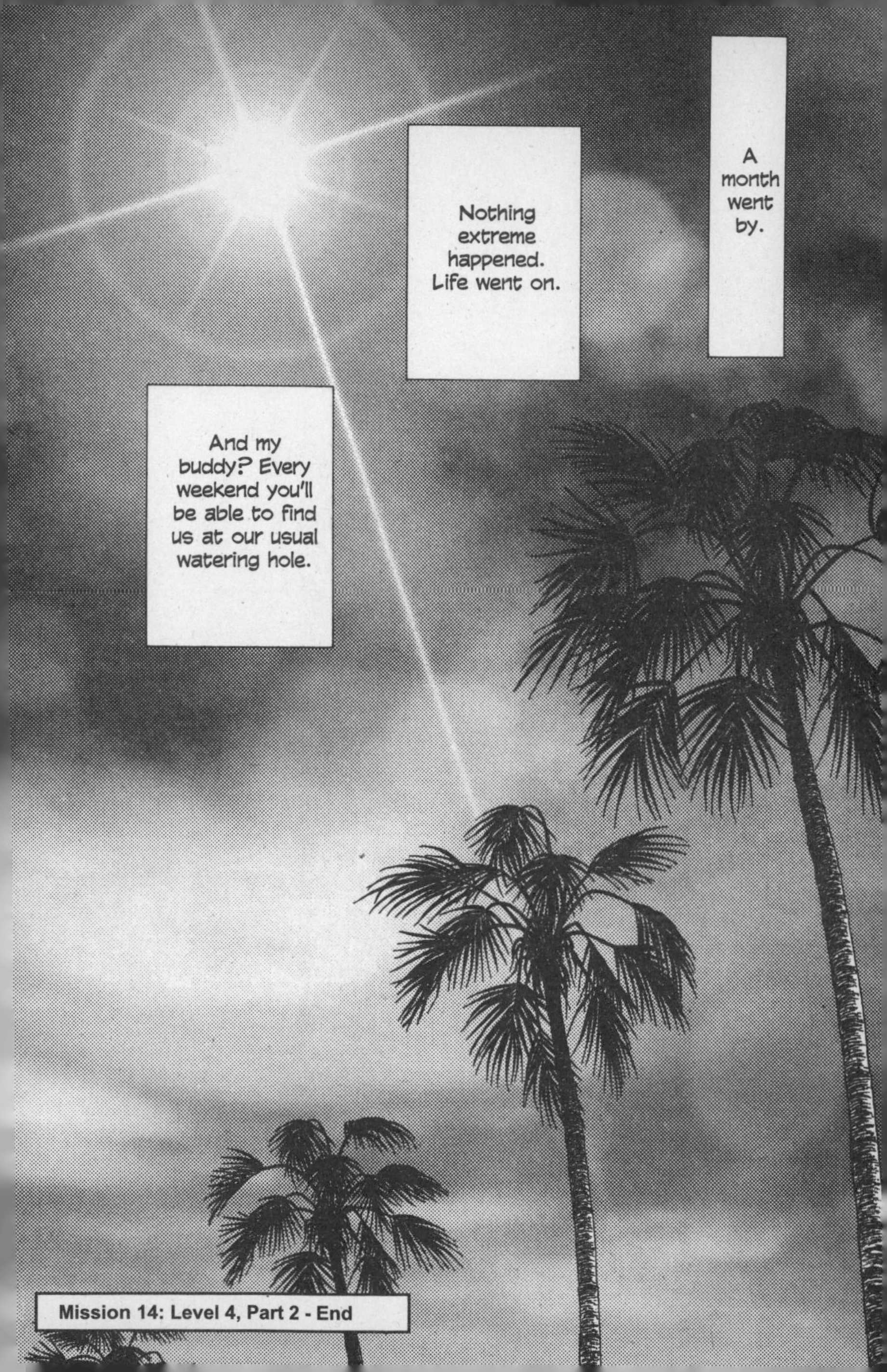
A month went by.
Nothing extreme happened. Life went on.
And my buddy? Every weekend you'll be able to find us at our usual watering hole.
Mission 14: Level 4, Part 2 - End

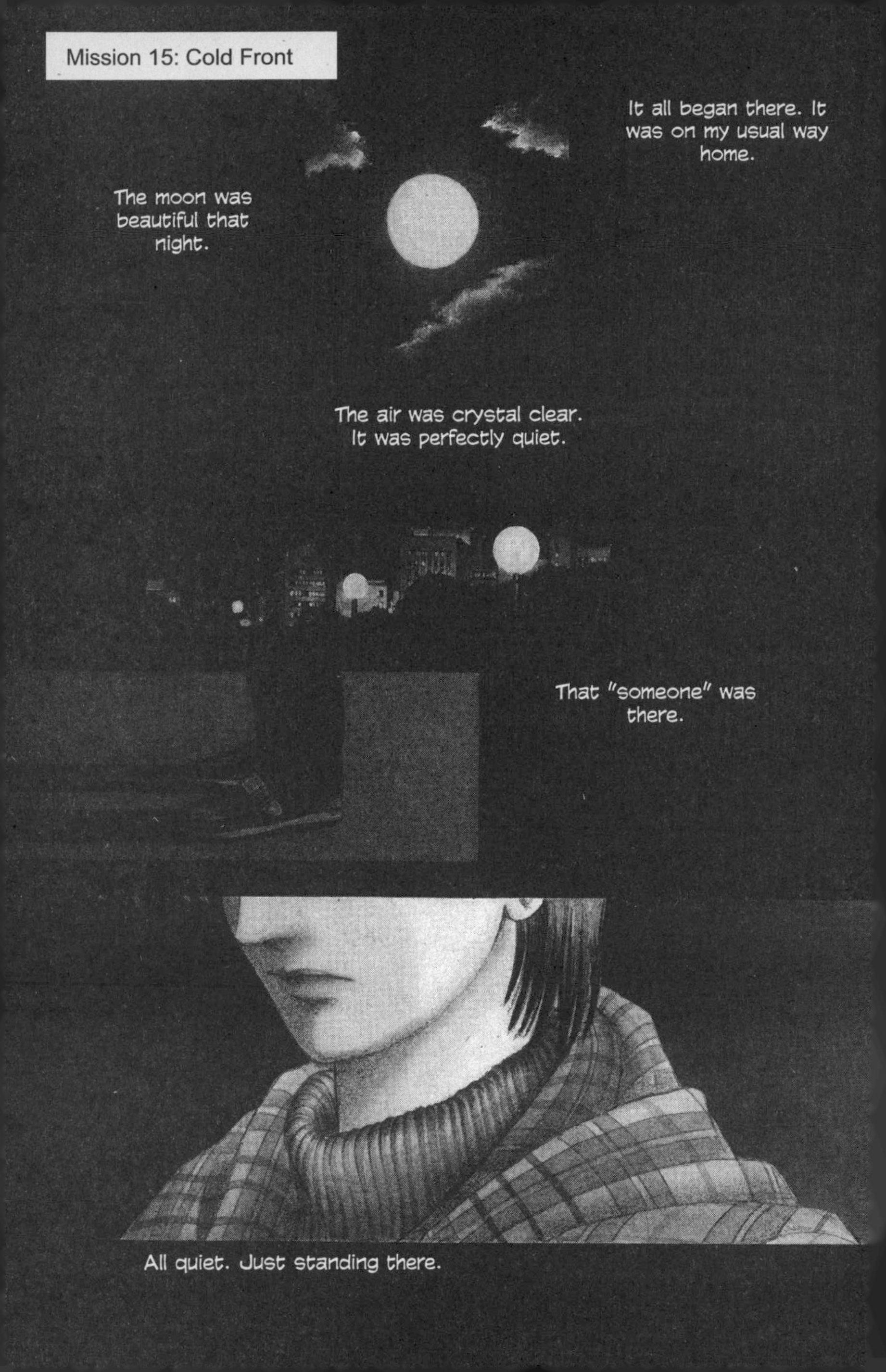
Mission 15: Cold Front
It all began there. It was on my usual way home.
The moon was beautiful that night.
The air was crystal clear. It was perfectly quiet.
That "someone" was there.
All quiet. Just standing there.

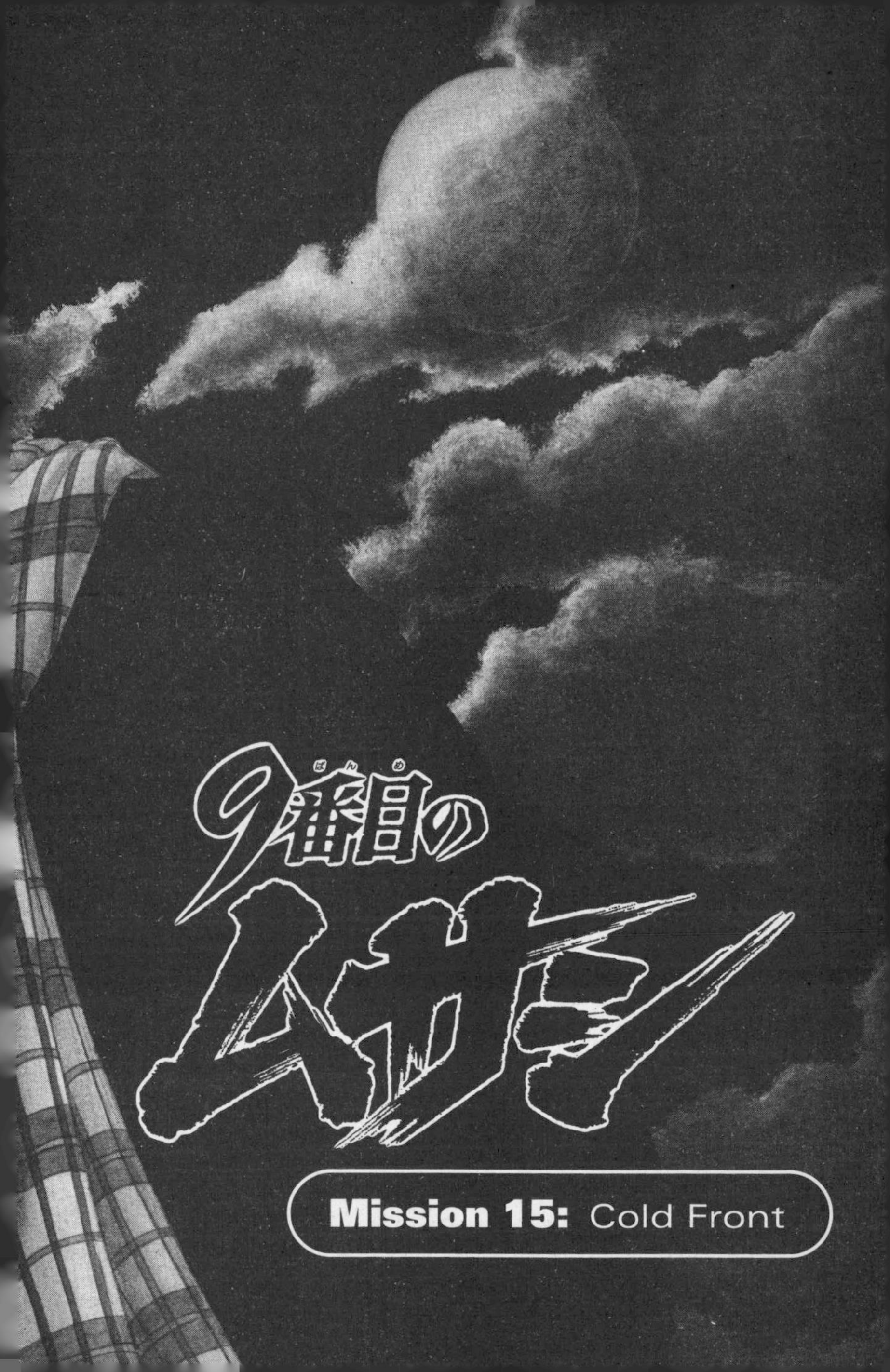
9番目のムサシ
Mission 15: Cold Front

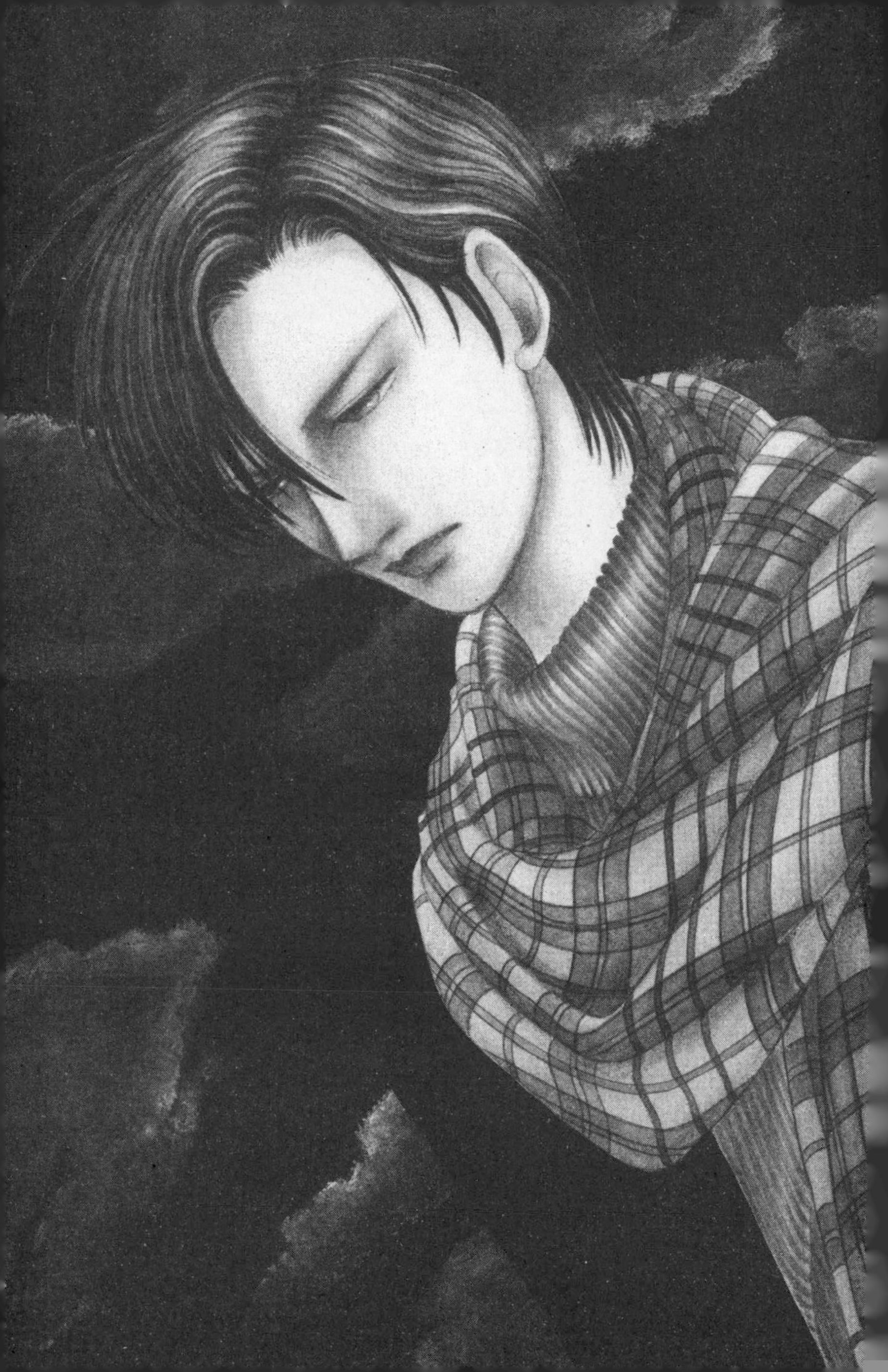

The history of mankind has
been one of wars. Race.
Religion. Philosophy.
The causes are untold.

The combatants have their own
justifications, but on occasion,
some create a volatile
situation that threatens to
destroy the world.

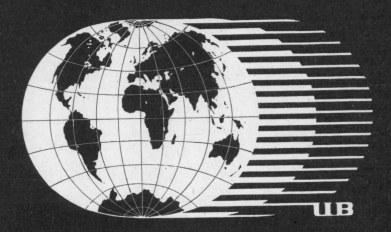

Ultimate Blue.
An organization shrouded in
complete secrecy. Also known
as "the other United Nations."
Nobody knows when it was
created. Nobody knows
where it is based.

The Blue of the Seas.
The Blue of the Skies.
The Blue of the Earth.

The last line of defense against chaos.

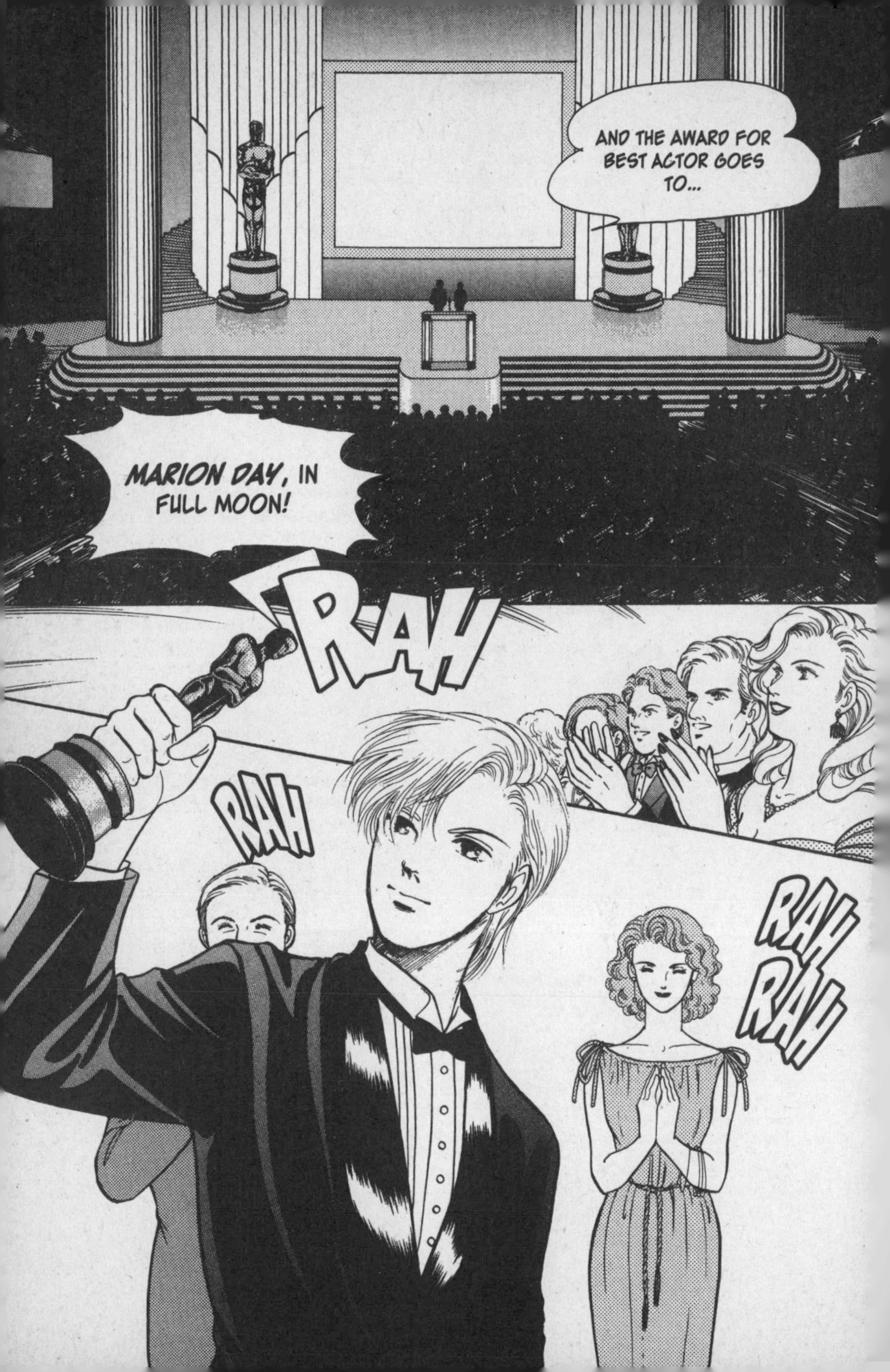
AND THE AWARD FOR BEST ACTOR GOES TO...
MARION DAY, IN FULL MOON!
RAH
RAH RAH
RAH

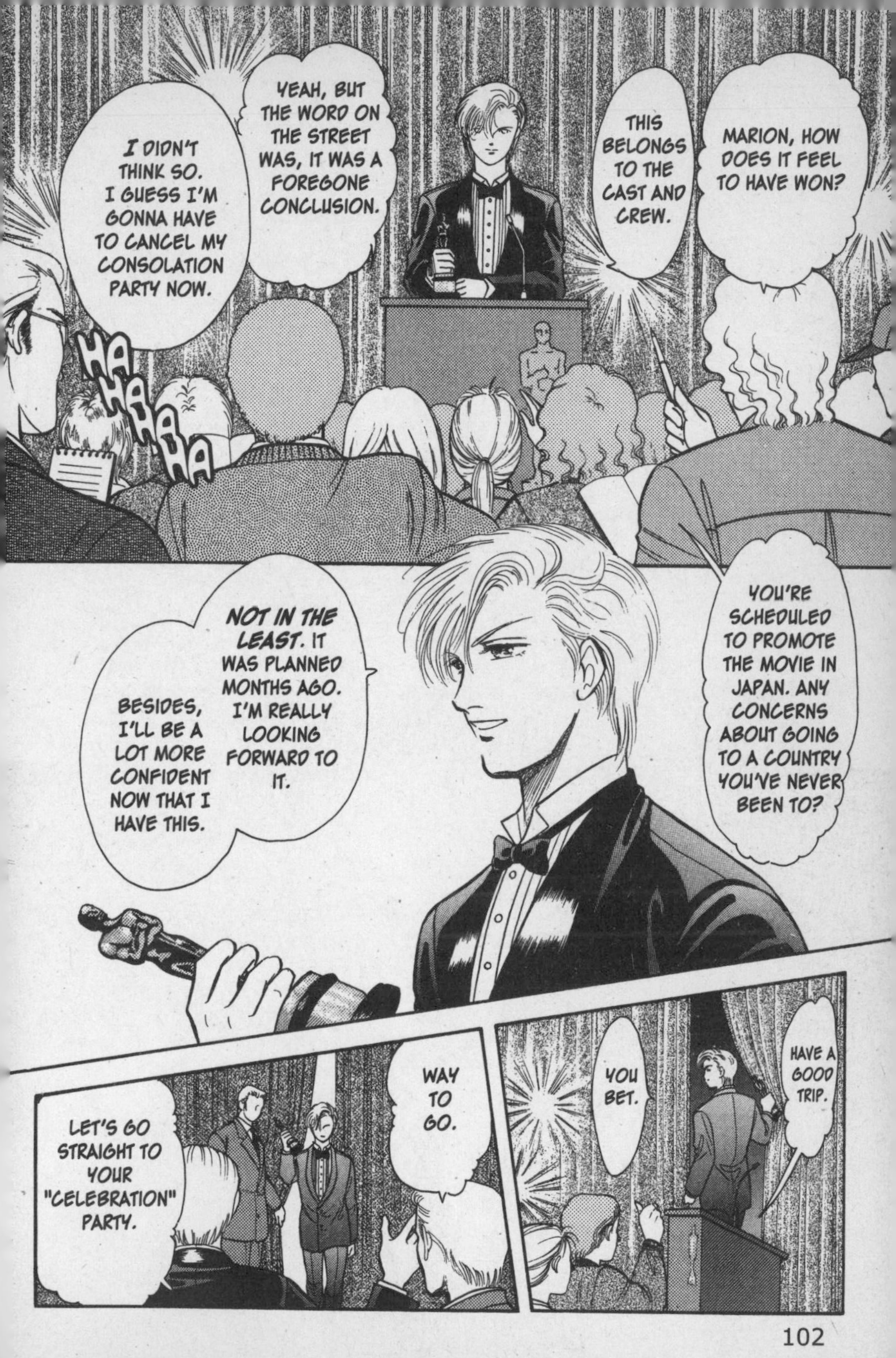
MARION, HOW DOES IT FEEL TO HAVE WON?
THIS BELONGS TO THE CAST AND CREW.
YEAH, BUT THE WORD ON THE STREET WAS, IT WAS A FOREGONE CONCLUSION.
I DIDN'T THINK SO. I GUESS I'M GONNA HAVE TO CANCEL MY CONSOLATION PARTY NOW.
HA HA HA HA HA
YOU'RE SCHEDULED TO PROMOTE THE MOVIE IN JAPAN. ANY CONCERNS ABOUT GOING TO A COUNTRY YOU'VE NEVER BEEN TO?
NOT IN THE LEAST. IT WAS PLANNED MONTHS AGO. I'M REALLY LOOKING FORWARD TO IT.
BESIDES, I'LL BE A LOT MORE CONFIDENT NOW THAT I HAVE THIS.
HAVE A GOOD TRIP.
YOU BET.
WAY TO GO.
LET'S GO STRAIGHT TO YOUR "CELEBRATION" PARTY.

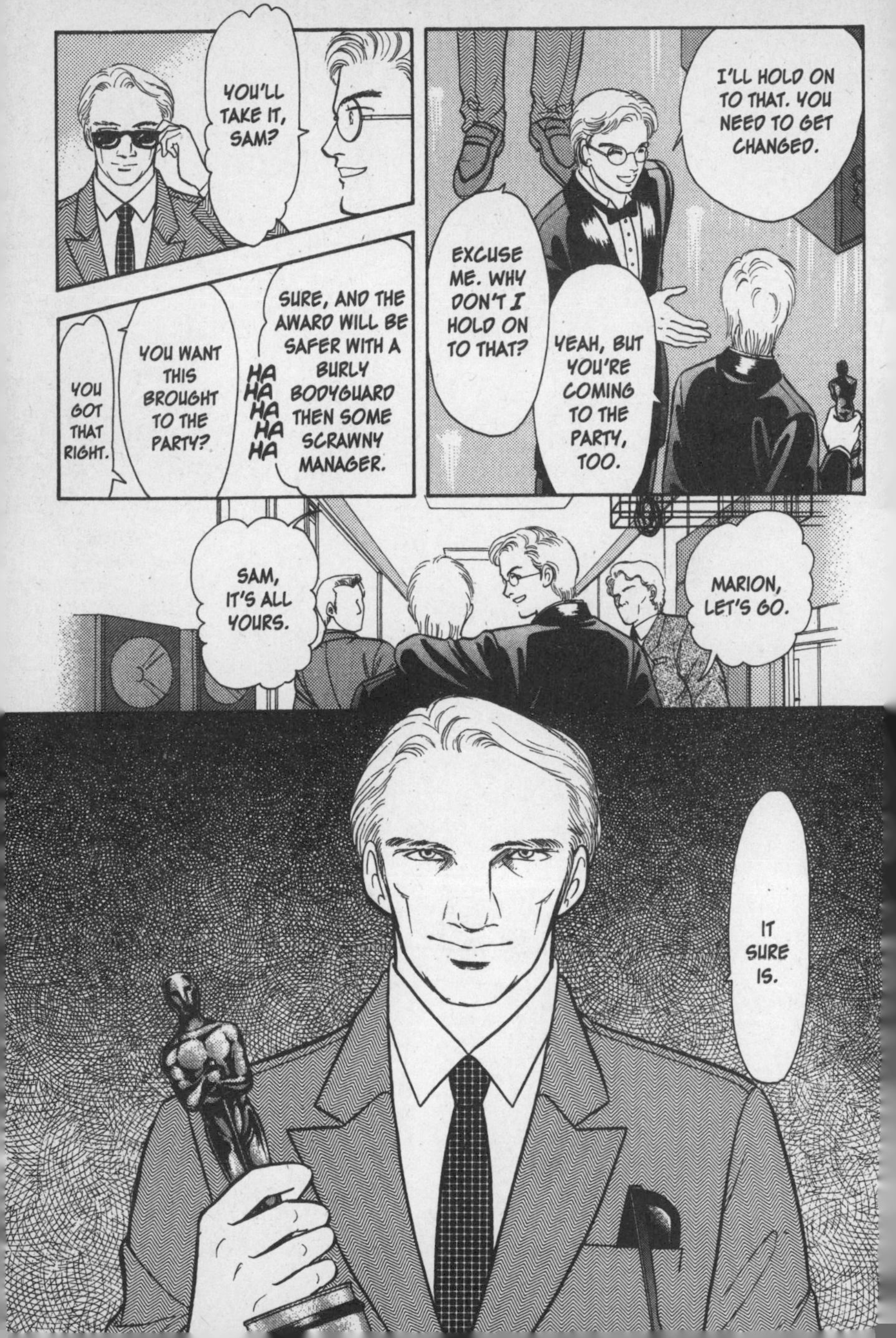
I'LL HOLD ON TO THAT. YOU NEED TO GET CHANGED.
YEAH, BUT YOU'RE COMING TO THE PARTY, TOO.
EXCUSE ME. WHY DON'T I HOLD ON TO THAT?
YOU'LL TAKE IT, SAM?
SURE, AND THE AWARD WILL BE SAFER WITH A BURLY BODYGUARD THEN SOME SCRAWNY MANAGER.
HA HA HA HA HA
YOU WANT THIS BROUGHT TO THE PARTY?
YOU GOT THAT RIGHT.
MARION, LET'S GO.
SAM, IT'S ALL YOURS.
IT SURE IS.

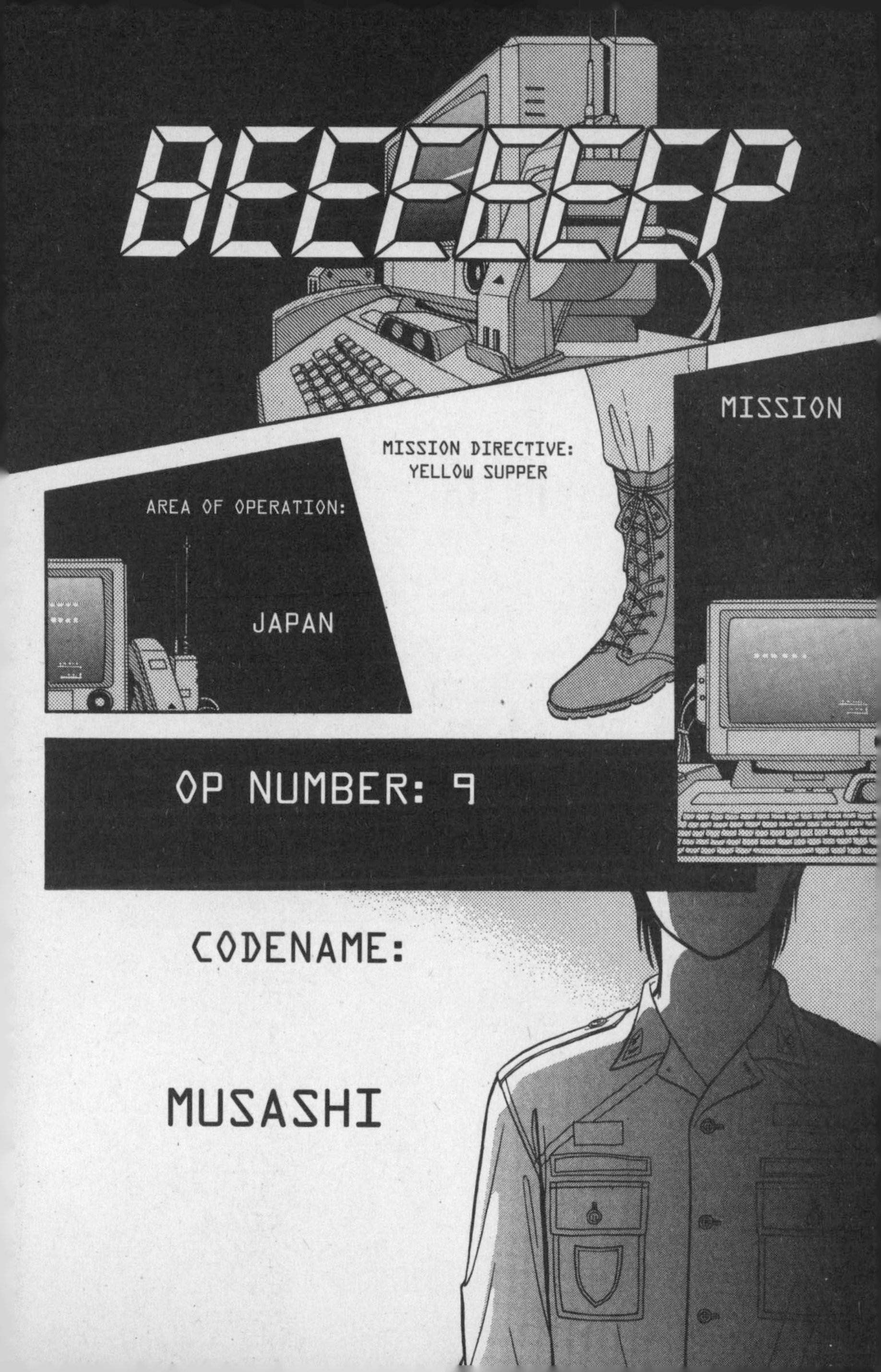
BEEEEEEP
MISSION
MISSION DIRECTIVE:
YELLOW SUPPER
AREA OF OPERATION:
JAPAN
OP NUMBER: 9
CODENAME:
MUSASHI

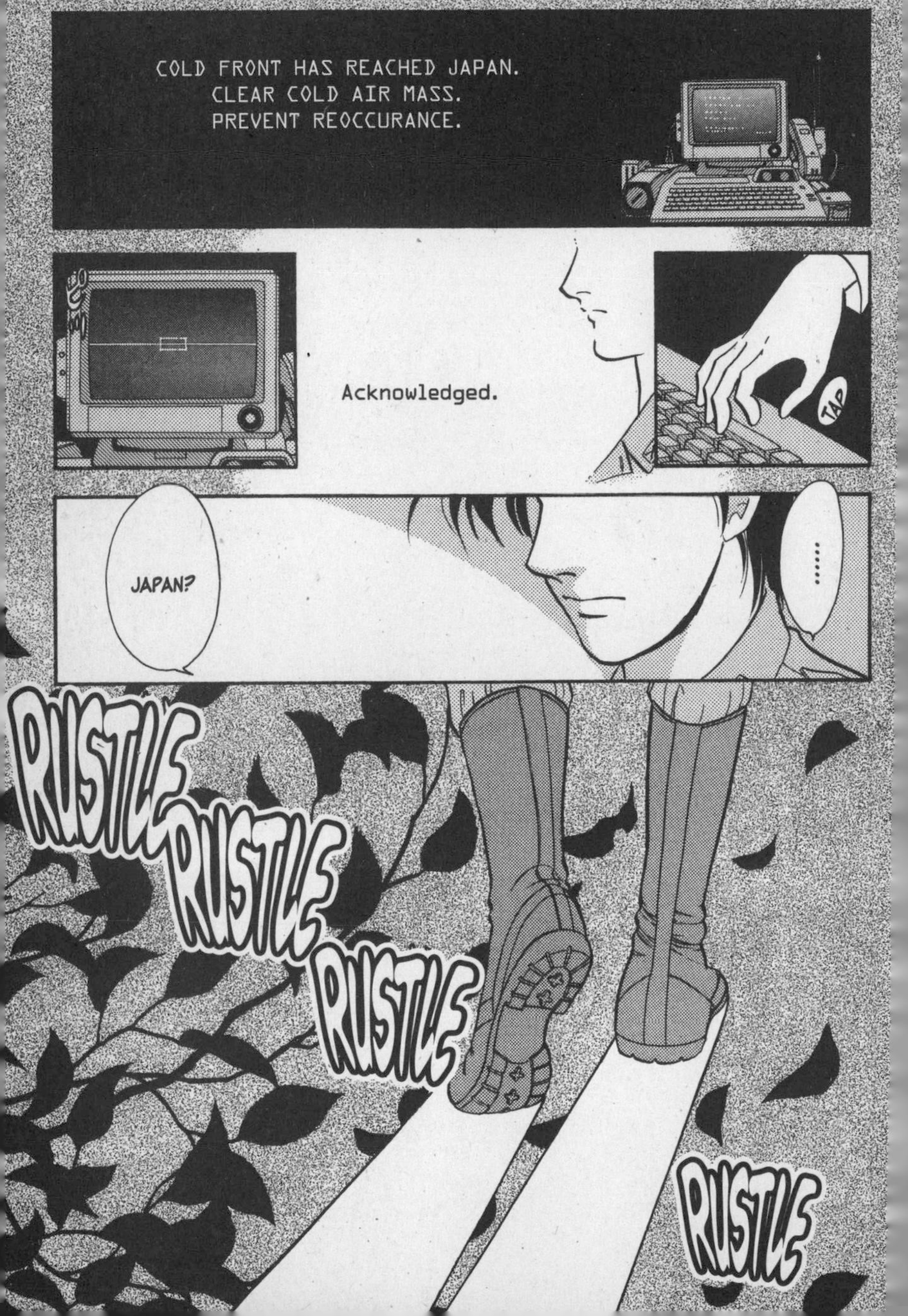
COLD FRONT HAS REACHED JAPAN.
CLEAR COLD AIR MASS.
PREVENT REOCCURANCE.
TAP
Acknowledged.
......
JAPAN?
RUSTLE
RUSTLE
RUSTLE
RUSTLE

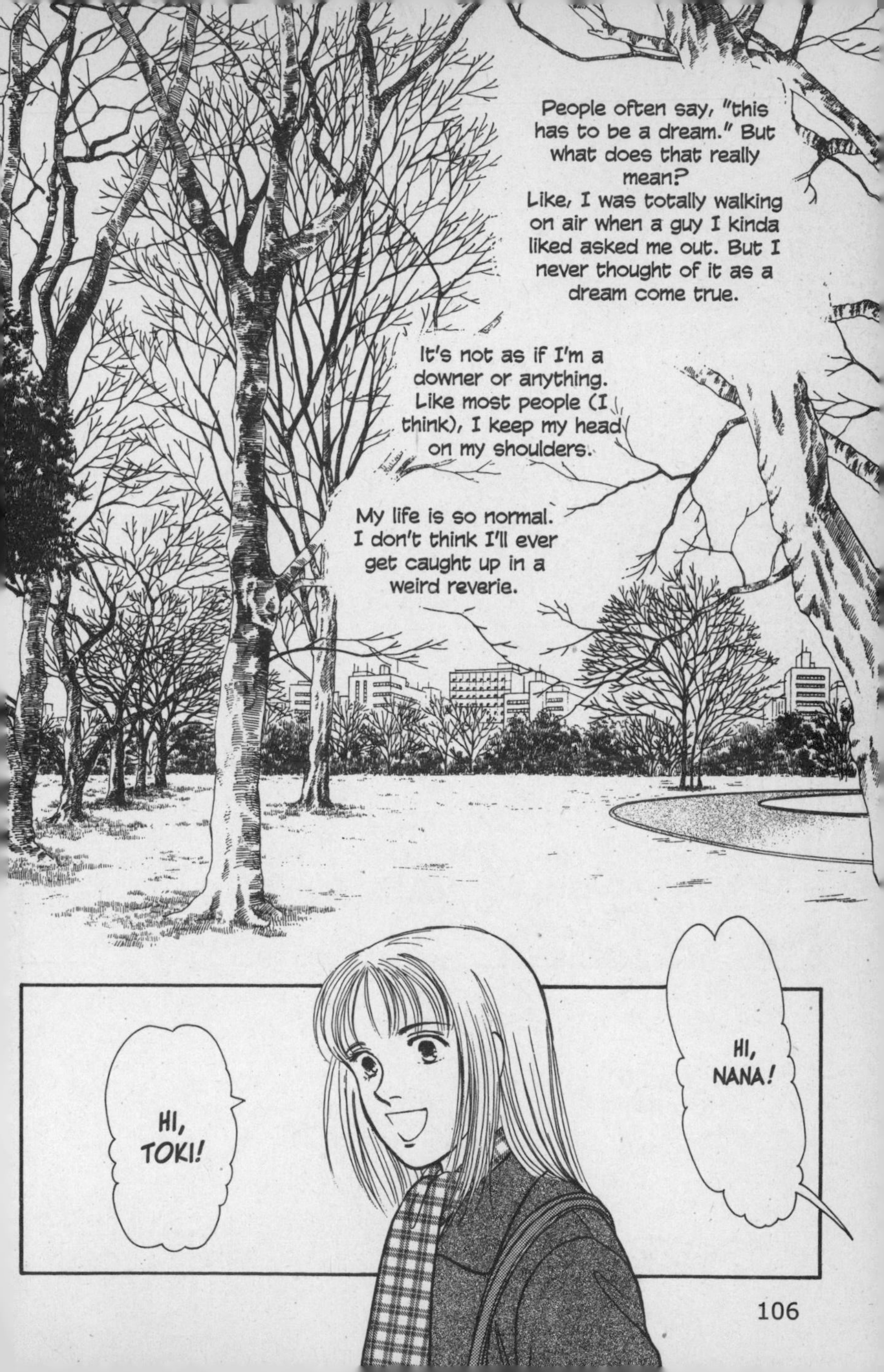
People often say, "this has to be a dream." But what does that really mean?
Like, I was totally walking on air when a guy I kinda liked asked me out. But I never thought of it as a dream come true.
It's not as if I'm a downer or anything. Like most people (I think), I keep my head on my shoulders.
My life is so normal. I don't think I'll ever get caught up in a weird reverie.
HI, NANA!
HI, TOKI!

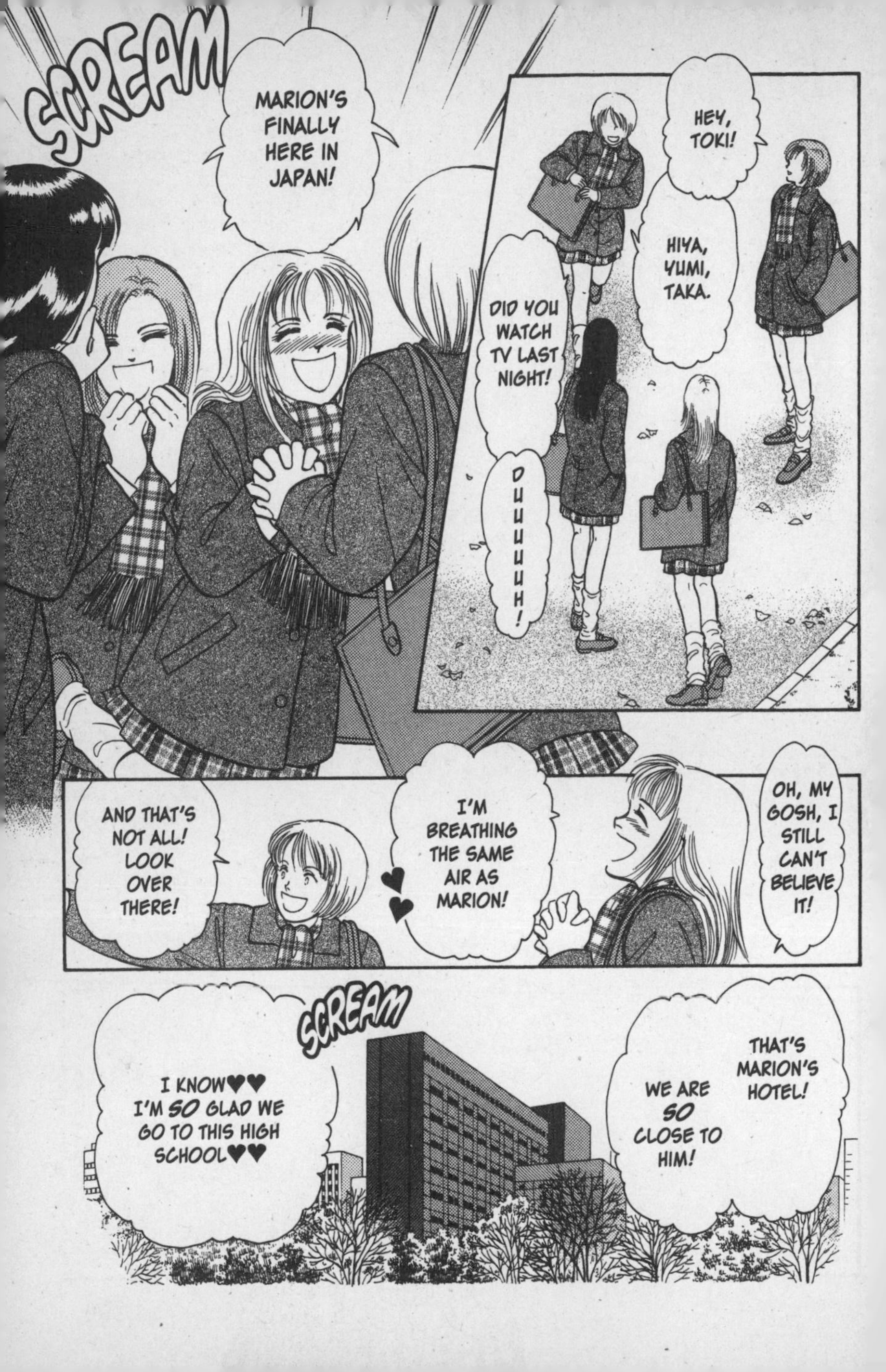
HEY, TOKI!
HIYA, YUMI, TAKA.
DID YOU WATCH TV LAST NIGHT!
DUUUUUUH!
SCREAM
MARION'S FINALLY HERE IN JAPAN!
OH, MY GOSH, I STILL CAN'T BELIEVE IT!
I'M BREATHING THE SAME AIR AS MARION! ♥♥
AND THAT'S NOT ALL! LOOK OVER THERE!
THAT'S MARION'S HOTEL!
WE ARE SO CLOSE TO HIM!
SCREAM
I KNOW♥♥ I'M SO GLAD WE GO TO THIS HIGH SCHOOL♥♥

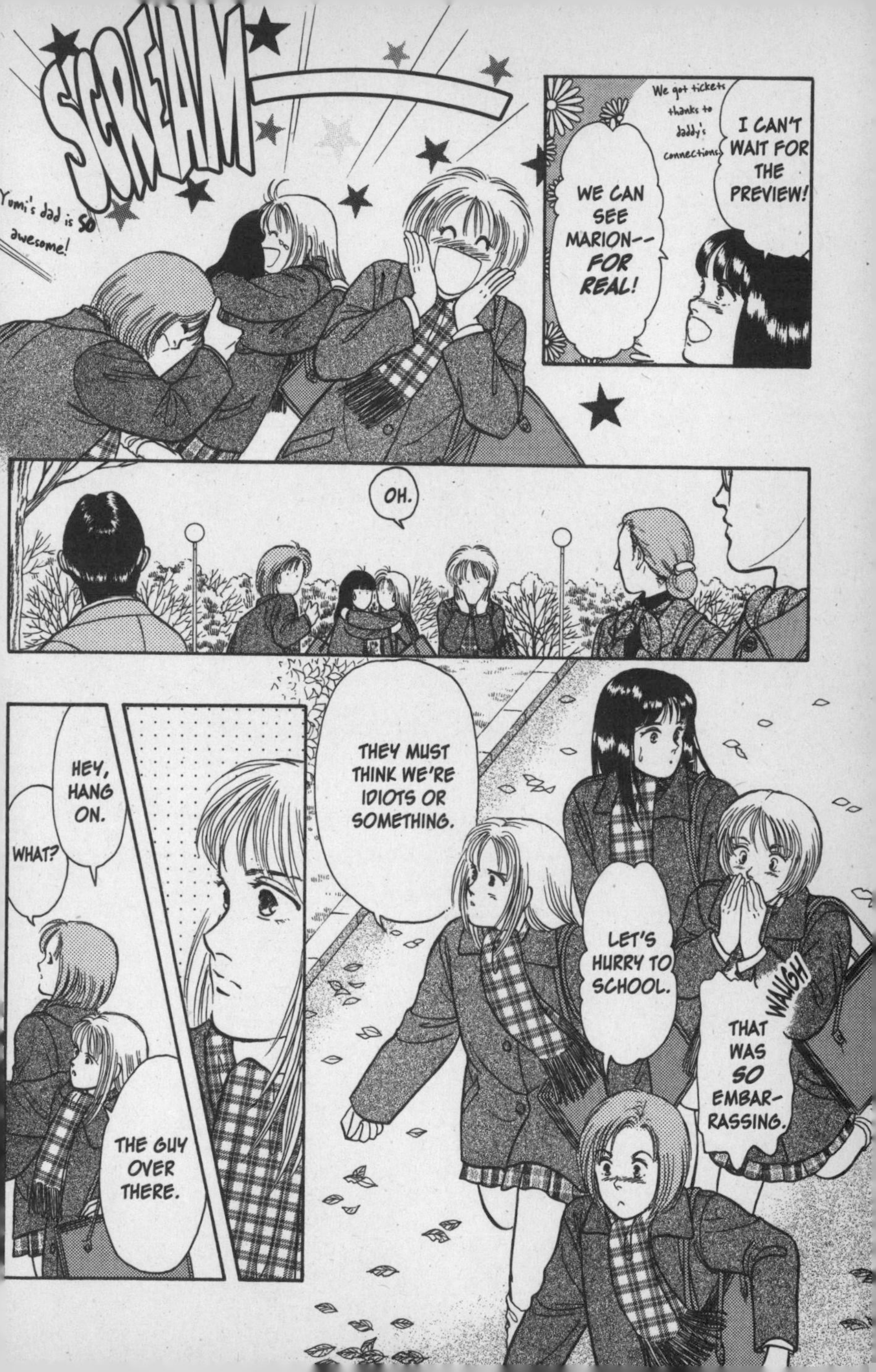

I CAN'T WAIT FOR THE PREVIEW!
We got tickets thanks to daddy's connections.
WE CAN SEE MARION--FOR REAL!
SCREAM
Yumi's dad is SO awesome!
OH.
THEY MUST THINK WE'RE IDIOTS OR SOMETHING.
LET'S HURRY TO SCHOOL.
WAUGH
THAT WAS SO EMBARRASSING.
HEY, HANG ON.
WHAT?
THE GUY OVER THERE.

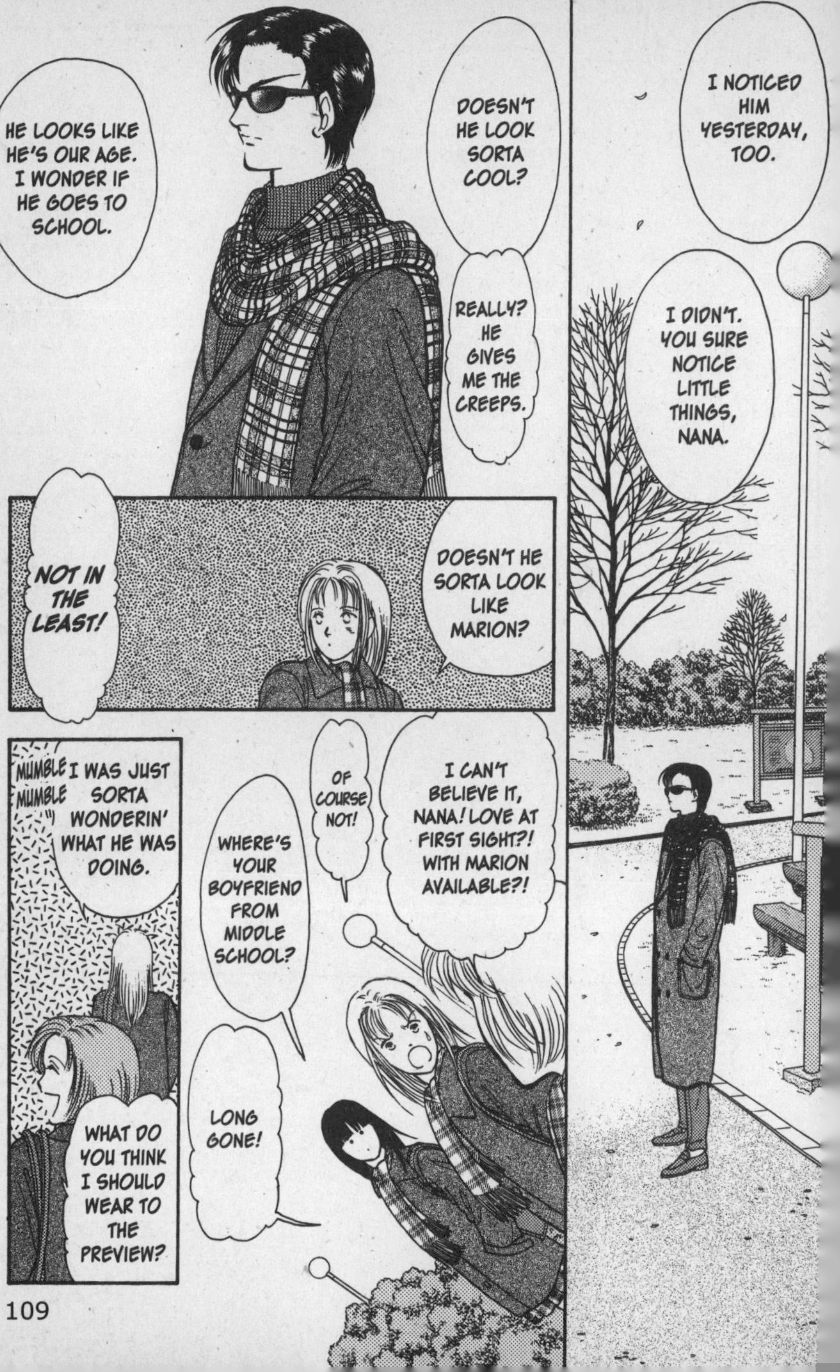
I NOTICED HIM YESTERDAY, TOO.
I DIDN'T. YOU SURE NOTICE LITTLE THINGS, NANA.
DOESN'T HE LOOK SORTA COOL?
REALLY? HE GIVES ME THE CREEPS.
HE LOOKS LIKE HE'S OUR AGE. I WONDER IF HE GOES TO SCHOOL.
DOESN'T HE SORTA LOOK LIKE MARION?
NOT IN THE LEAST!
I CAN'T BELIEVE IT, NANA! LOVE AT FIRST SIGHT?! WITH MARION AVAILABLE?!
OF COURSE NOT!
WHERE'S YOUR BOYFRIEND FROM MIDDLE SCHOOL?
LONG GONE!
MUMBLE MUMBLE
I WAS JUST SORTA WONDERIN' WHAT HE WAS DOING.
WHAT DO YOU THINK I SHOULD WEAR TO THE PREVIEW?

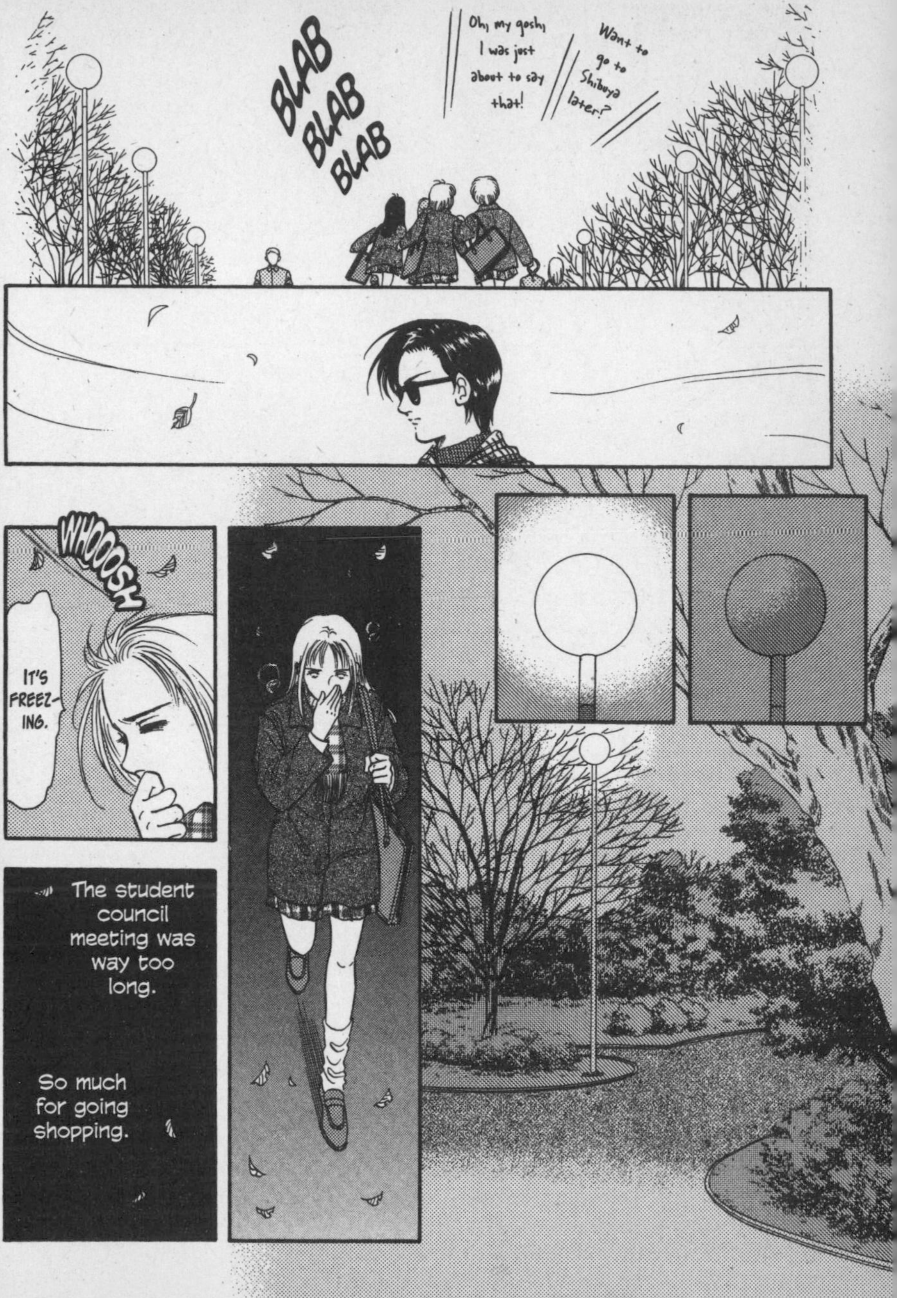
Want to go to Shibuya later?
Oh, my gosh, I was just about to say that!
BLAB BLAB BLAB
WHOOOSH
IT'S FREEZ-ING.
The student council meeting was way too long.
So much for going shopping.

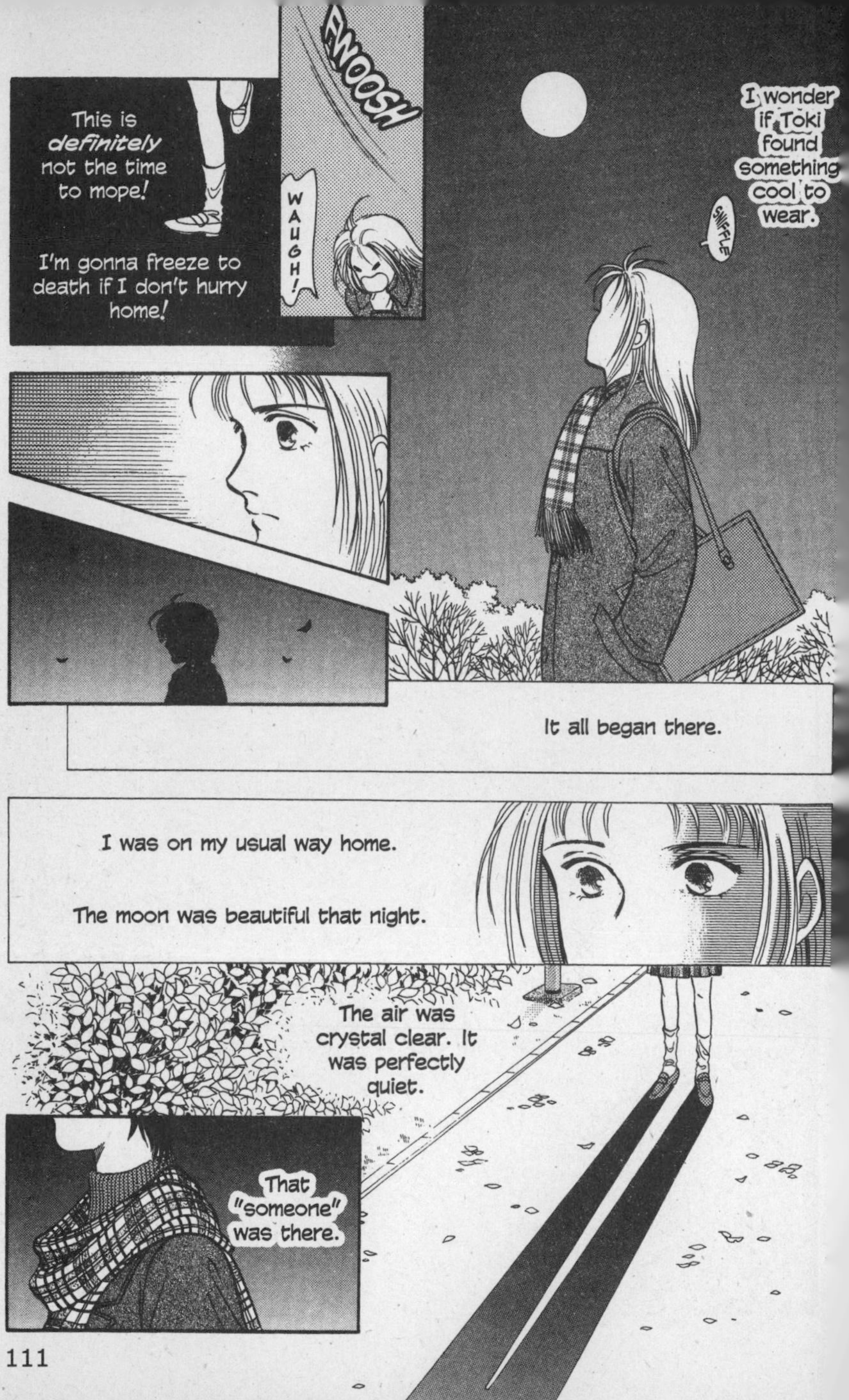
I wonder if Toki found something cool to wear.
SNIFFLE
FWOOSH
WAUGH!
This is *definitely* not the time to mope!
I'm gonna freeze to death if I don't hurry home!
It all began there.
I was on my usual way home.
The moon was beautiful that night.
The air was crystal clear. It was perfectly quiet.
That "someone" was there.

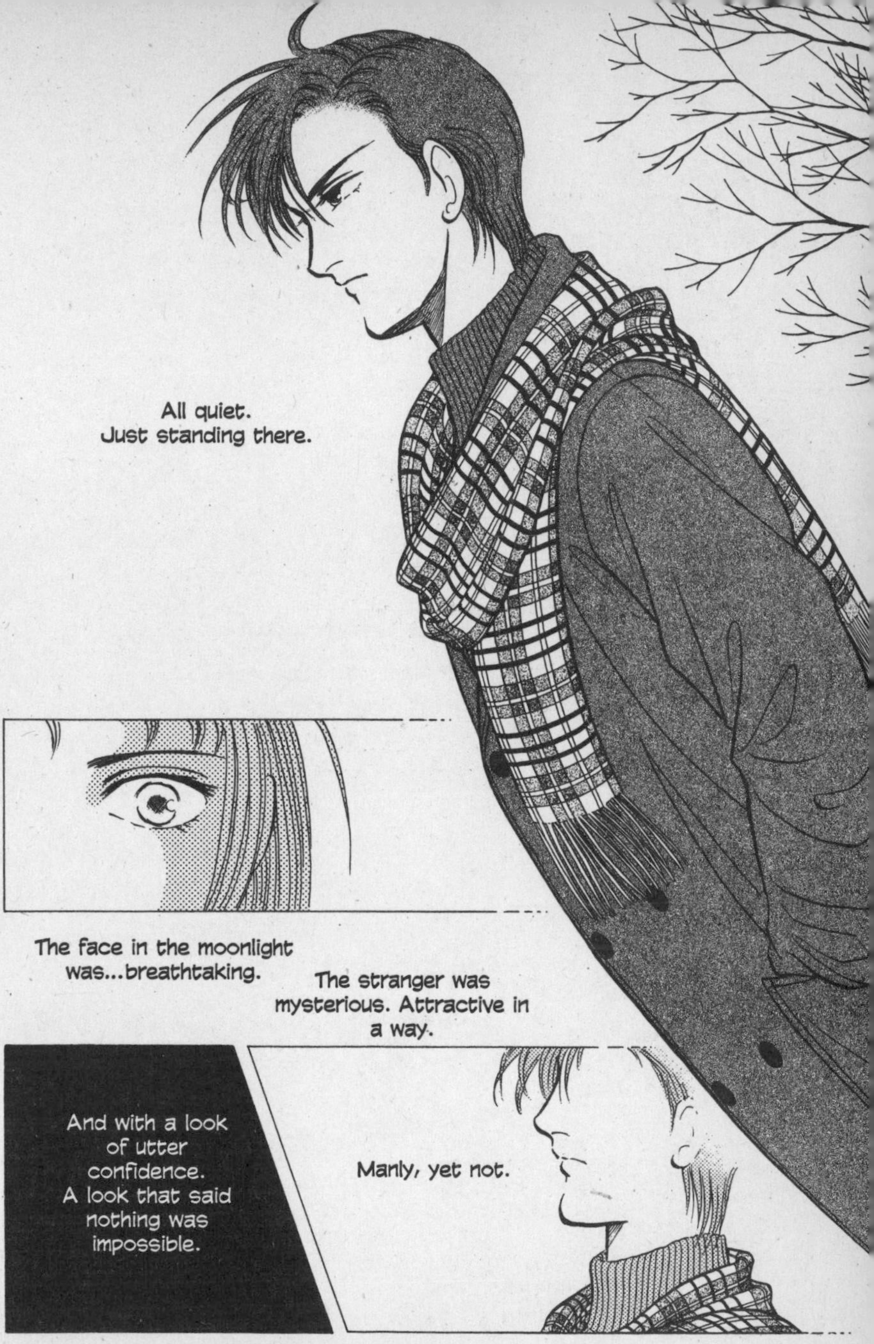
All quiet.
Just standing there.
The face in the moonlight
was...breathtaking.
The stranger was
mysterious. Attractive in
a way.
Manly, yet not.
And with a look
of utter
confidence.
A look that said
nothing was
impossible.

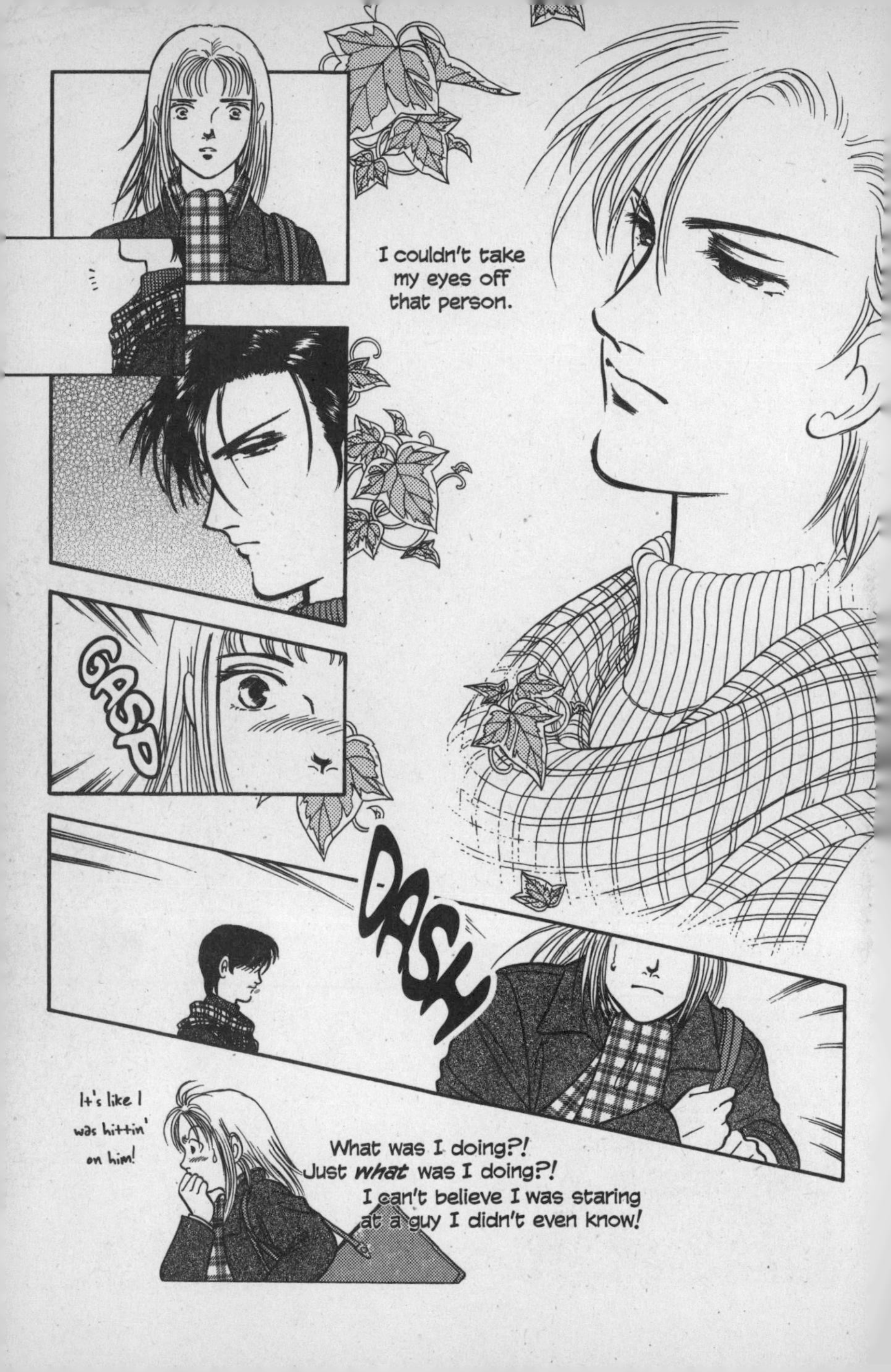
I couldn't take my eyes off that person.
GASP
DASH
What was I doing?! Just *what* was I doing?! I can't believe I was staring at a guy I didn't even know!
It's like I was hittin' on him!

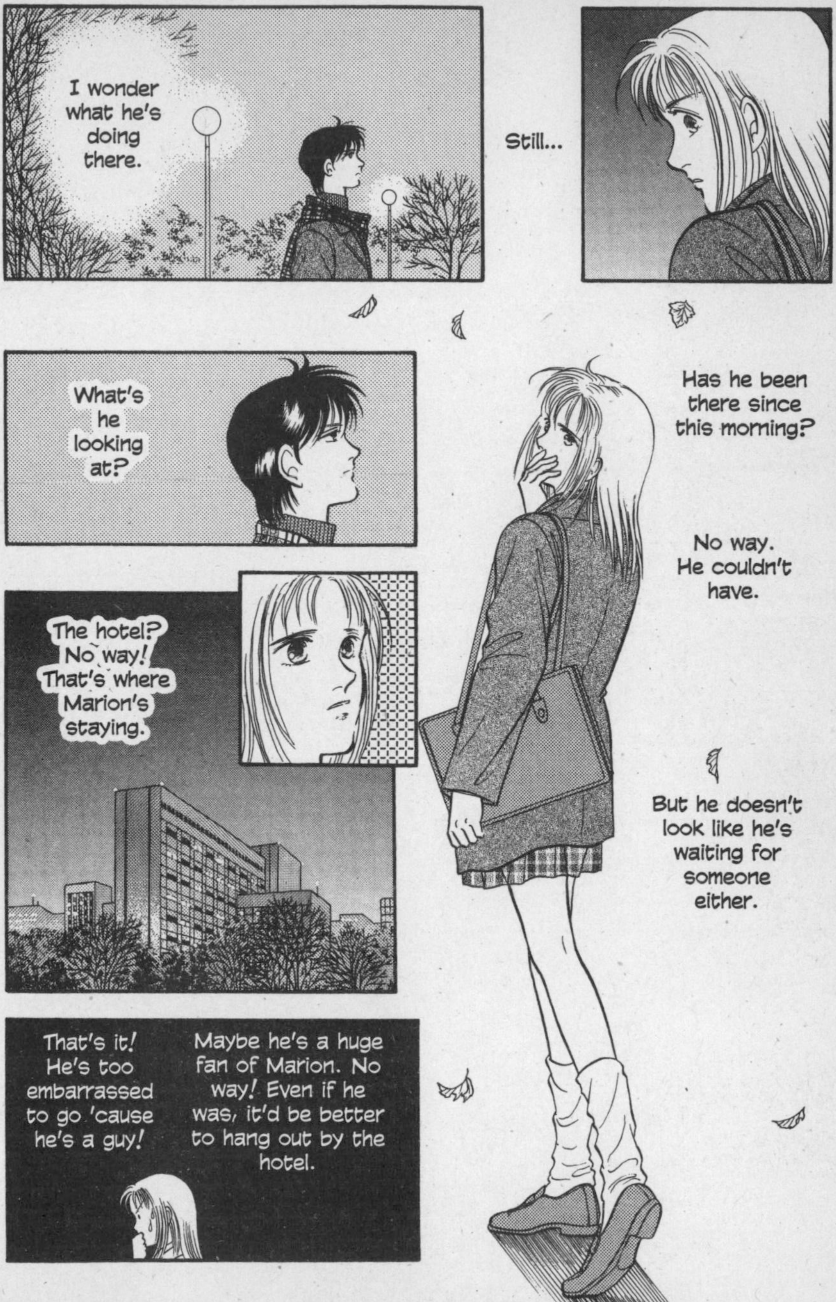
Still...
I wonder what he's doing there.
Has he been there since this morning?
No way. He couldn't have.
But he doesn't look like he's waiting for someone either.
What's he looking at?
The hotel? No way! That's where Marion's staying.
Maybe he's a huge fan of Marion. No way! Even if he was, it'd be better to hang out by the hotel.
That's it! He's too embarrassed to go 'cause he's a guy!

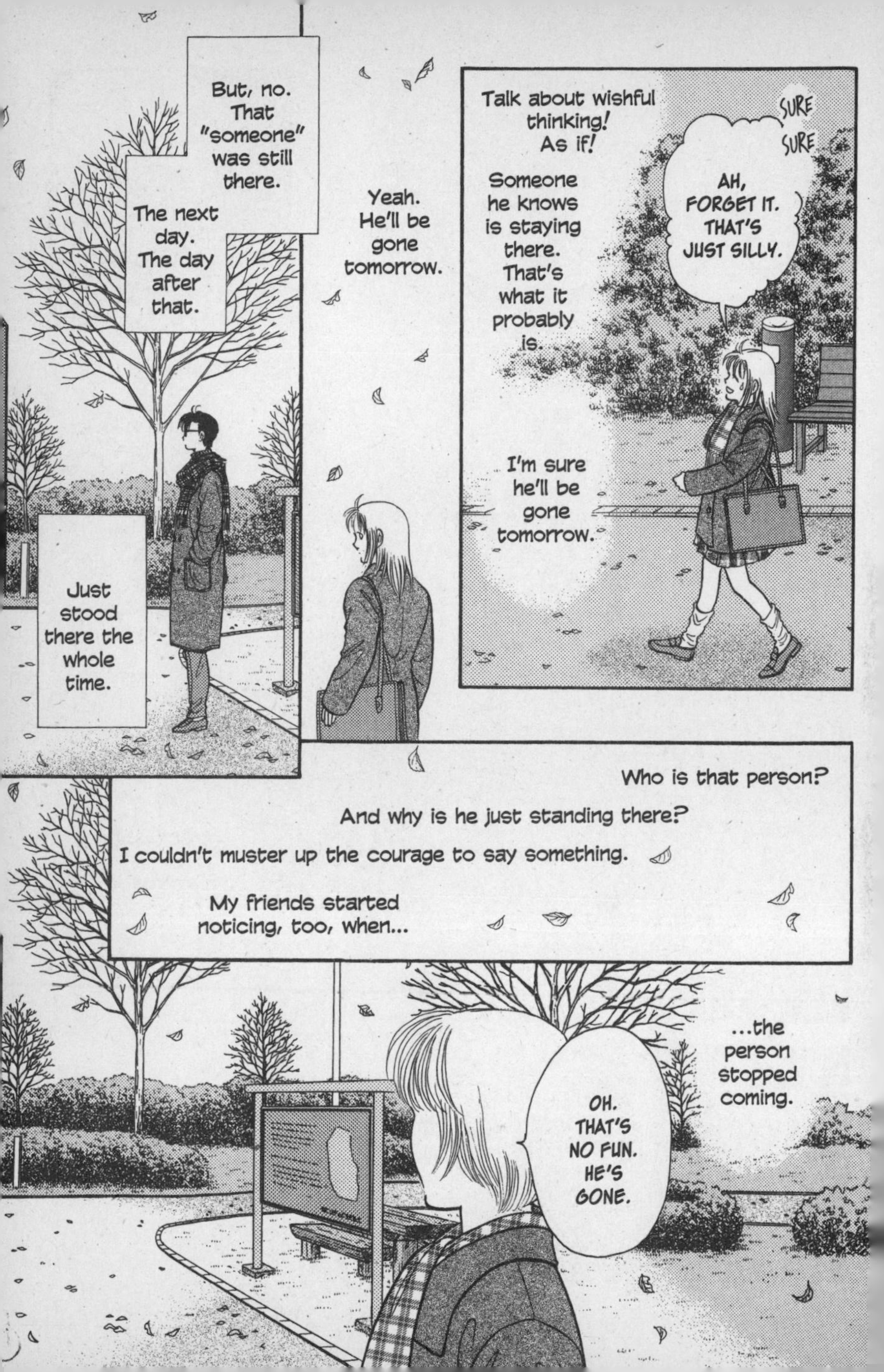
Talk about wishful thinking! As if!
Someone he knows is staying there. That's what it probably is.
SURE SURE
AH, FORGET IT. THAT'S JUST SILLY.
I'm sure he'll be gone tomorrow.
Yeah. He'll be gone tomorrow.
But, no. That "someone" was still there.
The next day. The day after that.
Just stood there the whole time.
Who is that person?
And why is he just standing there?
I couldn't muster up the courage to say something.
My friends started noticing, too, when...
...the person stopped coming.
OH. THAT'S NO FUN. HE'S GONE.

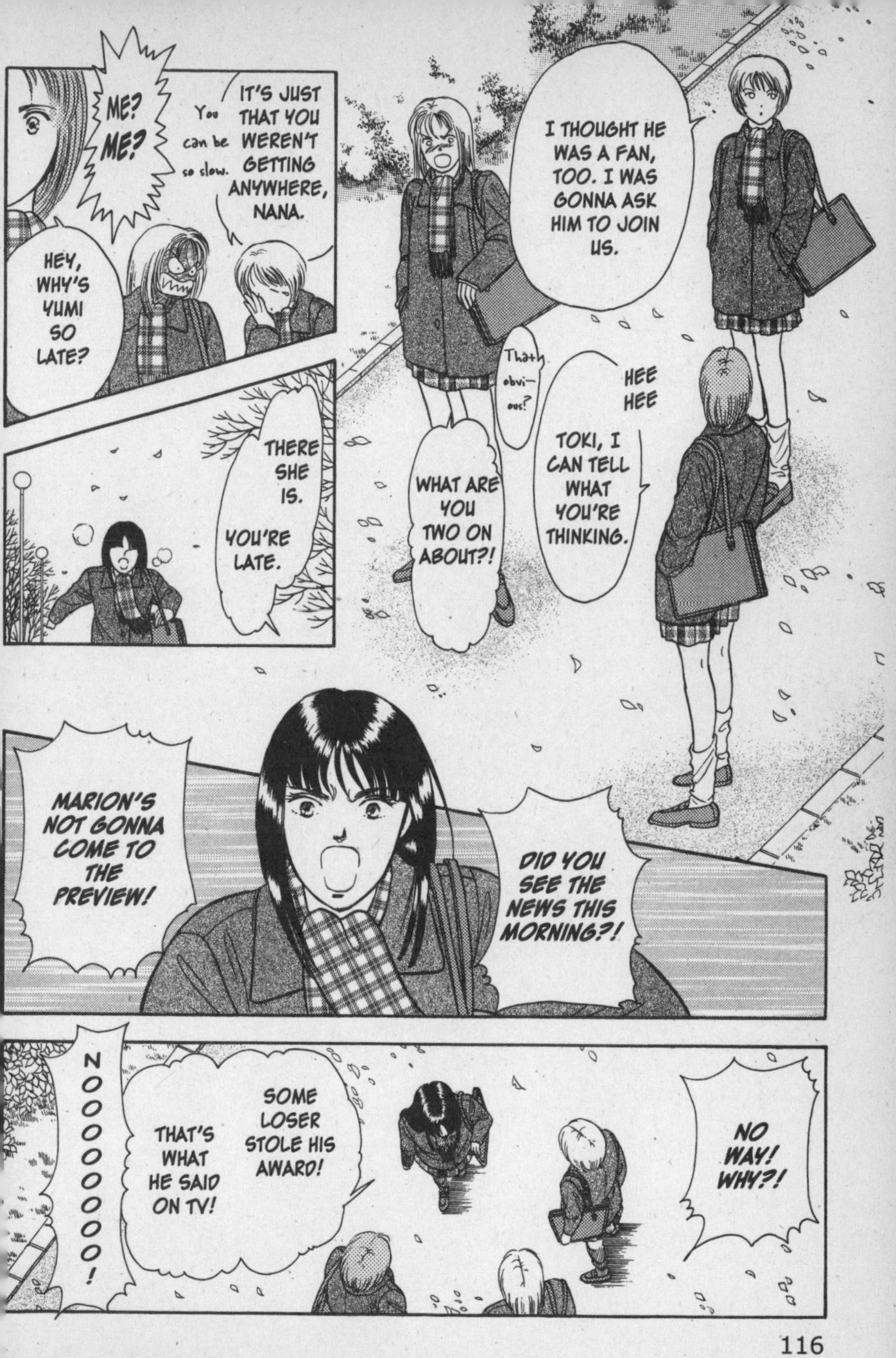
I THOUGHT HE WAS A FAN, TOO. I WAS GONNA ASK HIM TO JOIN US.
HEE HEE
TOKI, I CAN TELL WHAT YOU'RE THINKING.
That's obvi-ous?
WHAT ARE YOU TWO ON ABOUT?!
IT'S JUST THAT YOU WEREN'T GETTING ANYWHERE, NANA.
You can be so slow.
ME? ME?
HEY, WHY'S YUMI SO LATE?
THERE SHE IS.
YOU'RE LATE.
DID YOU SEE THE NEWS THIS MORNING?!
MARION'S NOT GONNA COME TO THE PREVIEW!
NO WAY! WHY?!
SOME LOSER STOLE HIS AWARD!
THAT'S WHAT HE SAID ON TV!
NOOOOOOOOOO!

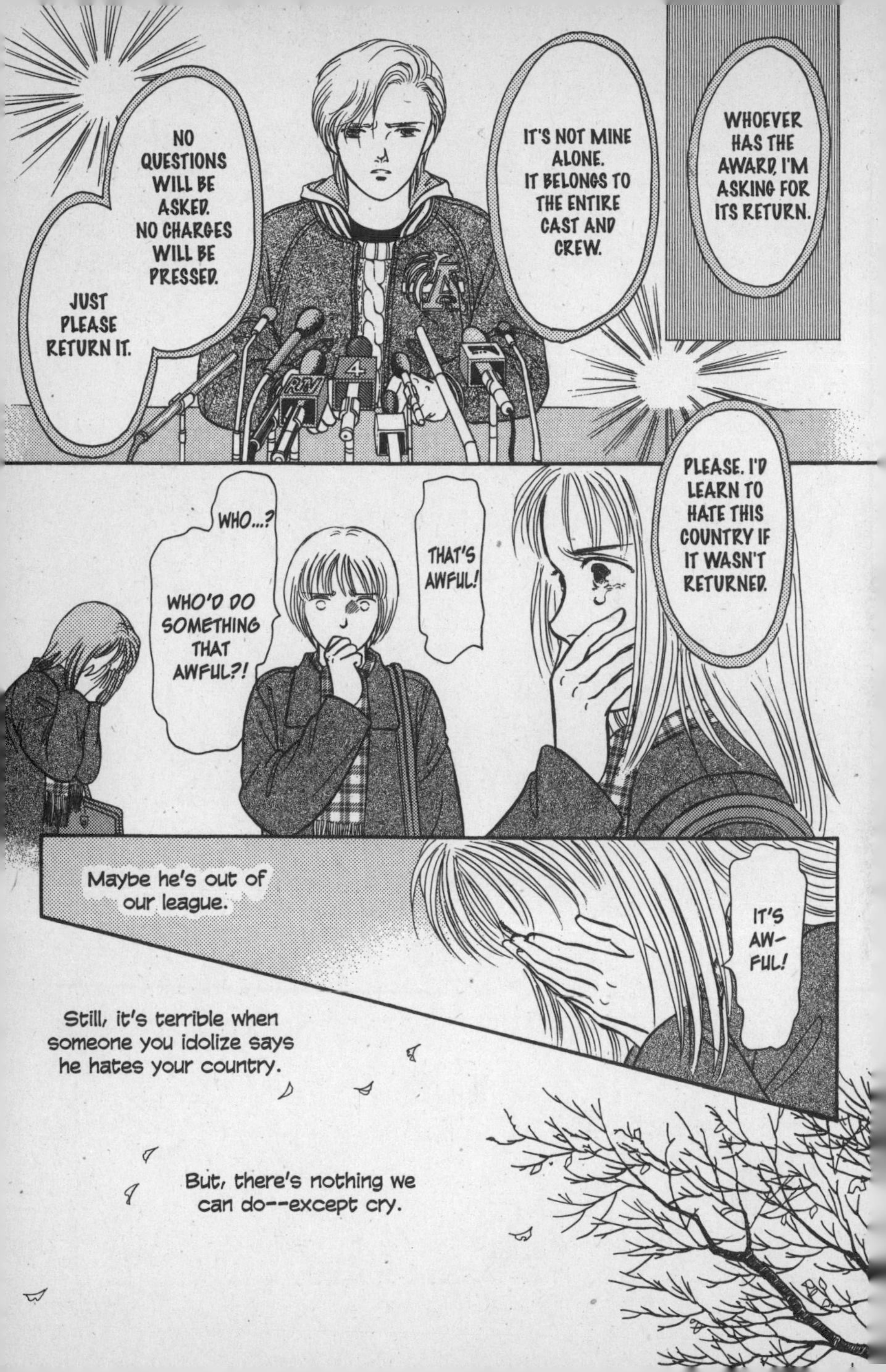
WHOEVER HAS THE AWARD, I'M ASKING FOR ITS RETURN.
IT'S NOT MINE ALONE. IT BELONGS TO THE ENTIRE CAST AND CREW.
NO QUESTIONS WILL BE ASKED. NO CHARGES WILL BE PRESSED.
JUST PLEASE RETURN IT.
PLEASE. I'D LEARN TO HATE THIS COUNTRY IF IT WASN'T RETURNED.
THAT'S AWFUL!
WHO...?
WHO'D DO SOMETHING THAT AWFUL?!
IT'S AW-FUL!
Maybe he's out of our league.
Still, it's terrible when someone you idolize says he hates your country.
But, there's nothing we can do--except cry.

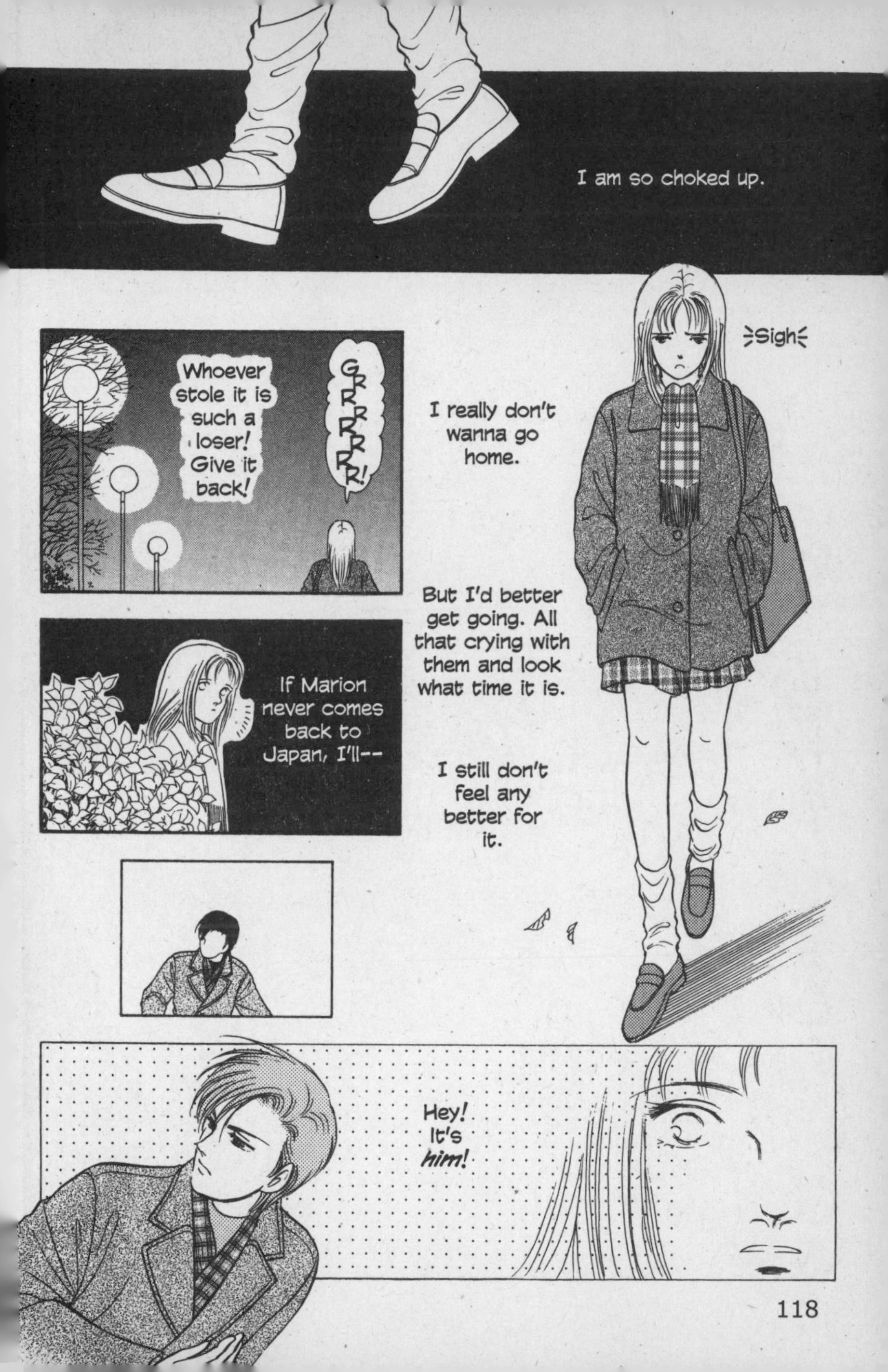

I am so choked up.
Sigh
I really don't wanna go home.
But I'd better get going. All that crying with them and look what time it is.
I still don't feel any better for it.
GRRRRRR!
Whoever stole it is such a loser! Give it back!
If Marion never comes back to Japan, I'll--
Hey! It's *him!*

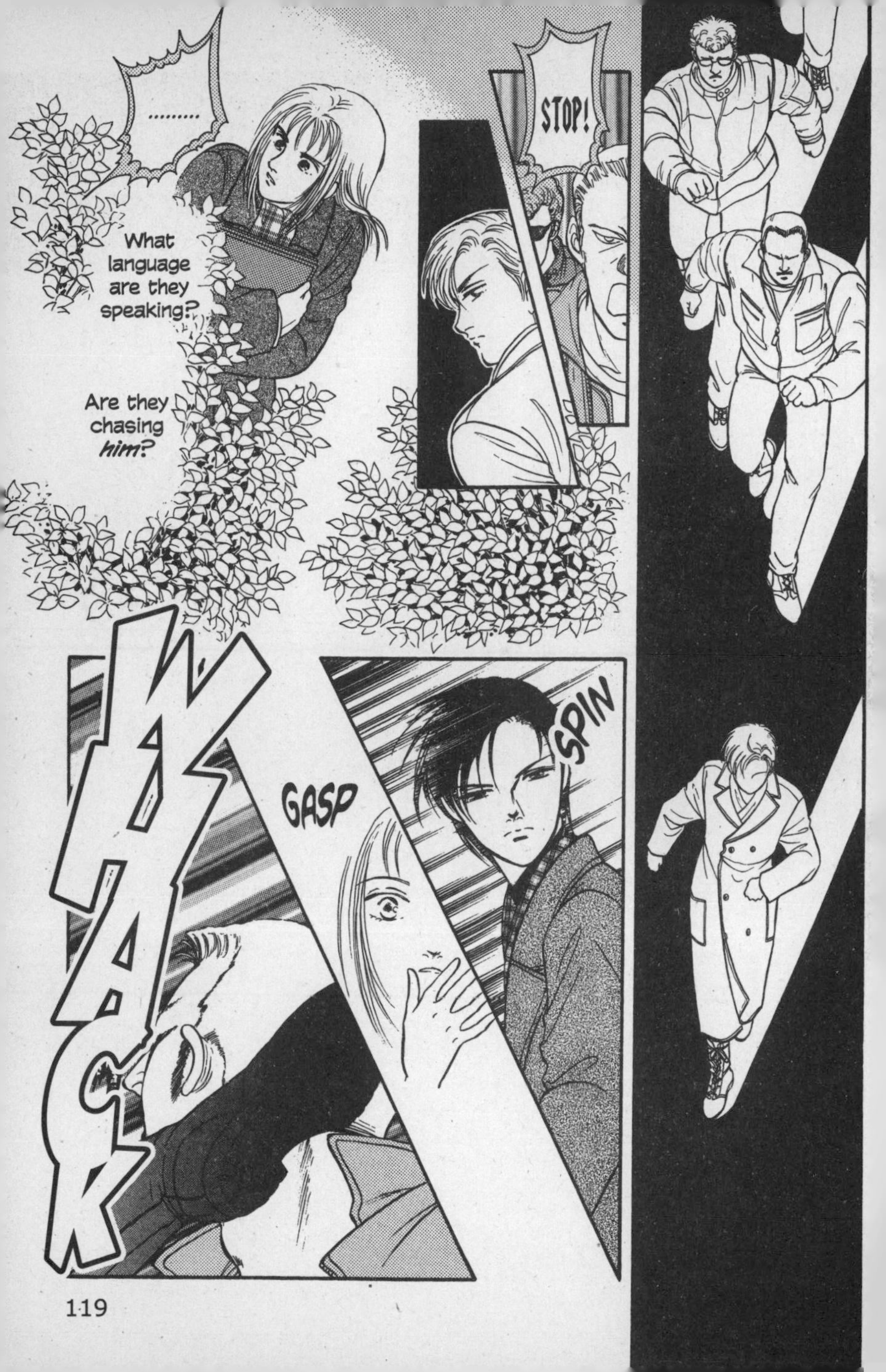
STOP!
....
What language are they speaking?
Are they chasing *him*?
SPIN
GASP
WHACK

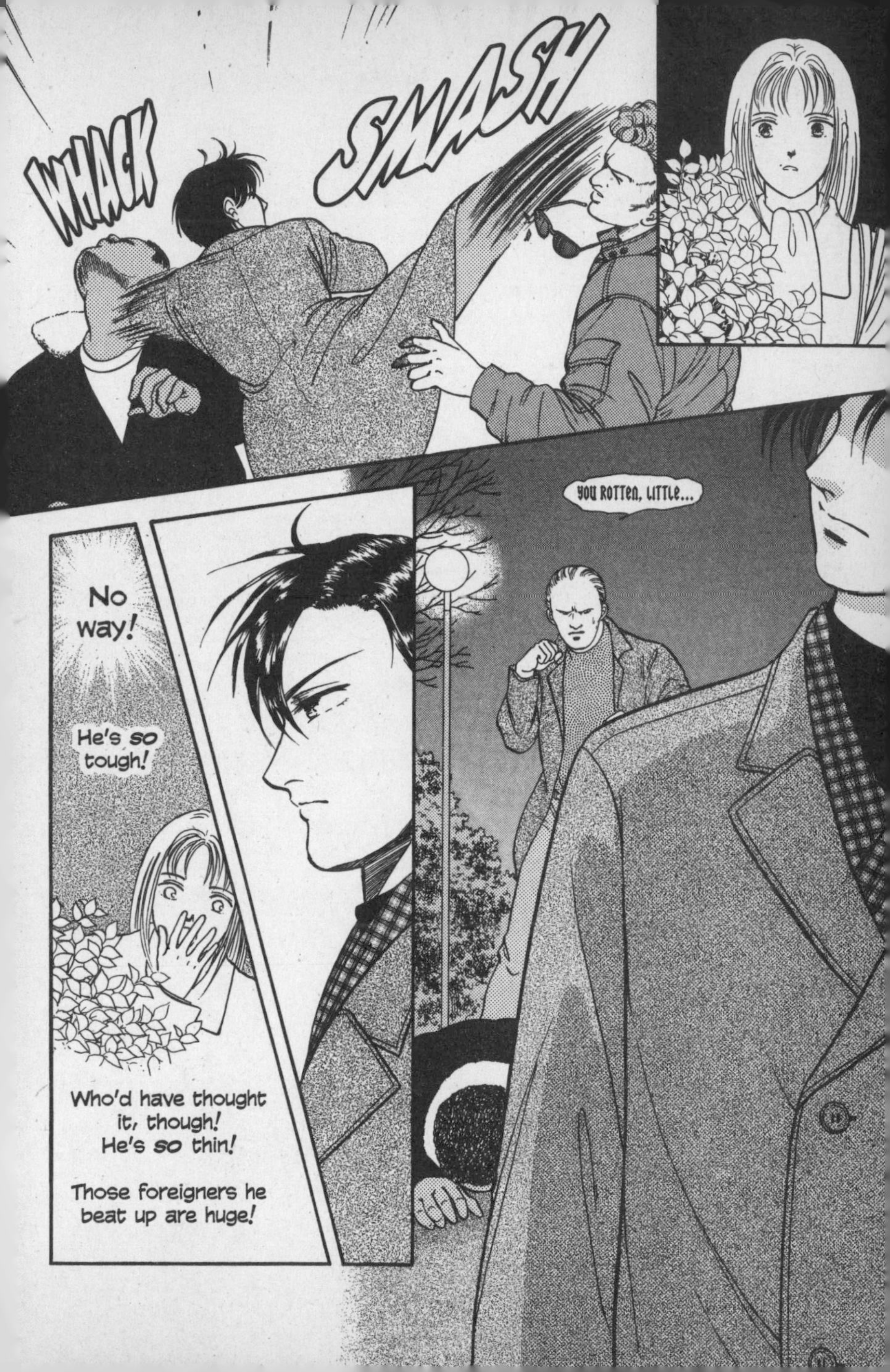
SMASH
WHACK
YOU ROTTEN, LITTLE...
No way!
He's so tough!
Who'd have thought it, though! He's so thin!
Those foreigners he beat up are huge!

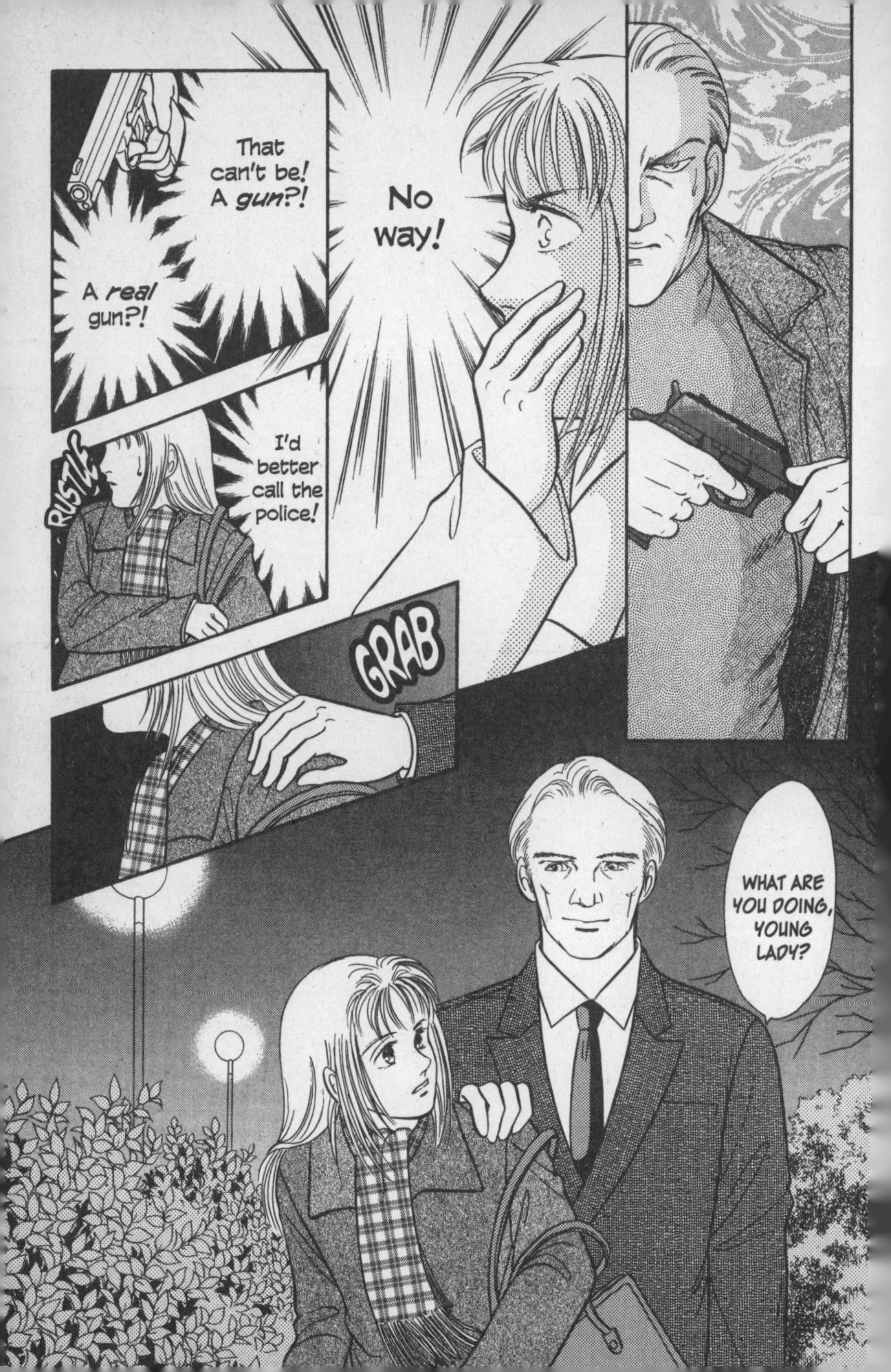
No way!
That can't be! A *gun*?!
A *real* gun?!
I'd better call the police!
RUSTLE
GRAB
WHAT ARE YOU DOING, YOUNG LADY?

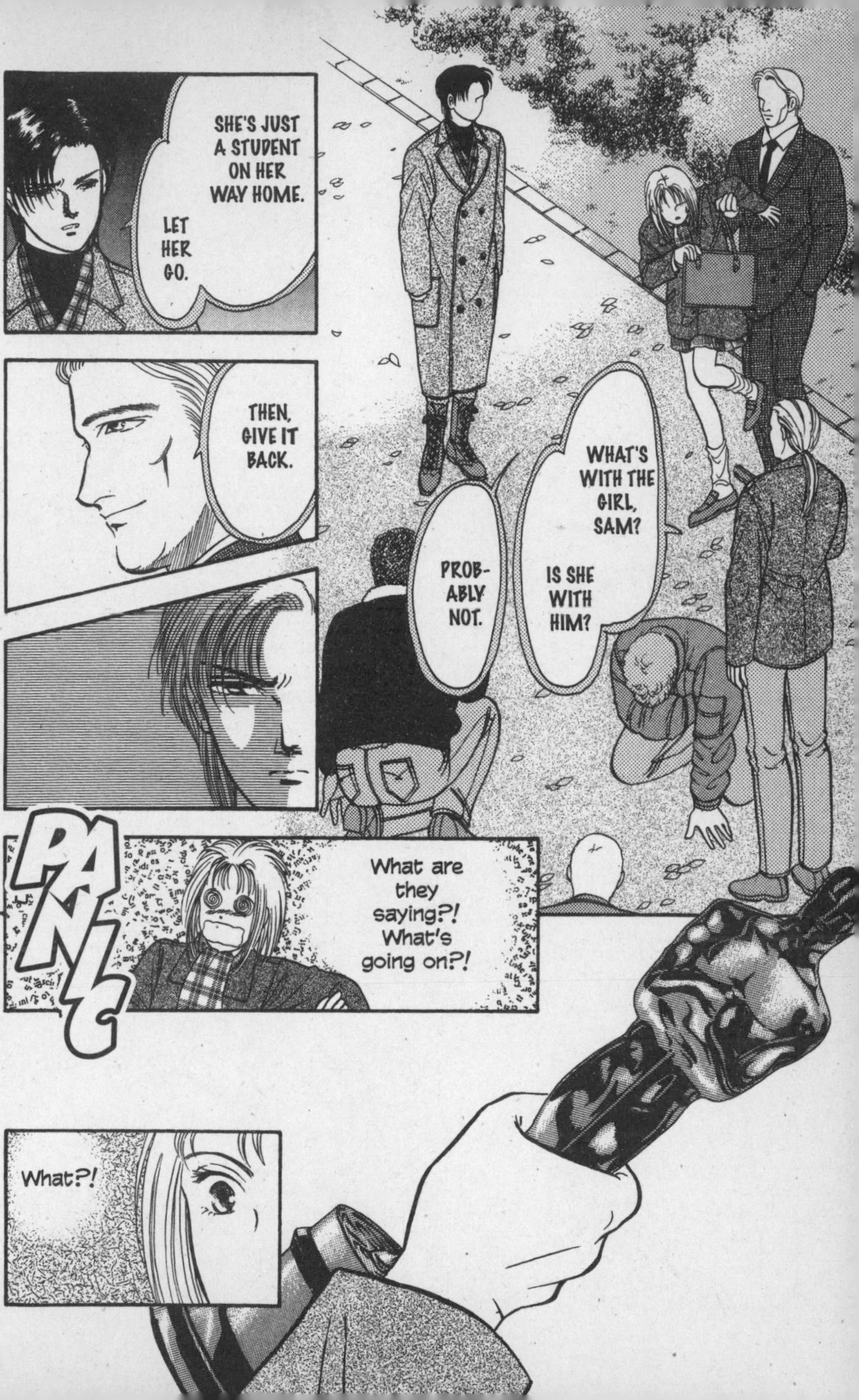
WHAT'S WITH THE GIRL, SAM?
IS SHE WITH HIM?
PROB-ABLY NOT.
SHE'S JUST A STUDENT ON HER WAY HOME.
LET HER GO.
THEN, GIVE IT BACK.
PANIC
What are they saying?! What's going on?!
What?!

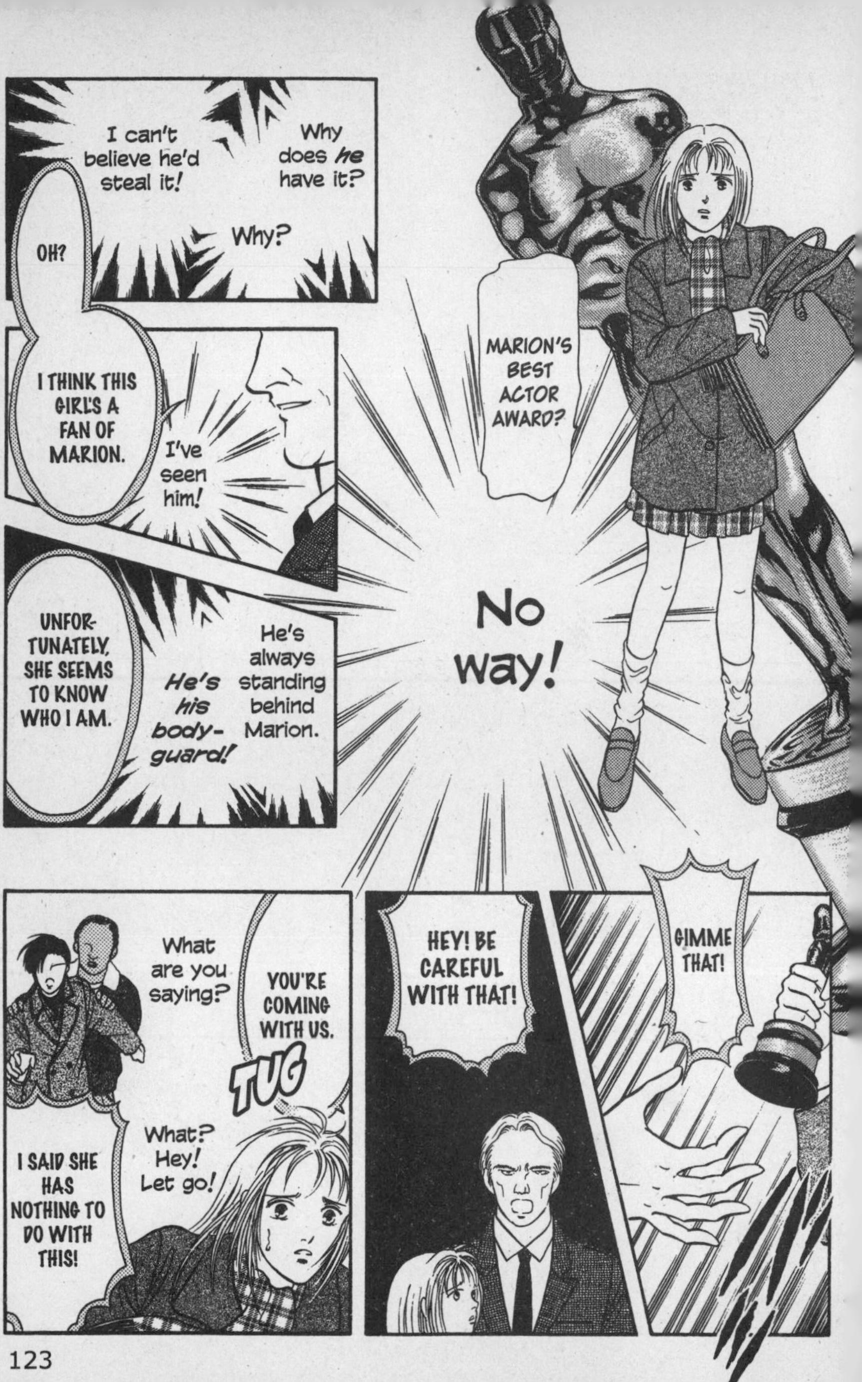
MARION'S BEST ACTOR AWARD?
No way!
Why does *he* have it?
I can't believe he'd steal it!
Why?
OH?
I've seen him!
I THINK THIS GIRL'S A FAN OF MARION.
He's always standing behind Marion.
He's his bodyguard!
UNFORTUNATELY, SHE SEEMS TO KNOW WHO I AM.
GIMME THAT!
HEY! BE CAREFUL WITH THAT!
YOU'RE COMING WITH US.
What are you saying?
TUG
What? Hey! Let go!
I SAID SHE HAS NOTHING TO DO WITH THIS!

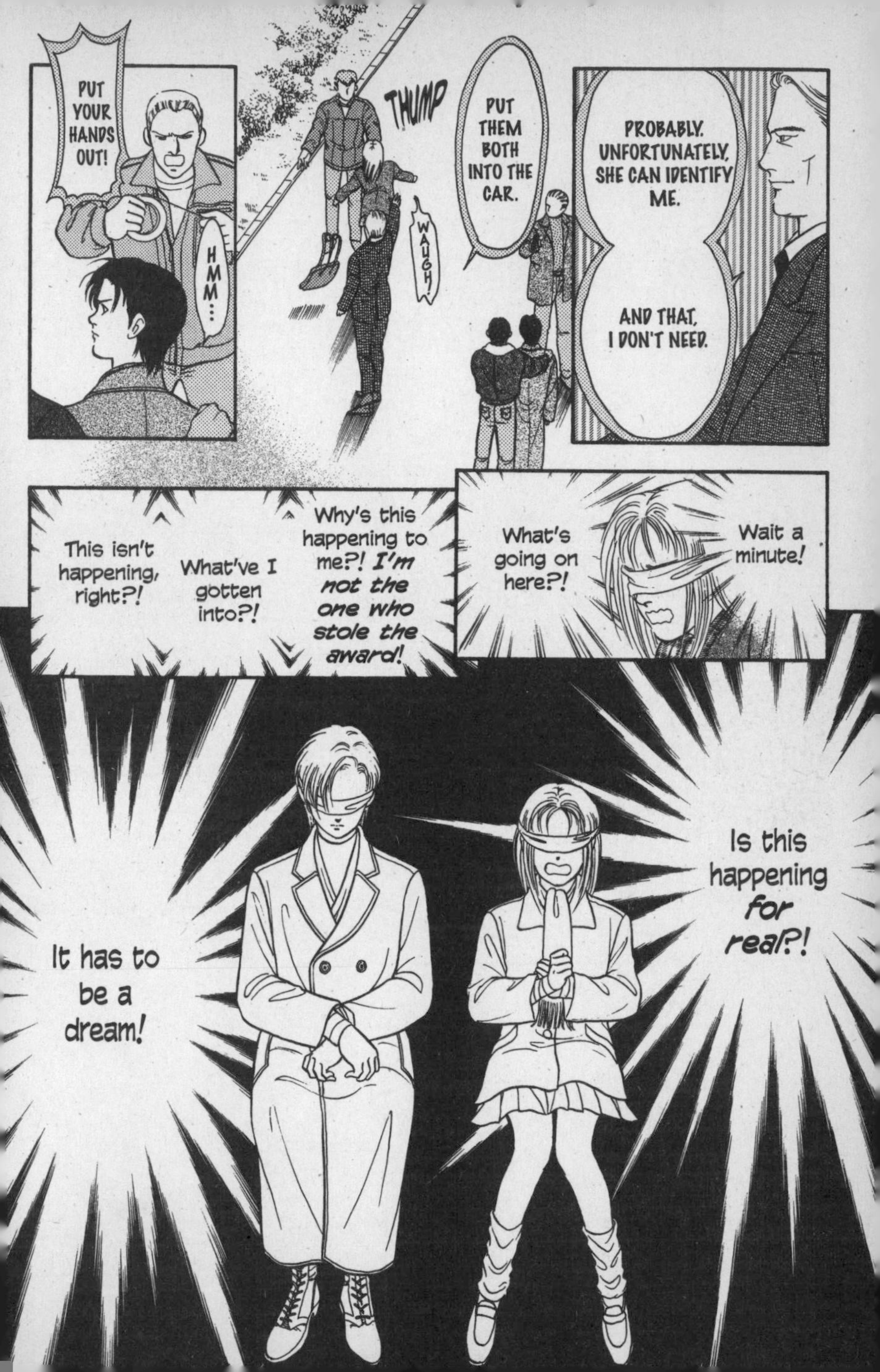
PROBABLY. UNFORTUNATELY, SHE CAN IDENTIFY ME.
AND THAT, I DON'T NEED.
PUT THEM BOTH INTO THE CAR.
THUMP
WAUGH!
PUT YOUR HANDS OUT!
HMM...
Wait a minute!
What's going on here?!
Why's this happening to me?! *I'm not the one who stole the award!*
What've I gotten into?!
This isn't happening, right?!
Is this happening *for real*?!
It has to be a dream!

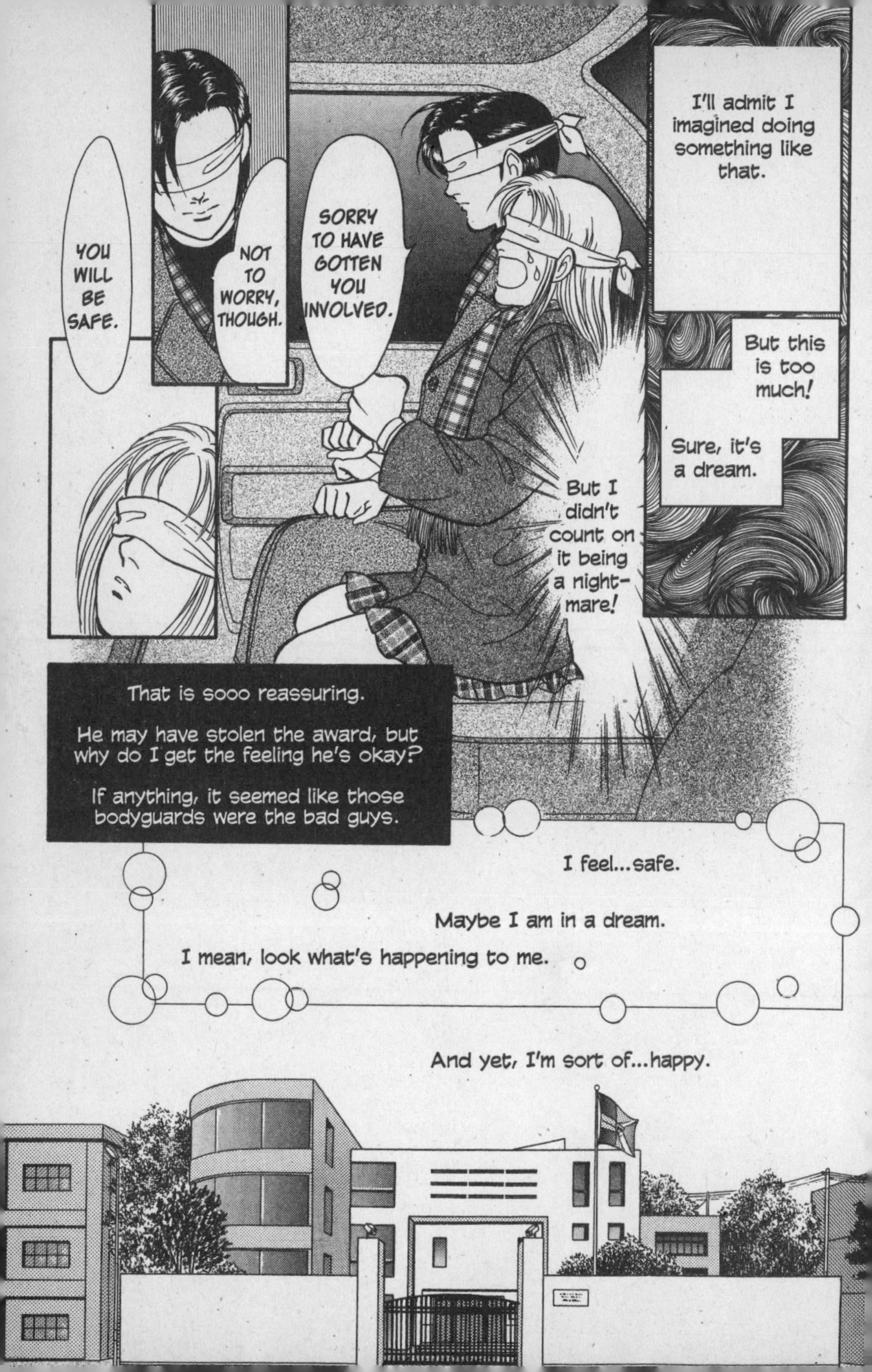
I'll admit I imagined doing something like that.
But this is too much!
Sure, it's a dream.
But I didn't count on it being a night-mare!
SORRY TO HAVE GOTTEN YOU INVOLVED.
NOT TO WORRY, THOUGH.
YOU WILL BE SAFE.
That is sooo reassuring.
He may have stolen the award, but why do I get the feeling he's okay?
If anything, it seemed like those bodyguards were the bad guys.
I feel...safe.
Maybe I am in a dream.
I mean, look what's happening to me.
And yet, I'm sort of...happy.

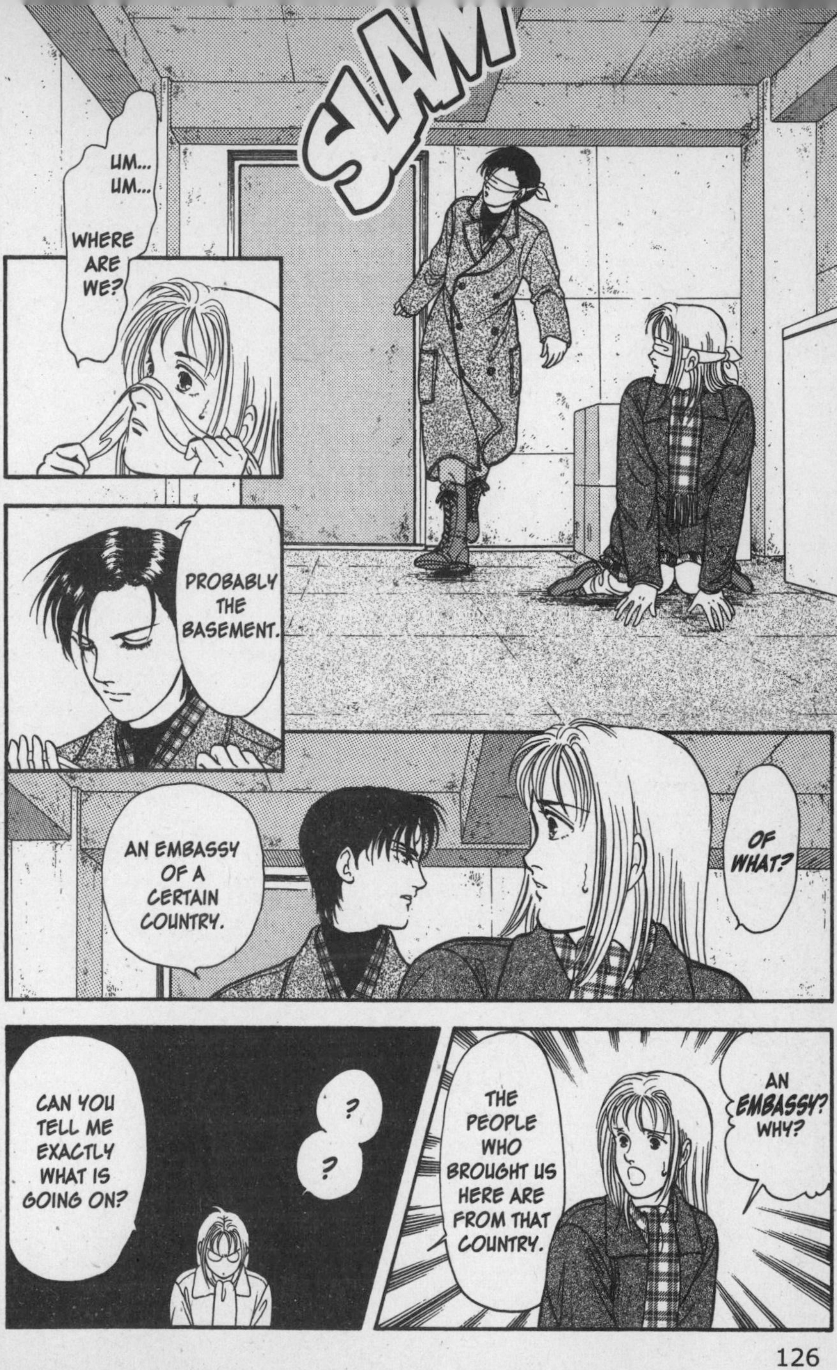
SLAM
UM... UM...
WHERE ARE WE?
PROBABLY THE BASEMENT.
OF WHAT?
AN EMBASSY OF A CERTAIN COUNTRY.
AN EMBASSY? WHY?
THE PEOPLE WHO BROUGHT US HERE ARE FROM THAT COUNTRY.
?
?
CAN YOU TELL ME EXACTLY WHAT IS GOING ON?

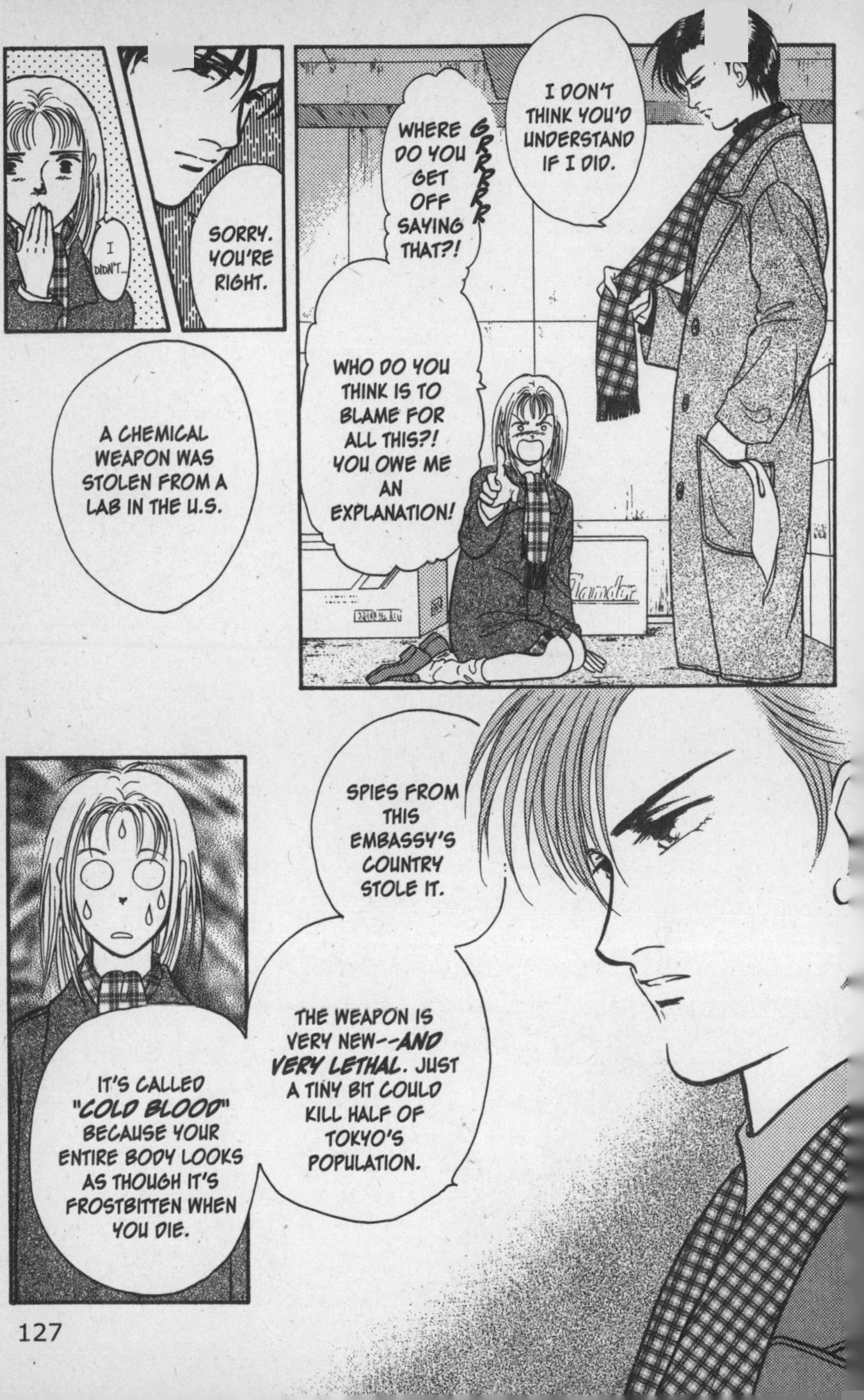
I DON'T THINK YOU'D UNDERSTAND IF I DID.
WHERE DO YOU GET OFF SAYING THAT?!
GRRRRR
WHO DO YOU THINK IS TO BLAME FOR ALL THIS?! YOU OWE ME AN EXPLANATION!
SORRY. YOU'RE RIGHT.
I DIDN'T...
A CHEMICAL WEAPON WAS STOLEN FROM A LAB IN THE U.S.
SPIES FROM THIS EMBASSY'S COUNTRY STOLE IT.
THE WEAPON IS VERY NEW--AND VERY LETHAL. JUST A TINY BIT COULD KILL HALF OF TOKYO'S POPULATION.
IT'S CALLED "COLD BLOOD" BECAUSE YOUR ENTIRE BODY LOOKS AS THOUGH IT'S FROSTBITTEN WHEN YOU DIE.

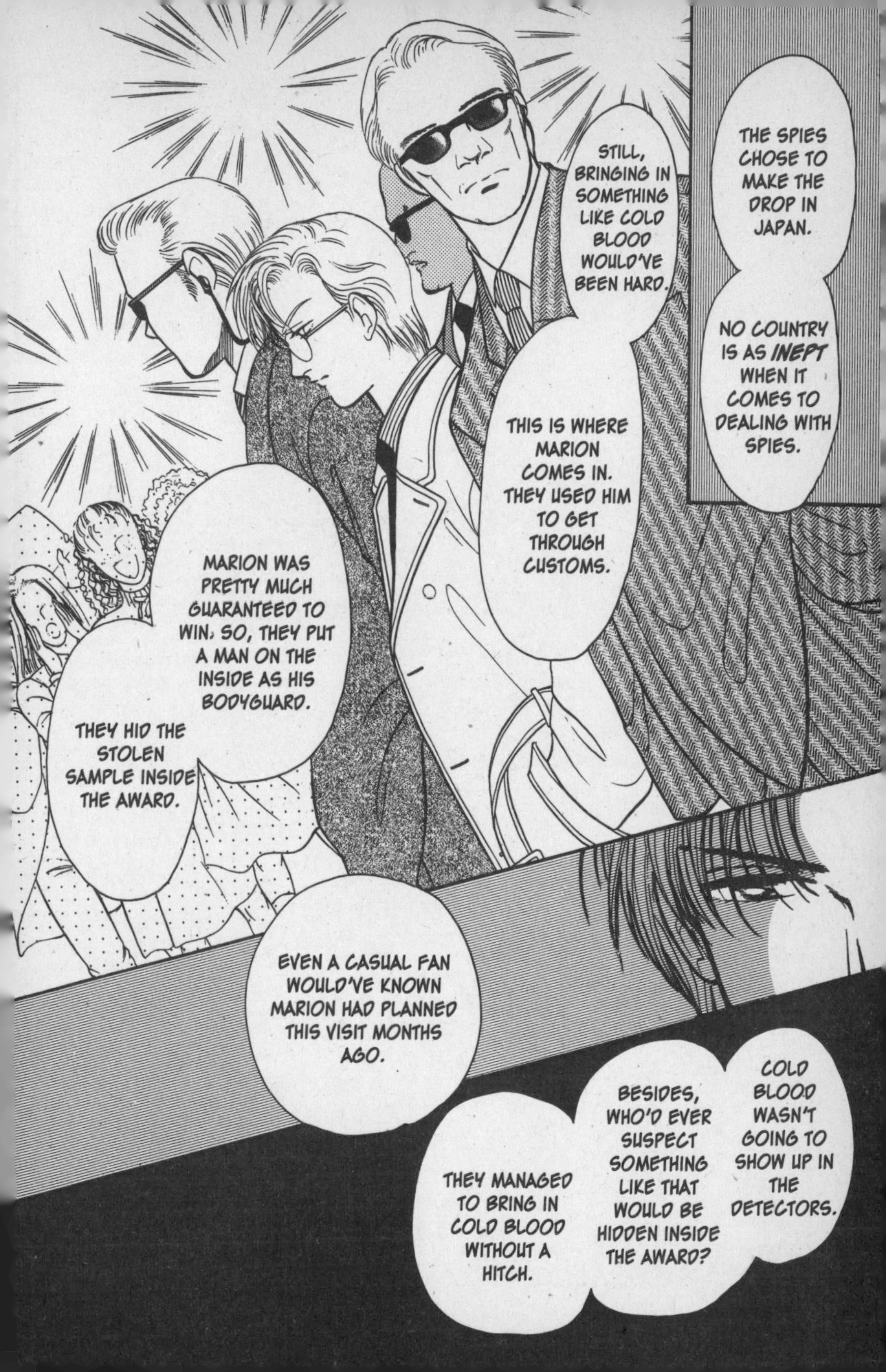
THE SPIES CHOSE TO MAKE THE DROP IN JAPAN.
NO COUNTRY IS AS *INEPT* WHEN IT COMES TO DEALING WITH SPIES.
STILL, BRINGING IN SOMETHING LIKE COLD BLOOD WOULD'VE BEEN HARD.
THIS IS WHERE MARION COMES IN. THEY USED HIM TO GET THROUGH CUSTOMS.
MARION WAS PRETTY MUCH GUARANTEED TO WIN. SO, THEY PUT A MAN ON THE INSIDE AS HIS BODYGUARD.
THEY HID THE STOLEN SAMPLE INSIDE THE AWARD.
EVEN A CASUAL FAN WOULD'VE KNOWN MARION HAD PLANNED THIS VISIT MONTHS AGO.
COLD BLOOD WASN'T GOING TO SHOW UP IN THE DETECTORS.
BESIDES, WHO'D EVER SUSPECT SOMETHING LIKE THAT WOULD BE HIDDEN INSIDE THE AWARD?
THEY MANAGED TO BRING IN COLD BLOOD WITHOUT A HITCH.

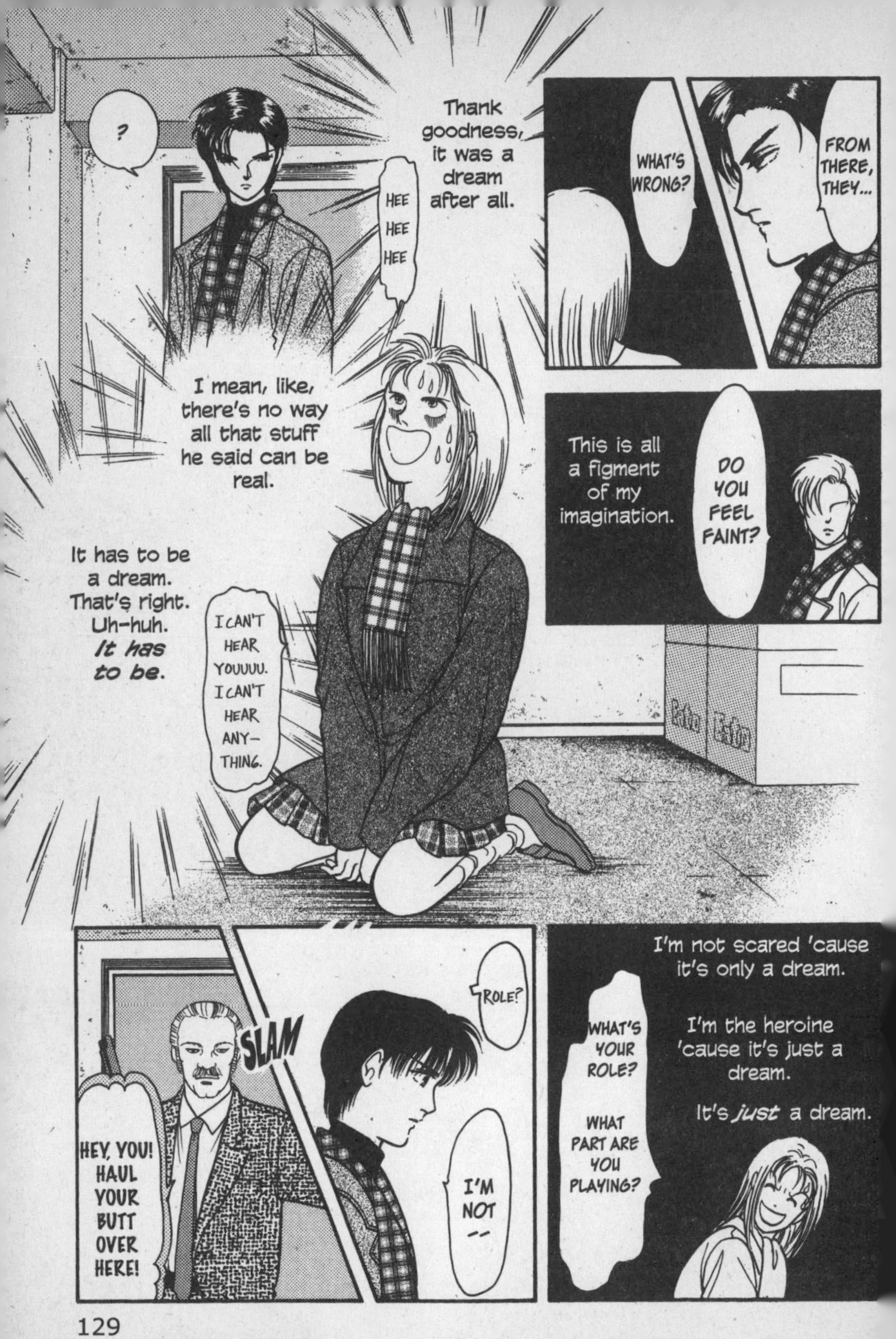
FROM THERE, THEY...
WHAT'S WRONG?
DO YOU FEEL FAINT?
This is all a figment of my imagination.
Thank goodness, it was a dream after all.
HEE HEE HEE
?
I mean, like, there's no way all that stuff he said can be real.
It has to be a dream. That's right. Uh-huh. *It has to be*.
I CAN'T HEAR YOUUUU. I CAN'T HEAR ANY-THING.
I'm not scared 'cause it's only a dream.
I'm the heroine 'cause it's just a dream.
It's *just* a dream.
WHAT'S YOUR ROLE?
WHAT PART ARE YOU PLAYING?
ROLE?
I'M NOT --
SLAM
HEY, YOU! HAUL YOUR BUTT OVER HERE!

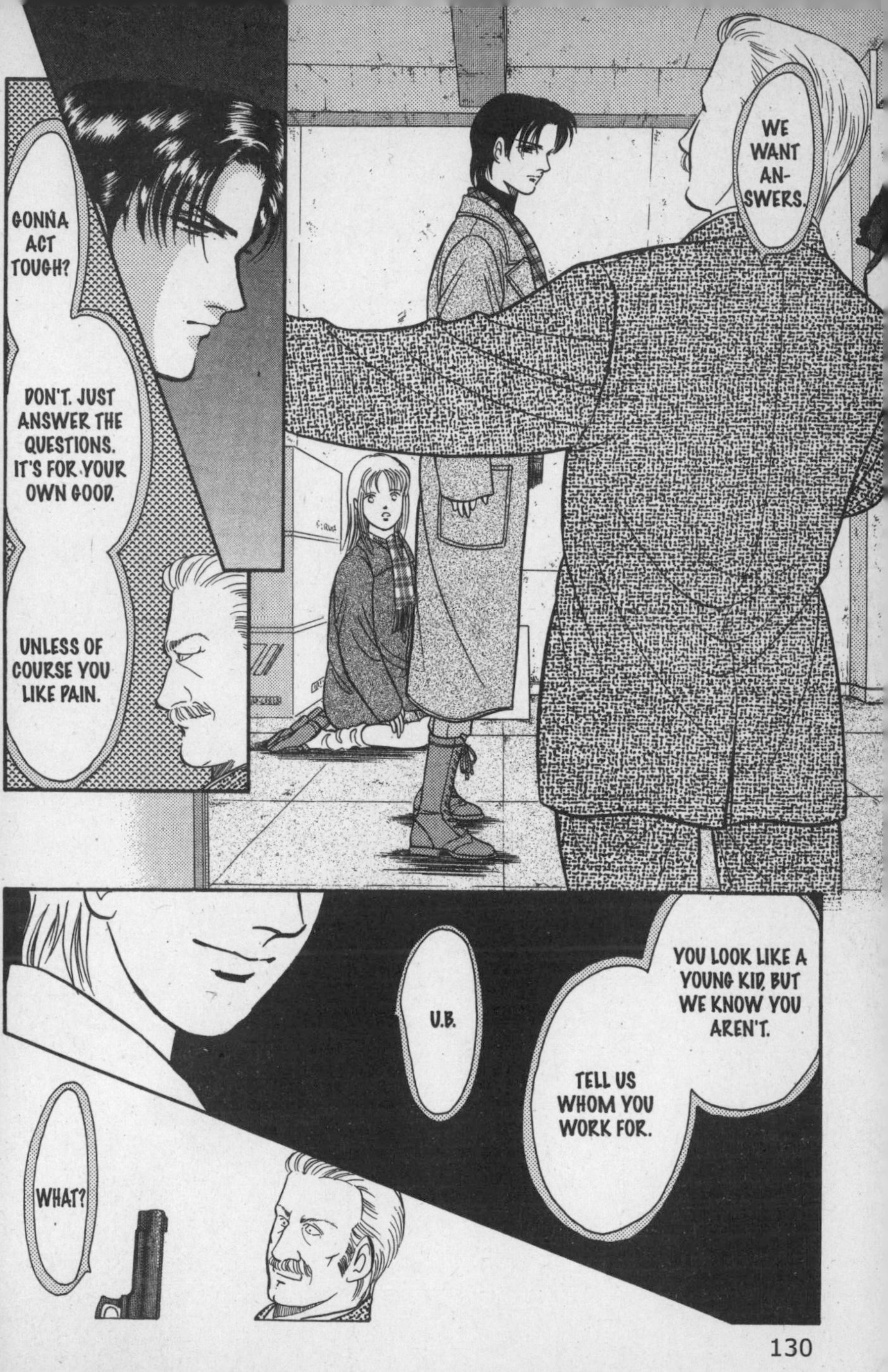
WE WANT AN-SWERS.
GONNA ACT TOUGH?
DON'T. JUST ANSWER THE QUESTIONS. IT'S FOR YOUR OWN GOOD.
UNLESS OF COURSE YOU LIKE PAIN.
YOU LOOK LIKE A YOUNG KID, BUT WE KNOW YOU AREN'T.
TELL US WHOM YOU WORK FOR.
U.B.
WHAT?

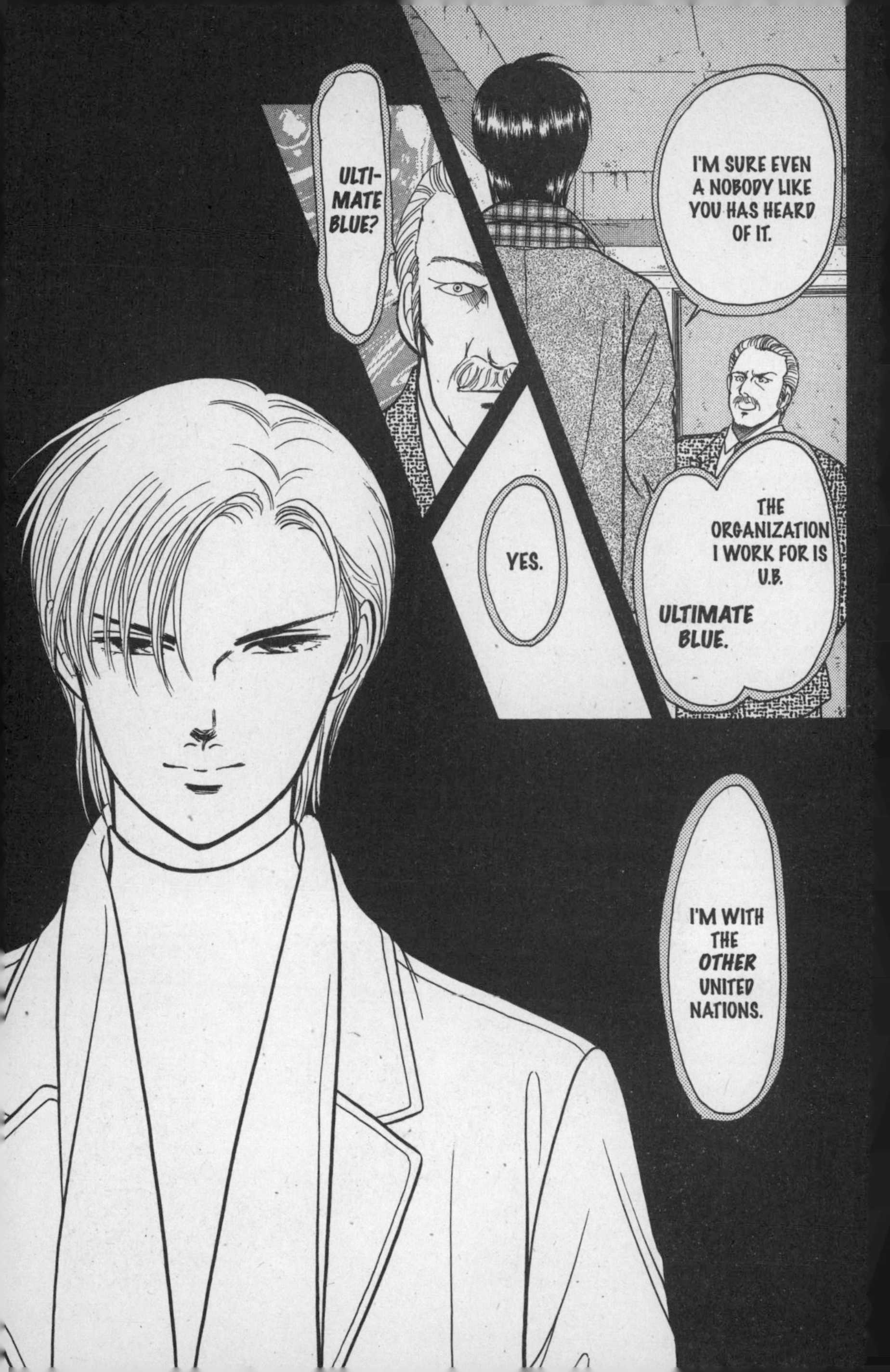
I'M SURE EVEN A NOBODY LIKE YOU HAS HEARD OF IT.
THE ORGANIZATION I WORK FOR IS U.B.
ULTIMATE BLUE.
ULTI-MATE BLUE?
YES.
I'M WITH THE *OTHER* UNITED NATIONS.

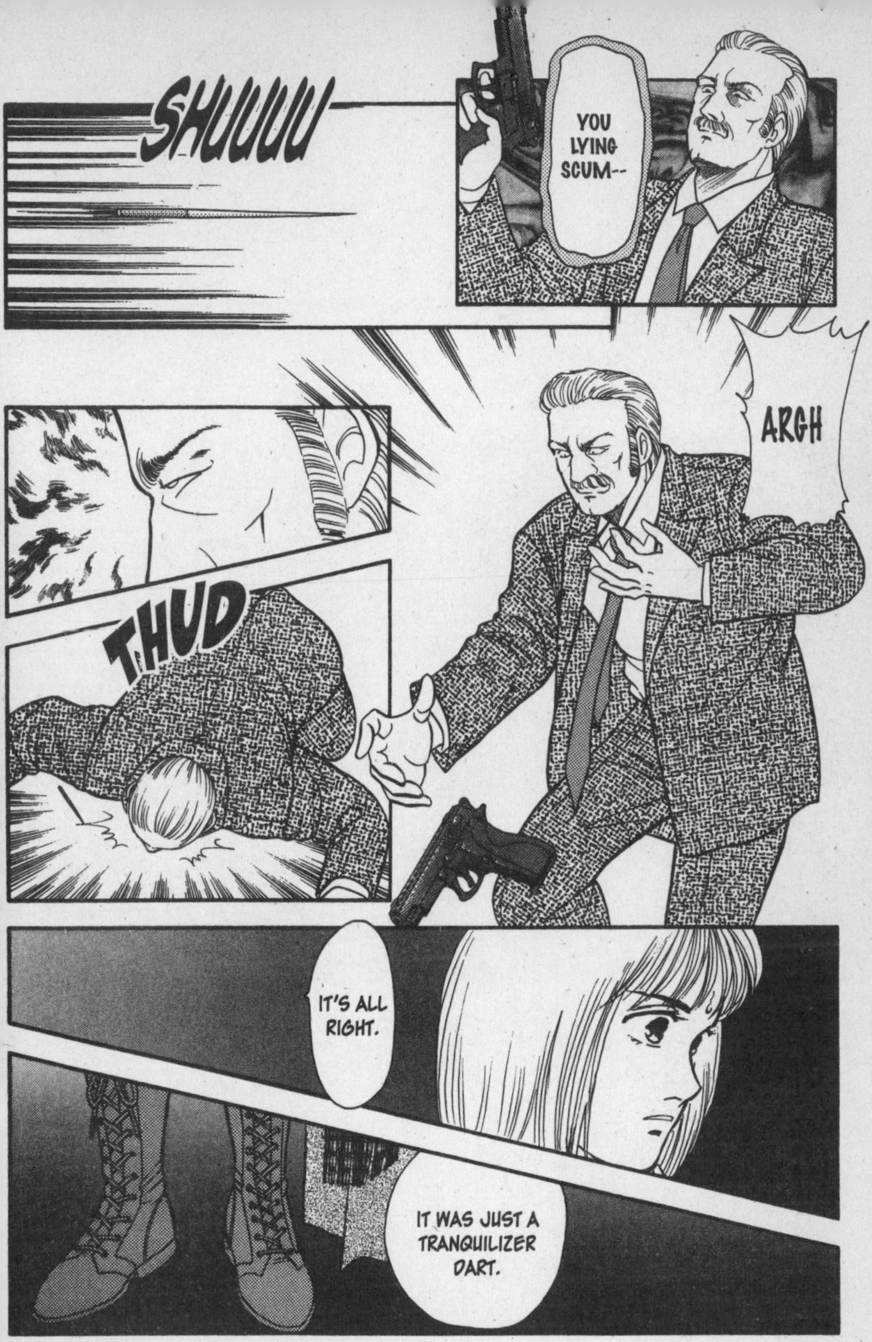
YOU LYING SCUM--
SHUUUUU
ARGH
THUD
IT'S ALL RIGHT.
IT WAS JUST A TRANQUILIZER DART.

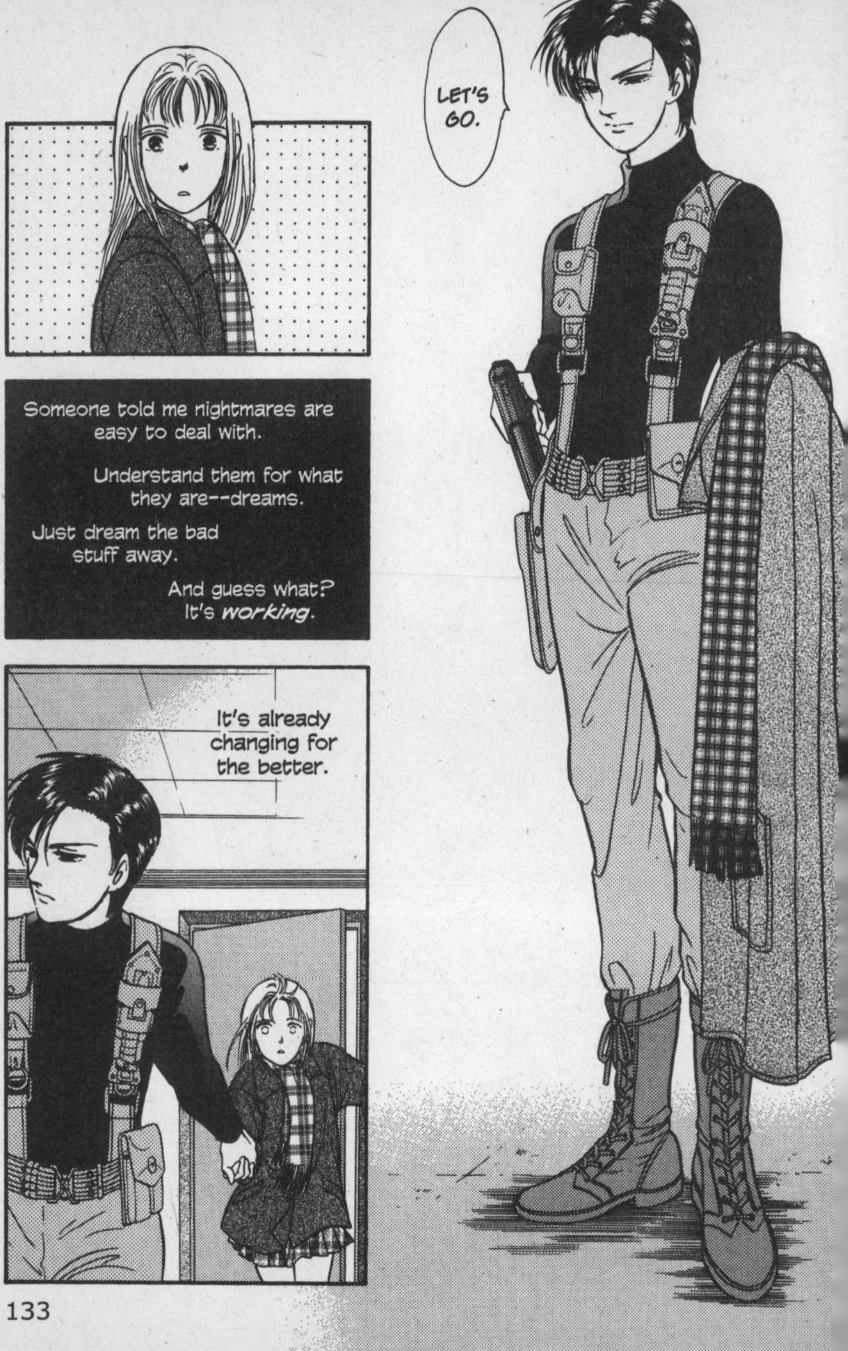
LET'S GO.
Someone told me nightmares are easy to deal with.
Understand them for what they are--dreams.
Just dream the bad stuff away.
And guess what? It's *working*.
It's already changing for the better.

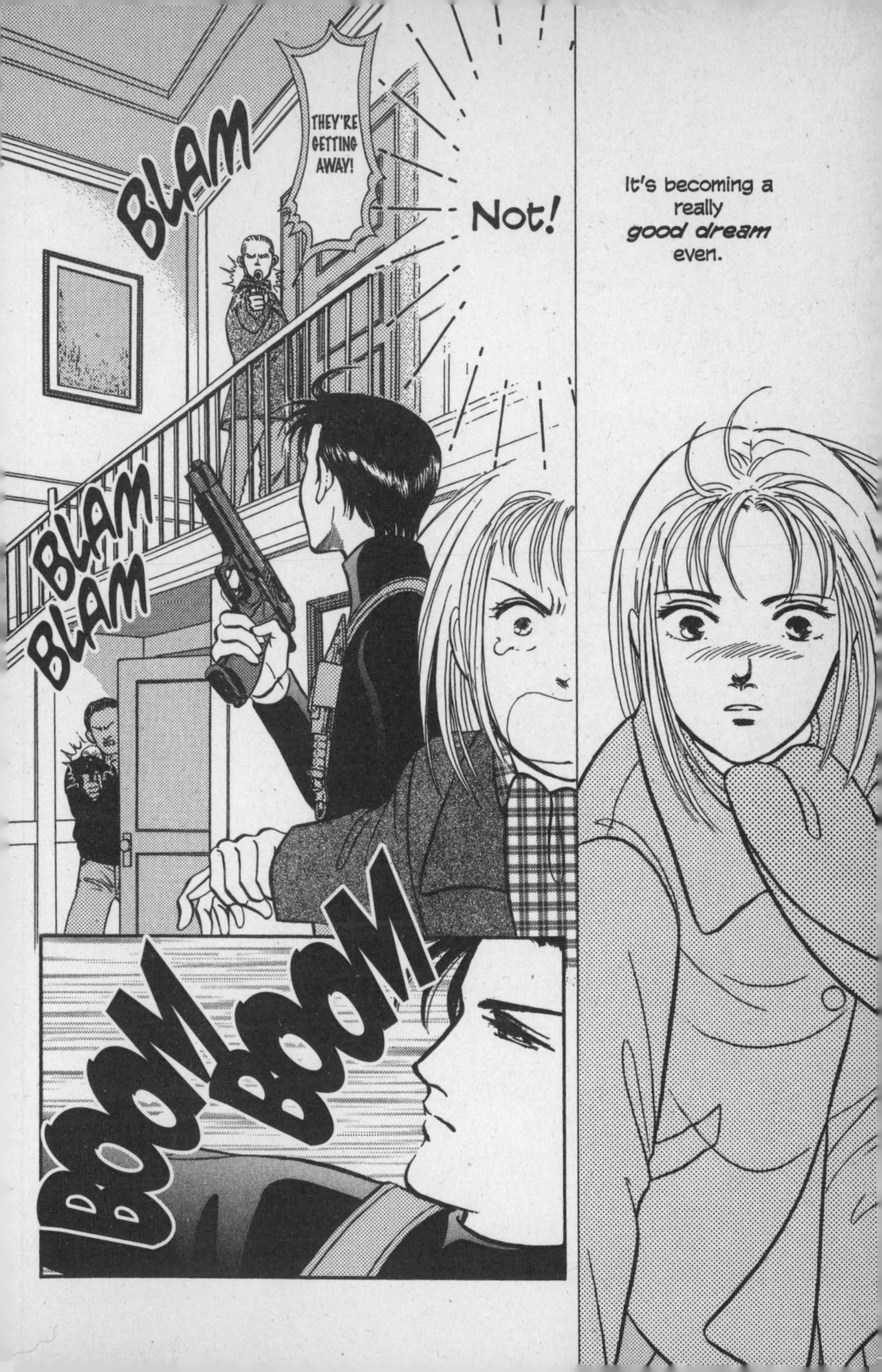
It's becoming a really good dream even.
THEY'RE GETTING AWAY!
Not!
BLAM
BLAM BLAM
BOOM BOOM

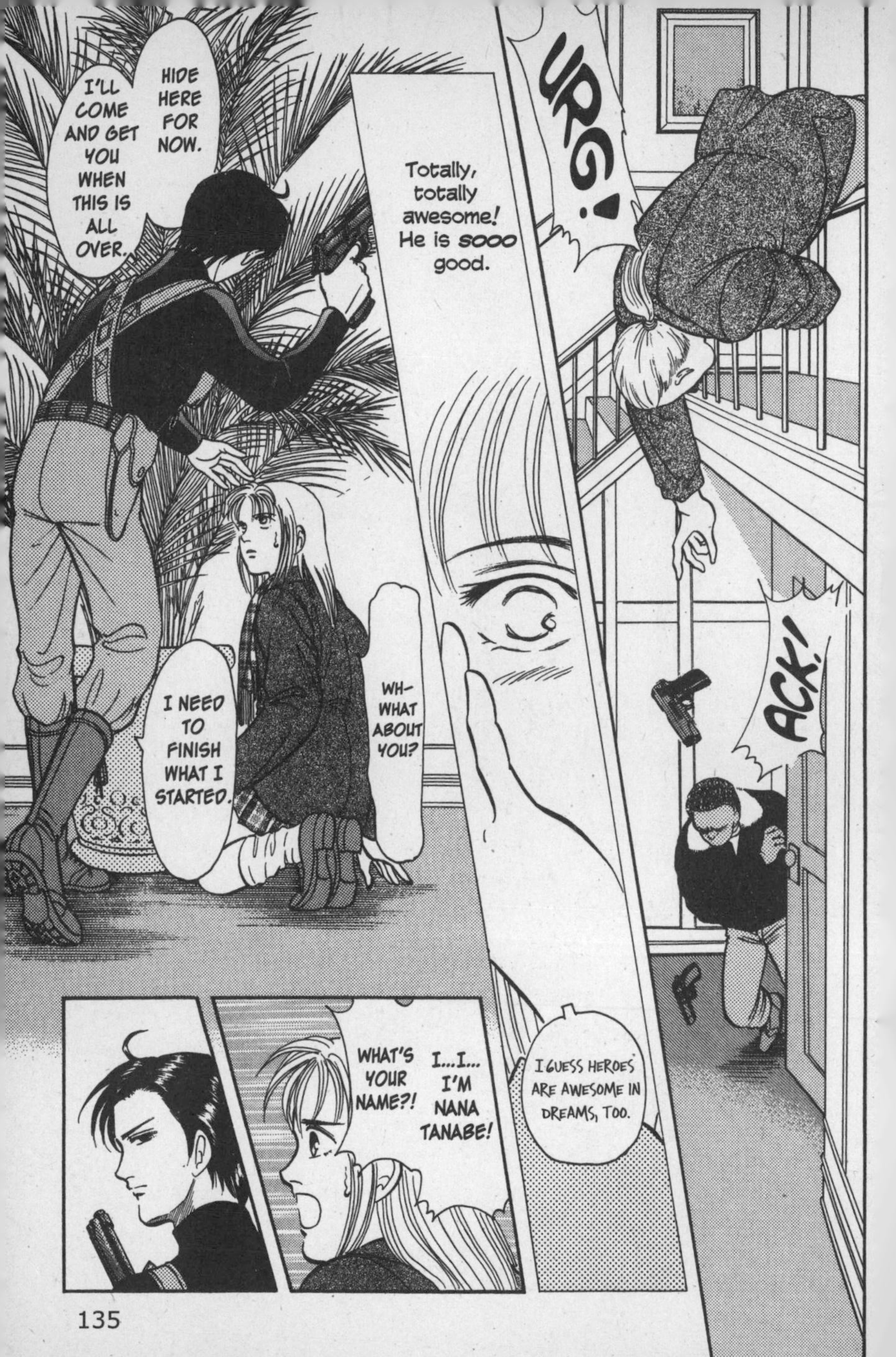
URG!
ACK!
Totally, totally awesome! He is sooo good.
I GUESS HEROES ARE AWESOME IN DREAMS, TOO.
HIDE HERE FOR NOW.
I'LL COME AND GET YOU WHEN THIS IS ALL OVER.
WH-WHAT ABOUT YOU?
I NEED TO FINISH WHAT I STARTED.
I...I... I'M NANA TANABE!
WHAT'S YOUR NAME?!

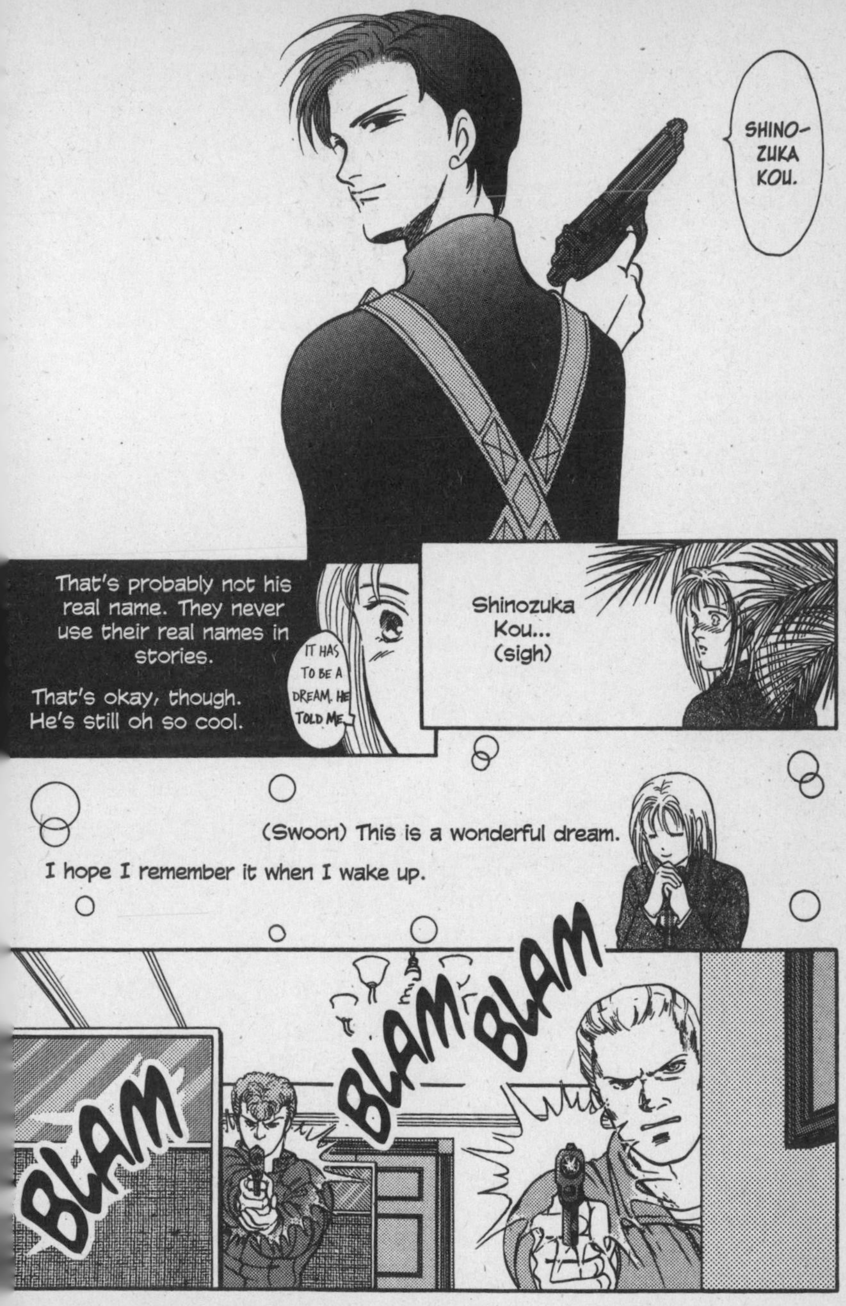
SHINOZUKA KOU.
Shinozuka Kou... (sigh)
IT HAS TO BE A DREAM. HE TOLD ME.
That's probably not his real name. They never use their real names in stories.
That's okay, though. He's still oh so cool.
(Swoon) This is a wonderful dream.
I hope I remember it when I wake up.
BLAM
BLAM
BLAM
BLAM

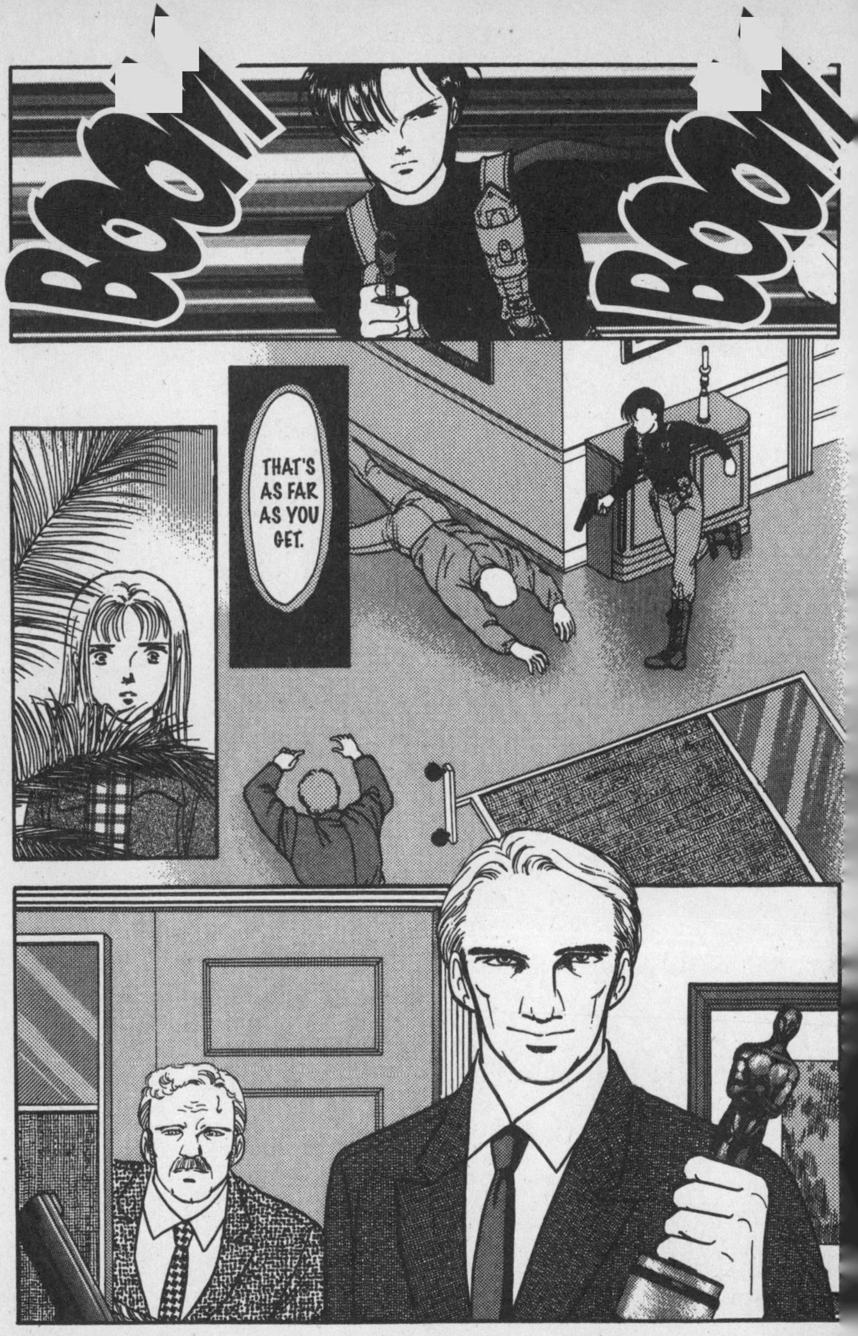
BOOM
BOOM
THAT'S AS FAR AS YOU GET.

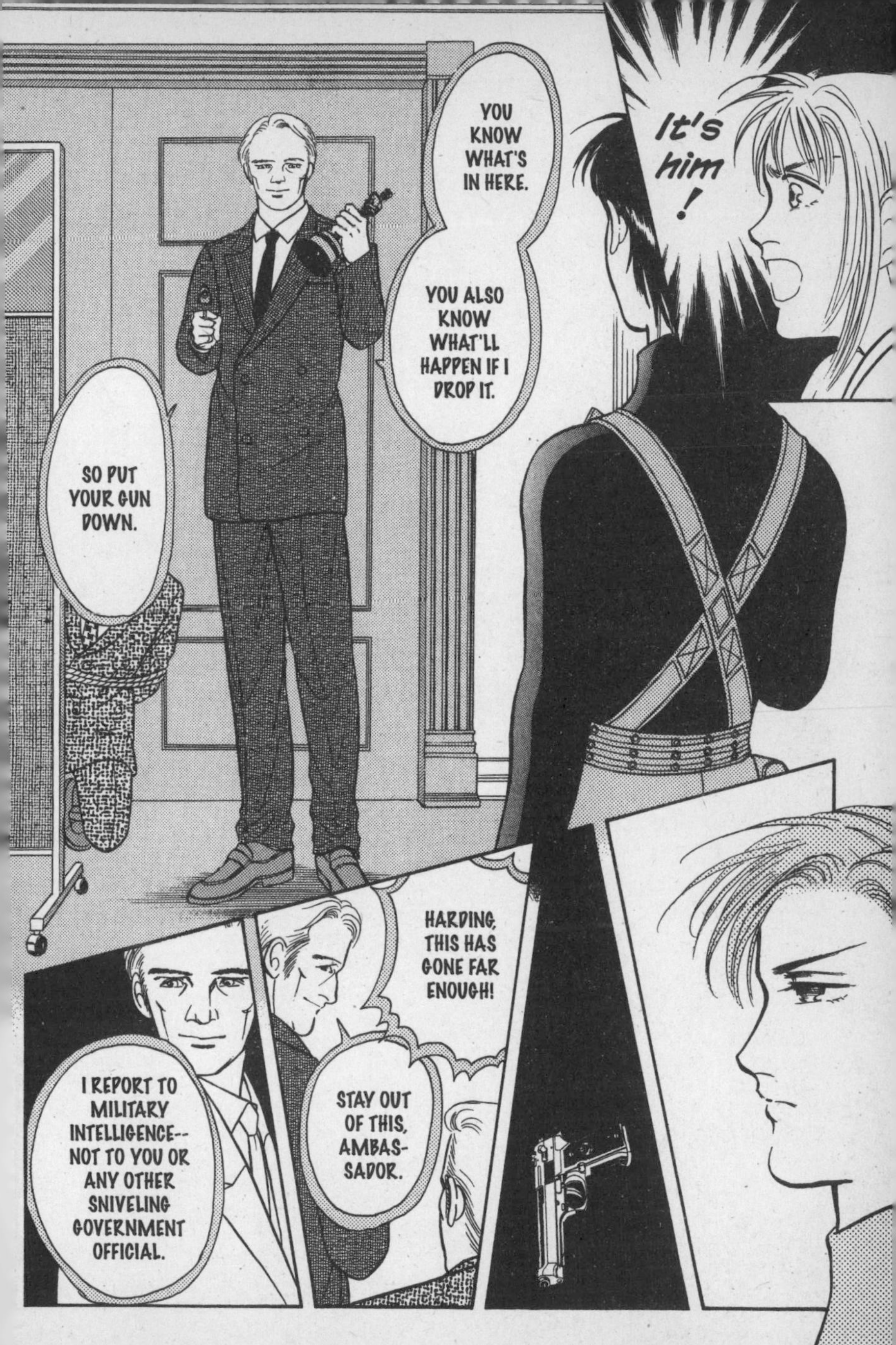
It's him!
YOU KNOW WHAT'S IN HERE.
YOU ALSO KNOW WHAT'LL HAPPEN IF I DROP IT.
SO PUT YOUR GUN DOWN.
HARDING, THIS HAS GONE FAR ENOUGH!
STAY OUT OF THIS, AMBAS-SADOR.
I REPORT TO MILITARY INTELLIGENCE-- NOT TO YOU OR ANY OTHER SNIVELING GOVERNMENT OFFICIAL.

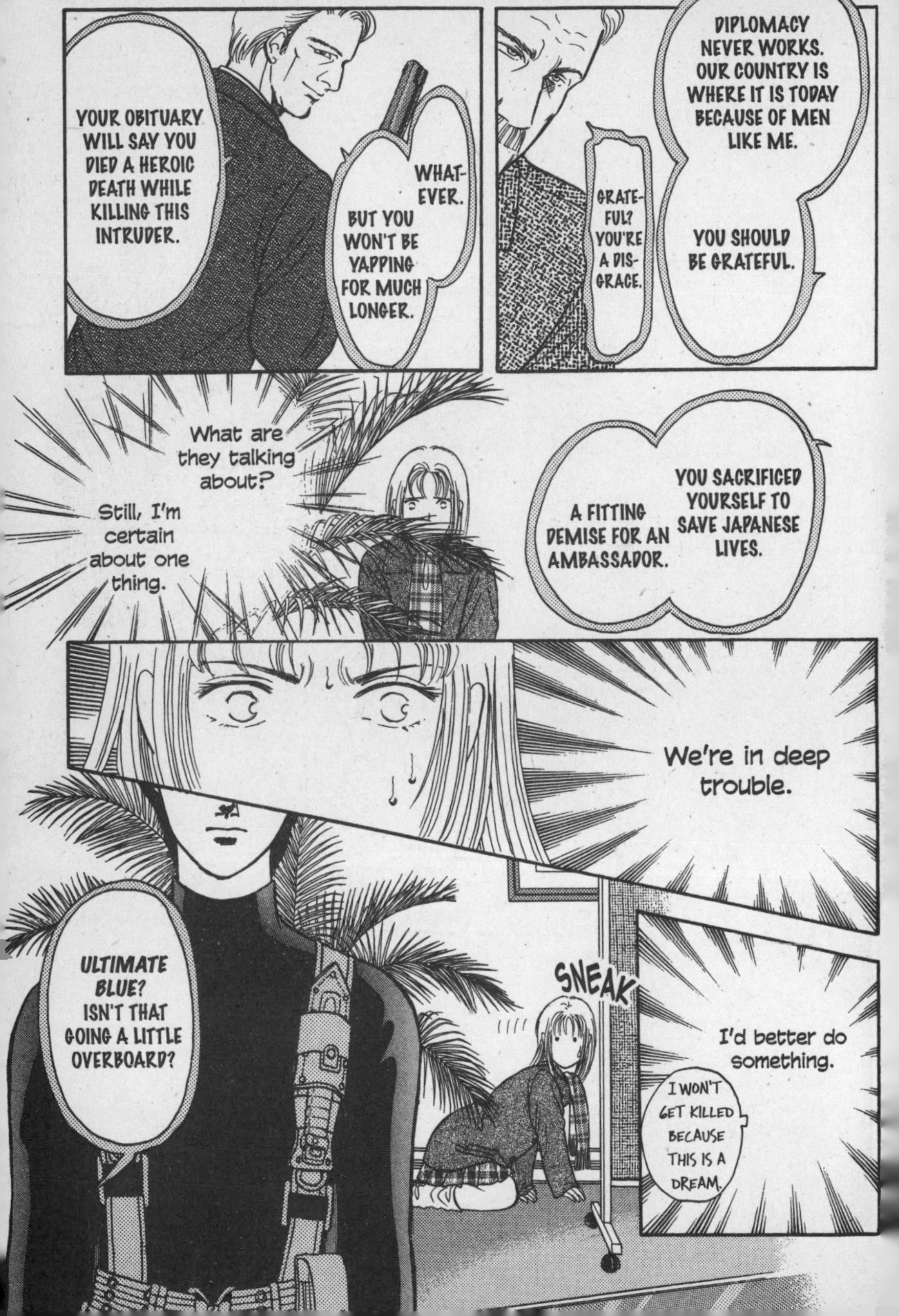
DIPLOMACY NEVER WORKS. OUR COUNTRY IS WHERE IT IS TODAY BECAUSE OF MEN LIKE ME.
YOU SHOULD BE GRATEFUL.
GRATEFUL? YOU'RE A DISGRACE.
WHATEVER.
BUT YOU WON'T BE YAPPING FOR MUCH LONGER.
YOUR OBITUARY WILL SAY YOU DIED A HEROIC DEATH WHILE KILLING THIS INTRUDER.
YOU SACRIFICED YOURSELF TO SAVE JAPANESE LIVES.
A FITTING DEMISE FOR AN AMBASSADOR.
What are they talking about?
Still, I'm certain about one thing.
We're in deep trouble.
I'd better do something.
I WON'T GET KILLED BECAUSE THIS IS A DREAM.
SNEAK
ULTIMATE BLUE? ISN'T THAT GOING A LITTLE OVERBOARD?

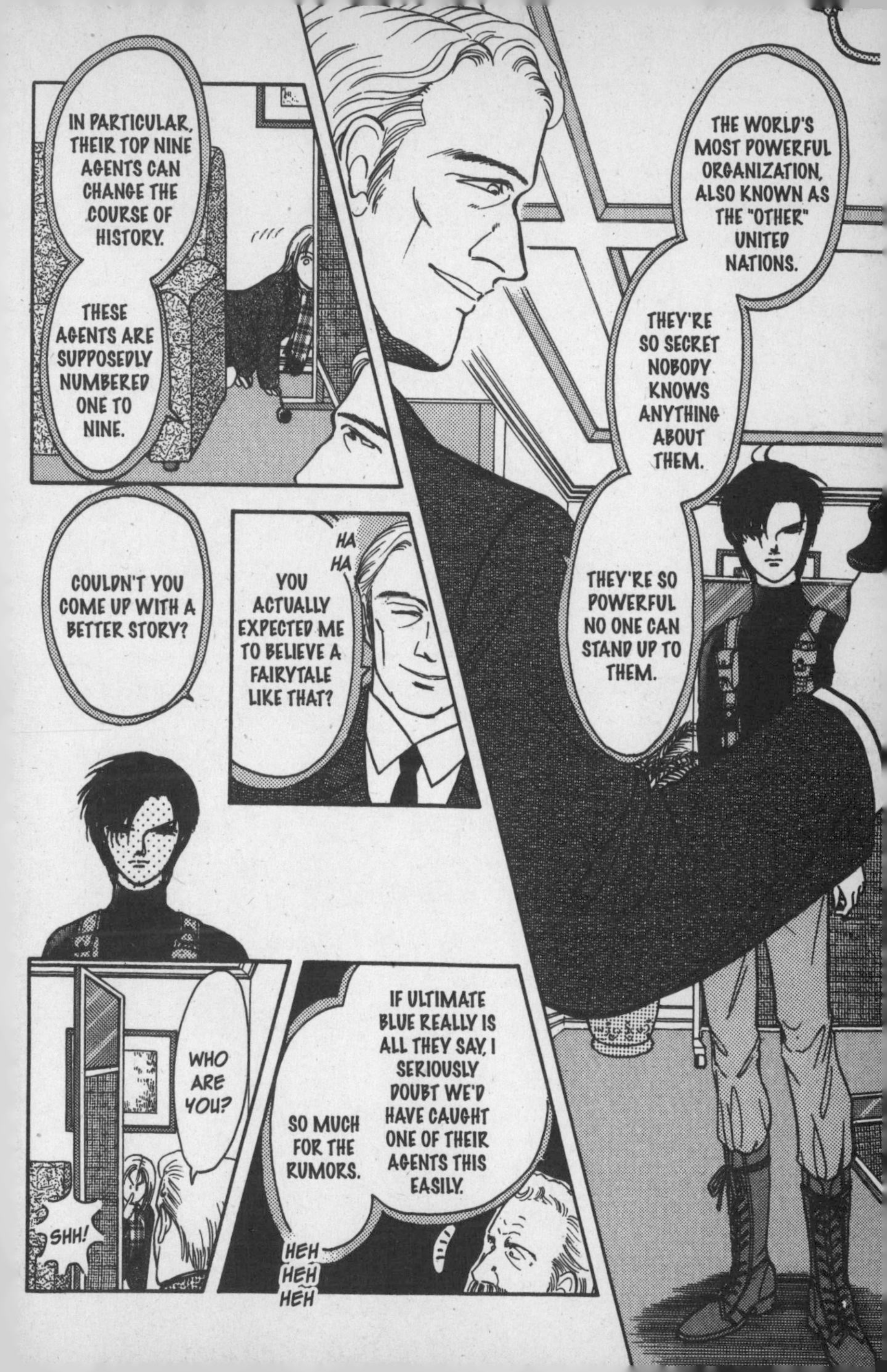
THE WORLD'S MOST POWERFUL ORGANIZATION, ALSO KNOWN AS THE "OTHER" UNITED NATIONS.
THEY'RE SO SECRET NOBODY KNOWS ANYTHING ABOUT THEM.
THEY'RE SO POWERFUL NO ONE CAN STAND UP TO THEM.
IN PARTICULAR, THEIR TOP NINE AGENTS CAN CHANGE THE COURSE OF HISTORY.
THESE AGENTS ARE SUPPOSEDLY NUMBERED ONE TO NINE.
HA HA
YOU ACTUALLY EXPECTED ME TO BELIEVE A FAIRYTALE LIKE THAT?
COULDN'T YOU COME UP WITH A BETTER STORY?
IF ULTIMATE BLUE REALLY IS ALL THEY SAY, I SERIOUSLY DOUBT WE'D HAVE CAUGHT ONE OF THEIR AGENTS THIS EASILY.
SO MUCH FOR THE RUMORS.
HEH HEH HEH
WHO ARE YOU?
SHH!

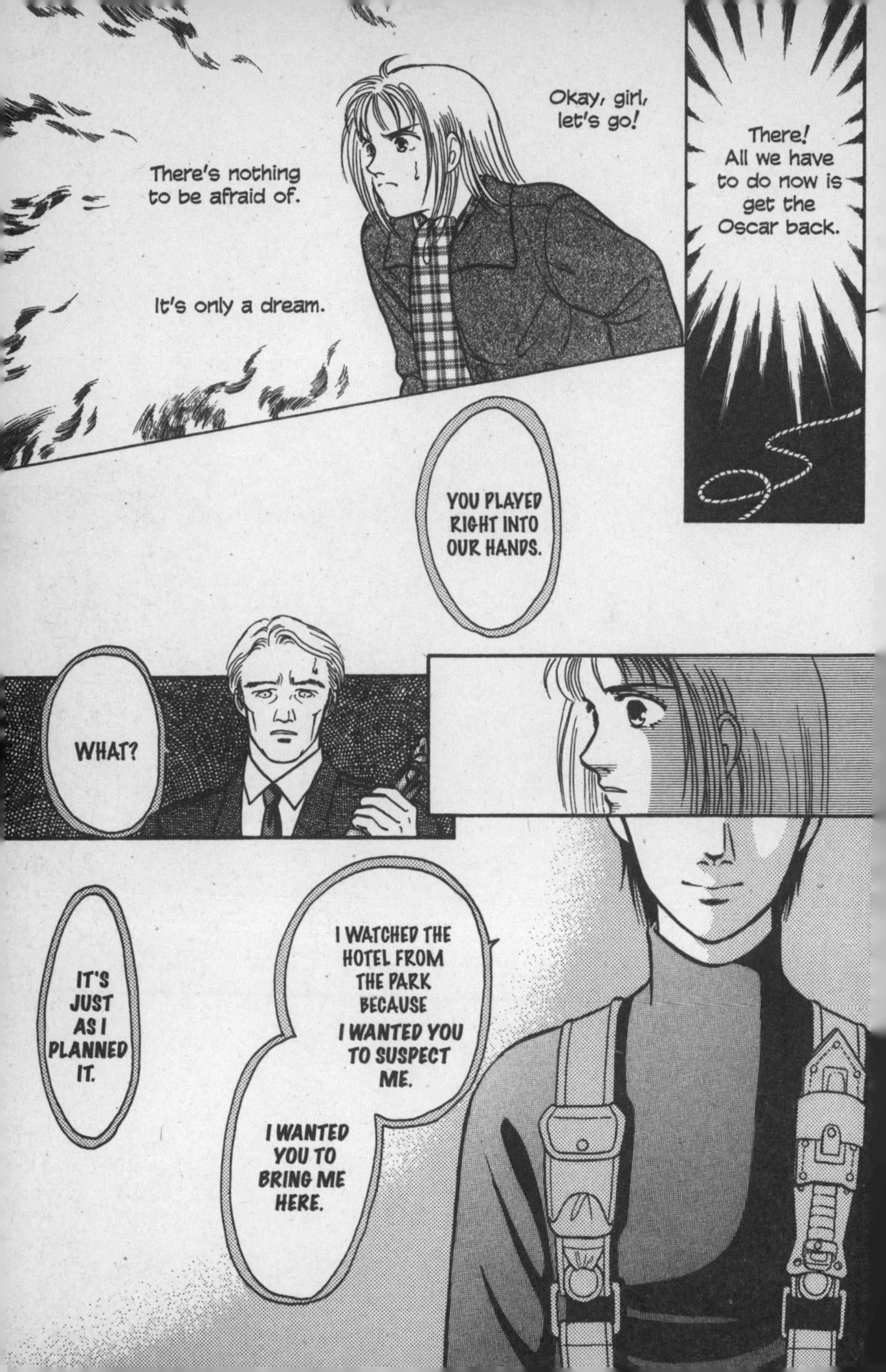
There! All we have to do now is get the Oscar back.
Okay, girl, let's go!
There's nothing to be afraid of.
It's only a dream.
YOU PLAYED RIGHT INTO OUR HANDS.
WHAT?
I WATCHED THE HOTEL FROM THE PARK BECAUSE I WANTED YOU TO SUSPECT ME.
I WANTED YOU TO BRING ME HERE.
IT'S JUST AS I PLANNED IT.

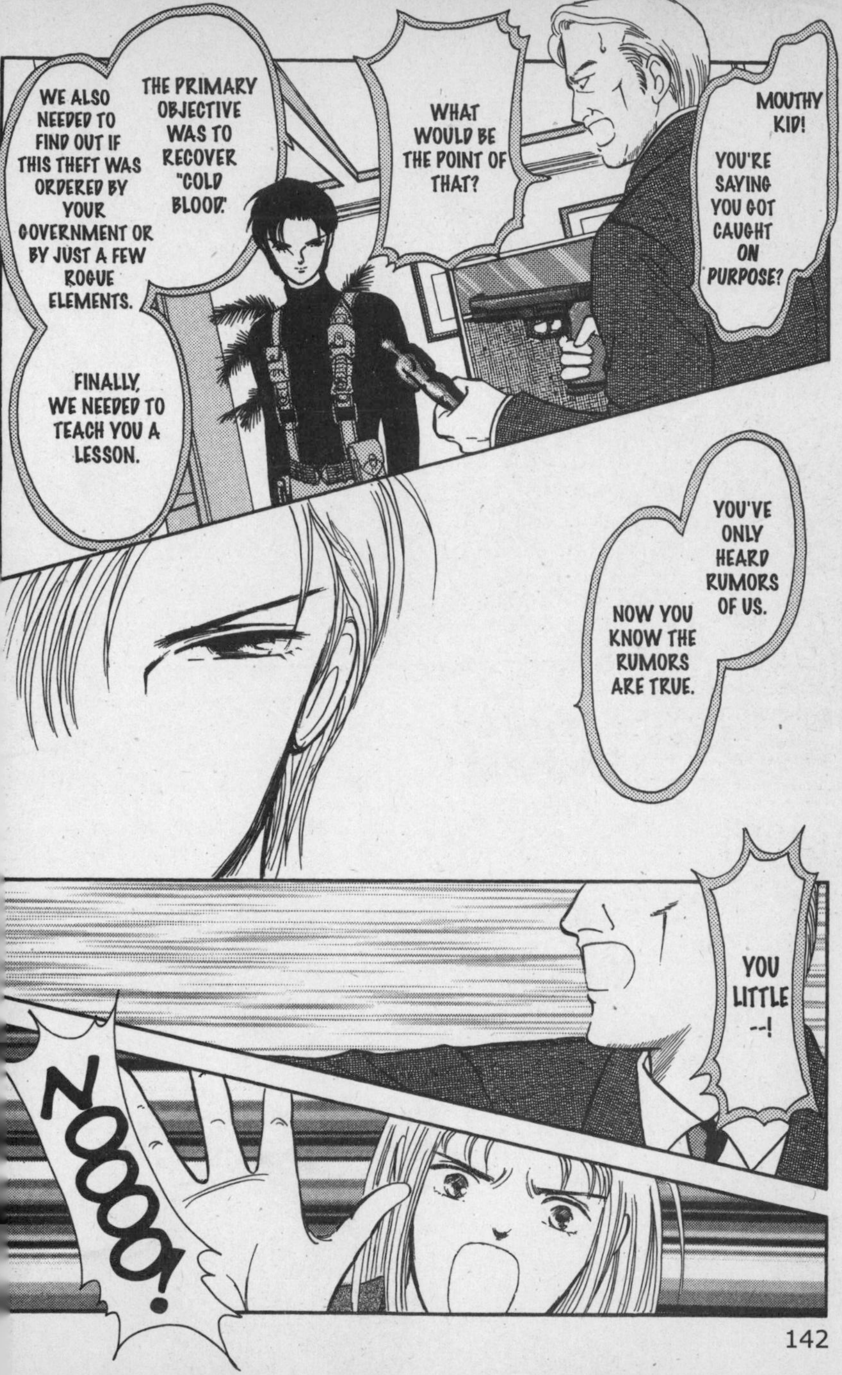
MOUTHY KID!
YOU'RE SAYING YOU GOT CAUGHT ON PURPOSE?
WHAT WOULD BE THE POINT OF THAT?
THE PRIMARY OBJECTIVE WAS TO RECOVER "COLD BLOOD."
WE ALSO NEEDED TO FIND OUT IF THIS THEFT WAS ORDERED BY YOUR GOVERNMENT OR BY JUST A FEW ROGUE ELEMENTS.
FINALLY, WE NEEDED TO TEACH YOU A LESSON.
YOU'VE ONLY HEARD RUMORS OF US.
NOW YOU KNOW THE RUMORS ARE TRUE.
YOU LITTLE --!
NOOOO!

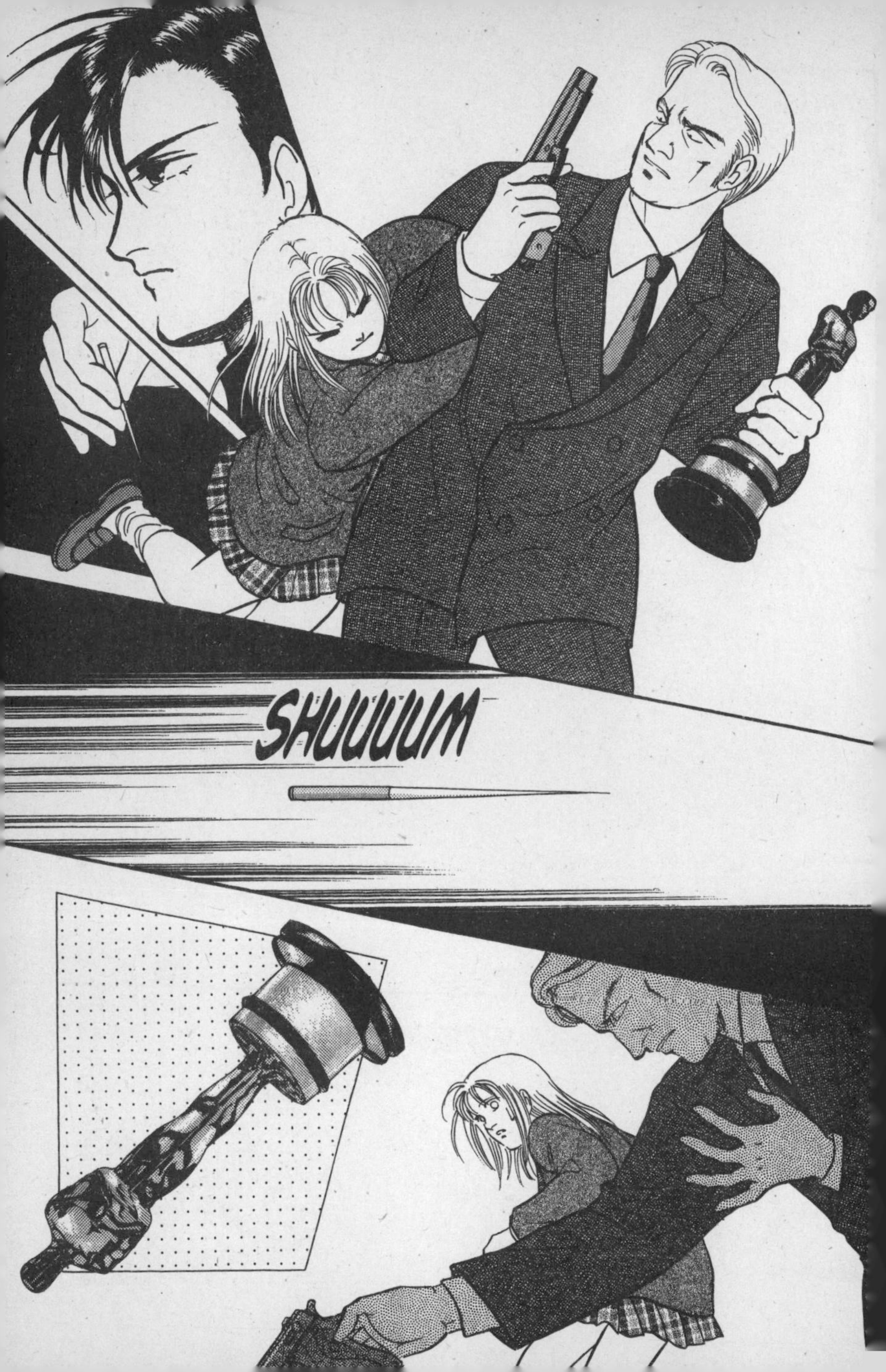
SHUUUUUM

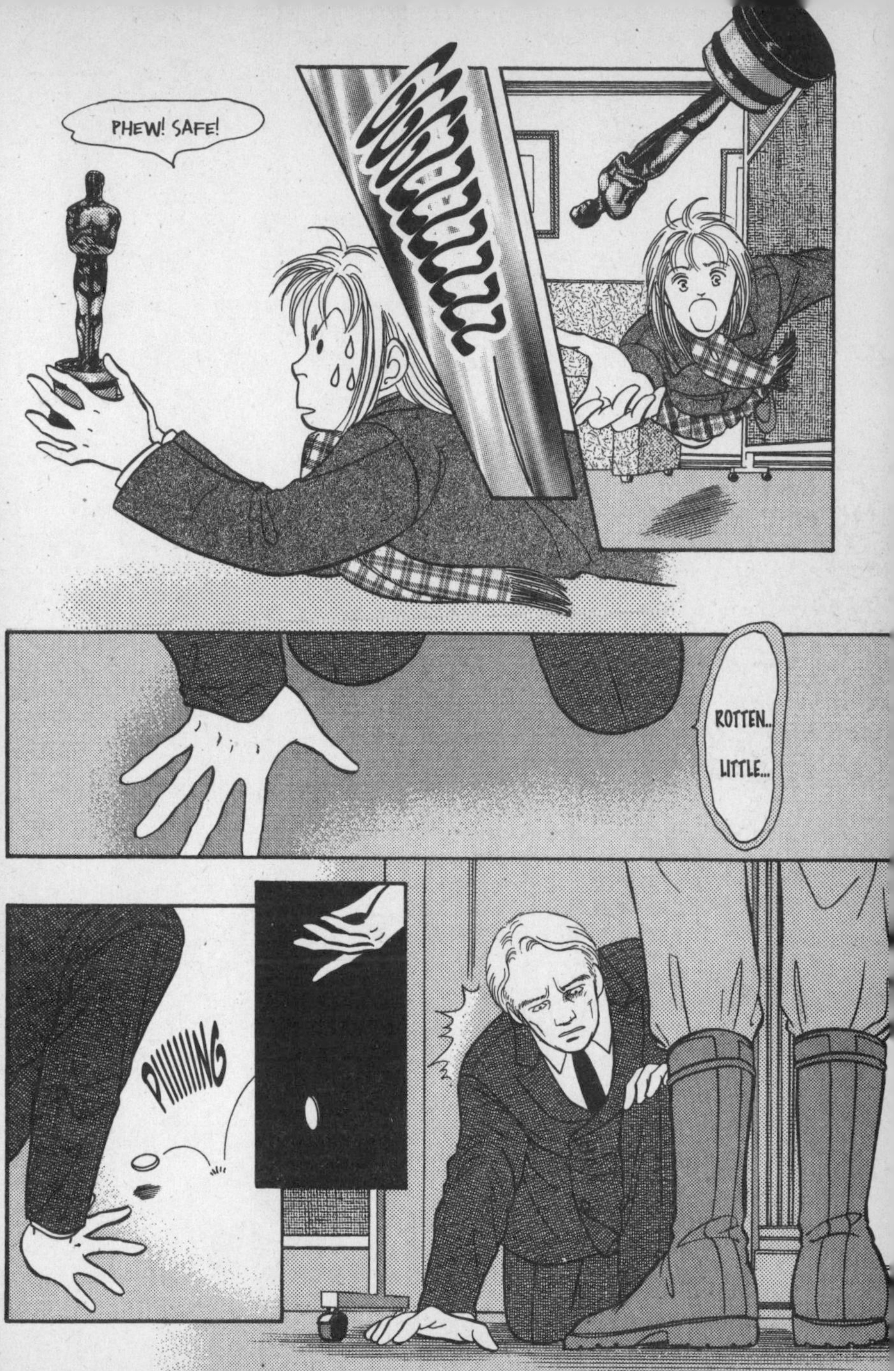
PHEW! SAFE!
ROTTEN.. LITTLE...
DIIIIING

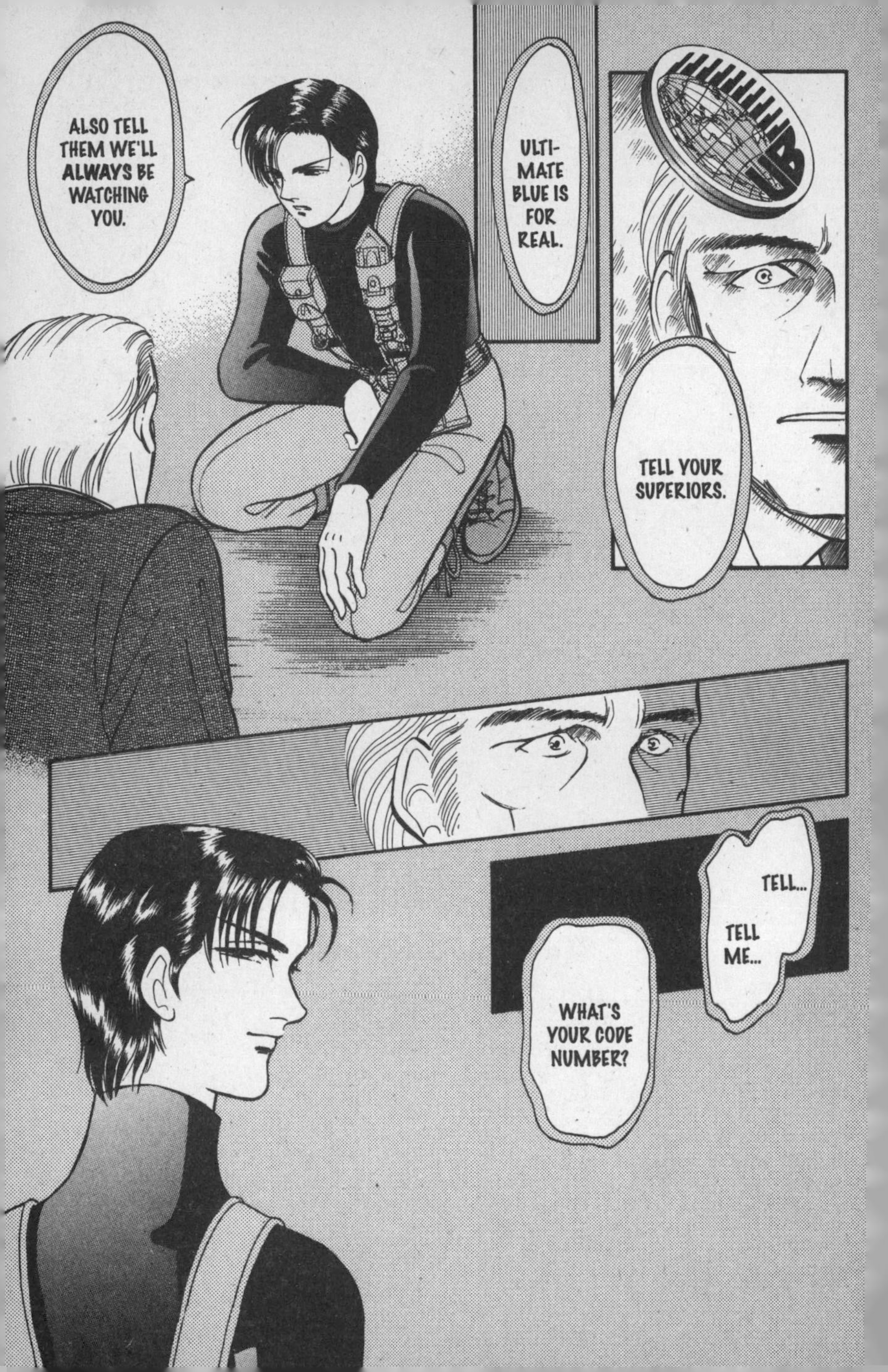
TELL YOUR SUPERIORS.
ULTI-MATE BLUE IS FOR REAL.
ALSO TELL THEM WE'LL ALWAYS BE WATCHING YOU.
TELL...
TELL ME...
WHAT'S YOUR CODE NUMBER?

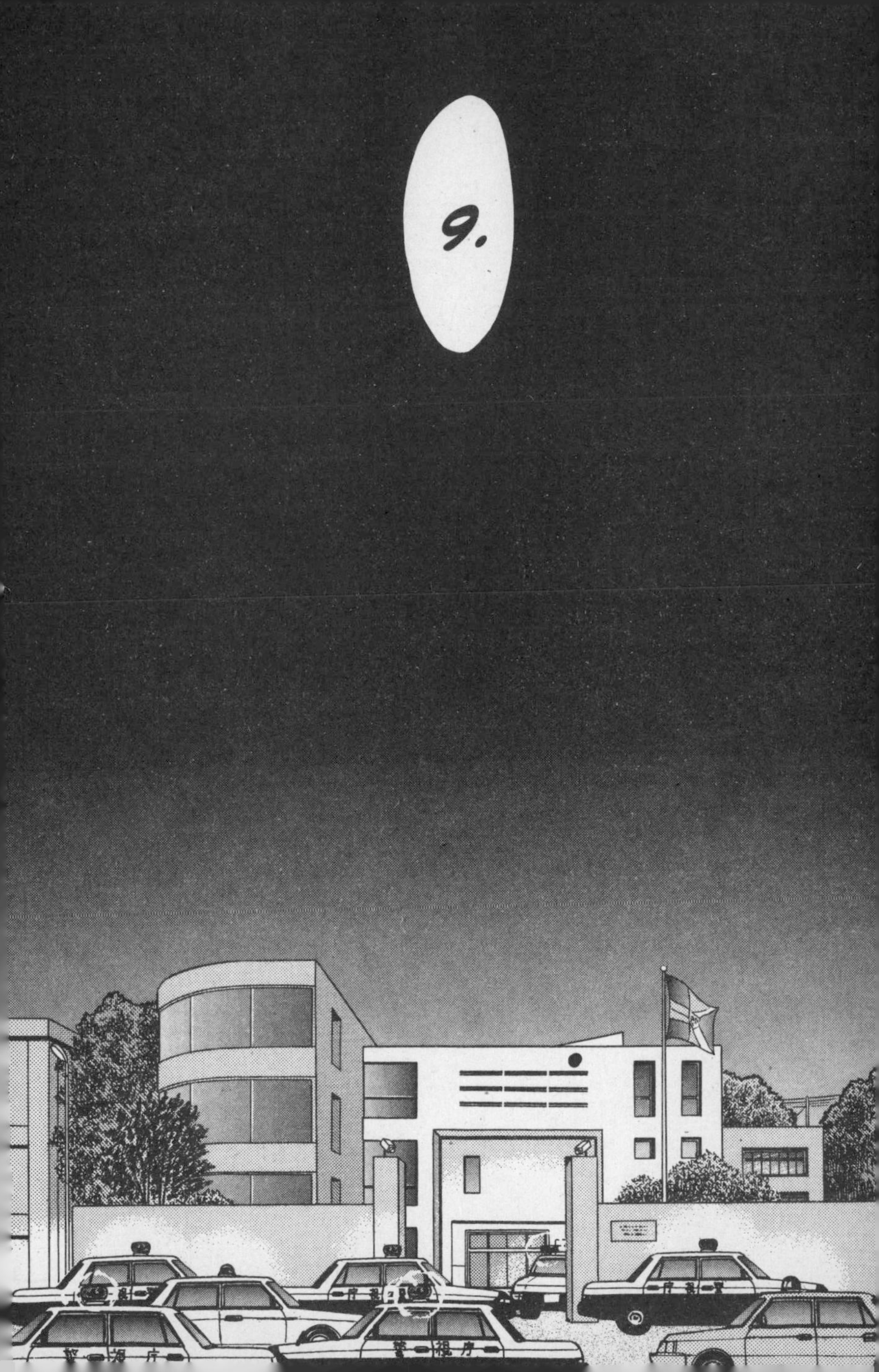
9.
警視庁

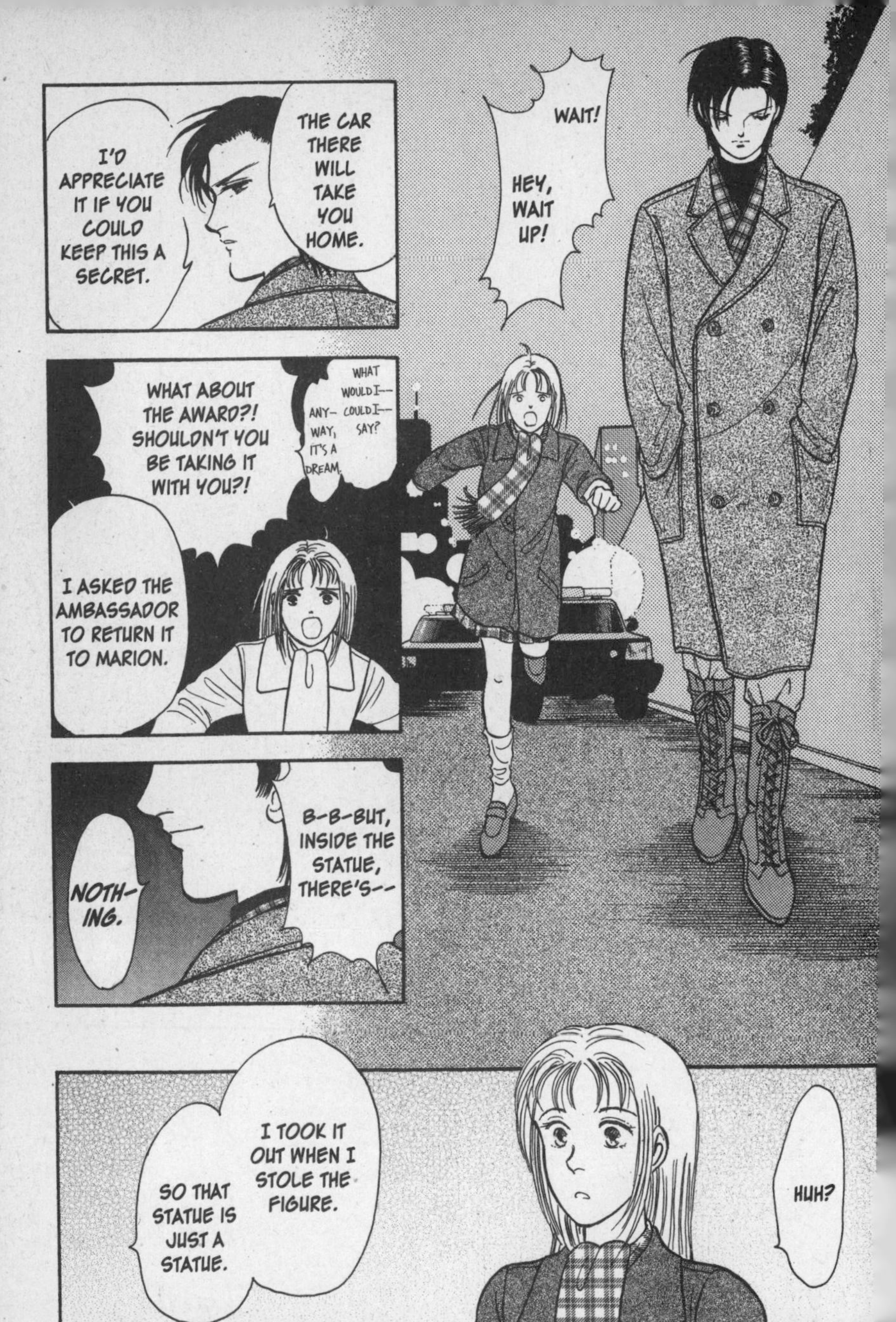
WAIT!
HEY, WAIT UP!
THE CAR THERE WILL TAKE YOU HOME.
I'D APPRECIATE IT IF YOU COULD KEEP THIS A SECRET.
WHAT WOULD I-- COULD I-- SAY?
ANY-WAY, IT'S A DREAM.
WHAT ABOUT THE AWARD?! SHOULDN'T YOU BE TAKING IT WITH YOU?!
I ASKED THE AMBASSADOR TO RETURN IT TO MARION.
B-B-BUT, INSIDE THE STATUE, THERE'S--
NOTHING.
HUH?
I TOOK IT OUT WHEN I STOLE THE FIGURE.
SO THAT STATUE IS JUST A STATUE.

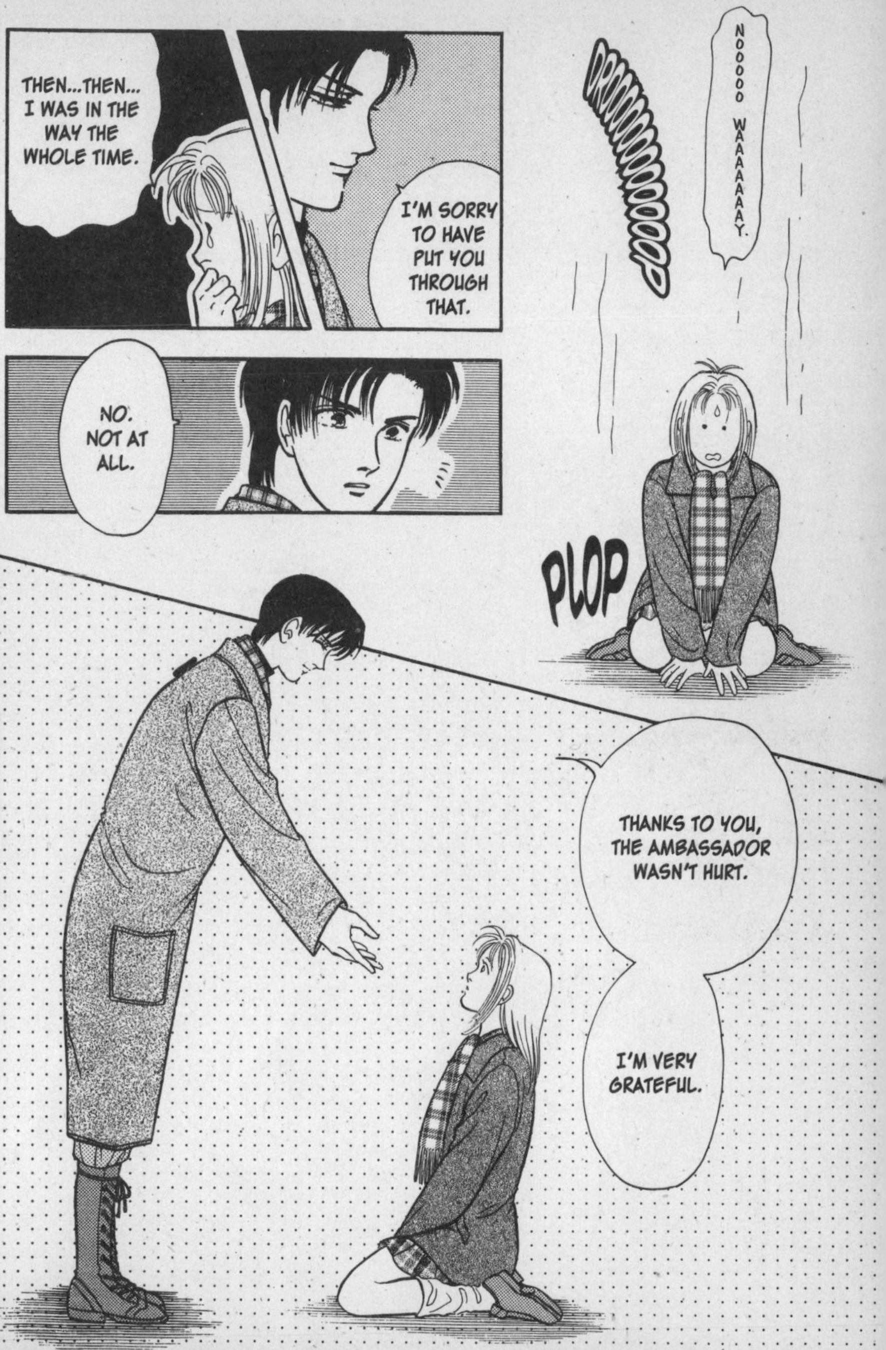
NOOOOO WAAAAAAAY.
DROOOOOOOOOOOOP
PLOP
I'M SORRY TO HAVE PUT YOU THROUGH THAT.
THEN...THEN... I WAS IN THE WAY THE WHOLE TIME.
NO. NOT AT ALL.
THANKS TO YOU, THE AMBASSADOR WASN'T HURT.
I'M VERY GRATEFUL.

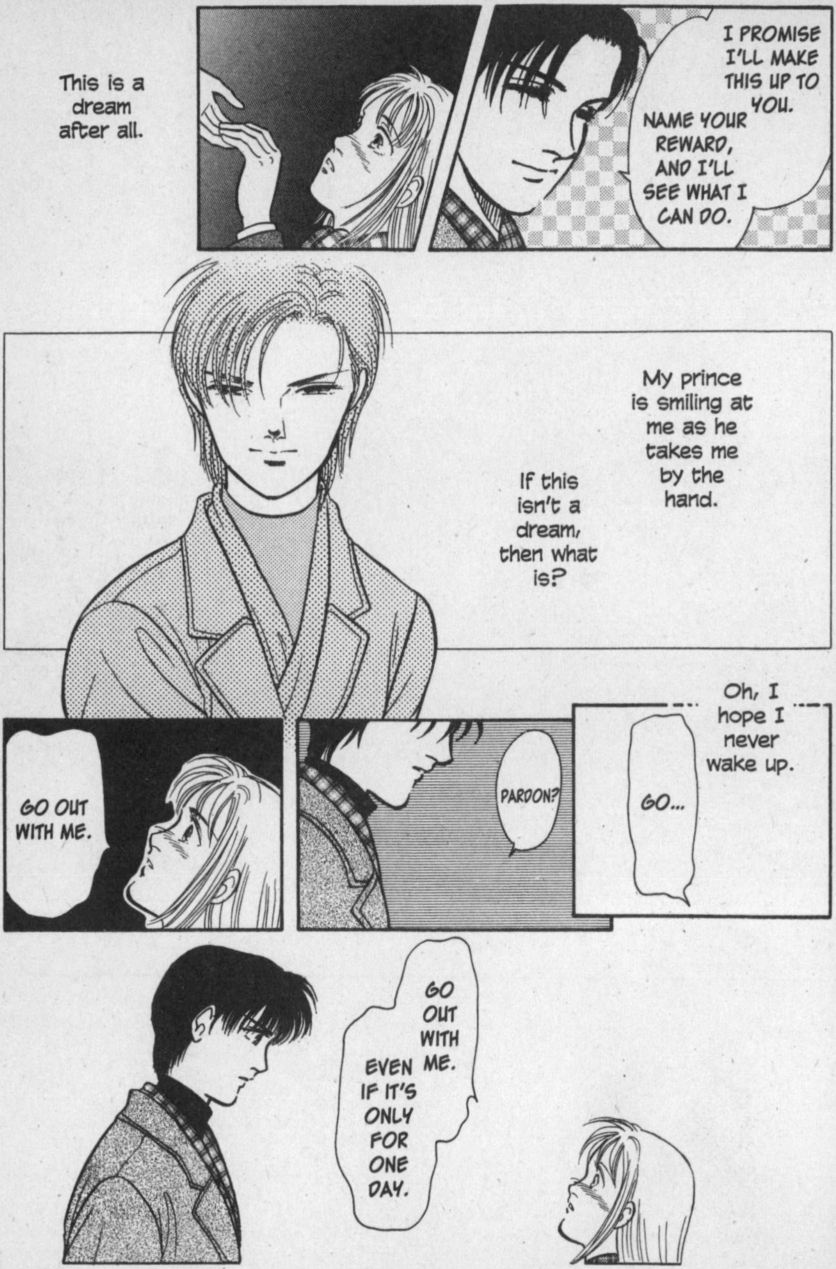
I PROMISE I'LL MAKE THIS UP TO YOU.
NAME YOUR REWARD, AND I'LL SEE WHAT I CAN DO.
This is a dream after all.
My prince is smiling at me as he takes me by the hand.
If this isn't a dream, then what is?
Oh, I hope I never wake up.
GO...
PARDON?
GO OUT WITH ME.
GO OUT WITH ME.
EVEN IF IT'S ONLY FOR ONE DAY.

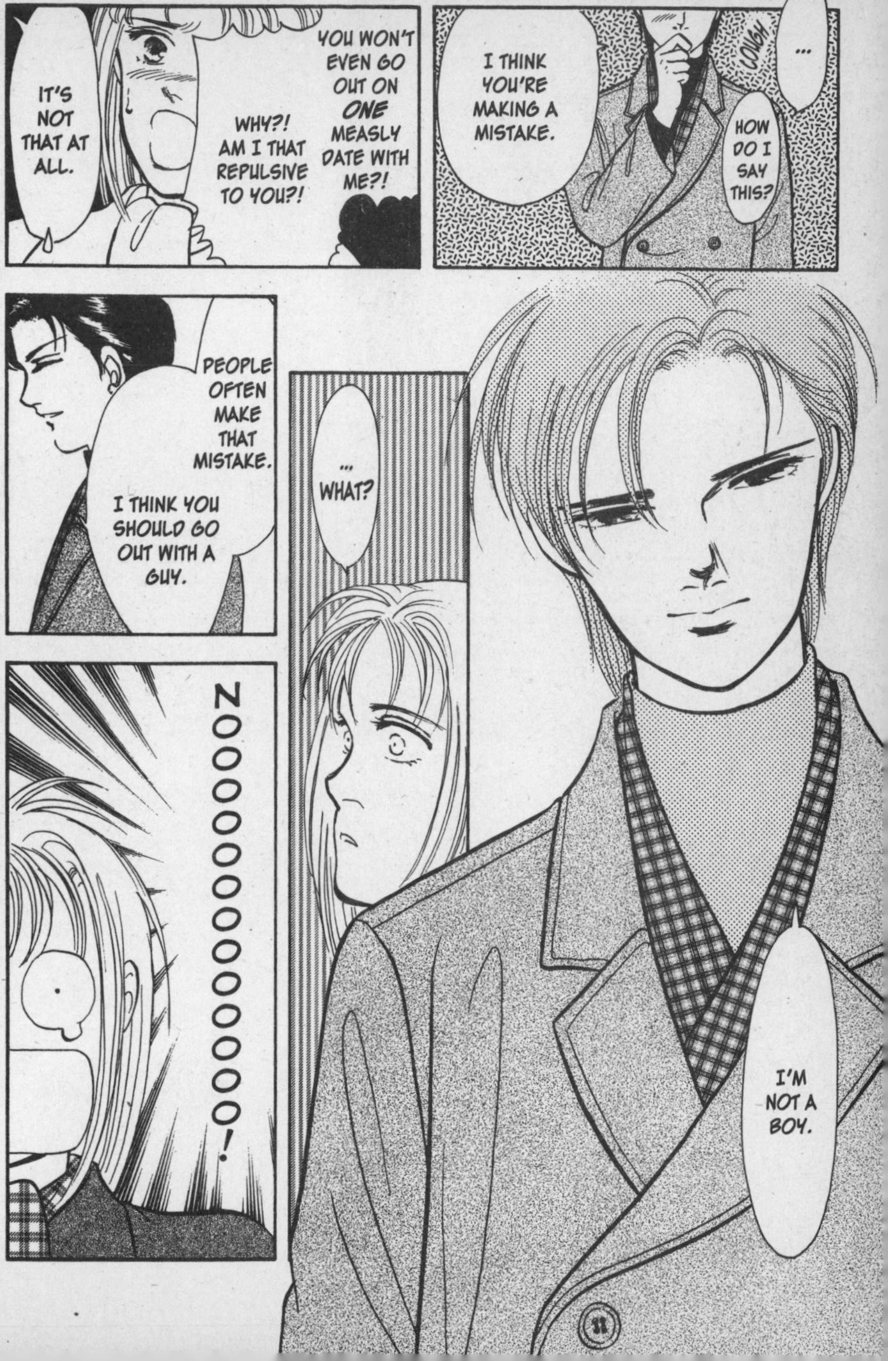
...
COUGH
HOW DO I SAY THIS?
I THINK YOU'RE MAKING A MISTAKE.
YOU WON'T EVEN GO OUT ON ONE MEASLY DATE WITH ME?!
WHY?! AM I THAT REPULSIVE TO YOU?!
IT'S NOT THAT AT ALL.
... WHAT?
I'M NOT A BOY.
PEOPLE OFTEN MAKE THAT MISTAKE.
I THINK YOU SHOULD GO OUT WITH A GUY.
NOOOOOOOOOOOOOO!

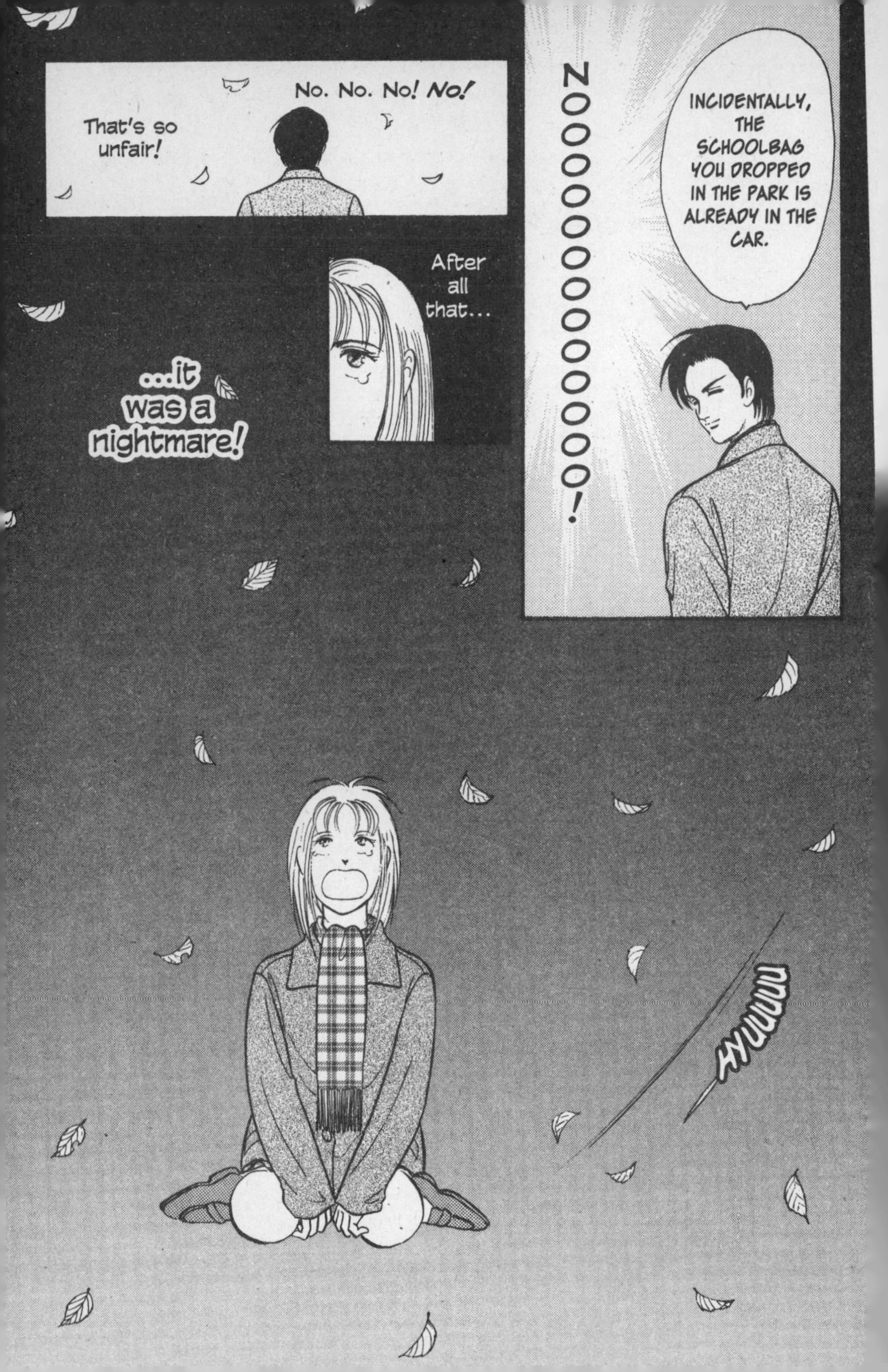
INCIDENTALLY, THE SCHOOLBAG YOU DROPPED IN THE PARK IS ALREADY IN THE CAR.
NOOOOOOOOOOOOO!
No. No. No! *No!*
That's so unfair!
After all that...
...it was a nightmare!
HYUUUUU

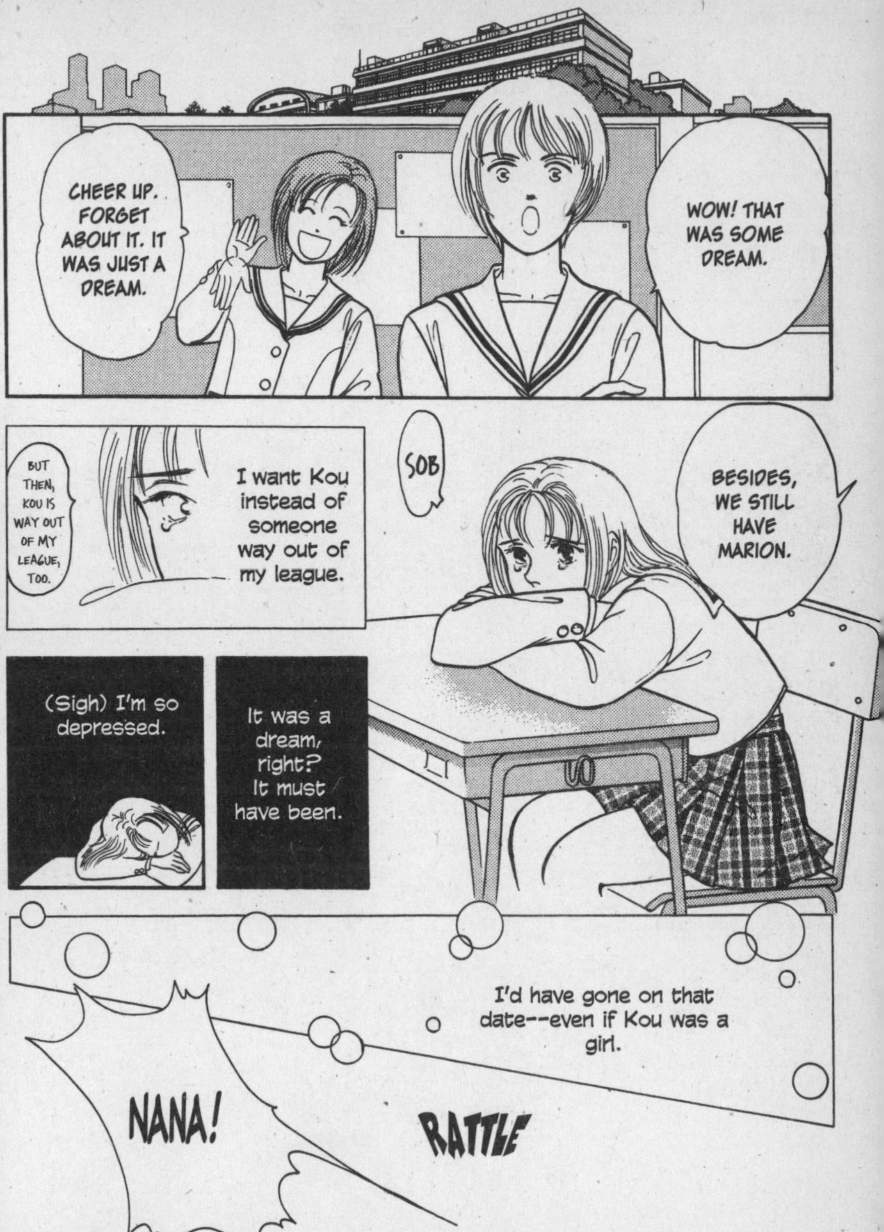
WOW! THAT WAS SOME DREAM.
CHEER UP. FORGET ABOUT IT. IT WAS JUST A DREAM.
BESIDES, WE STILL HAVE MARION.
SOB
I want Kou instead of someone way out of my league.
BUT THEN, KOU IS WAY OUT OF MY LEAGUE, TOO.
It was a dream, right? It must have been.
(Sigh) I'm so depressed.
I'd have gone on that date--even if Kou was a girl.
RATTLE
NANA!

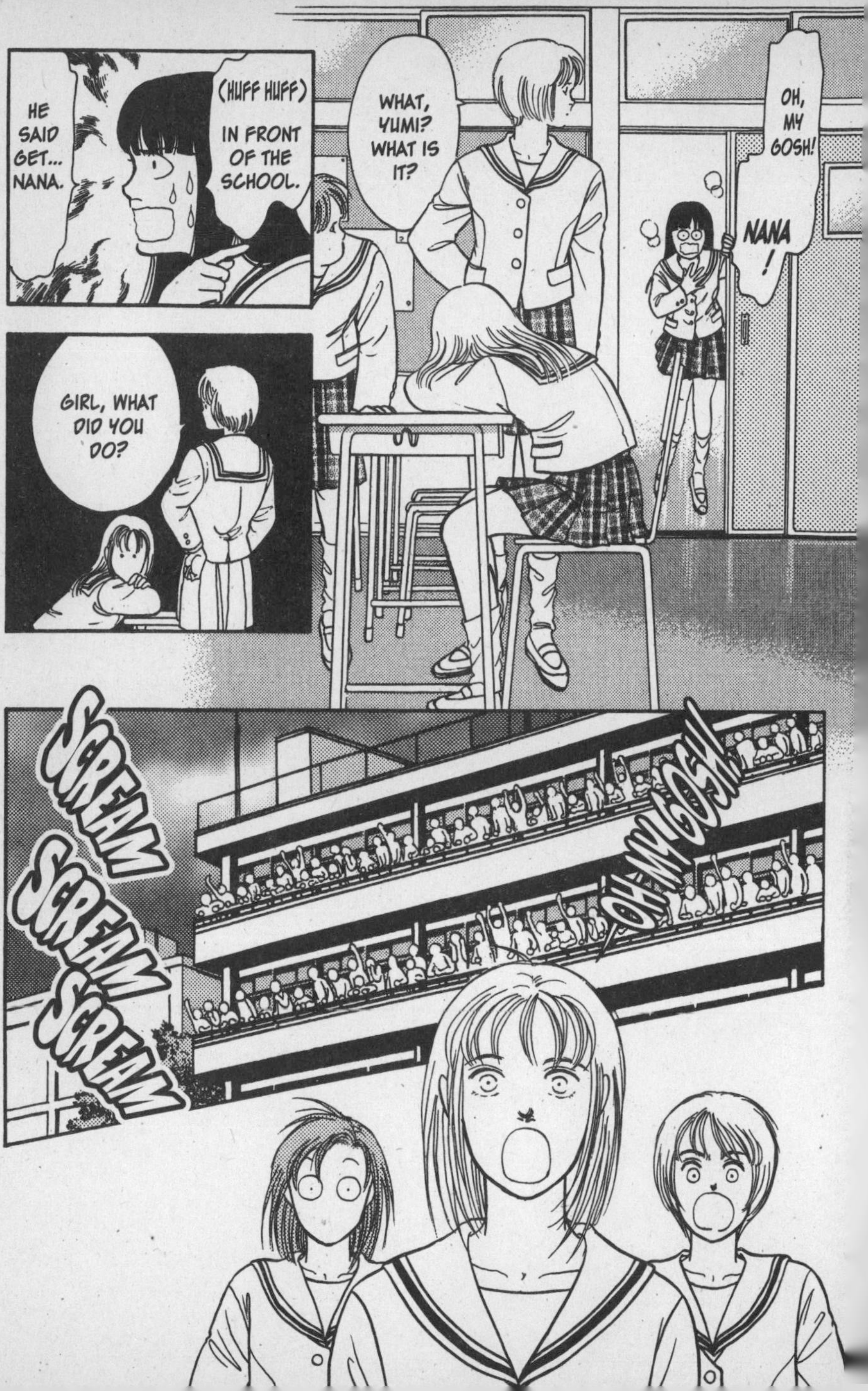
OH, MY GOSH!
NANA!
WHAT, YUMI? WHAT IS IT?
(HUFF HUFF)
IN FRONT OF THE SCHOOL.
HE SAID GET... NANA.
GIRL, WHAT DID YOU DO?
OH MY GOSH!
SCREAM SCREAM SCREAM

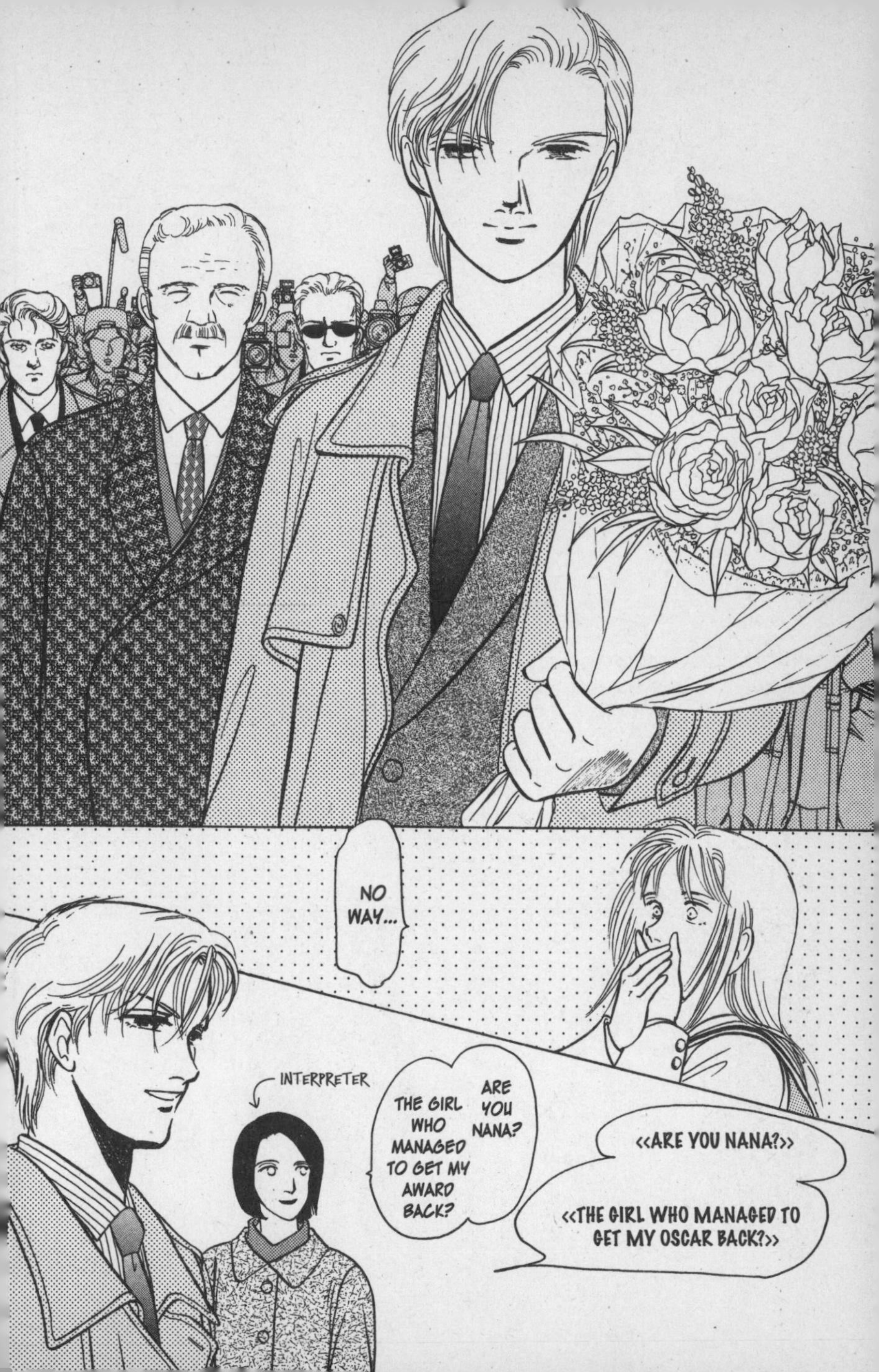
NO WAY...
<<ARE YOU NANA?>>
<<THE GIRL WHO MANAGED TO GET MY OSCAR BACK?>>
ARE YOU NANA?
THE GIRL WHO MANAGED TO GET MY AWARD BACK?
INTERPRETER

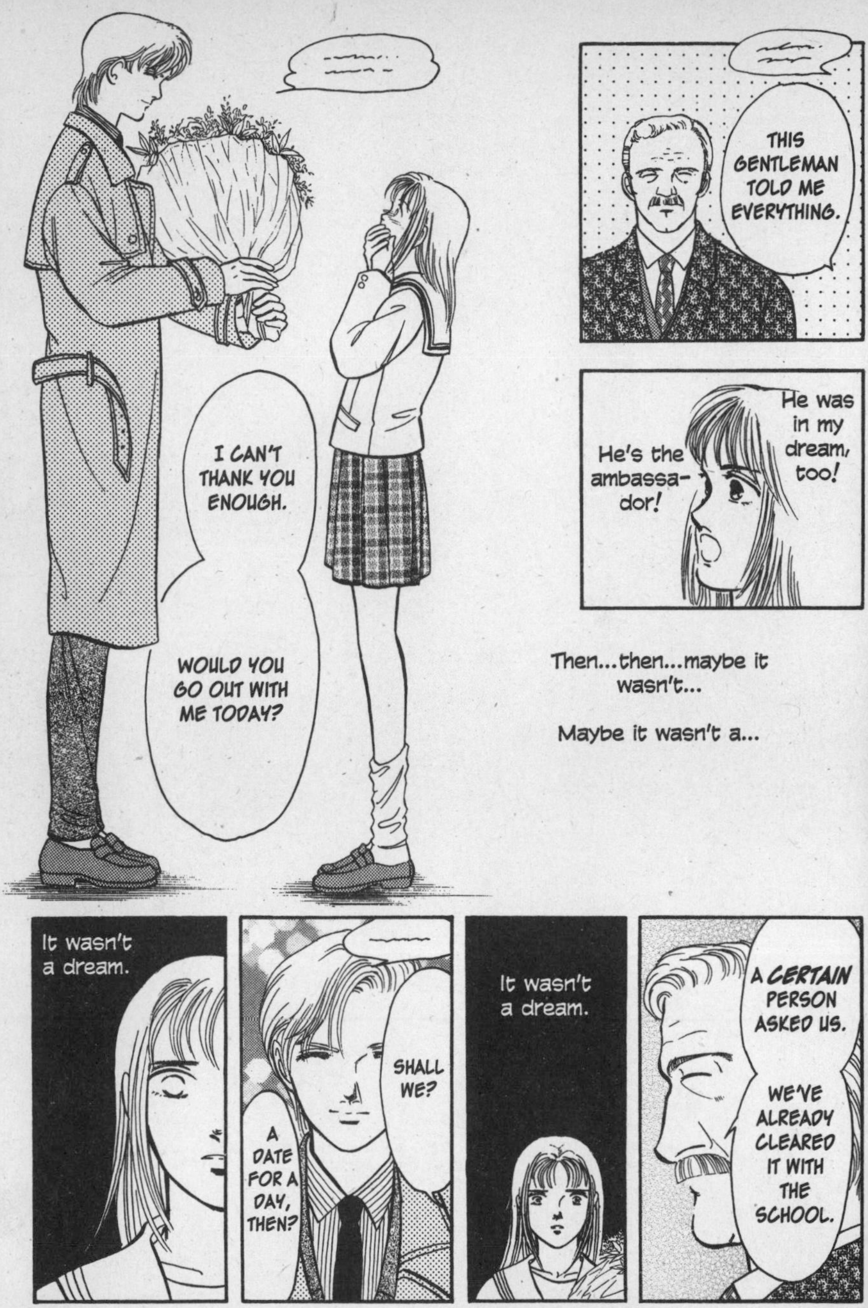
THIS GENTLEMAN TOLD ME EVERYTHING.
He was in my dream, too!
He's the ambassador!
Then...then...maybe it wasn't...
Maybe it wasn't a...
I CAN'T THANK YOU ENOUGH.
WOULD YOU GO OUT WITH ME TODAY?
A CERTAIN PERSON ASKED US.
WE'VE ALREADY CLEARED IT WITH THE SCHOOL.
It wasn't a dream.
SHALL WE?
A DATE FOR A DAY, THEN?
It wasn't a dream.

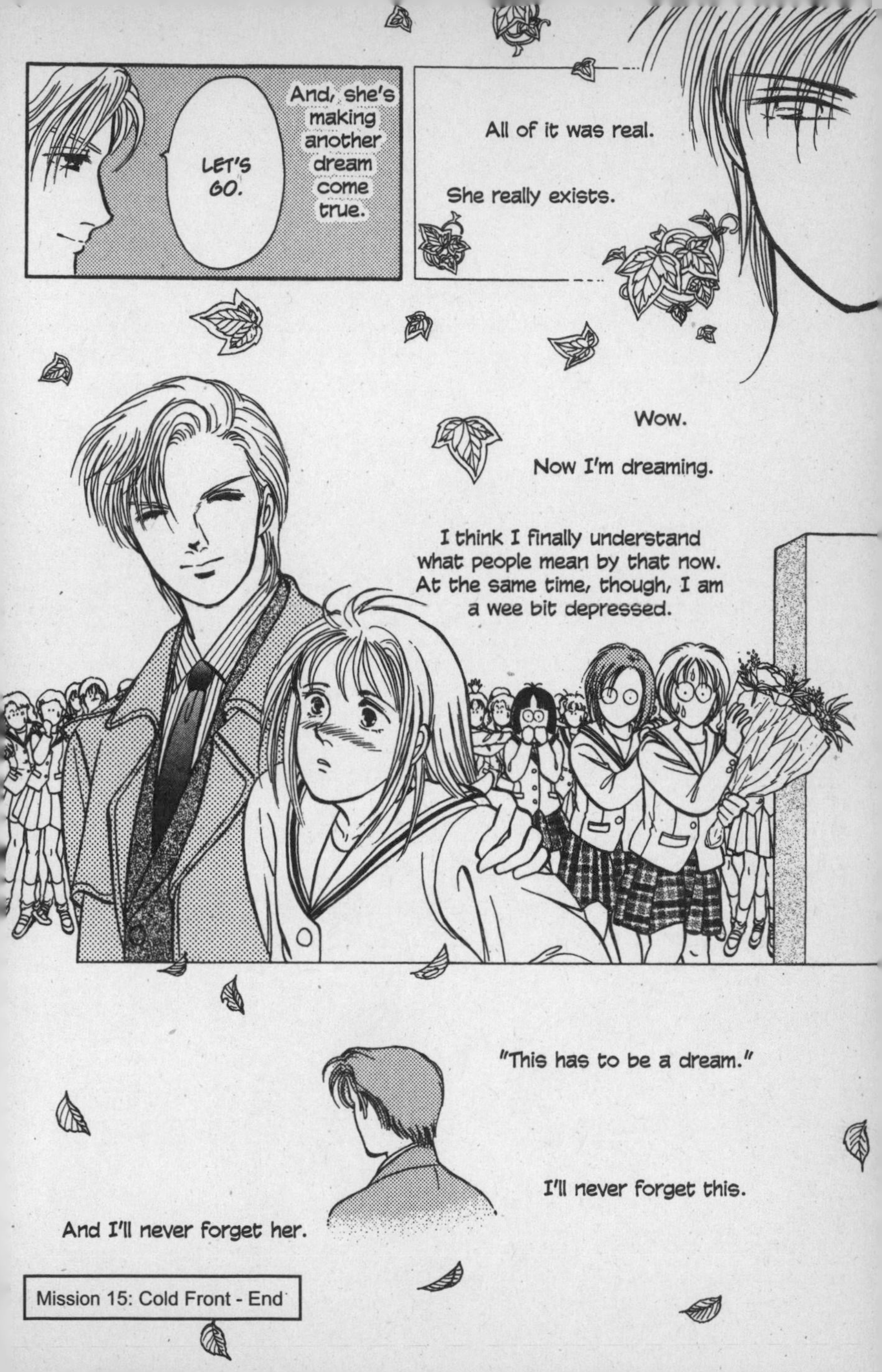
All of it was real.
She really exists.
And, she's making another dream come true.
LET'S GO.
Wow.
Now I'm dreaming.
I think I finally understand what people mean by that now. At the same time, though, I am a wee bit depressed.
"This has to be a dream."
I'll never forget this.
And I'll never forget her.
Mission 15: Cold Front - End

UB

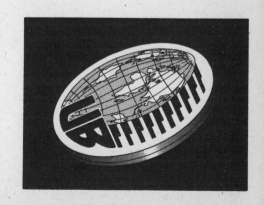

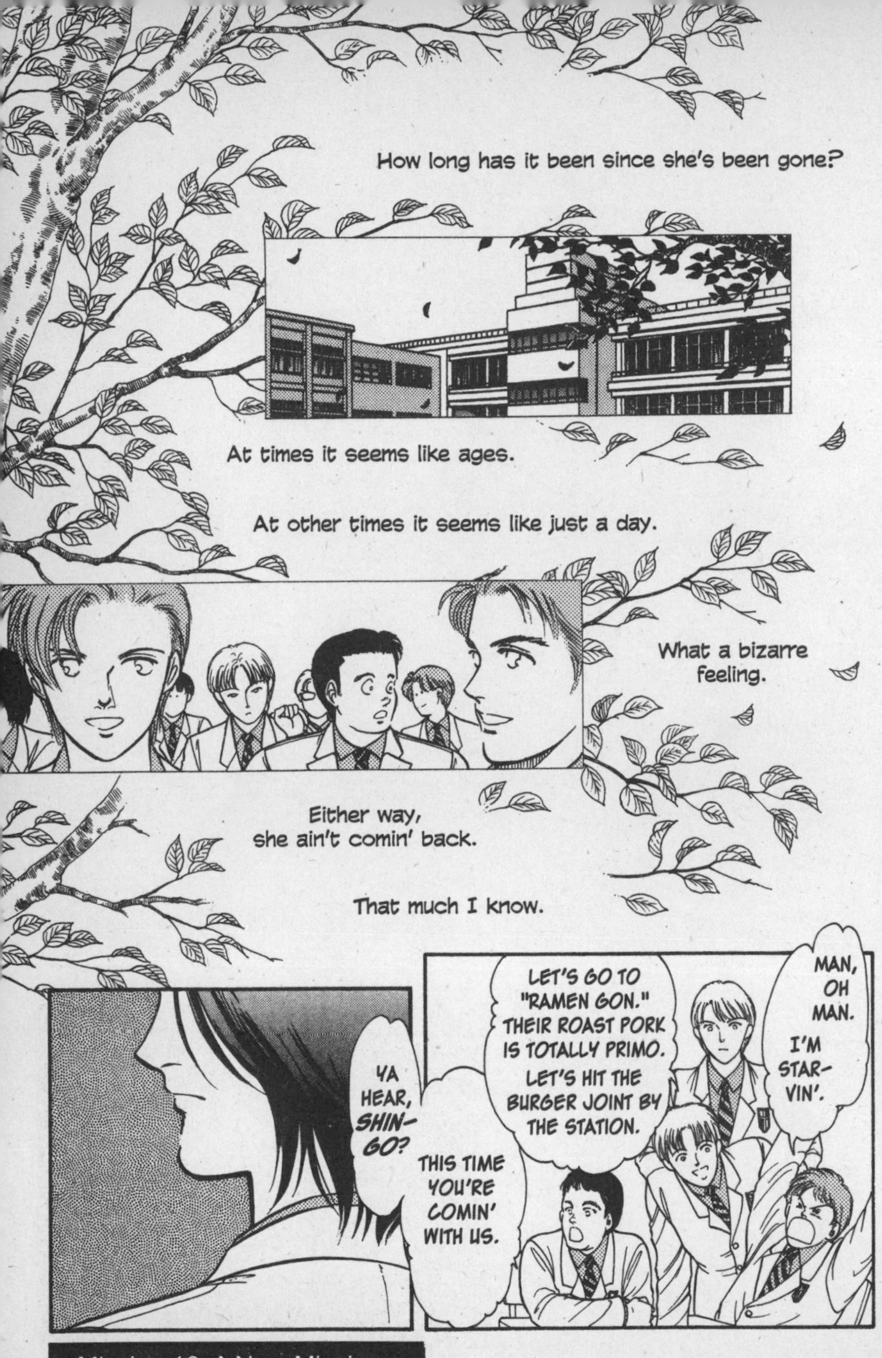
How long has it been since she's been gone?
At times it seems like ages.
At other times it seems like just a day.
What a bizarre feeling.
Either way, she ain't comin' back.
That much I know.
MAN, OH MAN.
I'M STAR-VIN'.
LET'S GO TO "RAMEN GON." THEIR ROAST PORK IS TOTALLY PRIMO.
LET'S HIT THE BURGER JOINT BY THE STATION.
THIS TIME YOU'RE COMIN' WITH US.
YA HEAR, SHIN-GO?

Mission 16: A New Mission

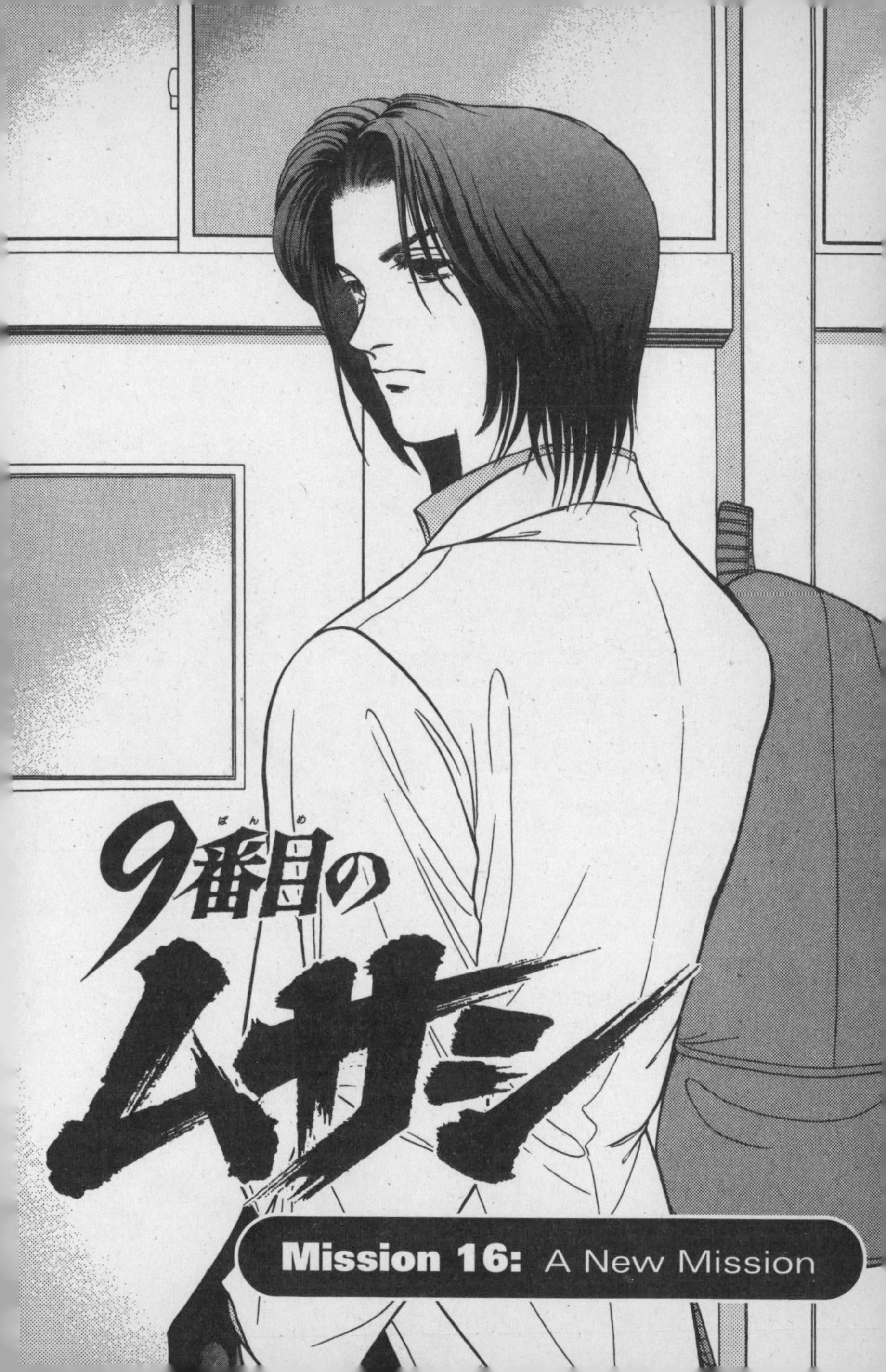
9番目のムサシ
Mission 16: A New Mission

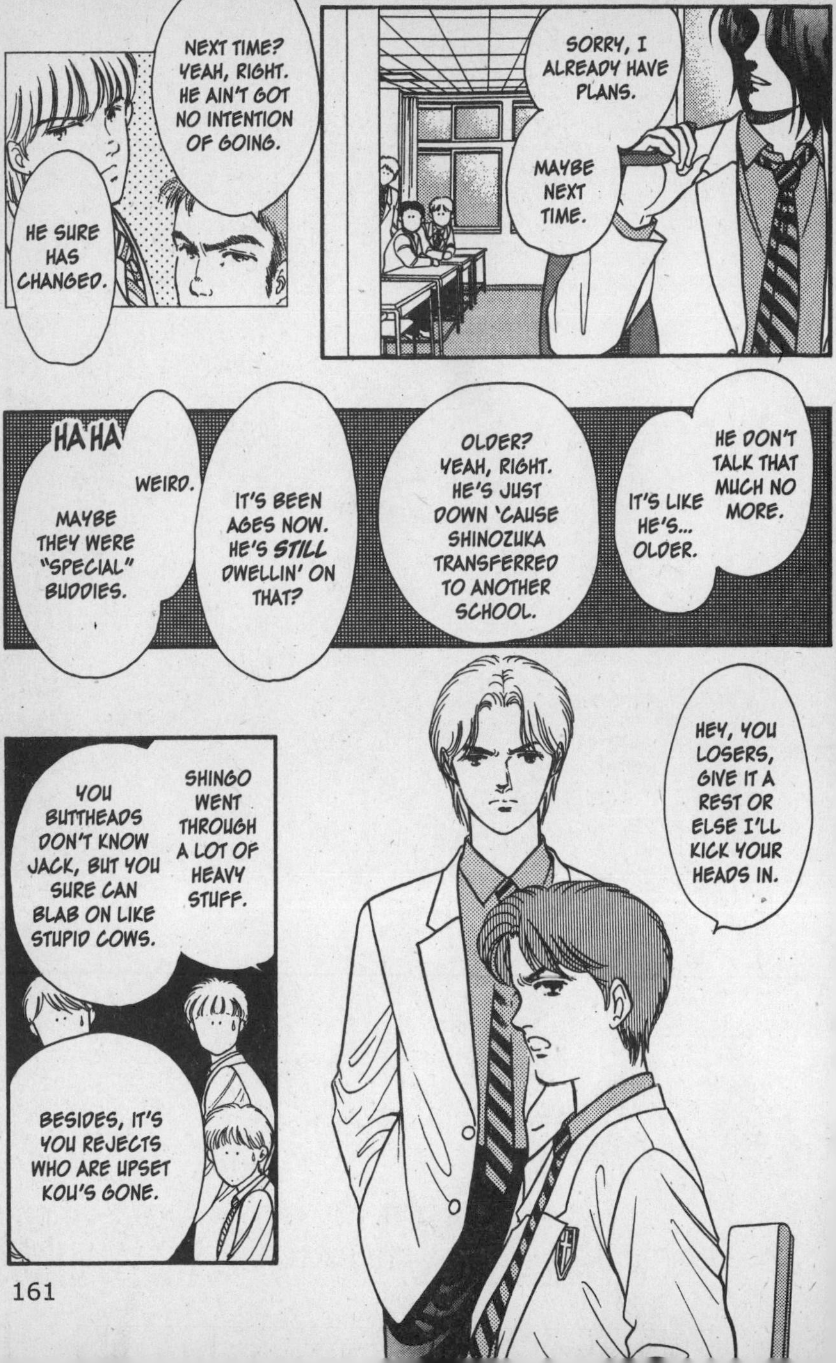
SORRY, I ALREADY HAVE PLANS.
MAYBE NEXT TIME.
NEXT TIME? YEAH, RIGHT. HE AIN'T GOT NO INTENTION OF GOING.
HE SURE HAS CHANGED.
HE DON'T TALK THAT MUCH NO MORE.
IT'S LIKE HE'S... OLDER.
OLDER? YEAH, RIGHT. HE'S JUST DOWN 'CAUSE SHINOZUKA TRANSFERRED TO ANOTHER SCHOOL.
IT'S BEEN AGES NOW. HE'S *STILL* DWELLIN' ON THAT?
WEIRD.
HA HA
MAYBE THEY WERE "SPECIAL" BUDDIES.
HEY, YOU LOSERS, GIVE IT A REST OR ELSE I'LL KICK YOUR HEADS IN.
SHINGO WENT THROUGH A LOT OF HEAVY STUFF.
YOU BUTTHEADS DON'T KNOW JACK, BUT YOU SURE CAN BLAB ON LIKE STUPID COWS.
BESIDES, IT'S YOU REJECTS WHO ARE UPSET KOU'S GONE.

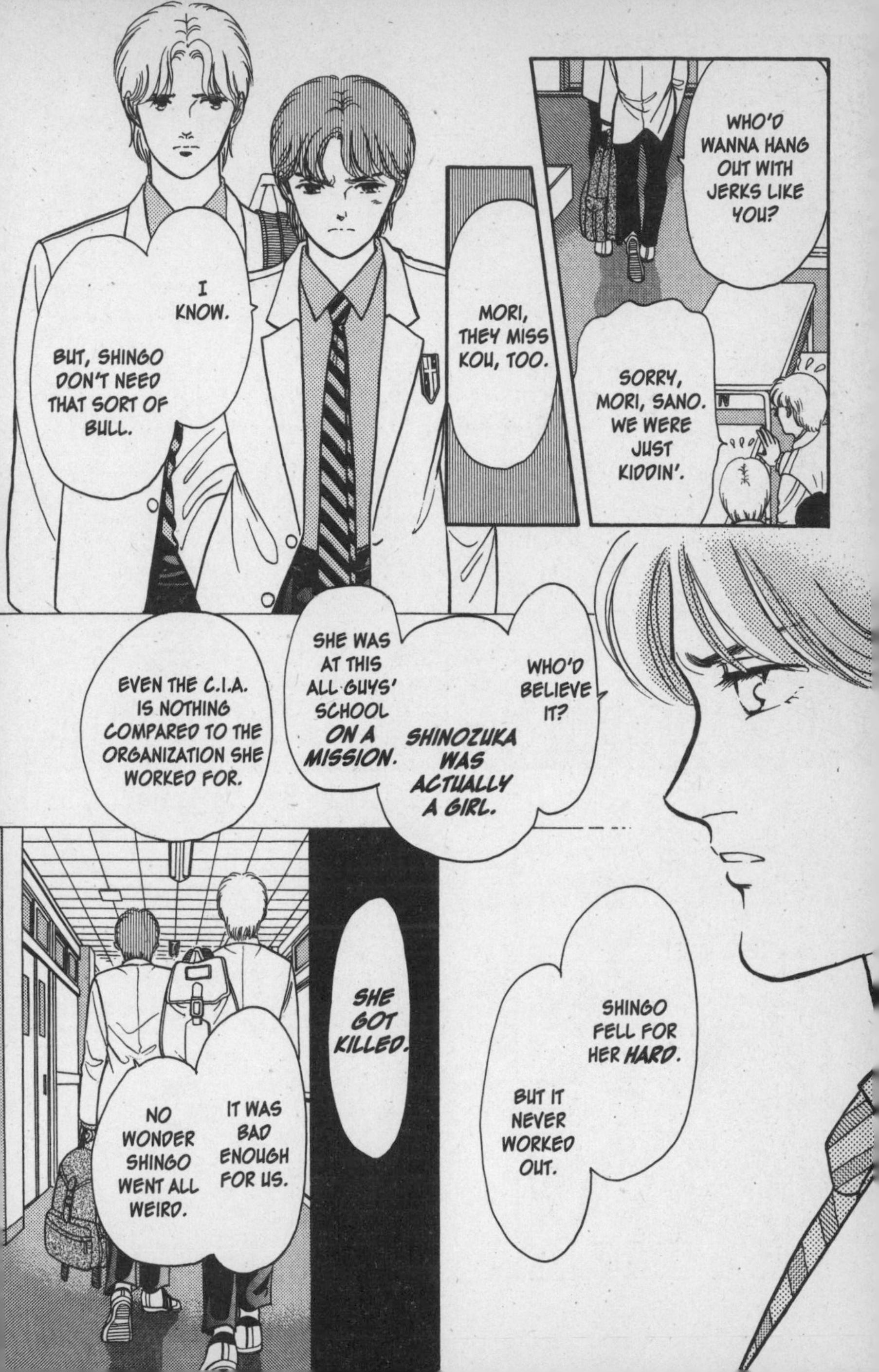
WHO'D WANNA HANG OUT WITH JERKS LIKE YOU?
SORRY, MORI, SANO. WE WERE JUST KIDDIN'.
MORI, THEY MISS KOU, TOO.
I KNOW.
BUT, SHINGO DON'T NEED THAT SORT OF BULL.
WHO'D BELIEVE IT?
SHINOZUKA WAS ACTUALLY A GIRL.
SHE WAS AT THIS ALL-GUYS' SCHOOL ON A MISSION.
EVEN THE C.I.A. IS NOTHING COMPARED TO THE ORGANIZATION SHE WORKED FOR.
SHINGO FELL FOR HER HARD.
BUT IT NEVER WORKED OUT.
SHE GOT KILLED.
IT WAS BAD ENOUGH FOR US.
NO WONDER SHINGO WENT ALL WEIRD.

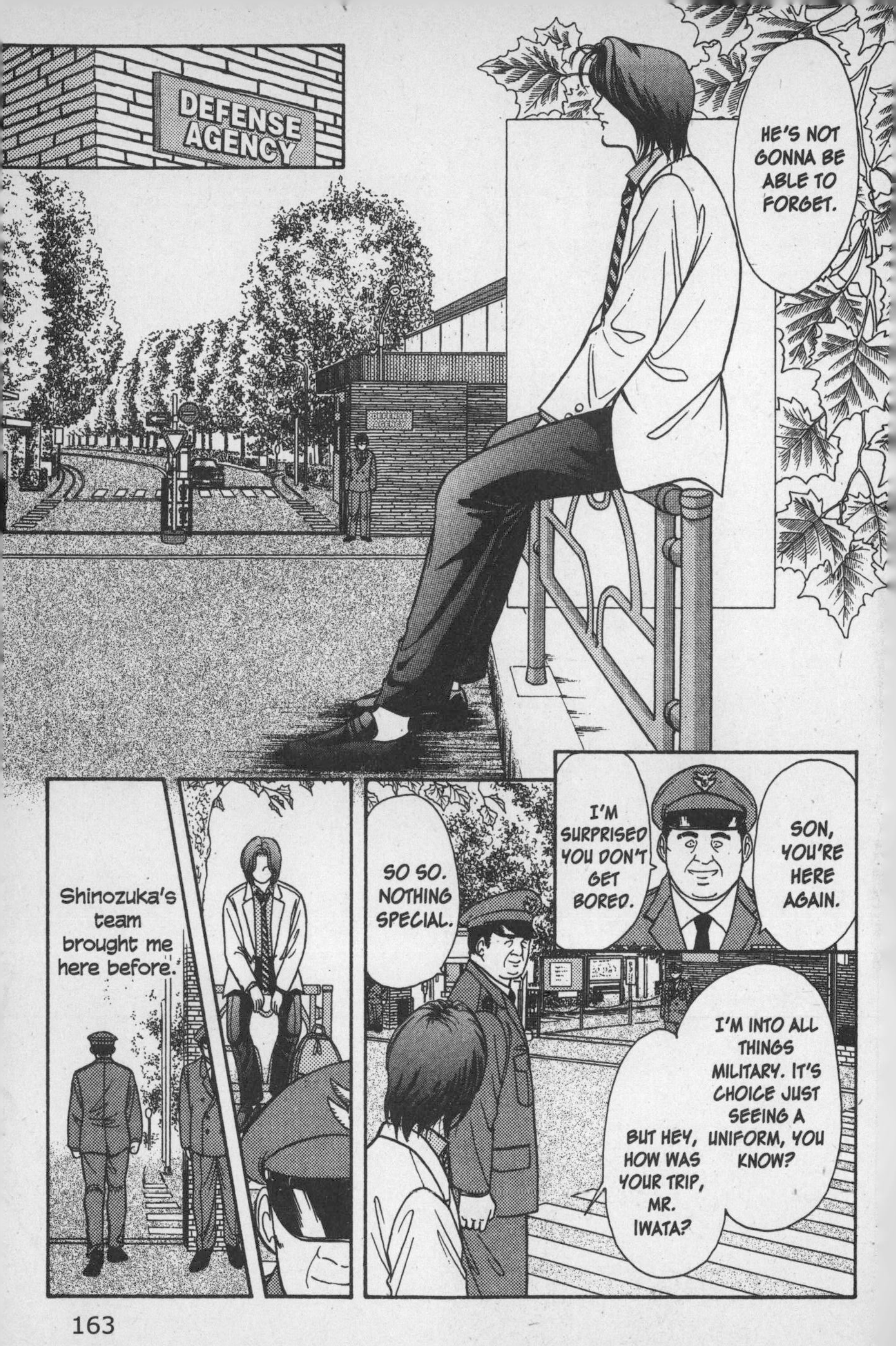
HE'S NOT GONNA BE ABLE TO FORGET.
DEFENSE AGENCY
SON, YOU'RE HERE AGAIN.
I'M SURPRISED YOU DON'T GET BORED.
I'M INTO ALL THINGS MILITARY. IT'S CHOICE JUST SEEING A UNIFORM, YOU KNOW?
BUT HEY, HOW WAS YOUR TRIP, MR. IWATA?
SO SO. NOTHING SPECIAL.
Shinozuka's team brought me here before.

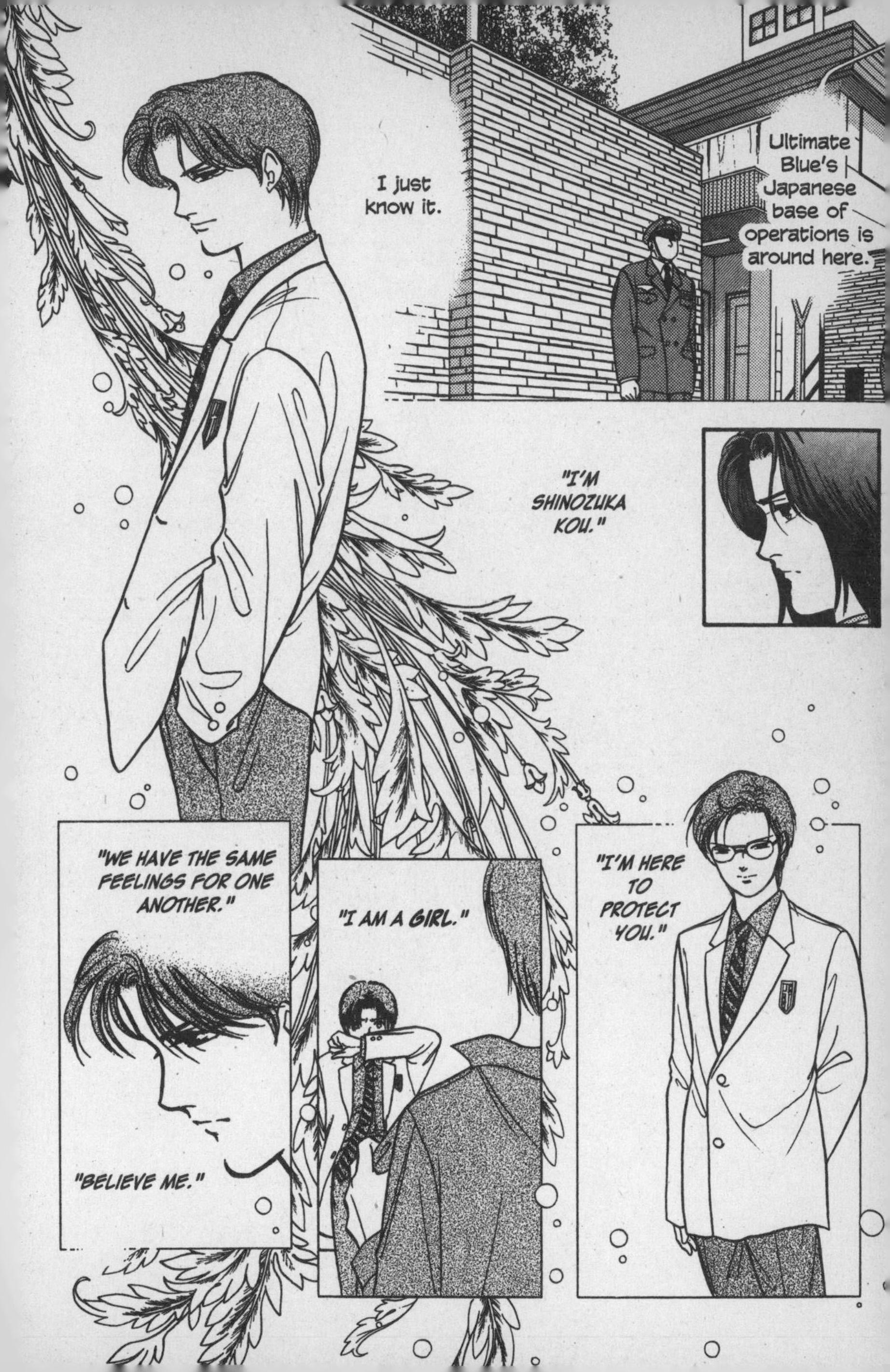
Ultimate Blue's Japanese base of operations is around here.
I just know it.
"I'M SHINOZUKA KOU."
"I'M HERE TO PROTECT YOU."
"I AM A GIRL."
"WE HAVE THE SAME FEELINGS FOR ONE ANOTHER."
"BELIEVE ME."

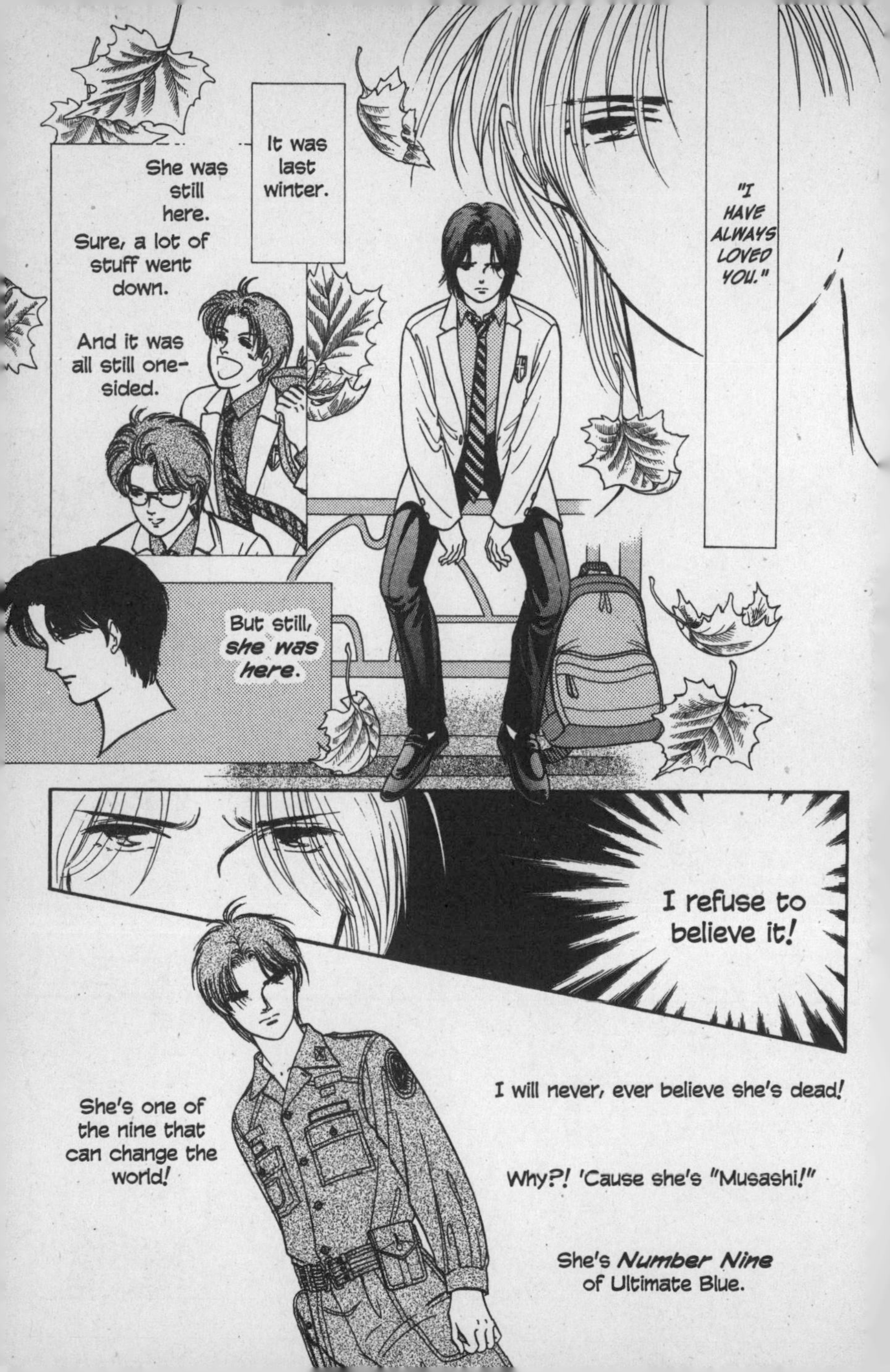
"I HAVE ALWAYS LOVED YOU."
It was last winter.
She was still here.
Sure, a lot of stuff went down.
And it was all still one-sided.
But still, *she was here*.
I refuse to believe it!
I will never, ever believe she's dead!
Why?! 'Cause she's "Musashi!"
She's *Number Nine* of Ultimate Blue.
She's one of the nine that can change the world!

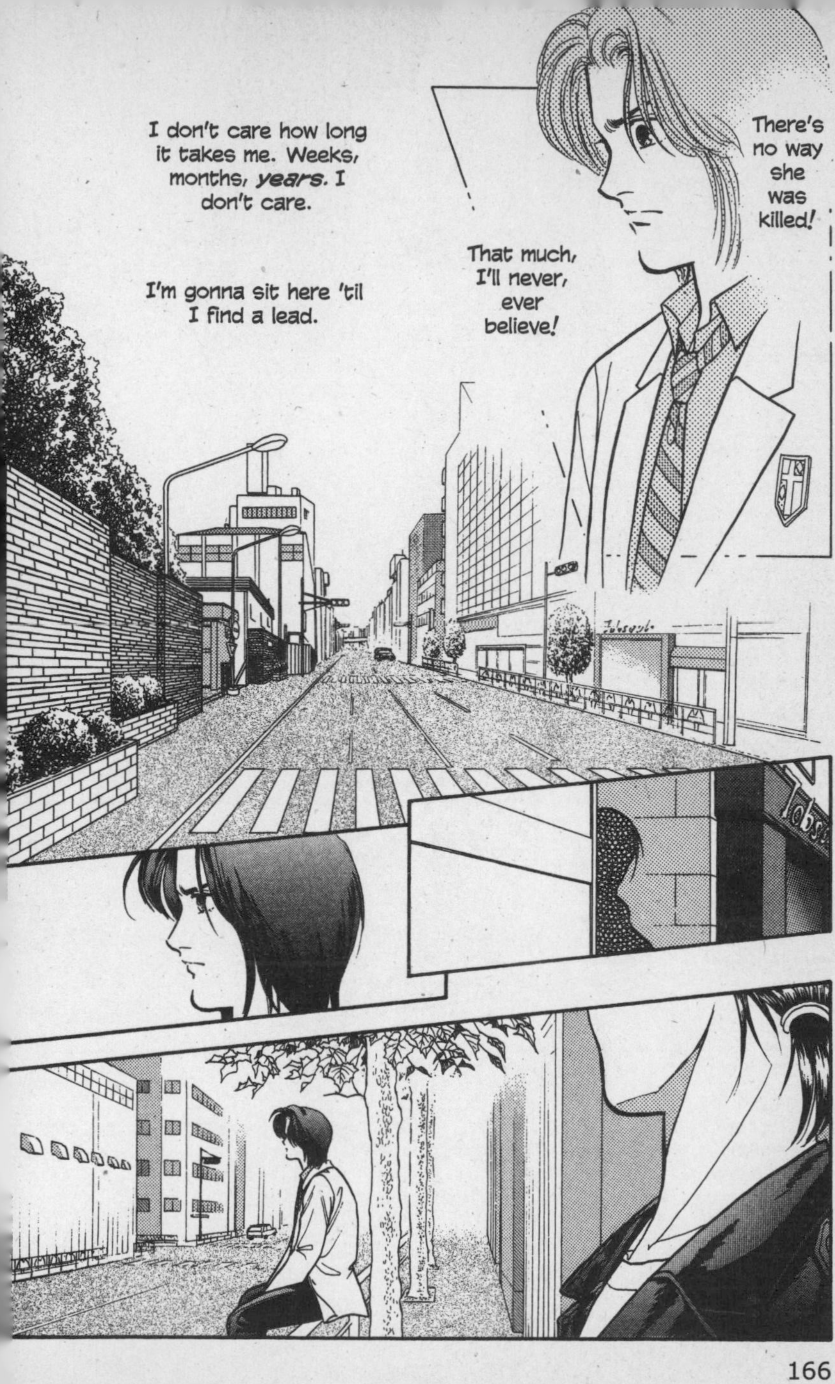
There's no way she was killed!
That much, I'll never, ever believe!
I don't care how long it takes me. Weeks, months, *years*. I don't care.
I'm gonna sit here 'til I find a lead.

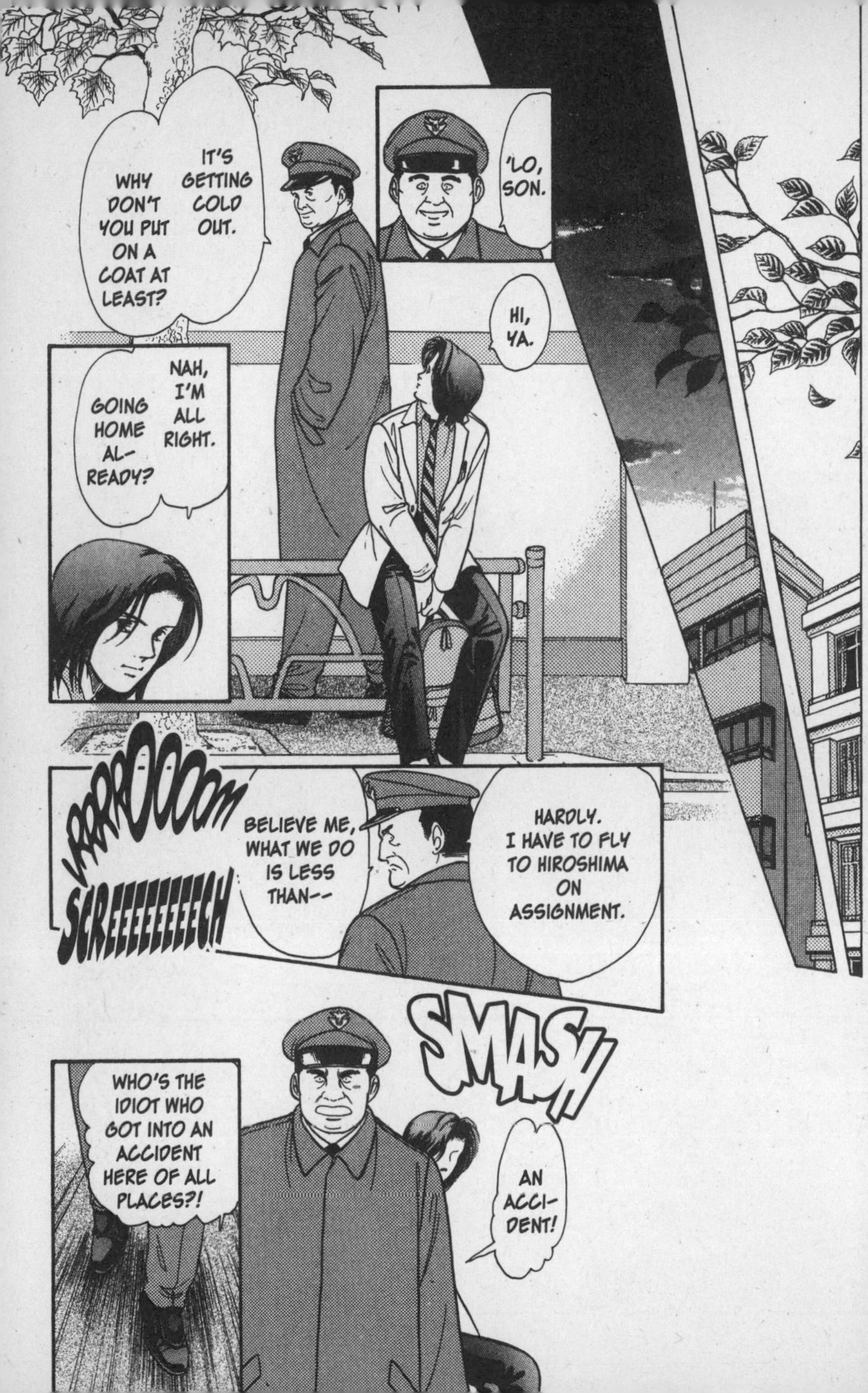
'LO, SON.
HI, YA.
IT'S GETTING COLD OUT.
WHY DON'T YOU PUT ON A COAT AT LEAST?
NAH, I'M ALL RIGHT.
GOING HOME AL-READY?
HARDLY. I HAVE TO FLY TO HIROSHIMA ON ASSIGNMENT.
BELIEVE ME, WHAT WE DO IS LESS THAN--
VRRRROOOOOM
SCREEEEEEEEECH!
SMASH
AN ACCI-DENT!
WHO'S THE IDIOT WHO GOT INTO AN ACCIDENT HERE OF ALL PLACES?!

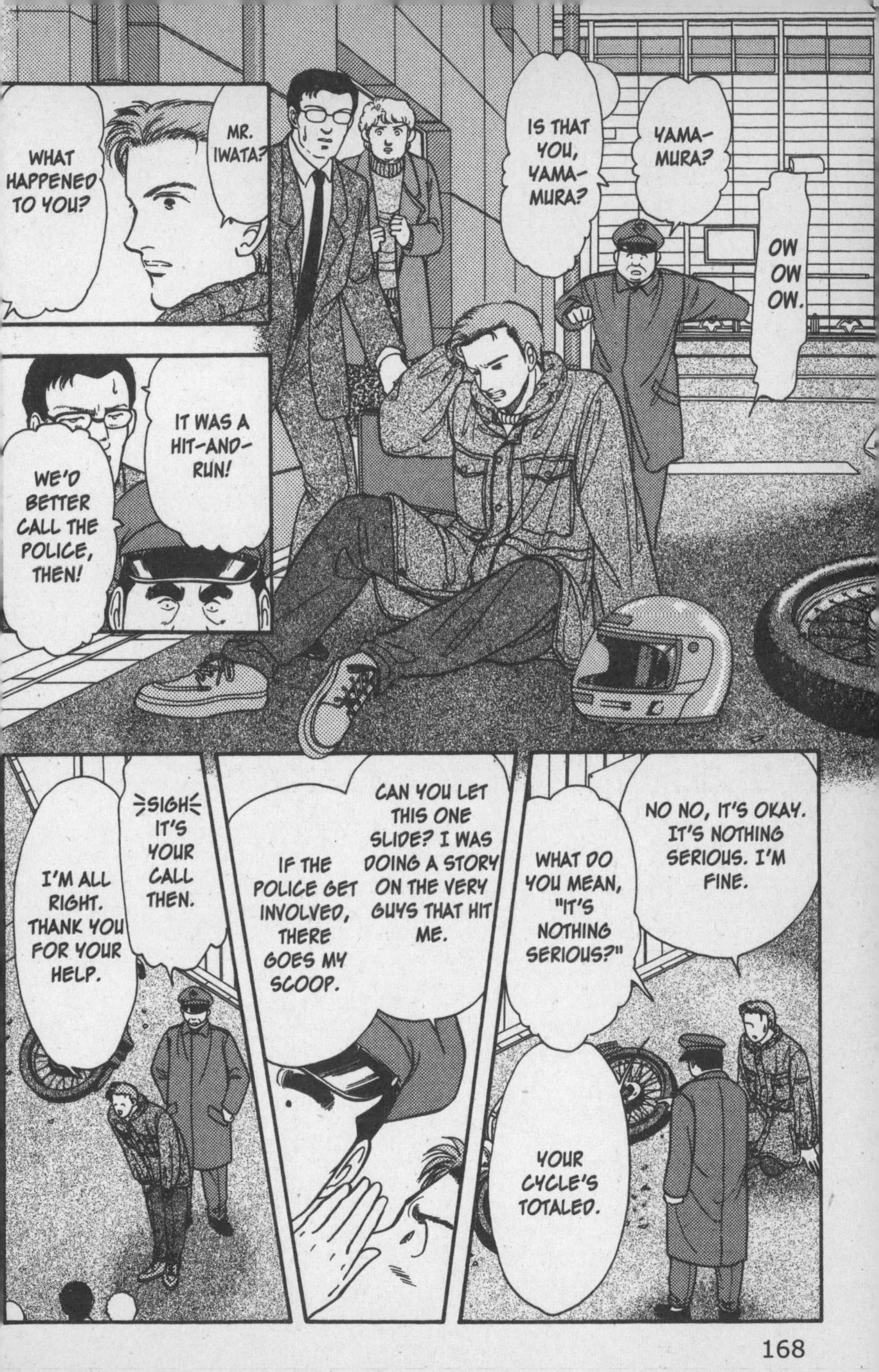
OW OW OW.
YAMA-MURA?
IS THAT YOU, YAMA-MURA?
MR. IWATA?
WHAT HAPPENED TO YOU?
IT WAS A HIT-AND-RUN!
WE'D BETTER CALL THE POLICE, THEN!
NO NO, IT'S OKAY. IT'S NOTHING SERIOUS. I'M FINE.
WHAT DO YOU MEAN, "IT'S NOTHING SERIOUS?"
YOUR CYCLE'S TOTALED.
CAN YOU LET THIS ONE SLIDE? I WAS DOING A STORY ON THE VERY GUYS THAT HIT ME.
IF THE POLICE GET INVOLVED, THERE GOES MY SCOOP.
≡SIGH≡ IT'S YOUR CALL THEN.
I'M ALL RIGHT. THANK YOU FOR YOUR HELP.

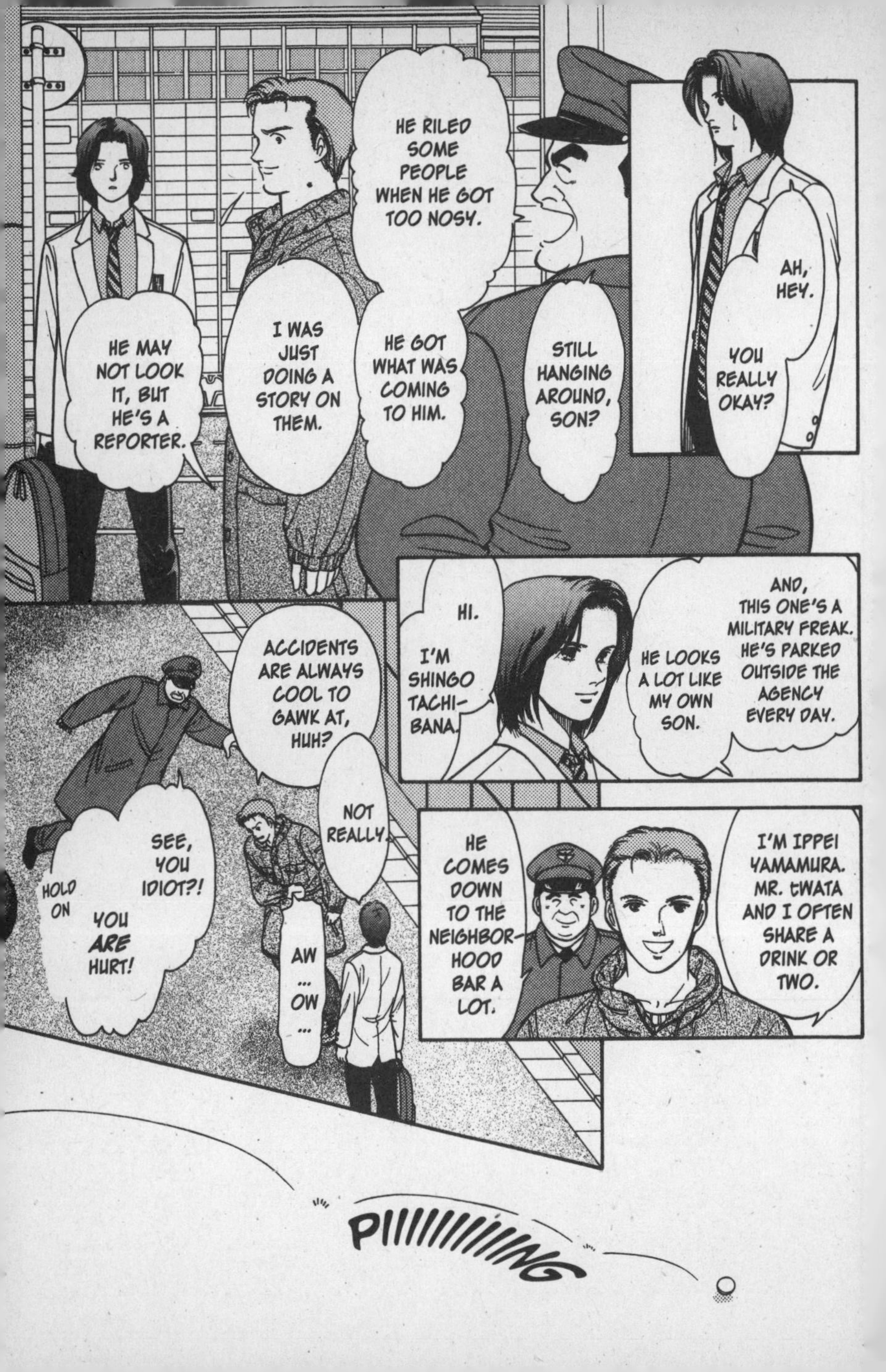
AH, HEY.
YOU REALLY OKAY?
STILL HANGING AROUND, SON?
HE RILED SOME PEOPLE WHEN HE GOT TOO NOSY.
HE GOT WHAT WAS COMING TO HIM.
I WAS JUST DOING A STORY ON THEM.
HE MAY NOT LOOK IT, BUT HE'S A REPORTER.
AND, THIS ONE'S A MILITARY FREAK. HE'S PARKED OUTSIDE THE AGENCY EVERY DAY.
HE LOOKS A LOT LIKE MY OWN SON.
HI.
I'M SHINGO TACHIBANA.
I'M IPPEI YAMAMURA. MR. IWATA AND I OFTEN SHARE A DRINK OR TWO.
HE COMES DOWN TO THE NEIGHBORHOOD BAR A LOT.
ACCIDENTS ARE ALWAYS COOL TO GAWK AT, HUH?
NOT REALLY.
AW ... OW ...
SEE, YOU IDIOT?!
HOLD ON
YOU **ARE** HURT!
PIIIIIIIIIING

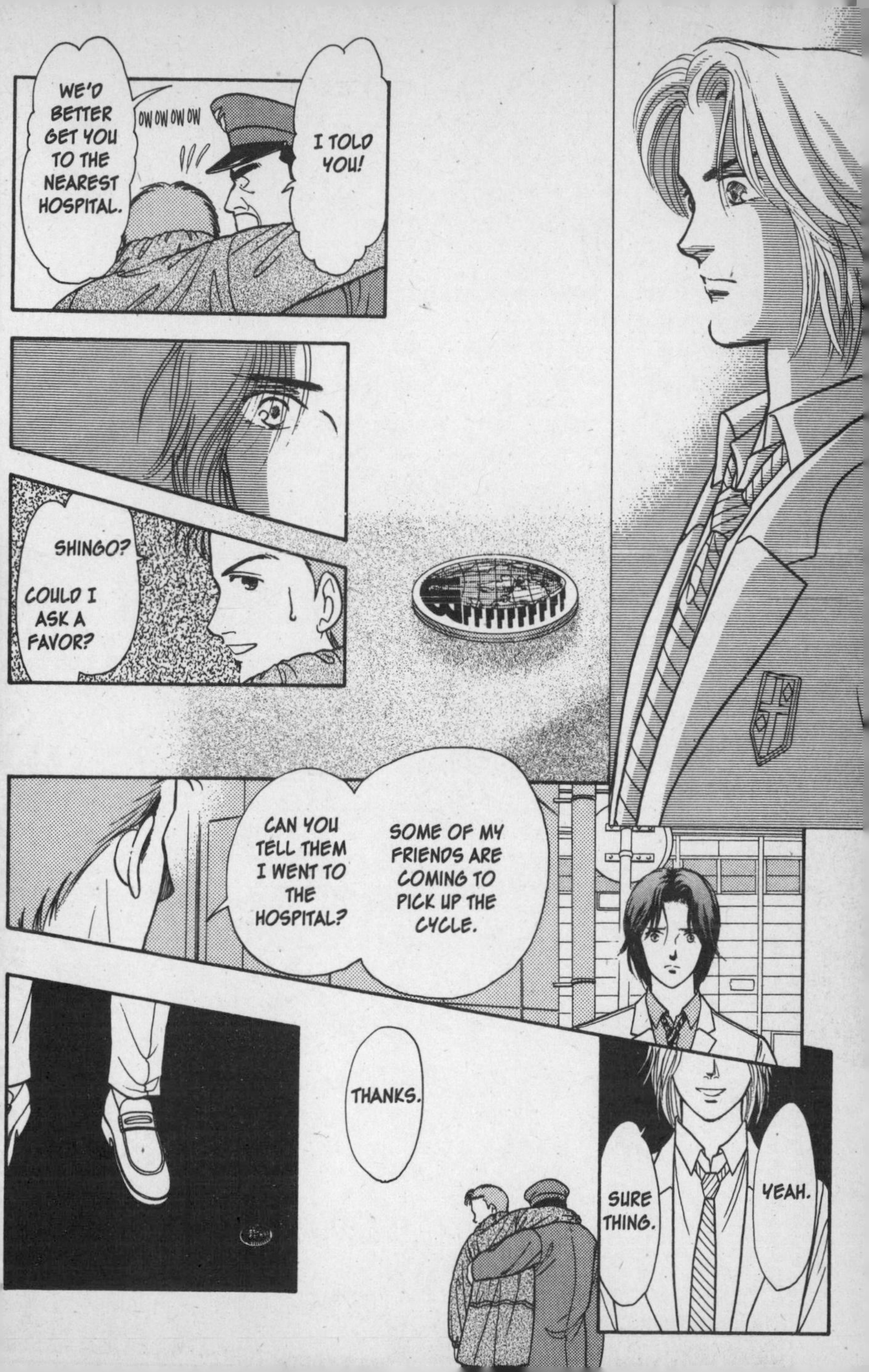
I TOLD YOU!
OW OW OW OW
WE'D BETTER GET YOU TO THE NEAREST HOSPITAL.
SHINGO?
COULD I ASK A FAVOR?
SOME OF MY FRIENDS ARE COMING TO PICK UP THE CYCLE.
CAN YOU TELL THEM I WENT TO THE HOSPITAL?
YEAH.
SURE THING.
THANKS.

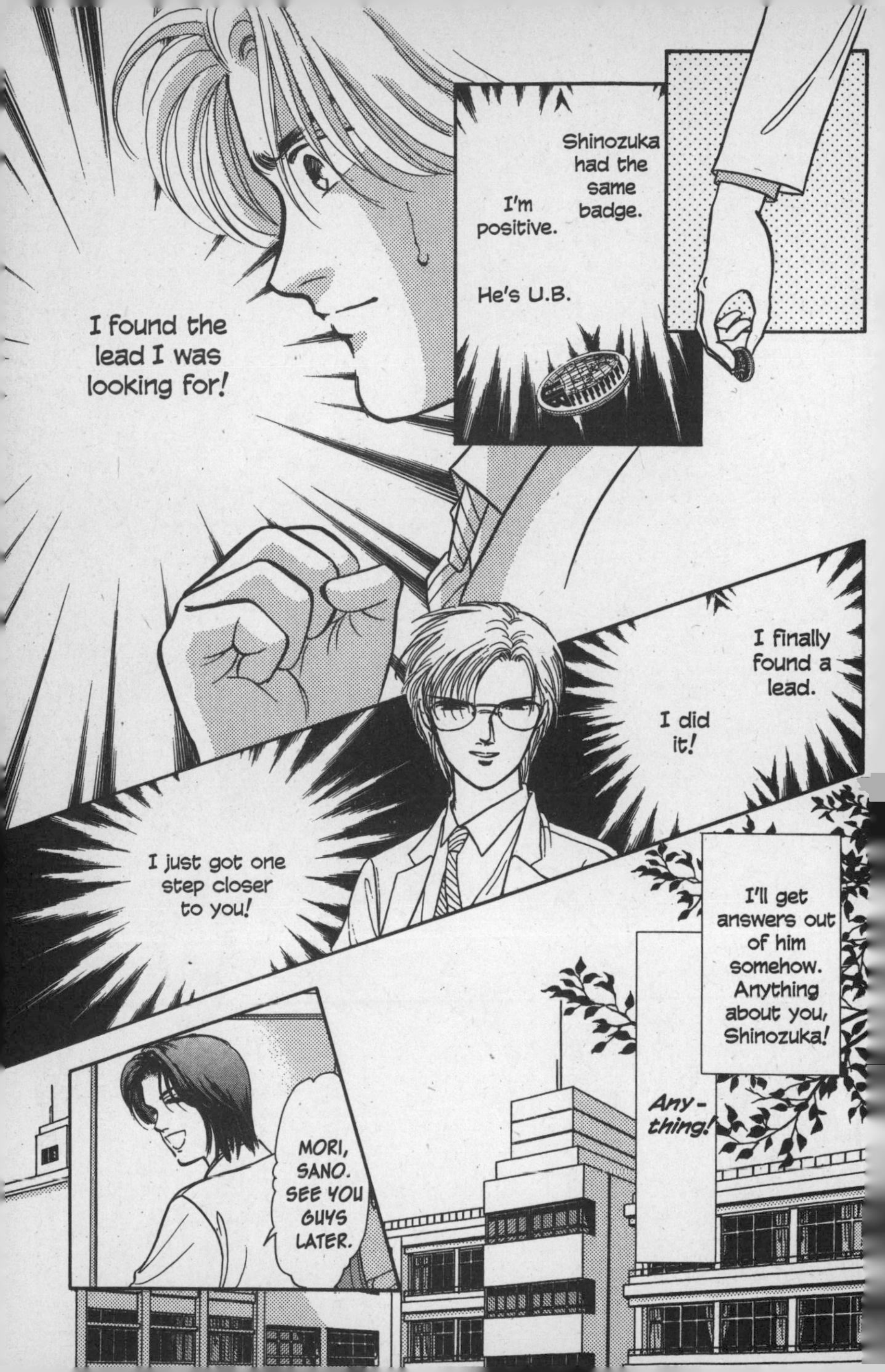
Shinozuka had the same badge.
I'm positive.
He's U.B.
I found the lead I was looking for!
I finally found a lead.
I did it!
I just got one step closer to you!
I'll get answers out of him somehow. Anything about you, Shinozuka!
Any-thing!
MORI, SANO. SEE YOU GUYS LATER.

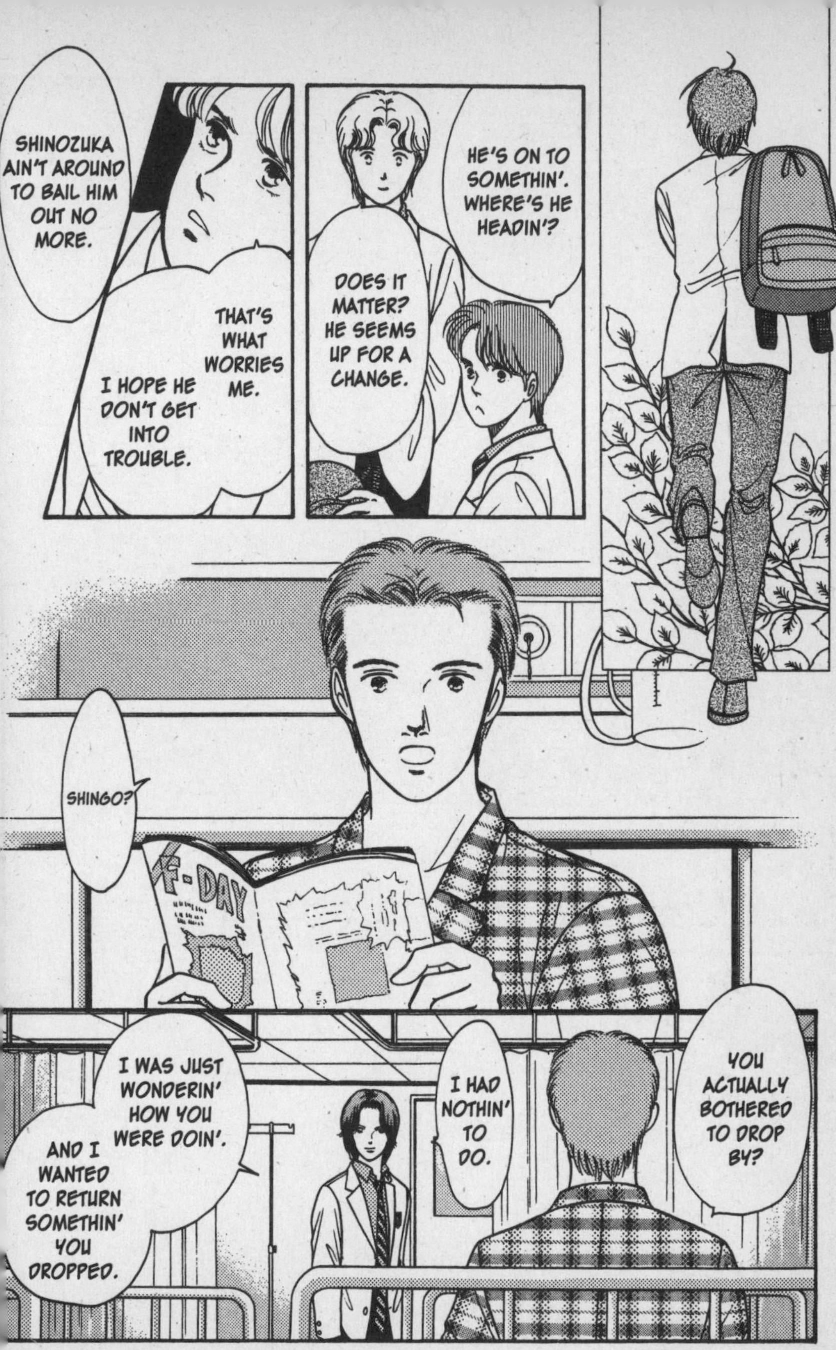
HE'S ON TO SOMETHIN'. WHERE'S HE HEADIN'?
DOES IT MATTER? HE SEEMS UP FOR A CHANGE.
SHINOZUKA AIN'T AROUND TO BAIL HIM OUT NO MORE.
THAT'S WHAT WORRIES ME.
I HOPE HE DON'T GET INTO TROUBLE.
SHINGO?
F-DAY
YOU ACTUALLY BOTHERED TO DROP BY?
I HAD NOTHIN' TO DO.
I WAS JUST WONDERIN' HOW YOU WERE DOIN'.
AND I WANTED TO RETURN SOMETHIN' YOU DROPPED.

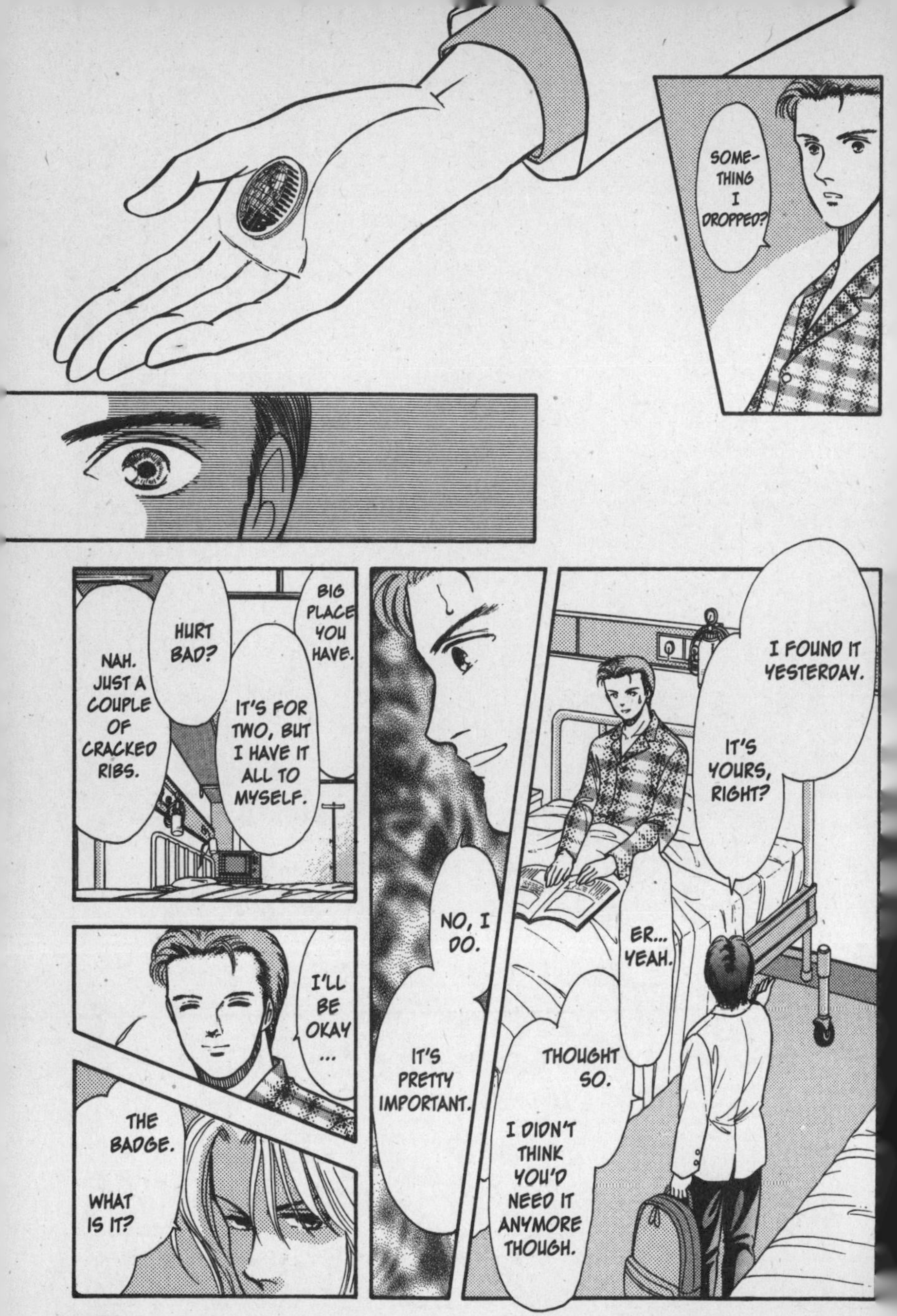
SOME-THING I DROPPED?
I FOUND IT YESTERDAY.
IT'S YOURS, RIGHT?
ER... YEAH.
THOUGHT SO.
I DIDN'T THINK YOU'D NEED IT ANYMORE THOUGH.
NO, I DO.
IT'S PRETTY IMPORTANT.
BIG PLACE YOU HAVE.
IT'S FOR TWO, BUT I HAVE IT ALL TO MYSELF.
HURT BAD?
NAH. JUST A COUPLE OF CRACKED RIBS.
I'LL BE OKAY ...
THE BADGE.
WHAT IS IT?

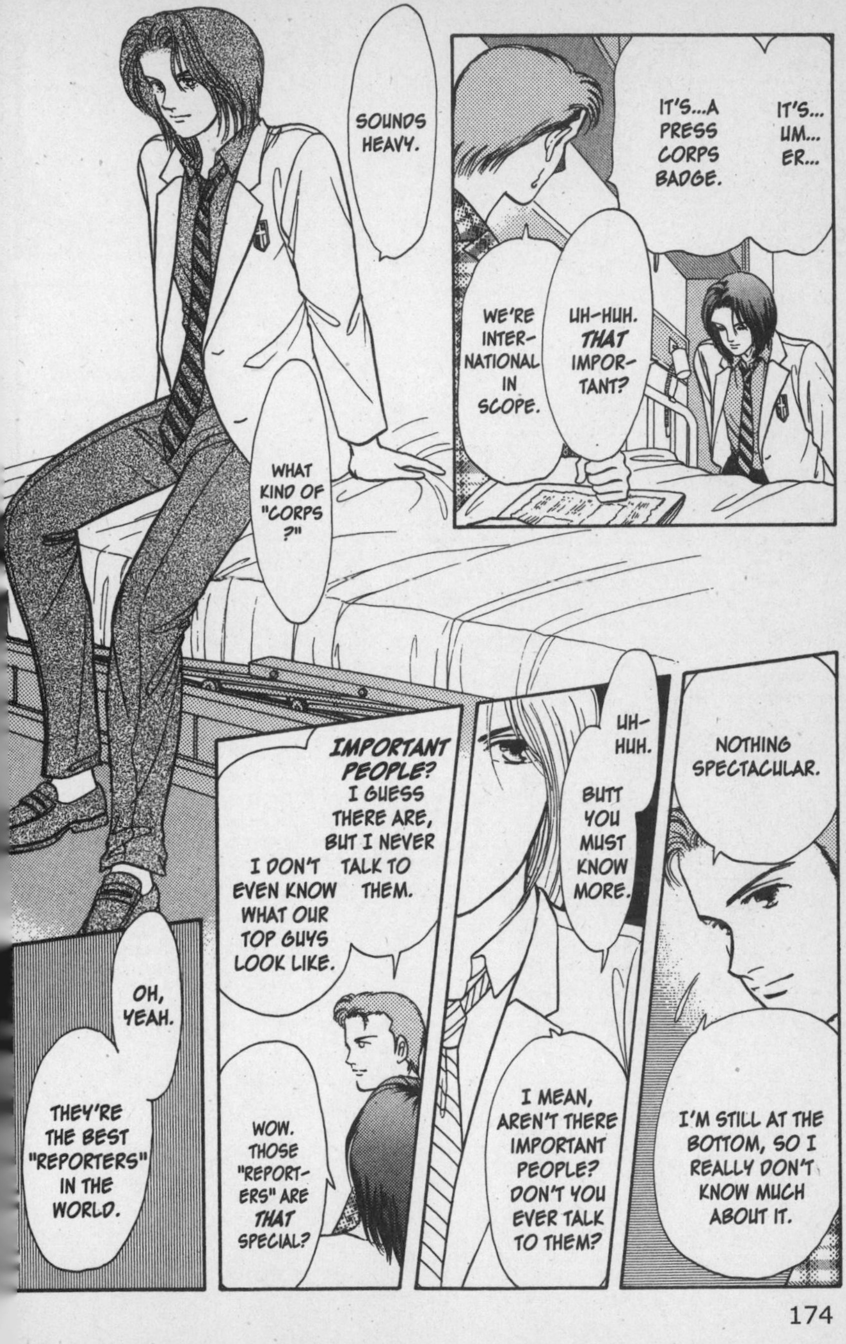
IT'S... UM... ER...
IT'S...A PRESS CORPS BADGE.
UH-HUH. *THAT* IMPORTANT?
WE'RE INTER-NATIONAL IN SCOPE.
SOUNDS HEAVY.
WHAT KIND OF "CORPS?"
NOTHING SPECTACULAR.
I'M STILL AT THE BOTTOM, SO I REALLY DON'T KNOW MUCH ABOUT IT.
UH-HUH.
BUTT YOU MUST KNOW MORE.
I MEAN, AREN'T THERE IMPORTANT PEOPLE? DON'T YOU EVER TALK TO THEM?
IMPORTANT PEOPLE? I GUESS THERE ARE, BUT I NEVER TALK TO THEM.
I DON'T EVEN KNOW WHAT OUR TOP GUYS LOOK LIKE.
WOW. THOSE "REPORT-ERS" ARE *THAT* SPECIAL?
OH, YEAH.
THEY'RE THE BEST "REPORTERS" IN THE WORLD.

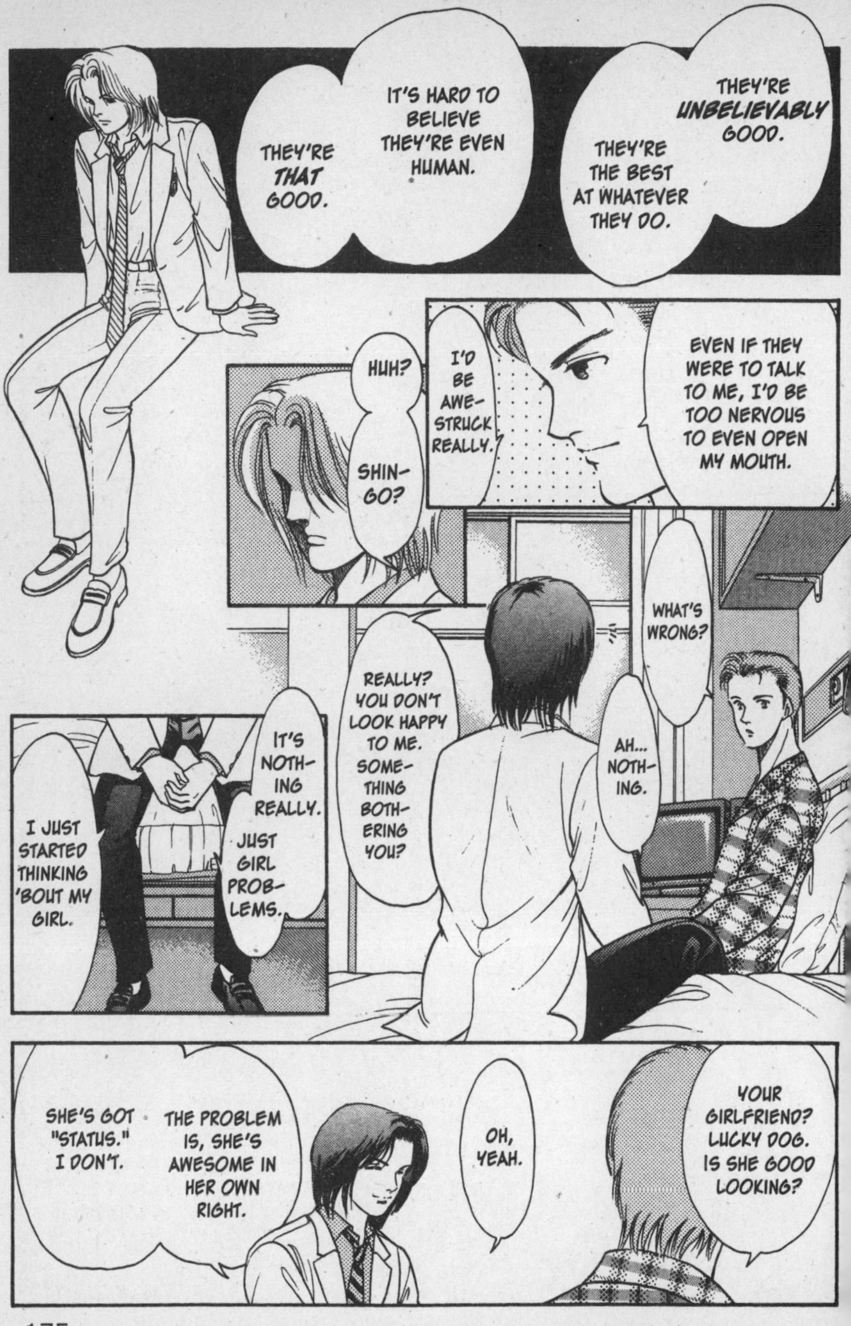
THEY'RE *UNBELIEVABLY* GOOD.
THEY'RE THE BEST AT WHATEVER THEY DO.
IT'S HARD TO BELIEVE THEY'RE EVEN HUMAN.
THEY'RE *THAT* GOOD.
EVEN IF THEY WERE TO TALK TO ME, I'D BE TOO NERVOUS TO EVEN OPEN MY MOUTH.
I'D BE AWE-STRUCK REALLY.
HUH?
SHIN-GO?
WHAT'S WRONG?
AH... NOTHING.
REALLY? YOU DON'T LOOK HAPPY TO ME. SOMETHING BOTHERING YOU?
IT'S NOTHING REALLY.
JUST GIRL PROBLEMS.
I JUST STARTED THINKING 'BOUT MY GIRL.
YOUR GIRLFRIEND? LUCKY DOG. IS SHE GOOD LOOKING?
OH, YEAH.
THE PROBLEM IS, SHE'S AWESOME IN HER OWN RIGHT.
SHE'S GOT "STATUS." I DON'T.

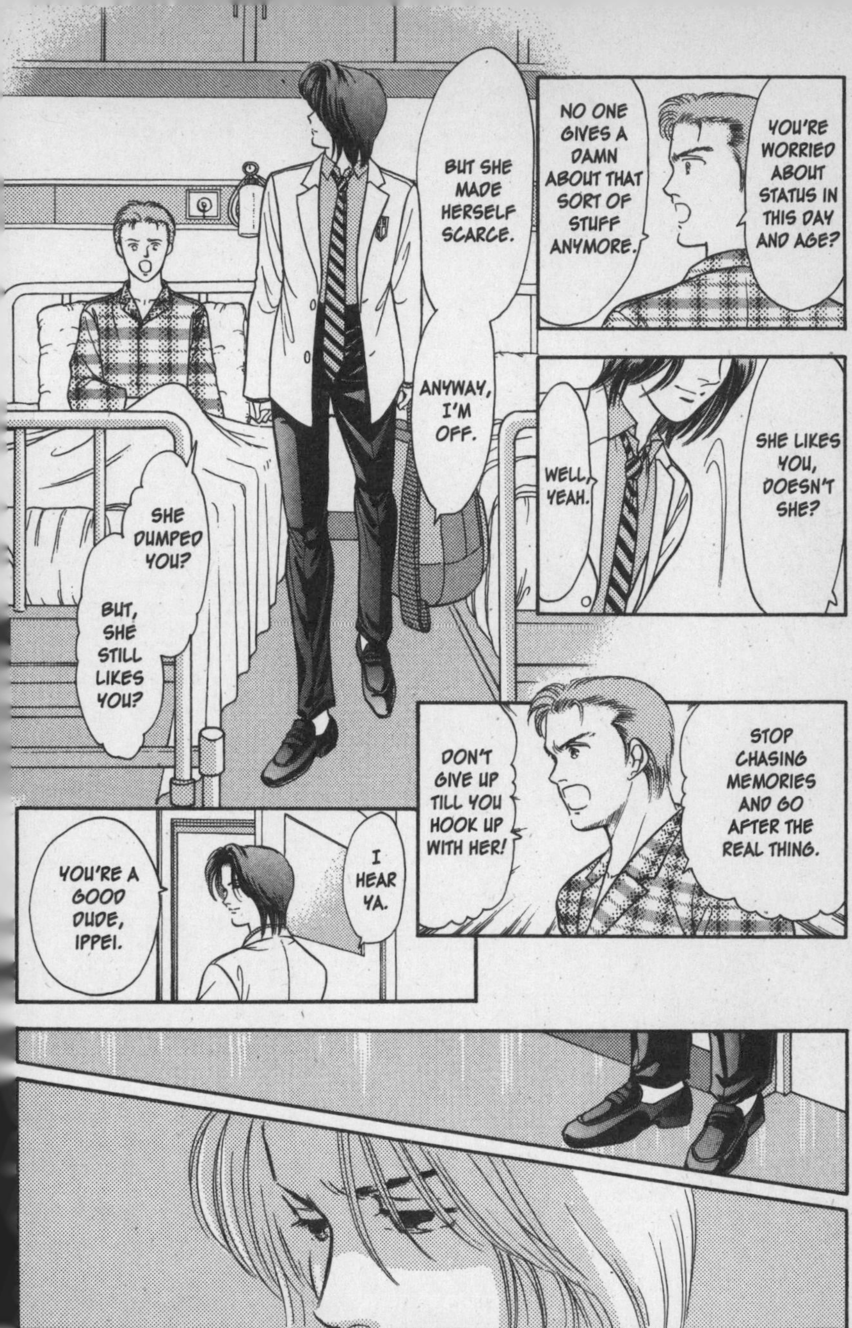

YOU'RE WORRIED ABOUT STATUS IN THIS DAY AND AGE?
NO ONE GIVES A DAMN ABOUT THAT SORT OF STUFF ANYMORE.
SHE LIKES YOU, DOESN'T SHE?
WELL, YEAH.
BUT SHE MADE HERSELF SCARCE.
ANYWAY, I'M OFF.
SHE DUMPED YOU?
BUT, SHE STILL LIKES YOU?
STOP CHASING MEMORIES AND GO AFTER THE REAL THING.
DON'T GIVE UP TILL YOU HOOK UP WITH HER!
I HEAR YA.
YOU'RE A GOOD DUDE, IPPEI.

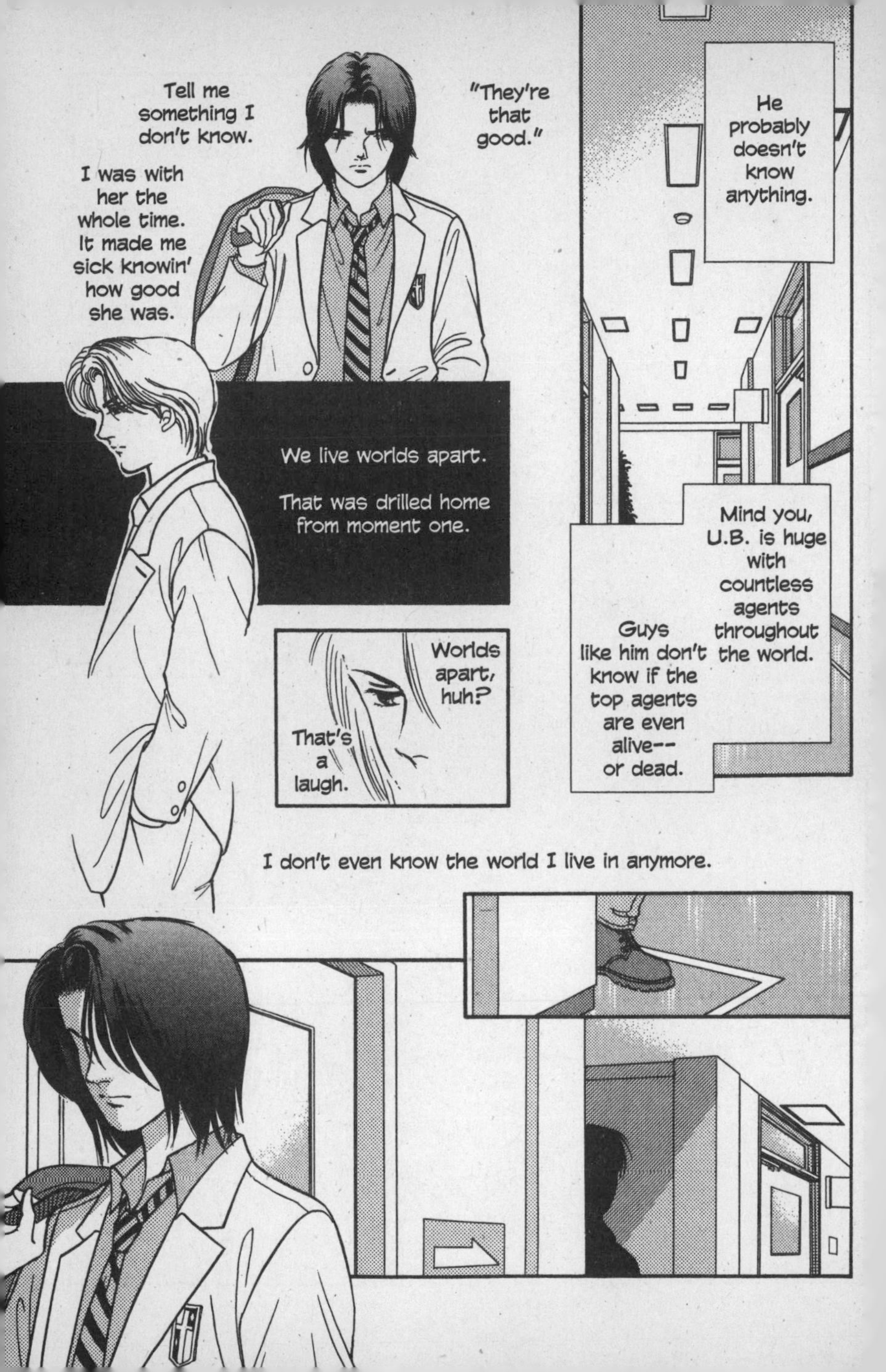
He probably doesn't know anything.
Mind you, U.B. is huge with countless agents throughout the world.
Guys like him don't know if the top agents are even alive-- or dead.
"They're that good."
Tell me something I don't know.
I was with her the whole time. It made me sick knowin' how good she was.
We live worlds apart.
That was drilled home from moment one.
Worlds apart, huh?
That's a laugh.
I don't even know the world I live in anymore.

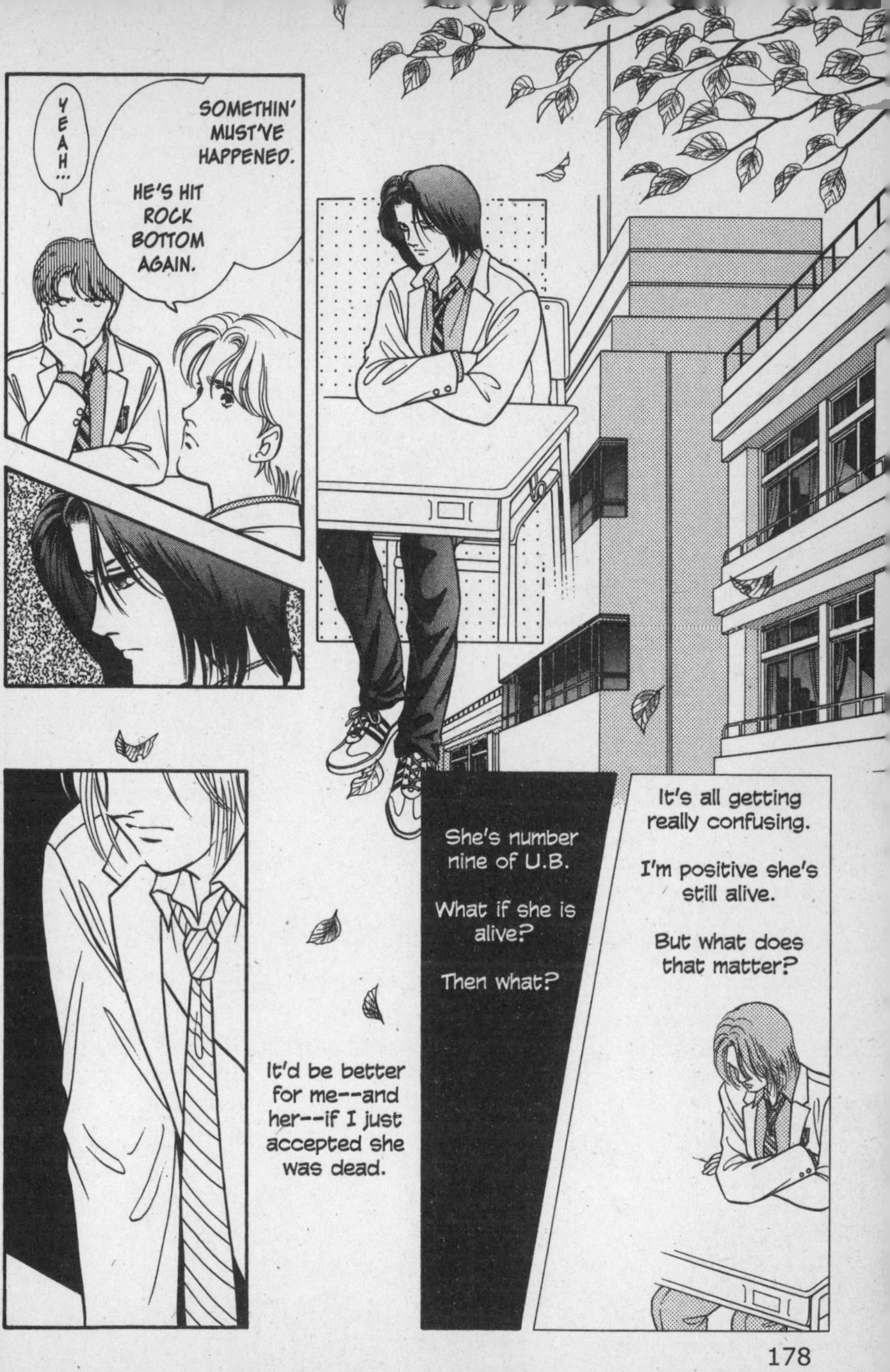
SOMETHIN' MUST'VE HAPPENED.
HE'S HIT ROCK BOTTOM AGAIN.
YEAH...
It's all getting really confusing.
I'm positive she's still alive.
But what does that matter?
She's number nine of U.B.
What if she is alive?
Then what?
It'd be better for me--and her--if I just accepted she was dead.

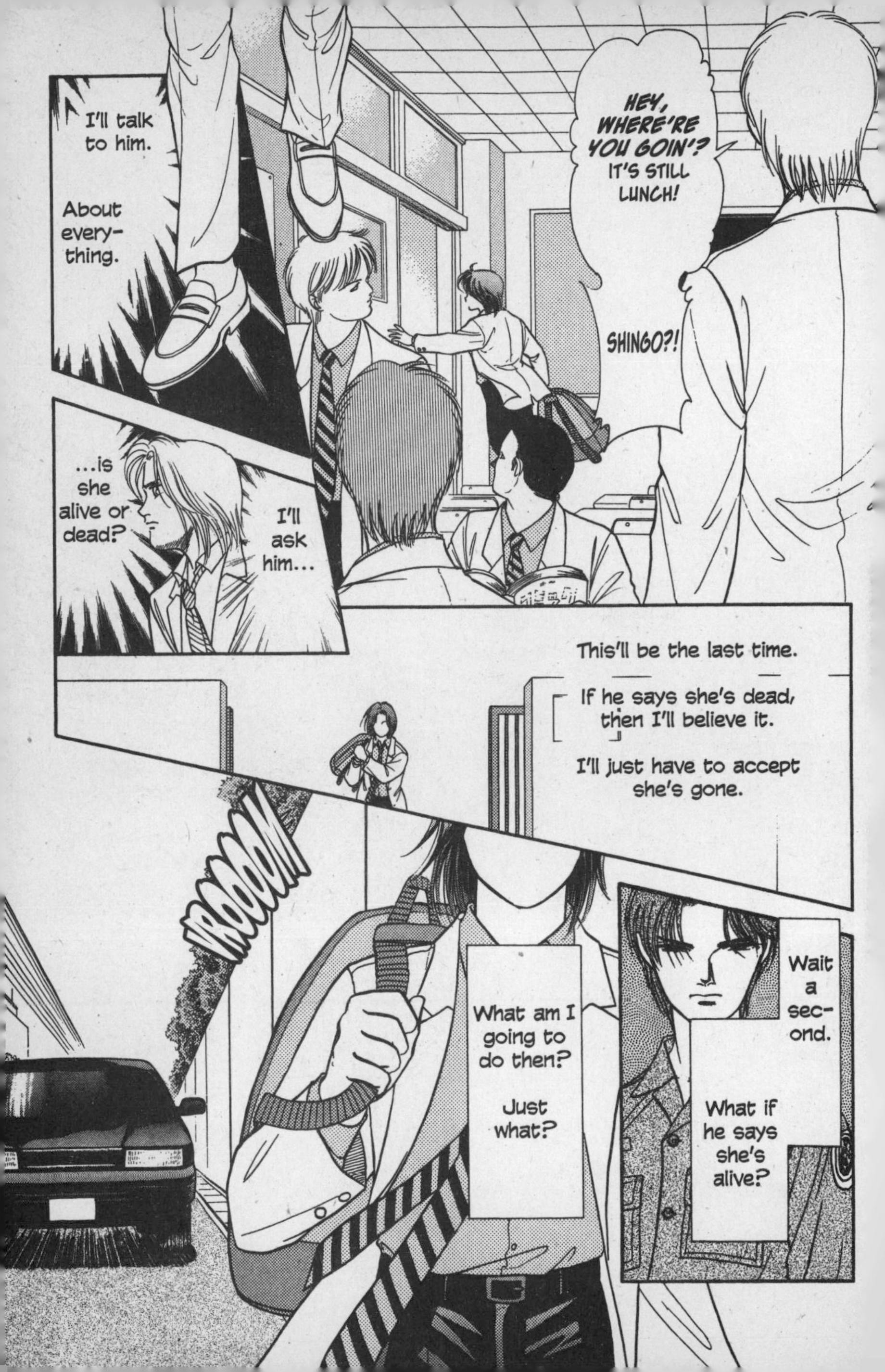
HEY, WHERE'RE YOU GOIN'? IT'S STILL LUNCH!
SHINGO?!
I'll talk to him.
About every-thing.
I'll ask him...
...is she alive or dead?
This'll be the last time.
If he says she's dead, then I'll believe it.
I'll just have to accept she's gone.
Wait a sec-ond.
What if he says she's alive?
VROOOM
What am I going to do then?
Just what?

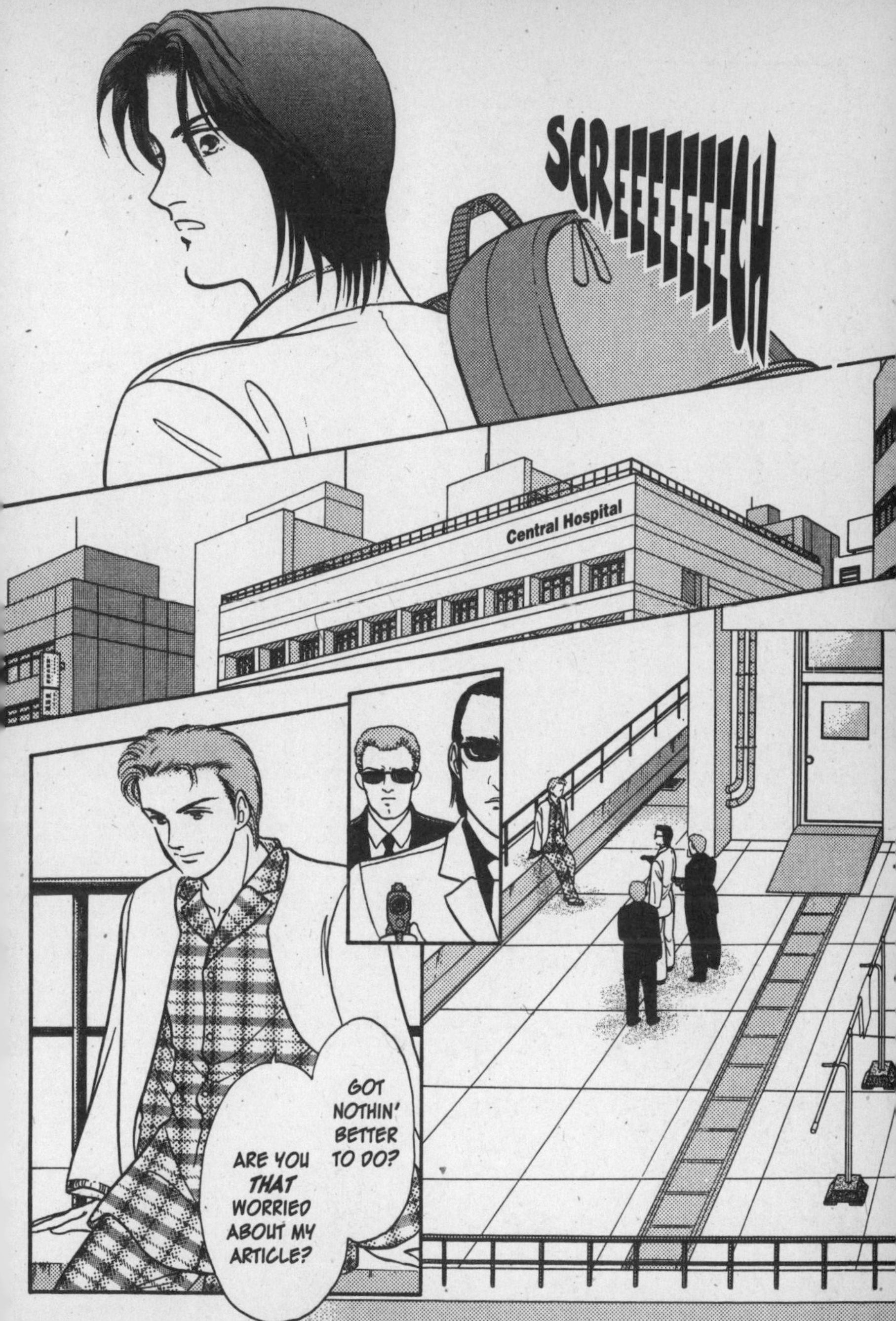
SCREEEEEEECH
Central Hospital
GOT NOTHIN' BETTER TO DO?
ARE YOU *THAT* WORRIED ABOUT MY ARTICLE?

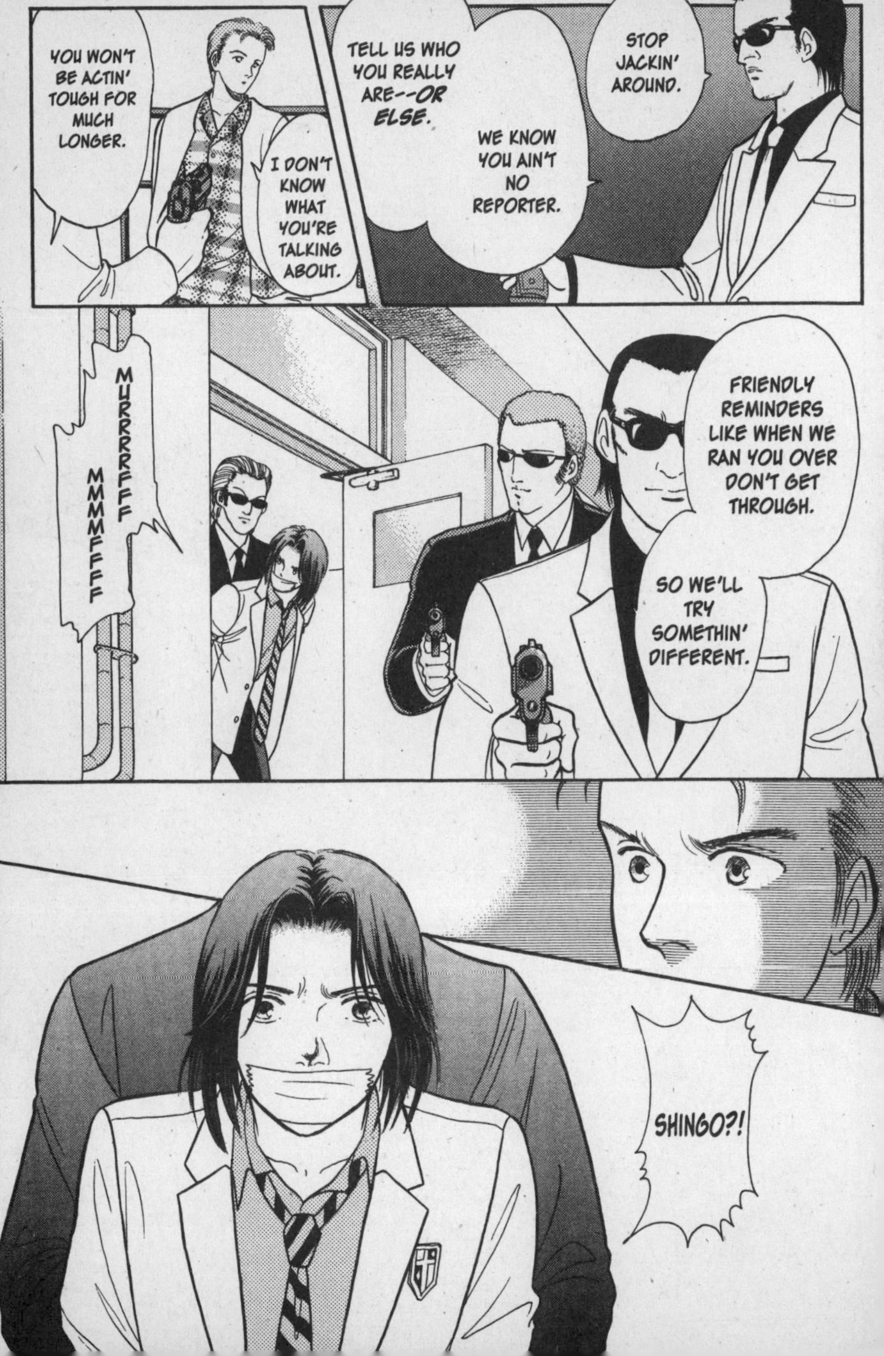
STOP JACKIN' AROUND.
TELL US WHO YOU REALLY ARE--OR ELSE.
WE KNOW YOU AIN'T NO REPORTER.
I DON'T KNOW WHAT YOU'RE TALKING ABOUT.
YOU WON'T BE ACTIN' TOUGH FOR MUCH LONGER.
FRIENDLY REMINDERS LIKE WHEN WE RAN YOU OVER DON'T GET THROUGH.
SO WE'LL TRY SOMETHIN' DIFFERENT.
MURRRRFFF
MMMMFFFF
SHINGO?!

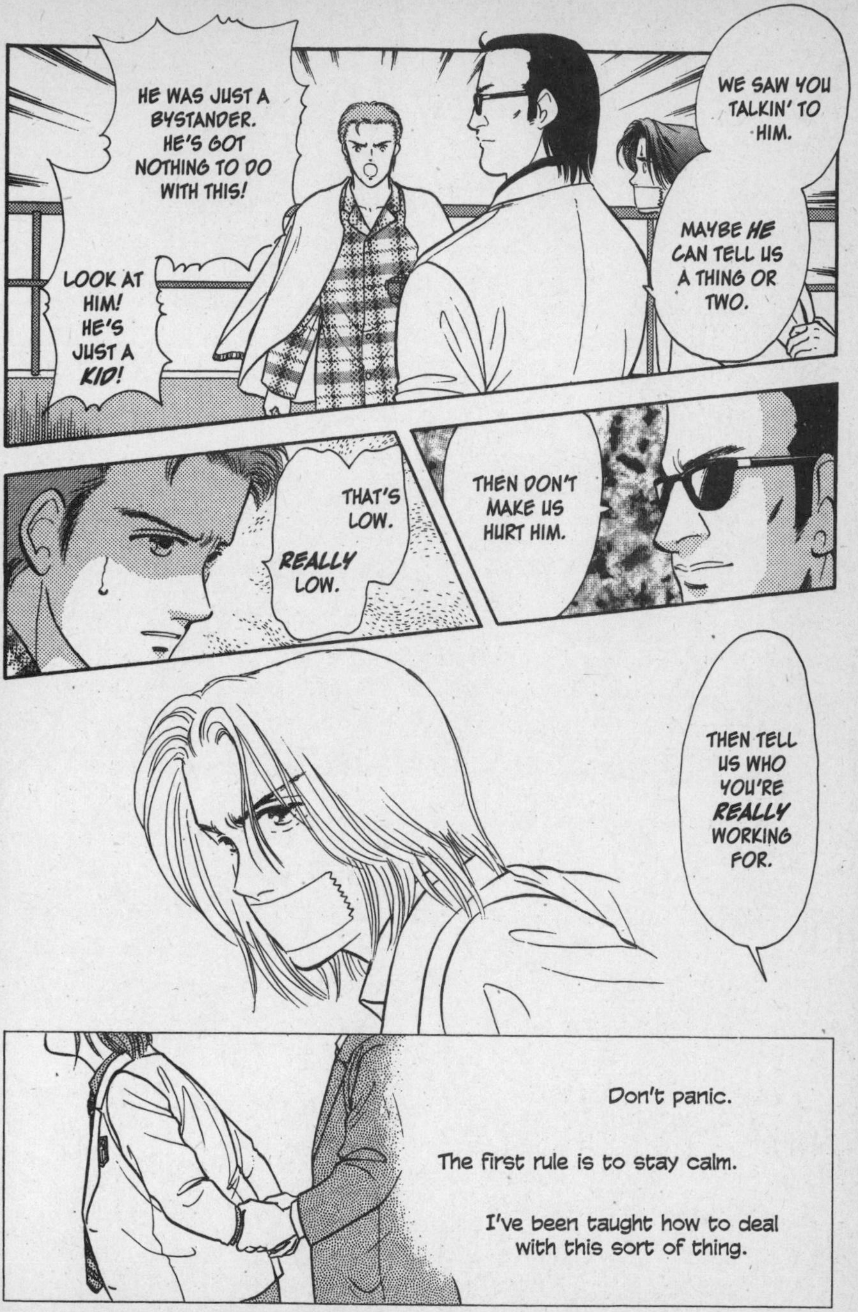
WE SAW YOU TALKIN' TO HIM.
MAYBE *HE* CAN TELL US A THING OR TWO.
HE WAS JUST A BYSTANDER. HE'S GOT NOTHING TO DO WITH THIS!
LOOK AT HIM! HE'S JUST A *KID!*
THEN DON'T MAKE US HURT HIM.
THAT'S LOW.
REALLY LOW.
THEN TELL US WHO YOU'RE *REALLY* WORKING FOR.
Don't panic.
The first rule is to stay calm.
I've been taught how to deal with this sort of thing.

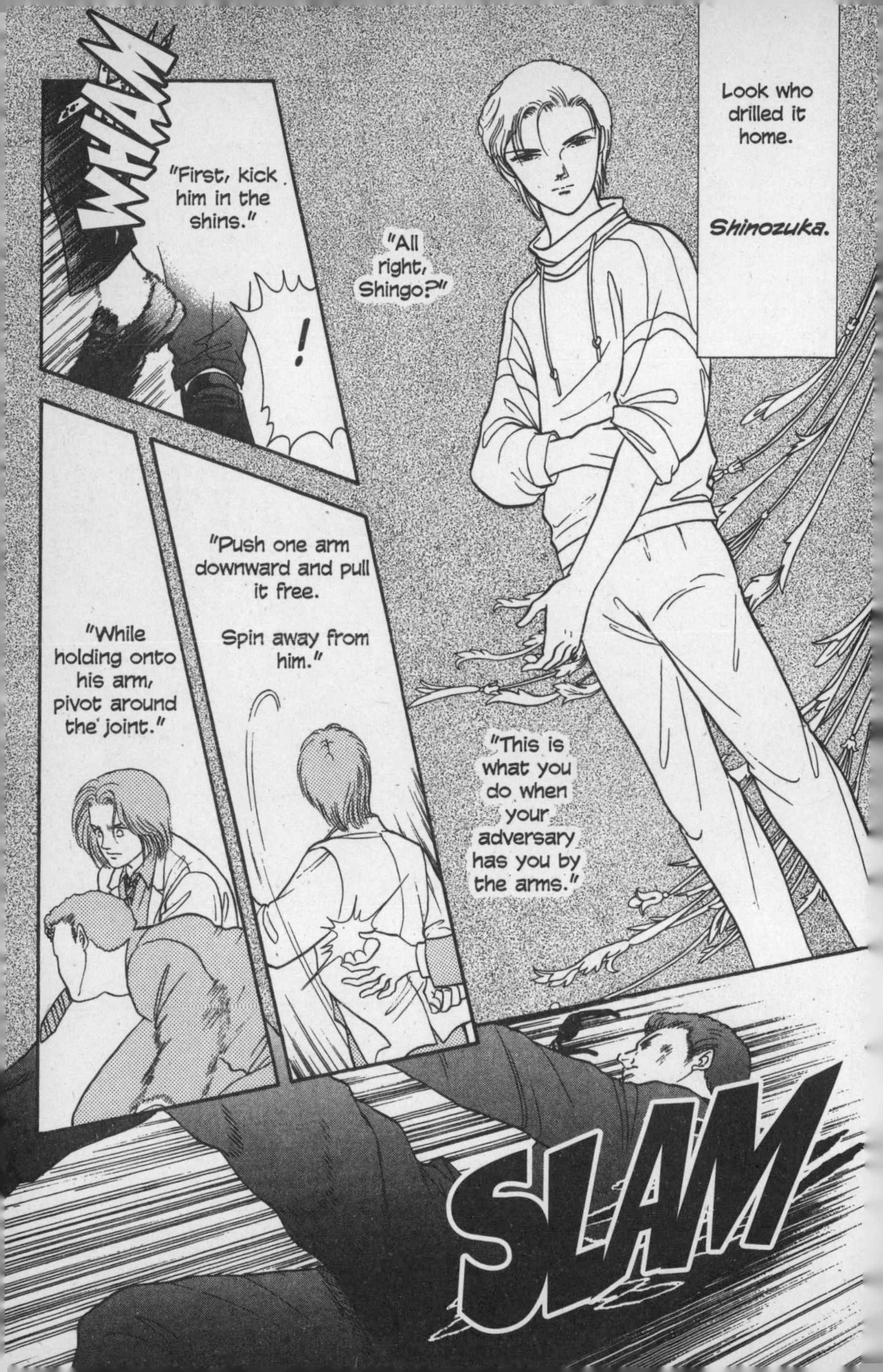

Look who drilled it home.
Shinozuka.
"All right, Shingo?"
"This is what you do when your adversary has you by the arms."
WHAM
"First, kick him in the shins."
!
"Push one arm downward and pull it free.
Spin away from him."
"While holding onto his arm, pivot around the joint."
SLAM

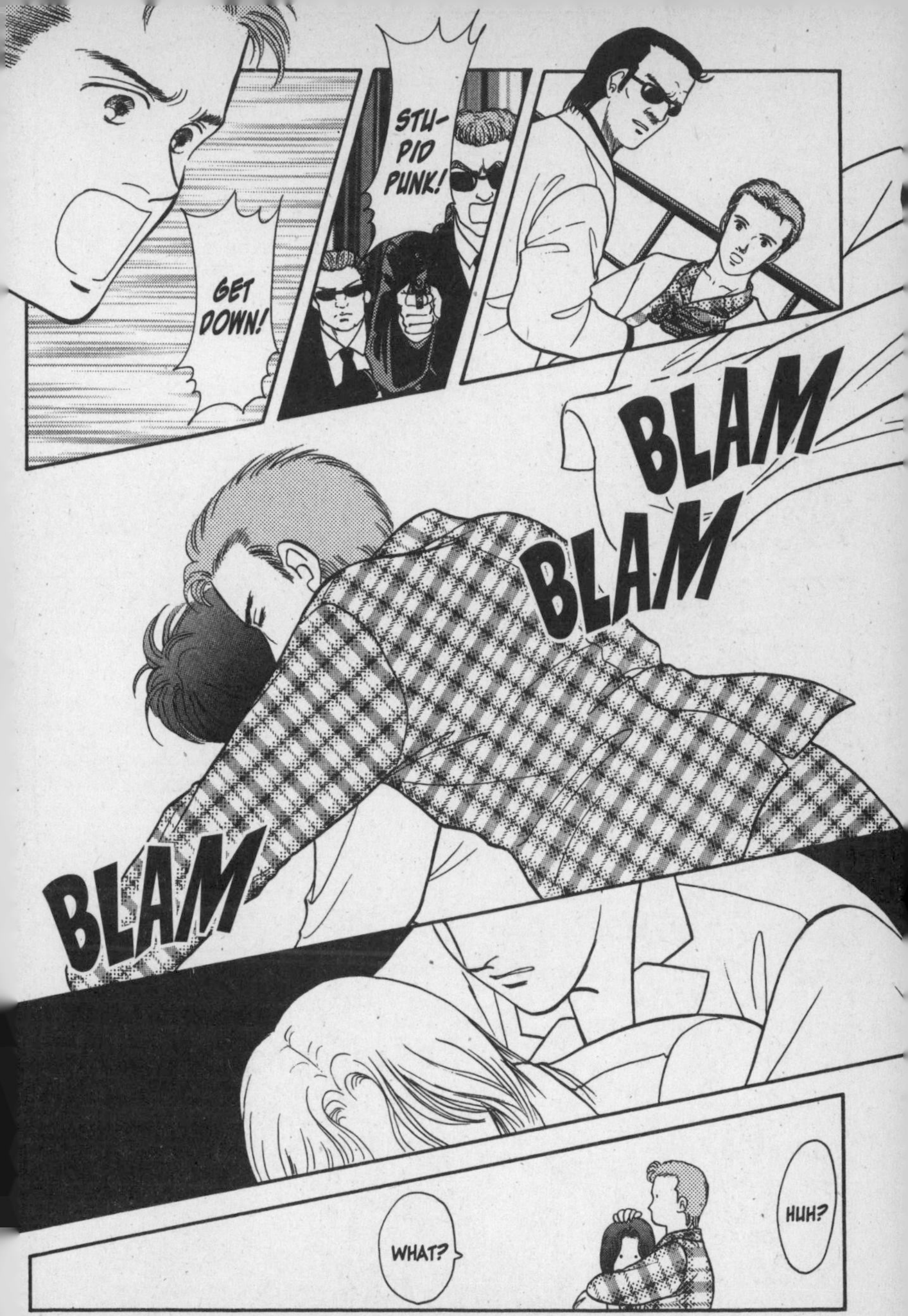
STU-PID PUNK!
GET DOWN!
BLAM
BLAM
BLAM
HUH?
WHAT?

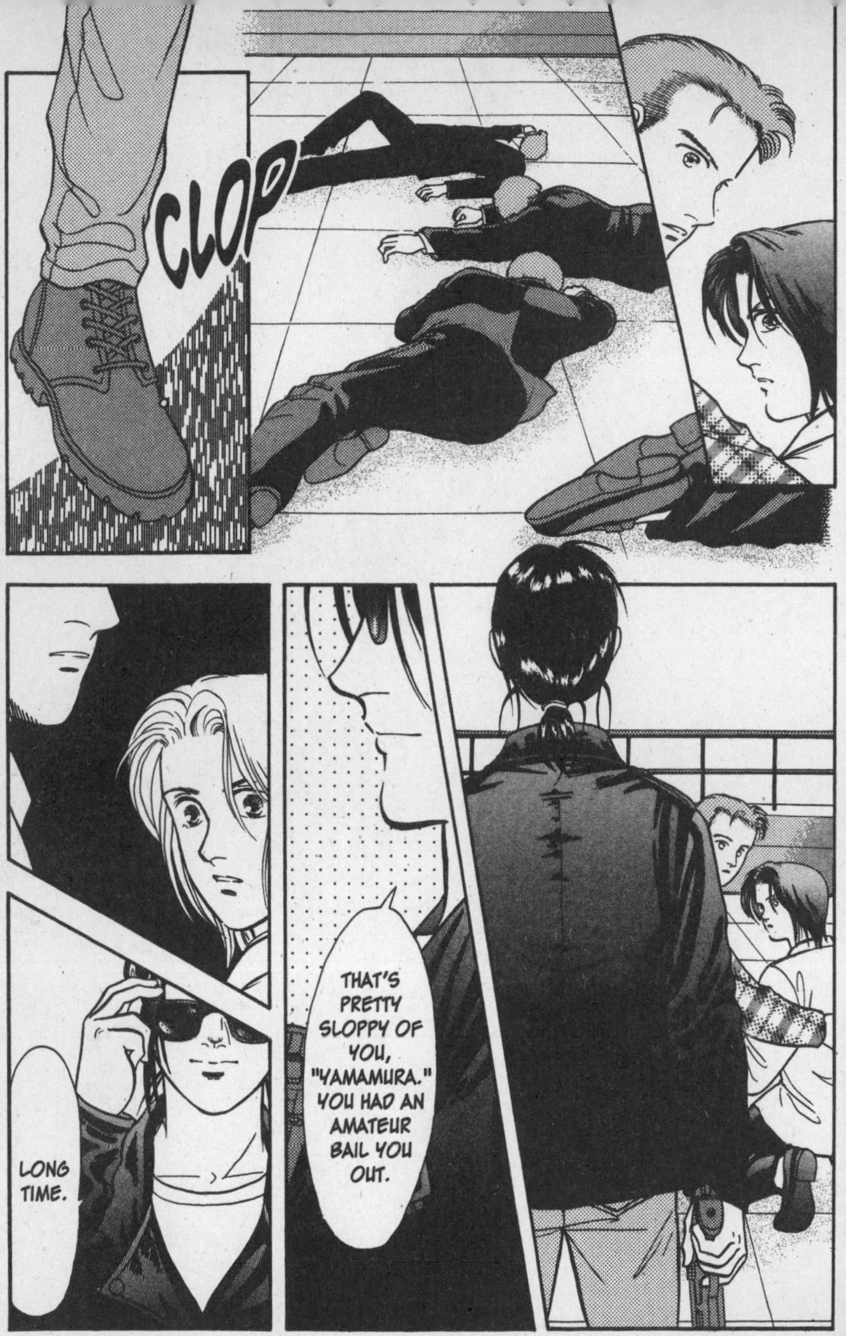
CLOP
THAT'S PRETTY SLOPPY OF YOU, "YAMAMURA." YOU HAD AN AMATEUR BAIL YOU OUT.
LONG TIME.

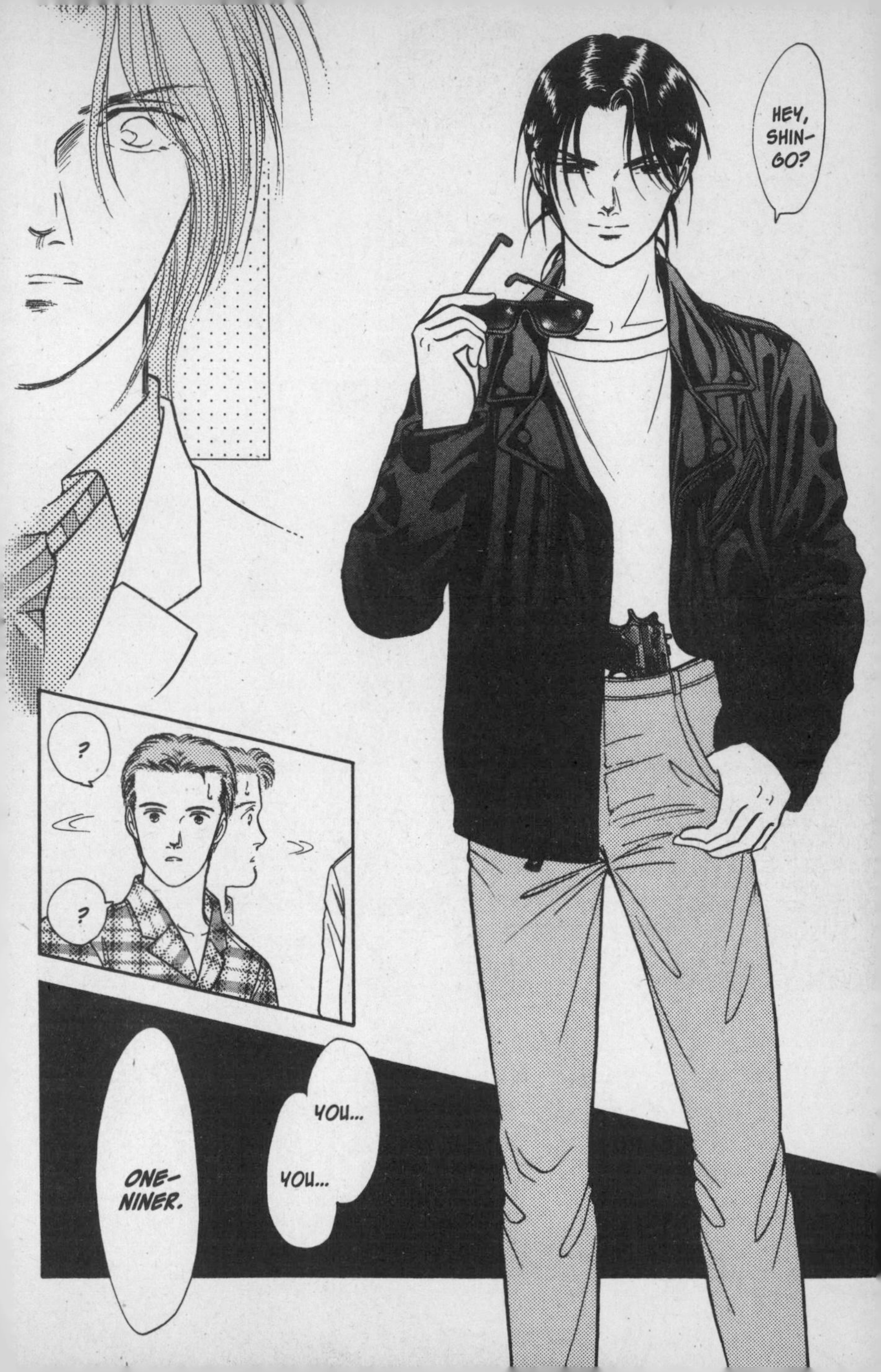
HEY, SHIN-GO?
?
?
YOU...
YOU...
ONE-NINER.

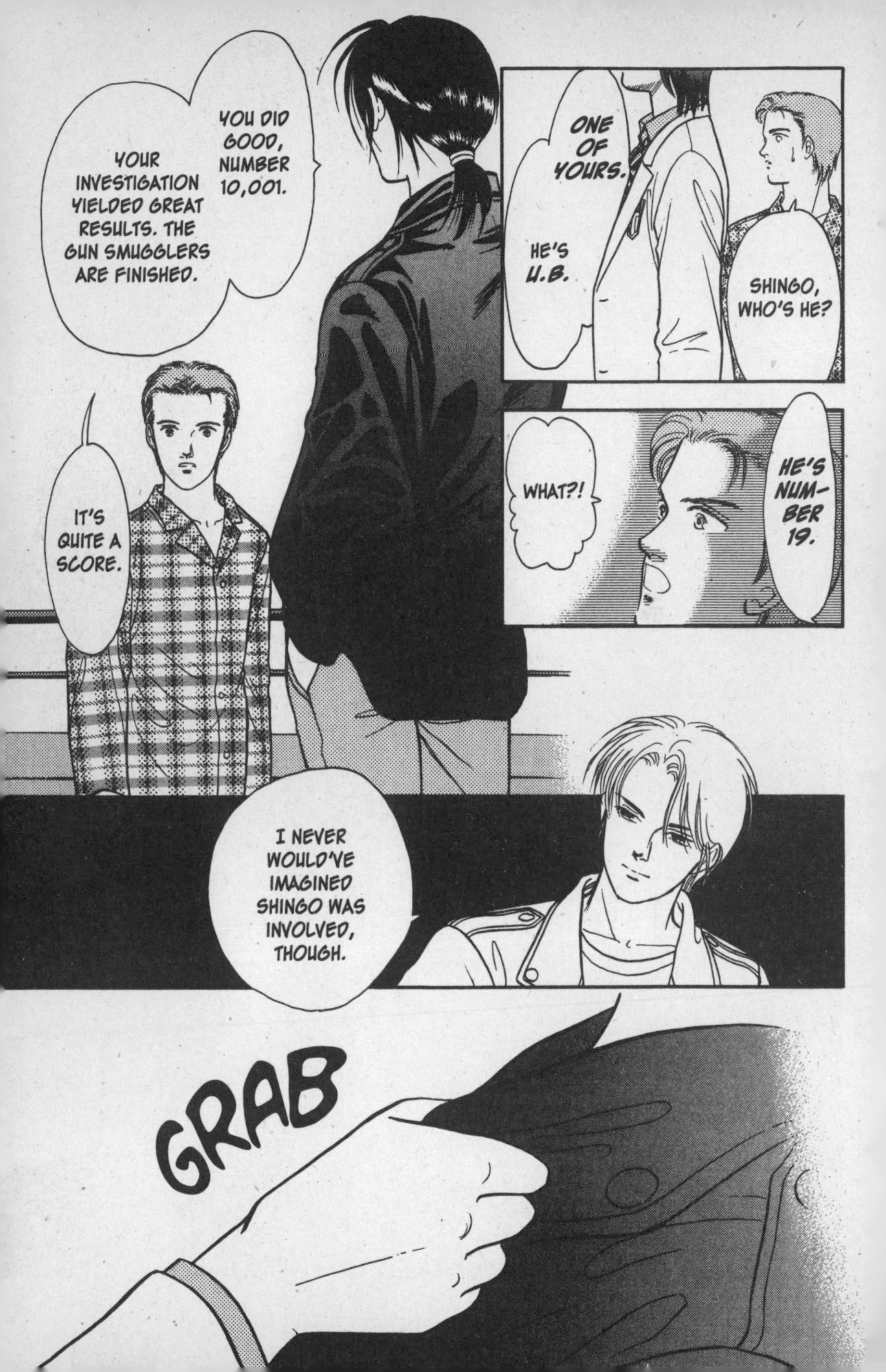
SHINGO, WHO'S HE?
ONE OF YOURS. HE'S U.B.
HE'S NUM-BER 19.
WHAT?!
YOU DID GOOD, NUMBER 10,001.
YOUR INVESTIGATION YIELDED GREAT RESULTS. THE GUN SMUGGLERS ARE FINISHED.
IT'S QUITE A SCORE.
I NEVER WOULD'VE IMAGINED SHINGO WAS INVOLVED, THOUGH.
GRAB

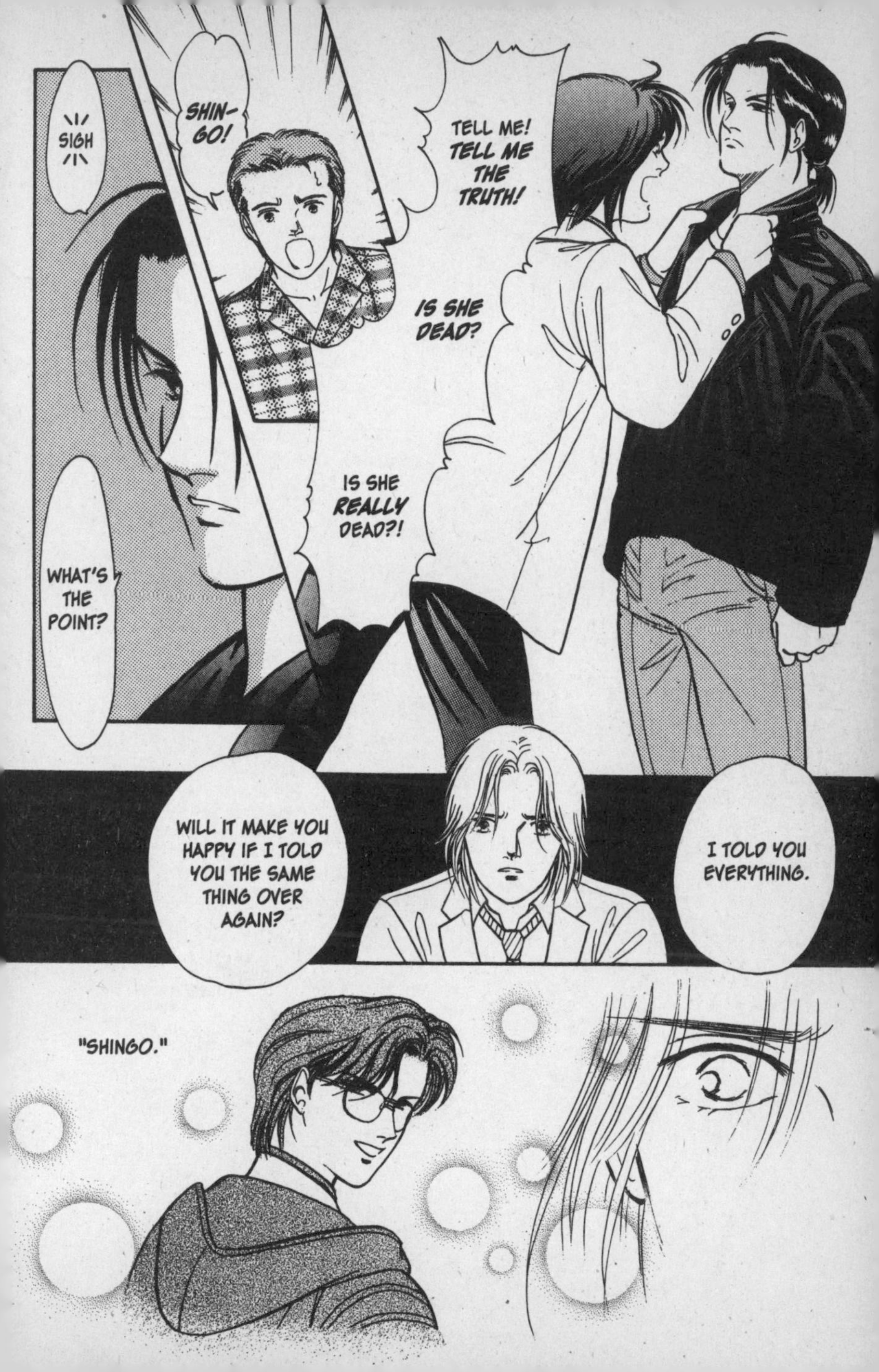
TELL ME! TELL ME THE TRUTH!
IS SHE DEAD?
IS SHE REALLY DEAD?!
SHIN-GO!
SIGH
WHAT'S THE POINT?
I TOLD YOU EVERYTHING.
WILL IT MAKE YOU HAPPY IF I TOLD YOU THE SAME THING OVER AGAIN?
"SHINGO."

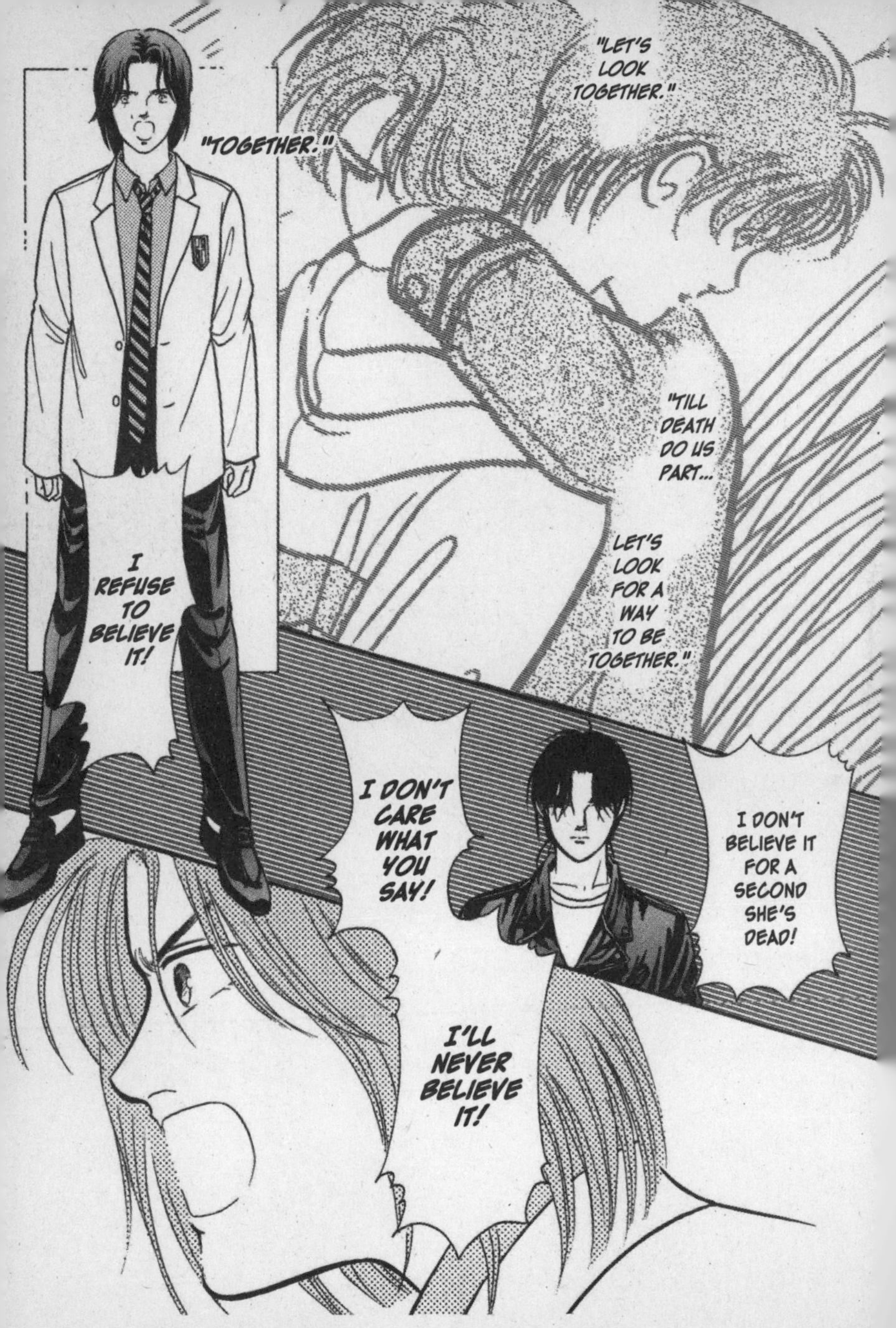
"LET'S LOOK TOGETHER."
"TILL DEATH DO US PART...
LET'S LOOK FOR A WAY TO BE TOGETHER."
"TOGETHER."
I REFUSE TO BELIEVE IT!
I DON'T BELIEVE IT FOR A SECOND SHE'S DEAD!
I DON'T CARE WHAT YOU SAY!
I'LL NEVER BELIEVE IT!

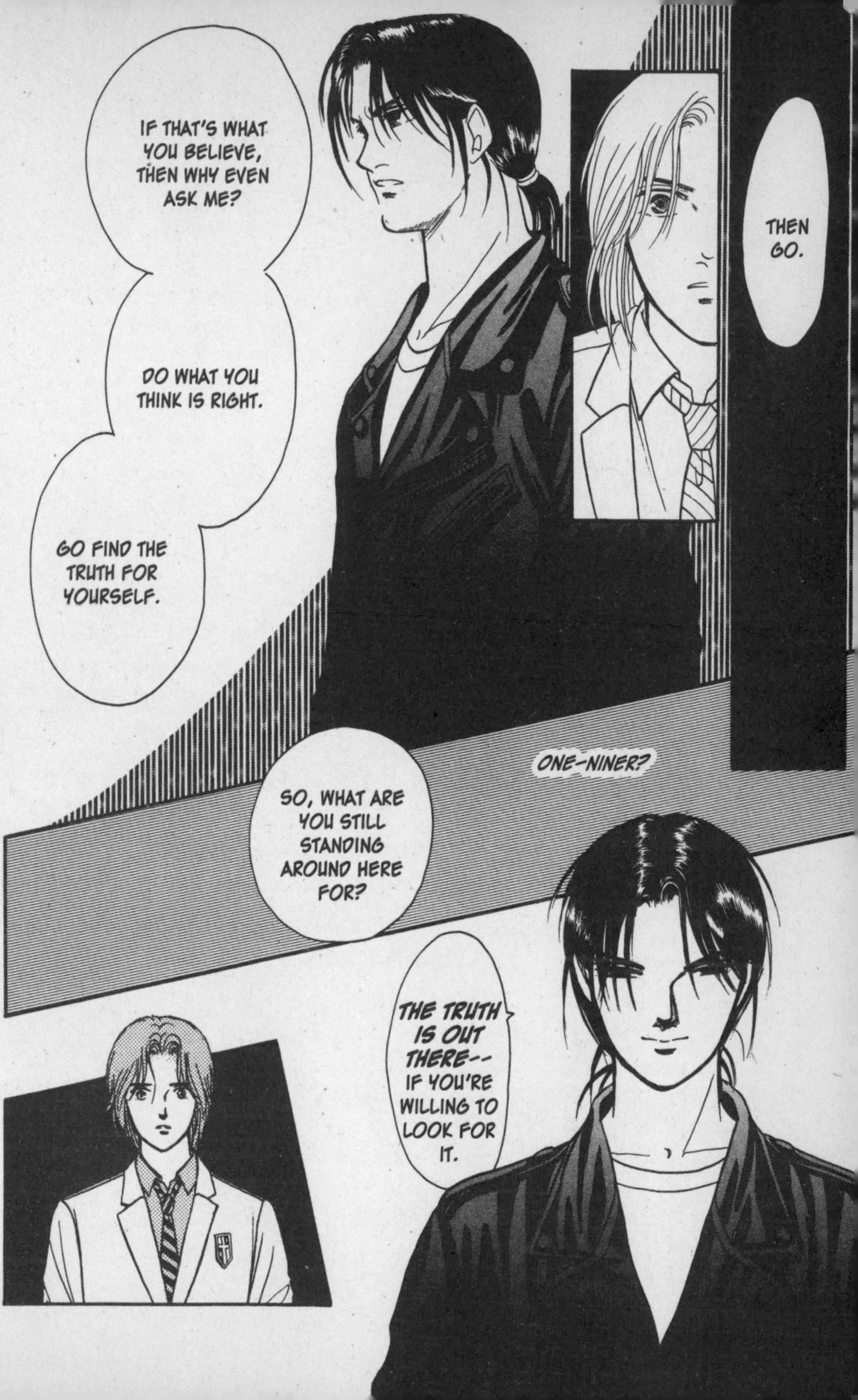
THEN GO.
IF THAT'S WHAT YOU BELIEVE, THEN WHY EVEN ASK ME?
DO WHAT YOU THINK IS RIGHT.
GO FIND THE TRUTH FOR YOURSELF.
ONE-NINER?
SO, WHAT ARE YOU STILL STANDING AROUND HERE FOR?
THE TRUTH IS OUT THERE-- IF YOU'RE WILLING TO LOOK FOR IT.

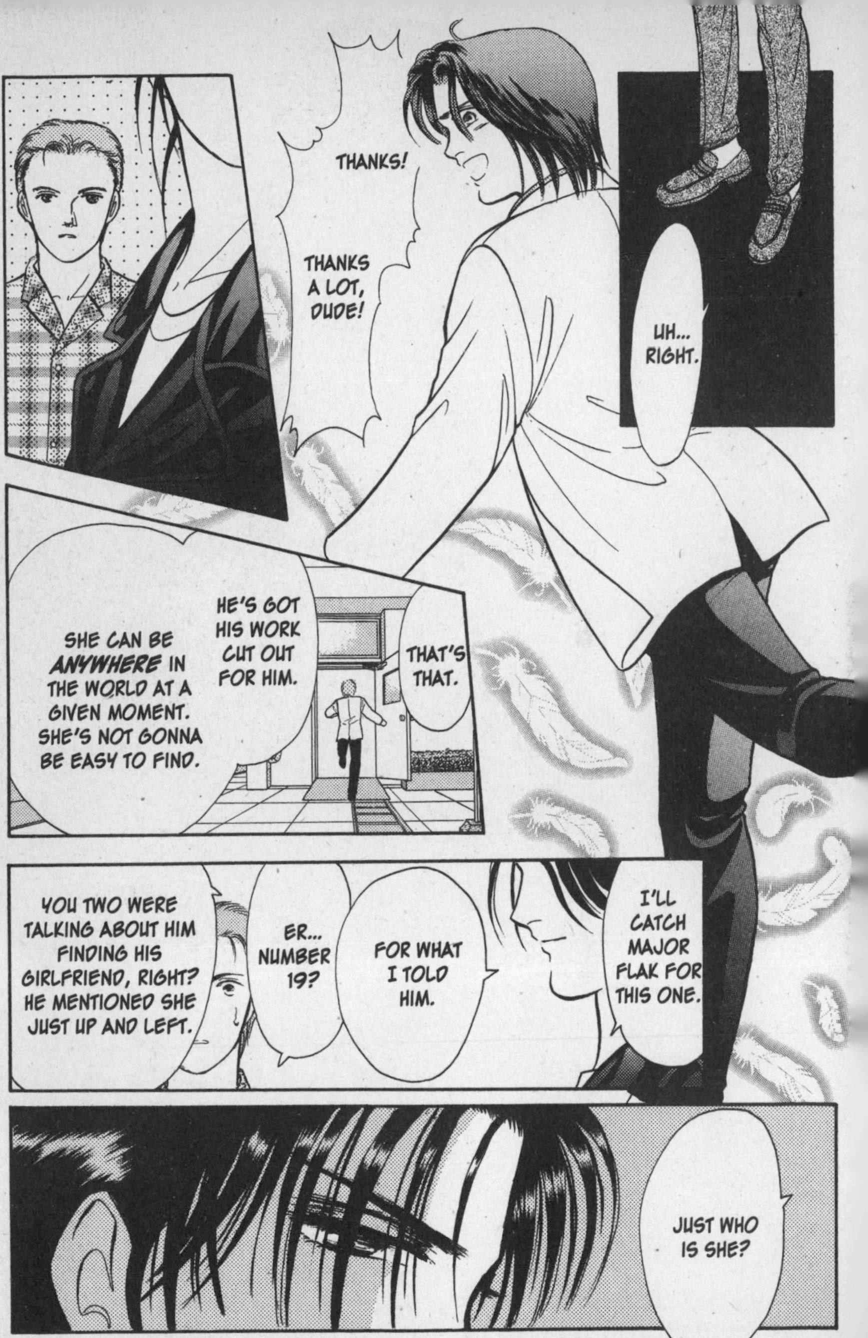
THANKS!
THANKS A LOT, DUDE!
UH... RIGHT.
THAT'S THAT.
HE'S GOT HIS WORK CUT OUT FOR HIM.
SHE CAN BE ANYWHERE IN THE WORLD AT A GIVEN MOMENT. SHE'S NOT GONNA BE EASY TO FIND.
I'LL CATCH MAJOR FLAK FOR THIS ONE.
FOR WHAT I TOLD HIM.
ER... NUMBER 19?
YOU TWO WERE TALKING ABOUT HIM FINDING HIS GIRLFRIEND, RIGHT? HE MENTIONED SHE JUST UP AND LEFT.
JUST WHO IS SHE?

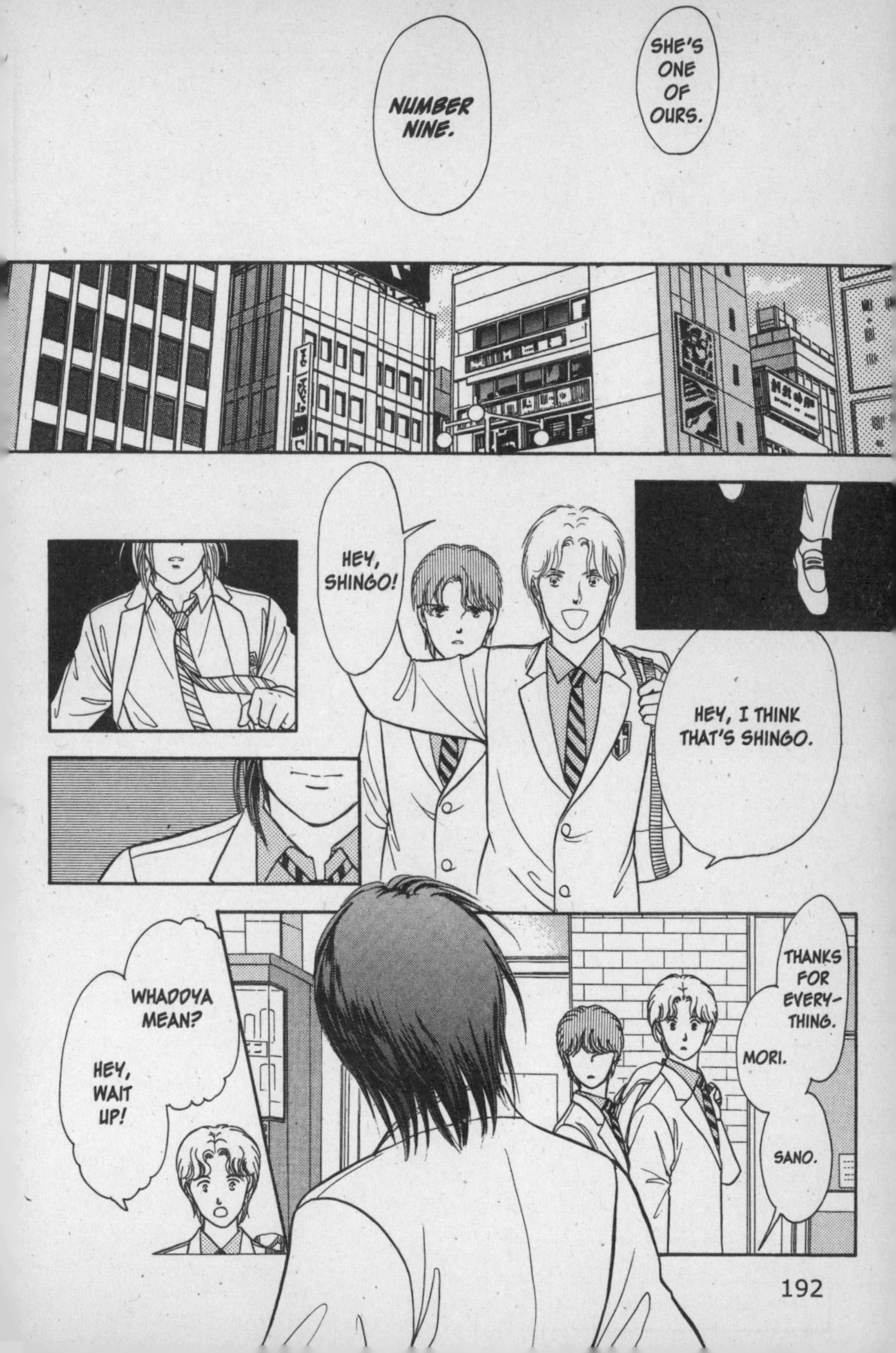
SHE'S ONE OF OURS.
NUMBER NINE.
HEY, I THINK THAT'S SHINGO.
HEY, SHINGO!
THANKS FOR EVERY-THING.
MORI.
SANO.
WHADDYA MEAN?
HEY, WAIT UP!

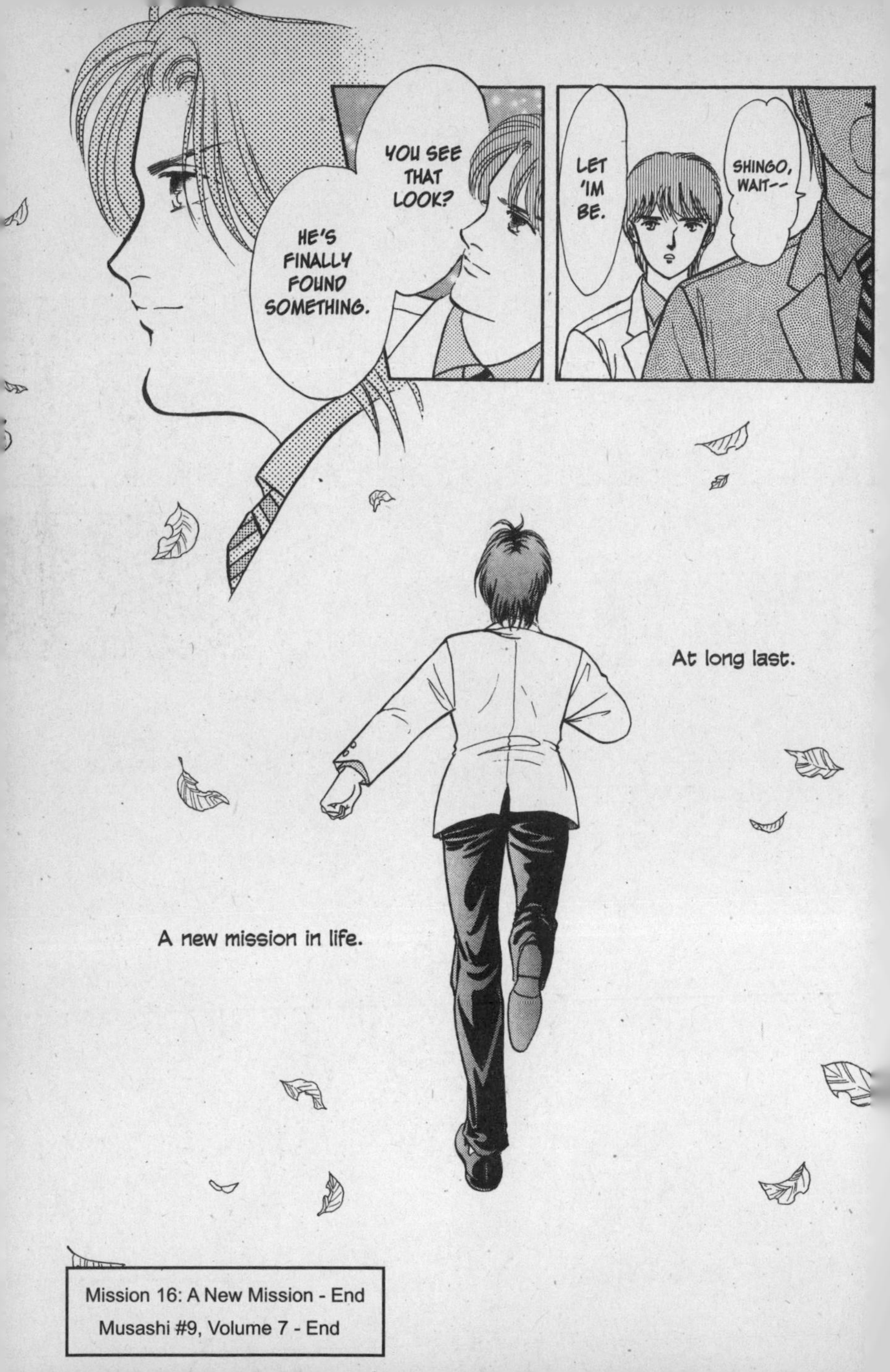
SHINGO, WAIT--
LET 'IM BE.
YOU SEE THAT LOOK?
HE'S FINALLY FOUND SOMETHING.
At long last.
A new mission in life.
Mission 16: A New Mission - End
Musashi #9, Volume 7 - End

cmx

In the next
volume of

MUSASHI # 9

Volume 8

**By Miyuki
Takahashi**

**Available in
August**

A helicopter carrying
top-secret plans crashes.
Musashi faces off against
armed terrorists who'll
stop at nothing to retrieve
the plans. As Musashi
works to recover the plan,
gang warfare erupts,
distracting her further
from her goal. It's another
race against time and a
struggle against the odds
for Ultimate Blue's
top agent.

KYUBANME NO MUSASHI Vol. 8 © 1996 Miyuki Takahashi/AKITASHOTEN.

cmxmanga.com

cmx

KYUBANME NO MUSASHI Volume 7 © 1996 by Miyuki Takahashi. All rights reserved. First Published in Japan in 1996 by AKITA PUBLISHING CO.,LTD., Tokyo.

MUSASHI #9 Volume 7, published by WildStorm Productions, an imprint of DC Comics, 888 Prospect St. #240, La Jolla, CA 92037. English Translation © 2006. All Rights Reserved. English translation rights in U.S.A. arranged with AKITA PUBLISHING CO.,LTD., Tokyo, through Tuttle-Mori Agency, Inc., Tokyo. The stories, characters, and incidents mentioned in this magazine are entirely fictional. Printed on recyclable paper. WildStorm does not read or accept unsolicited submissions of ideas, stories or artwork. Printed in Canada.

 DC Comics, a Warner Bros. Entertainment Company.

Translation and Adaptation by
Tony Ogasawara

William F. Schuch — Lettering
Larry Berry — Design
Jim Chadwick — Editor

ISBN: 1-4012-0850-4
ISBN-13: 978-1-4012-0850-5

FLIP IT!!

All the pages in this book were created—and are printed here—in Japanese RIGHT-to-LEFT format. No artwork has been reversed, so you can read the stories the way the creators meant for them to be read.

RIGHT TO LEFT?!

Traditional Japanese manga starts at the upper right-hand corner, and moves right-to-left as it goes down the page. Follow this guide for an easy understanding.

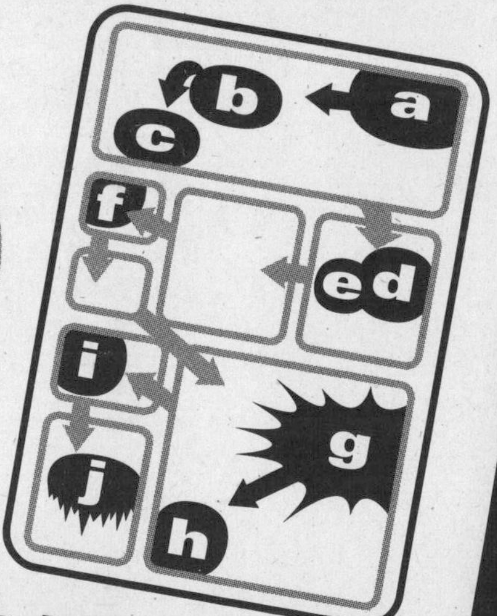
a
b
c
ed
f
g
h
i
j

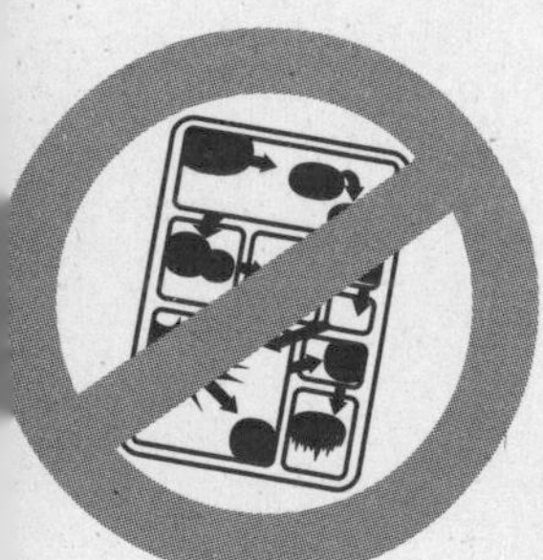

Catch the latest at cmxmanga.com!